Free Expression in Canada:

Surrendered to Diversity and Multiculturalism

Robert Ivan Martin

Foreword by Julian Porter, Q.C.

Also By Robert Ivan Martin

Personal Freedom and the Law in Tanzania
Controls and the Canadian Media
Critical Perspectives on the Constitution
A Sourcebook of Canadian Media Law
Media Law
Access to Information in Developing Countries
Speaking Freely: Expression and the Law in the Commonwealth
The Most Dangerous Branch: How the Supreme Court of Canada Has
Undermined Our Law and Our Democracy

ISBN 978-0-9827734-9-9

STAIRWAY≡PRESS

www.stairwaypress.com
1500A East College Way #554
Mount Vernon, WA 98273

Cover design by Guy Corp, www.grafixCORP.com
The front cover painting and chapter icon by Norman Rockwell—
used under license with permission of the Rockwell estate.

To **Asha Mary Martin** with love and in confident expectation of the many wonderful things you will accomplish.

AUTHOR'S PREFACE

THE BEGINNING IS usually the best place to start.

In January of 1975 I was teaching in the Faculty of Law of the University of Nairobi and was well into my eighth year of living outside Canada. It occurred to me that perhaps it was time to return to Canada and, having two very small sons, it was clear that finding a job in Canada was essential. I was invited to deliver a paper at a conference at the State University of New York in Albany and, after the conference, headed north in search of a job.

The search took me to London, Ontario where I met David Johnston, then the Dean of the Faculty of Law of the University of Western Ontario and now His Excellency the Right Honourable David Johnston, Governor General and Commander in Chief of Canada. He was interested in offering me a job, but was uncertain as to what I might teach. He discussed this question with Andy MacFarlane, then the Dean of the School of Journalism at Western. They agreed that I could teach "Journalism and the Law", then a required course in the M.A. in Journalism programme. Consequently, I was offered a joint appointment in the School of Journalism and the Faculty of Law.

When I started at Western in September of 1975, I knew absolutely nothing about "Journalism and the Law". If Dr. Johnson were right, as he usually was, when he said, "Nothing concentrates the mind like the prospect of a hanging", then nothing creates as powerful an incentive for learning a subject as being required to teach a course in it. Under Andy MacFarlane's direction and buoyed by his encouragement, I actually began to learn something about the law and the mass media. Andy ceased to be the Dean of the Journalism School in 1981. After his departure from the deanship, the School went steadily downhill, disappearing in 1998. Andy's death in 2002 was a terrible loss to both journalism and journalism education in Canada.

The first person to thank concerning this volume is Ian Holloway, until recently, the Dean of the Faculty of Law at Western. Though I am no longer employed in the Law Faculty, he was generous enough to make a law student available as a research assistant. That student, Leeanne Melnyk, of the U.W.O. Law class of 2010, did a superb job. She found all the material I wanted and presented it to me neatly arranged in binders with tabs. Her work was thorough and painstaking and completely lawyer-like.

I worked from a printout of the Second Edition of an earlier book, *Media Law,* on which I made corrections and improvements and to which I added information necessary to bring the whole thing up to date. My friend, Geri Akiens, did all the necessary keyboarding and did it with great skill and very pleasantly. Marianne Welch's retirement was a major loss to the scholarly capacity of the U.W.O. Law Faculty. She has prepared the Bibliography, Index and Table of Cases for my last three books. Her skill is beyond praise. The final thanks go to Barb Fetchison of the U.W.O. Law Library. The time I spent working in the Law Library would have been vastly less productive without her capable and generous assistance. Even after I left London, she continued to assist me in overcoming gaps in my capacity for on-line research. She also completed the Bibliography which Marianne Welch had started and did so in a fashion which was strikingly thorough and meticulous.

I owe a special debt of thanks to my dear friend Kristine Perz. She offered very generous and capable assistance at an extremely difficult point in the gestation of the book, being instrumental in putting the final version together.

It is a pleasure to thank my sons, Ivan and Dawson, for their constant support and encouragement. I am highly biased about this, but do understand that being a parent is the supreme experience of human life. It is a great blessing to be the father of two such fine men.

The book is dedicated to my granddaughter, Asha. I thank her for all the happiness she has brought into my life over the past six and a half years.

Jan Hoffman and Mario Contini were unfailingly pleasant and helpful on many occasions. While this book began its life as the third edition of *Media Law,* that has changed completely. I was doing this work during a period which many have described as "The war on free expression". My strong support for free expression, plus my concomitant hostility towards those attacking it, began to occupy a greater and greater place in the manuscript. Irretrievable breakdown with Irwin Law resulted.

Beginning in 2010, I rewrote the book completely. As I hope the reader will come to realize, contemporary Canada supports neither free thinking, nor free expression. Consequently, an impressive array of Canadian publishers rejected the manuscript. Being in possession of a finished manuscript which does not have a publisher is not an experience I recommend. But fortunately, in October of 2011, I discovered Stairway Press. Ken Coffman, the publisher at Stairway Press, and I hit it off immediately. We quickly established a pleasant and productive working relationship. I have developed great admiration and respect for Ken.

Robert Ivan Martin
Guelph, Ontario
April 2012

Table of Contents

FOREWORD

Free Expression in Canada provides a clear and comprehensive analysis of how Canada's laws approach freedom of expression. It covers the evolution of judicial attitudes to limits on speech. Rob Martin's lucidity will make you contemplate the whole horizon of the law. As a lawyer practicing in this field since 1965 I have learned a great deal from his survey of the law.

A journalist must read this book. It emphasizes the necessity of resisting orthodox thought. As Rob Martin says: "free expression demands from each journalist both nurturing and jealous protection."

Enjoy the book. You'll be the wiser for it.

—Julian Porter, Queen's Counsel and co-author of *Canadian Libel Practice*

INTRODUCTION

The Purpose and Scope of the Book

THIS BOOK HAS two distinct, but complimentary, objectives. It aims, first, to set out a clear, complete and up–to-date exposition of the law as it relates to the mass media and to the people who work in them. At the same time, the book seeks to analyse the state of free expression in contemporary Canada. Free expression is under attack today[1] and the book attempts to place both free expression and the attacks against it in their proper social and ideological contexts.

The author is deeply committed to free expression[2] and, consequently, is hostile towards those who are attacking it. My work on this book had progressed quite far before I had the good fortune to read Stephen Braun's important and valuable study, *Democracy off Balance: Freedom of Expression and Hate Propaganda Law*

---

[1] Stefan Braun, the author of *Democracy off Balance: Freedom of Expression and Hate Propaganda Laws in Canada,* Toronto, University of Toronto Press, 2004, a work which canvasses many of the same questions as does this one, raised the astute and disturbing question, "Can anyone really feel safe from rapacious censors?". See his *Free Speech: Beware of the 'system works' test,* Winnipeg Free Press, 8 May 2010.

[2] As an illustration, see Robert Martin, *Speaking Freely: Expression and the Law in the Commonwealth,* Toronto, Irwin Law, 1999. See also, Robert Martin, *Promoting Freedom of Expression in the Commonwealth,* (2002) 366 The Round Table 521.

in Canada.[3] Reading Braun induced me to rethink a number of matters, in particular, the general direction being pursued by those who attack free expression. What Braun identified as the "progressive left" was, for him, the leading force supporting the assault on free expression.[4] This position on the part of the "progressive left" flows naturally from its attachment to structuralist social analysis. From a structuralist perspective, intolerance and discrimination are simply manifestations of structures of socio-economic domination and exploitation.[5] Braun has argued that, "...progressive critics would substitute found social truths, fixed public meanings, and final political triumphs for the political process".[6] Andrew Klavan sought to analyse the success which the neologism "Islamophobia" has achieved as a technique for stifling public discourse[7] and observed, "One of the cleverest tricks of the cultural left is demonizing perfectly reasonable actions and opinions by giving them sinister names".[8]

By the latter part of 2010, it appeared to have become impermissible to say anything critical about Islam or about Muslims. Mark Steyn, a Canadian writer who has attempted to warn the West about the threat from Islam, discovered that the site at which he had been booked to speak in London, Ontario cancelled the booking[9]. As it turned out, the event went ahead

---

[3] See, note 1, above.

[4] *Ibid.,* pp. 3-4.

[5] *Ibid.,* p.18.

[6] *Ibid.,* p.19.

[7] Robert Fulford, *Lessons of 9/11*, National Post, 11 September 2010.

[8] Andrew Klavan, *Name-Calling*, City Journal, 27 August 2010.

[9] Kate Dubinski, *Charges fly over venue's snub of author*, London Free Press, 22 October 2010. Another writer for the same paper believed that ensuring no-one's feelings might ever be hurt should be the dominant consideration. See, Vasco Castelo, *Why not accommodate feelings?*, *Ibid.,* 30 October 2010. The speech by Steyn was moved to another venue in London.

quietly, and without incident, at another location.[10] Juan Williams was a news analyst for National Public Radio in the United States. He was sacked for expressing his feelings of unease and hostility about jihadis[11].

Charles Krauthammer has recognised the way in which this trick of demonising opinions with which one does not agree has become a multi-purpose deus ex machina.[12]

It was particularly astute and original of Stefan Braun both to have noticed and to have articulated the manipulative, misleading and question-begging way in which the perceived antinomy between free expression and the suppression of "hate" is most commonly presented. As he put it:

> *Framing the cause against intolerance, ignorance and prejudice in the language of hate as progressive censors do can become a straitjacket on more nuanced and balanced thinking. Once the problematic is successfully packaged in the socially singular and politically absolute language of hate, the case for censorship becomes almost self-evident.[13]*

How on earth can a thinking, adult citizen be expected to respond to the question, "Which side are you on? Do you favour 'free expression' or 'hate'?" For Braun, "An abridgement of the

---

[10] Jonathan Sher, *'Weak, opportunistic' Islam will fell West, Steyn says*, London Free Press, 2 November 2010.

[11] *Remarks over Muslims cost top US radio host his job*, National Post, 22 October 2010. See also, Lorne Gunter, *Liberals defend sanctity of free speech for liberals only, Ibid.* and Andrew Klavan, *Juan Williams told the truth*, City Journal 22 October 2010.

[12] Charles Krauthammer, *When in doubt, blame bigotry*, National Post, 28 August 2010.

[13] *Democracy off Balance*, at p. 8. This question is discussed in more detail in Chapter 4.

'individual' right of anyone to political communication is an abridgement of the right of everyone to political self-determination."[14] As Braun views the matter, the progressive censors are a central element of "...a political movement that, at bottom, targets society at large for *cognitive correction*".[15] In this regard, it is important to note two thoughtful and disturbing observations made by Kenneth Minogue. He asserted that, "We must face up to the grim fact that the rulers we elect are losing patience with us"[16] and "...we are constantly being summoned to reform ourselves."[17]

To the extent that I am capable of understanding the way Canadians think, there does appear to me to be widespread belief in the existence of an inherent and necessary contradiction between free expression and equality. L.W. Sumner has published a rigourous and searching analysis of this question.[18] The thought of J.S. Mill[19], in particular his "harm" principle,[20] is at the centre of Sumner's analysis. The two forms of expression which Sumner found to be specially problematic are hate speech and pornography. He went to some length in addressing the question whether the state might justifiably limit either or both. The answer, which Sumner derived from Mill, is that the state may only seek to limit hate speech or pornography if it can be shown that each causes harm. It seemed to Sumner that the "harm"

---

[14] *Ibid.*, p. 37.

[15] (emphasis added) *Ibid.*, p. 26.

[16] Kenneth Minogue, *The Servile Mind: How democracy erodes the moral life,* Encounter Books, New York, 2010, p.2.

[17] *Ibid.*, at p.3. On the utility of seeking to stamp out words commonly referred to as "slurs", see, Ernie Lefore, *Speech and Harm*, New York Times, 7 November 2010.

[18] *The Hateful and the Obscene: Studies in the Limits of Free Expression,* Toronto, University of Toronto Press, 2004.

[19] *Ibid.*, pp.18 20.

[20] *Ibid.*, pp. 20-22.

resulting from hate speech might be found in various forms of "emotional distress", including feelings of humiliation, degradation, exclusion and self-hatred, as well as injuries to "self-esteem".[21] Sumner was not convinced that results such as these, which he characterised as "moral distress", [22] would provide a sufficient empirical basis to satisfy the "harm" criterion.[23] The matter of pornography was more problematic. Many, in particular the American academic, Catharine MacKinnon, have argued that, not only does pornography promote violence against women, it *is* violence against women.[24] Sumner concluded, "The question whether pornography causes sexual violence seems to be one for the social sciences to answer…such evidence as is available concerning the effects of pornography tends to be inconclusive, worse, there seems no likelihood of finding conclusive evidence."[25]

These two, mutually-reinforcing, perspectives of support for free expression and opposition to those who attack it will inform much of my analysis of free expression. It is important, at this point, to attempt to establish why free expression does, and should, matter in Canada. There would seem to be three broad sets of reasons that it does: first, free expression is *the* essential precondition to democratic politics, for, without free expression, there cannot be democracy[26].

Professor Ronald Dworkin has recently essayed a compelling

---

[21] *Ibid.,* at p.61.

[22] *Ibid.,* at p.158.

[23] *Ibid.,* at p.161.

[24] Catharine MacKinnon, *Only Words,* Cambridge, Mass., Harvard University Press, 1993.

[25] Note 18, at p.131.

[26] *Corporation of the Town of Halton Hills* v. *Kerouac* (2006) 80 O.R.(3d) 577.

and original argument in favour of free expression.[27] He asserted that free expression is "not just instrumental to democracy, but constitutive of that practice" and "...apart from this intimate relationship with democracy, it is a universal human right." He addressed, *en passant*, common arguments against free expression. He noted of the "malign consequences" of "bad speech", that "Many of these claims are inflated and some are absurd."[28] He continued, "...if free speech really is fundamental..., we must protect it even if it does have bad consequences, and...be prepared to explain why."[29] It seems that Dworkin was determined to go beyond instrumental arguments to assert that free expression is important for "reasons of basic principle" and "...a condition of human dignity". He went further, arguing:

> ...in a democracy, no one, however powerful or impotent, can have a right not to be insulted or offended." And concluded, "We might have the power to silence those we despise, but it would be at the cost of political legitimacy, which is more important than they are."[30]

The second set of reasons sees free expression as the most fundamental element in the European civilisation of which Canada is a fortunate legatee;[31] and, third, there is the brilliant and astute observation made by the Indian economist Dr Amartya Sen, who was awarded the Nobel Prize in 1998, that there has never been a

---

[27] Ronald Dworkin, *Foreword*, Ivan Hare and James Weinstein, editors, Extreme Speech and Democracy, Oxford, Oxford University Press, 2009, p.v., hereinafter *Extreme Speech*.

[28] *Extreme Speech* at p.vi.

[29] *Ibid.*, at p. vii.

[30] *Ibid.*, at pp. viii-ix.

[31] Salim Mansur, *Stifling Free Speech is not really free*, Toronto Sun, 10 February 2010.

famine in a country which respects free expression.[32] The core of Dr Sen's observation, as I understand it, is that, in a country where the ruled are able publically to disagree with and to criticise their rulers, that ability permits the ruled to place substantial and practical limits on the capacity of the rulers to inflict disasters upon them. Dr Sen's observation suggests that the desirability of free expression is neither purely, nor largely, a matter of abstraction, but is both concrete and practical.

A substantial part of the book will be taken up with describing the attacks on free expression in Canada today. More than description, however, is necessary. I will attempt to explain why free expression is under attack. Central to this analysis is my suggestion that Canada today is best understood as a totalitarian[33] theocracy[34]. That last sentence should not be interpreted as an assertion that Canada is, *tout court*, a totalitarian theocracy; it is, simply, a suggestion that, in order to understand Canada today and the place in it of freedom of expression, it may be helpful to

---

[32] See, Article XIX, Starving in Silence: A Report on Famine and Censorship, London, 1990, preface.

[33] It would be foolish and a serious dereliction of one's duties as a scholar, even to use the word "totalitarian", without making reference to Hannah Arendt's magisterial work, *The Origins of Totalitarianism*, Orlando, Florida, Houghton-Mifflin, Harcourt Publishing Company, 1985., hereinafter, *Origins*. Arendt was far too rigourous and intellectually sophisticated to have attempted a potted definition of "totalitarian". Whenever, in the course of this book, I use the word "totalitarian", I shall return to Arendt in an attempt justify its use.

[34] See, Benjamin A. Plotinsky, *The Varieties of Liberal Enthusiasm*, (2010) 20 City Journal, no.2 for an explication of the predominantly religious nature of much of the support for President Obama. Melanie Phillips noted the same phenomenon in her *The World Turned Upside Down*, note 38, at p. 10.

think of the country as a totalitarian theocracy.[35] I will not attempt to *prove* that Canada is, indeed, a totalitarian theocracy, even if such a thing were possible. It does seem to me that thinking of Canada as a totalitarian theocracy provides a practical and plausible framework to be used in attempting to understand the matters which will be discussed throughout this book. At the base of my notion that Canada can usefully be understood as a theocracy is something which, as I understand it, is properly described as a secular state religion of equality.[36] Kenneth Minogue has also used the phrase "religion of equality".[37] In her recent, magnificent work[38], Melanie Phillips identified ways of thinking which have become dominant in Western societies and observed of these ways of thinking:

> *Most fundamentally, they all involve the promotion of beliefs that purport to be unchallengeable truths, but are in fact ideologies in which evidence is manipulated, twisted and distorted to support and "prove" their governing idea. All are therefore based on false or unsupported beliefs that are presented as axiomatically true. Moreover, because each assumes itself to be proclaiming the sole and exclusive truth, it cannot permit any challenge to itself. It has to maintain at all costs the integrity of the falsehood. So all challenges have to be resisted through coercive means. Knowledge*

[35] In a similar vein, see Paul Edward Gottfried, *Multiculturalism and the Politics of Guilt: Toward a Secular Theocracy,* Columbia, MO, University of Missouri Press, 2002.

[36] Robert Fulford has written of "our religion of multiculturalism". See *The threatening honesty of Ayaan Hirsi Ali*, National Post, 12 June 2010.

[37] *The Servile Mind, op. cit.,* p.83.

[38] *The World Turned Upside Down: The Global Battle over God, Truth and Power,* New York and London, Encounter Books, 2010.

is thus forced to give way to power. Reason is replaced
by bullying, intimidation and the suppression of
debate.[39]

The Canadian secular state religion consists of a set of beliefs, beliefs which are accepted largely on faith and, consequently, assumed to be beyond debate. It is characterised as a state religion because it both informs and determines the way in which the organs of the state operate and, as a result, and this is where the idea of the theocracy being totalitarian becomes significant, other precepts and institutions must give way to the pursuit of equality.[40] The secular state religion of equality is, as we shall see, hostile towards free expression. This religion is arrayed at its most militant in opposition to "discrimination", which is perceived as the most evil and unforgiveable of all sins.[41]

The hostility towards free expression derives, to a large extent, from a conflation of words and deeds which, as I interpret it, lies at the core of the religion of equality. It appears, insofar as I am able to understand these matters, that, were I publically to express my hostility towards Fantasians, I would, thereby, be perceived to be "discriminating" against Fantasians. There appears to me to be a widespread belief that even a single act of "discrimination", left unchecked, leads inexorably to Auschwitz.

---

[39] *Ibid.*, at p. 97.

[40] *Bruker* v. *Marcovitz* [2007] 3 S.C.R. 607. In this case, a husband, Marcovitz, had agreed to give his wife, Bruker, a *ghet,* a divorce under Jewish religious law. Consequently, the wife sued the husband in an effort to oblige him to comply with his agreement. The husband argued that requiring him to do so would amount to interference with his freedom of religion. The Supreme Court of Canada held that, "The public interest in protecting equality rights...outweighs Marcovitz's religious freedom".

[41] *The Servile Mind, op.cit.*, pp.78 to 82.

This view might seem fantastic.[42] In this regard it will be useful to consult two books by the noted author and lecturer, Barbara Coloroso.[43] She has suggested that schoolyard bullying is the first step towards genocide.

Kenneth Minogue adroitly captured both the religious and the totalitarian elements of the prevailing orthodoxy when he described it as "…so complete that attitudes and acts falling inside and outside it can be specified merely as 'acceptable' and 'unacceptable'".[44]

The passage from Melanie Phillips, quoted above, provides a solid sense of the way the theocracy operates. The Canadian state religion is described as "secular", since it is a religion without a deity. Persons familiar with Marxist analysis will see this secular state religion as an important weapon in the class struggle, a significant means by which the dominant class retains its ideological and intellectual hold over the masses.[45] Christopher Lasch described this phenomenon as "a form of class warfare" through which the "enlightened elite (as it thinks of itself) seeks to impose its values on the unenlightened and to exclude the unenlightened from active participation in civic affairs."[46] What follows in this book should be interpreted, not as criticism of equality, but as criticism of theocracy.

---

[42] Teaching in a Canadian university, it began to become clear to me that, were I to characterize an analysis or an argument as "fantastic", students would think I was praising it.

[43] *The Bully, the Bullied and the Bystander: from preschool to high school—how parents and teachers can help break the cycle of violence,* New York, Harper Collins, 2003 and *Extraordinary Evil: A brief History of Genocide,* Toronto, Viking Canada, 2007.

[44] *The Servile Mind.,* at p. 220.

[45] Angelo M. Codeivilla, *America's Ruling Class—And the Perils of Revolution,* The American Spectator, 17 July 2010.

[46] Christopher Lasch, *The Revolt of the Elites and the Betrayal of Democracy,* New York, W.W. Norton, 1995, p. 20.

This book should be of interest to students, both journalism students and law students. Some study of the relevant law is a part of many Canadian journalism education programs; however, except for the Media Law course formerly offered at the University of Western Ontario, the matters discussed in this book are not addressed in Canadian law faculties. It would be useful, for journalism students, to supplement this book with a general introduction to the Canadian legal system.

The book should also be useful to working journalists, who might wish to keep themselves and their employers out of trouble, and to practising lawyers, many of whom will likely have limited knowledge of these areas of the law. The book should, in addition, be of value to Canadian citizens who cherish free expression and are disturbed by the attacks against it.

The subject matter of much of the book might be described as "Media Law". "Media law" is a phrase that requires some explanation. It is not a term of art, which is simply to say that it does not refer to a recognized, discrete area of the law such as contracts, torts, or constitutional law.

In fact, media law brings together elements from a number of different areas—most prominently criminal law, constitutional law, and the law of torts. What unites these elements is that, taken together, they represent the law which directly affects the mass media and the people working in the mass media. It is unfortunate, but necessary, to have to stress that the word "media" is the plural of "medium." Thus, it is not correct to state, as far too many people in Canada regularly do state, "the media is".

Another error which should be avoided is that of using "media" as a synonym for "reporters", as in "a large number of media arrived at the scene of the accident". In a similar vein, "bacteria" is the plural of bacterium, as "data" is the plural of datum. It may also be noted that "criteria" is the plural of criterion, and "phenomena" the plural of phenomenon. Those who are paying attention will have noticed, in Canada, an apparently inexorable process whereby English is being eroded and replaced by something which seems to me to merit characterisation as a barbarous and semi-literate pastiche. As someone who has felt lifelong affection and respect for the "sweet English tongue"[47], I find myself in a near-permanent state of anger, sadness and despair as I observe the endless indignities which are heaped on the language in Canada, in particular by ostensibly educated persons. This process appears to have two roots. The first is found in post modern feminism and the second in a widespread predilection for solipsistic ways of thinking. We will address each root in turn.

The starting point in understanding post modern feminism is its nihilism.[48] Every existing institution, relation or precept (including the language) was seen as hopelessly tainted by patriarchy and, thus, cried out to be extirpated. Feminists waged war on our language, in particular on any usage that appeared to them to promote one sex over the other. They demanded the adoption of what was called "non gender-specific" language. In the pastiche that passes for English, "gender" is used to mean "sex" and "sex" to mean "copulation". Feminists attacked the widespread use of "he" and "his" as if they were generic third person singular pronouns. That usage began to be replaced by "he or she" and "his or her". This was awkward and inelegant and was gradually discarded, with "they", "them" and "their" becoming the

---

[47] The phrase appears to have originated with the English poet, James Elroy Flecker.

[48] Elizabeth Fox-Genovese, *From Separate Spheres to Dangerous Streets: Postmodernist Feminism and the Problem of Order*, (1993) 60 Social Research 235.

commonly-used third person singular pronouns.[49] Throughout the rest of this volume, I shall use "she" and "her" as generic third person singular pronouns.

Solipsistic thinking appears to me to be a significant element in contemporary North American culture. Many North Americans seem to be convinced that each person is entitled to "…make up his own version of the universe".[50] And it must follow, that, if one perceives oneself as entitled to make up one's own version of the universe, then one must also be entitled to make up one's own version of the language.

I have made certain, possibly arbitrary, decisions about what is to be included, or not included, under the rubric "media law." In particular, I have not discussed questions relating to copyright or, more generally, to the law of intellectual property. These matters deserve a separate treatment of their own.[51] The vexed questions of hate propaganda and obscenity have important implications for the state of freedom of expression. The notion "hate propaganda" has expanded to the point where the phrase seems near meaningless; harmless expressions of opinion can cause individuals to become entrapped in the state's thought control machinery. Some discussion of judicial decisions relating to obscenity/pornography is found in Chapter 1. Issues relating to material which seems, in contemporary Canada, to be characterised almost whimsically as hate propaganda are addressed in Chapter 5 at the end of the book. These two matters should not be of direct, practical concern to persons working in the mass

---

[49] This barbarism has even found its way into Canadian legislation, see *Anti-Terrorism Act*, S.C. 2001, c. 41, s. 16 (3).

[50] Hadley Arkes, *Liberalism and the Law*, in Hilton Kramer and Roger Kimball, eds., *The Betrayal of Liberalism*, Chicago, Ivan R. Dee, 1999, p.96.

[51] David Vaver, *Intellectual Property Law: Copyright, Patents, Trade-Marks*, Toronto, Irwin Law, 1997.

media, who, I assume, do not engage in producing such material.

Media law should, and does, apply equally to all media of communication. Most of the material in this book deals with newspapers, radio, and television—the media where legal issues have arisen. I do not specifically address issues relating to the use of computers or on-line computer services, because these areas have not yet been dealt with directly by our legal system. There is some discussion, in Chapter 4, of liability for defamatory material published over the Internet. Nonetheless, there is no reason of principle or of logic for treating on-line computer services differently from any other medium of communication.

If the Government of Canada were to decide to treat on-line computer services as broadcasting and bring them under the regulatory authority of the CRTC, this could be accomplished quite simply. The desirability of this step is discussed in Chapter 5.

In 1968 it was decided that cable distribution systems for television should be regulated as broadcasting. This was accomplished by amending the definition of broadcasting in the *Broadcasting Act* so as to include cable systems.[52] The Government of Canada does already, to a degree, regulate on-line computer services. In 2002 the *Criminal Code* was amended to make it an offence to view child pornography on a computer.[53] I can only assume, for example, that a libel published through the Internet would be dealt with in much the same way that a libel published in a newspaper is.

The central concept around which this book is organized is free expression.[54] First, however, we need to clarify a number of definitions or questions. The most important of these addresses

---

[52] See *Broadcasting Act*, 1968, S.C. 1967-68, c. 25, s. 3(d).

[53] See *Criminal Law Amendment Act*, 2001, S.C. 2002, c. 13, s. 5(3).

[54] For a full exposition of the meaning of freedom of expression, see Robert Martin, *Promoting Freedom of Expression in the Commonwealth*, (2002) 366 The Roundtable 521.

distinctions amongst four different, though related, notions: freedom of speech, freedom of the press, freedom of expression, and freedom of information. It is essential to keep the four separate, even though they are sometimes used interchangeably. Although they relate to similar things, they are not identical.

Freedom of speech is probably the phrase with the longest tradition. It is found in the first amendment to the U.S. Constitution: "Congress shall make no law…abridging the freedom of speech." Freedom of speech addresses the ability of individuals to communicate ideas and information without interference from the state. When we talk about interference by the state, as a legal notion, we are referring to the imposition of prior restraint. Freedom of speech has typically meant the freedom to publish—publish being used here in its widest possible meaning as writing, speaking, printing, or broadcasting ideas and information—without prior restraint imposed by the state. A prior restraint is any state-created limit whereby individuals must seek some form of official permission before they may lawfully publish material. Two examples, one from an old Supreme Court of Canada decision and one from my former university, will illustrate what is meant.

The Supreme Court decision is from the 1953 case *Saumur v. Quebec (City).*[55] *Saumur* was one of a series of cases where notions of civil liberties developed in a long struggle between, primarily, the Jehovah's Witnesses and the Quebec government of Maurice Duplessis. The decision dealt with a municipal by-law in Quebec City which said that anyone who wished to distribute any kind of printed material on the streets had first to take the material to the chief of police. The chief would look the material over and decide whether it was acceptable. If the chief decided the material was acceptable, it could lawfully be distributed; if he decided the material was not acceptable, it could not. Such a power is a classic

---

[55] [1953] 2 S.C.R. 299.

example of a prior restraint. Whenever you have to have the permission of a state official before you may publish—before you can print, write, or speak—you have a prior restraint. The Court struck the law down.

At my former university there was a system called Poster Pollution. If anyone wanted to put a flyer, poster, or handbill on a bulletin board anywhere on the campus, she was required first to submit the material to the University Students' Council. The Council decided whether it was acceptable and, if it was, put a dated Poster Pollution stamp on it. Students acting for the Students' Council patrolled the bulletin boards and, if they discovered anything that did not have the required stamp or that had an expired stamp, they would pull it down. The Quebec law was struck down because it had been challenged in court. Poster Pollution is equally unacceptable, but has not been formally challenged.

Traditionally, then, freedom of speech meant the ability to publish, write, speak, or print without prior restraint. Censorship, strictly defined, is any form of prior restraint. Thus, when we speak of censorship as a legal concept, we mean prior restraint.

Freedom of the press is a related notion, but it is not identical. Freedom of the press includes the absence of prior restraint, but there can be circumstances where distinctions, even contradictions, may arise between freedom of speech and freedom of the press. An example is found in a 1979 decision of the Supreme Court of Canada, *Gay Alliance Toward Equality* v. *Vancouver Sun*.[56] The title of the Vancouver group, Gay Alliance Toward Equality, expressed its politics and its objectives. It sought to take out a classified advertisement in the Vancouver Sun. The ad read: "Subs[cribe] to GAY TIDE, gay lib[eration]

---

[56] *Sub nom. British Columbia (Human Rights Commission)* v. *Vancouver Sun*, [1979] 2 S.C.R. 435.

paper," followed by the cost of a subscription and a street address in Vancouver. That was all. There were no extravagant graphics or exuberant political statements. The Vancouver Sun, however, declined to print the ad. The Alliance took a complaint to the British Columbia Human Rights Commission on the basis that the classified advertising pages of a newspaper were a service or facility customarily available to the public and, as a result, the Commission had jurisdiction to deal with the matter under the British Columbia Human Rights legislation. The Commission ordered the Sun to print the advertisement. The Sun took the Commission to court, and the case ended up before the Supreme Court. In the event, the Court decided that the Commission did not have the necessary legal authority to make such an order.

For our purposes, the case points up a contradiction between the freedom of speech of the Gay Alliance Toward Equality and the freedom of the press of the Vancouver Sun. Many people have argued that if freedom of speech is to be meaningful in the kind of society in which we live, it must include some notion of access to the mass media. It does seem that "access to the mass media" can only mean, in practice, positive censorship.[57] If freedom of speech simply means that I can set up my soapbox in the corner of a field and rave at the blue sky, with no access to the mass media, it may not be a practical or useful freedom. Given the role that the mass media play, access to them is crucial if one is going to communicate one's ideas or information effectively.

Dworkin addressed this point, suggesting that, "…we must try to find other ways of providing those without money or influence a real chance to make their voices heard."[58]

Thus, freedom of speech for the Gay Alliance Toward Equality, in the circumstances of the case just discussed, meant having its classified advertisement appear in the Vancouver Sun.

---

[57] See p. 39.
[58] *Extreme Speech,* at p.viii.

But, while freedom of the press contains elements of free speech, it also ensures that the managers or proprietors of a newspaper, journal, radio station, or television network are free to have the last word about what they will or will not print or broadcast. Freedom of the press must mean that no one outside a newspaper, for example, can set editorial policy for that newspaper. In the circumstances of this case, freedom of the press for the Vancouver Sun meant that it should be free to choose whether to run the ad or not. The simple point is that, while freedom of speech and freedom of the press may often appear to be synonymous, there can be instances, as in *Gay Alliance*, where there is tension or even direct contradiction between the two.

Freedom of expression is the specific phrase used in the *Canadian Charter of Rights and Freedoms*.[59] Freedom of expression contains many of the basic elements of freedom of speech, but it is a consciously broader and more expansive notion. While freedom of speech protects the communication of information and ideas through speaking, writing, printing, or publishing, freedom of expression may also protect the communication of ideas or opinions through purely physical acts. For example, the Supreme Court of Canada has decided that picketing during a labour dispute is a form of expression.[60] Thus, freedom of expression may include more than would traditionally be regarded as falling within freedom of speech. The obvious question is whether we dilute the significance of free speech by adding to it protection for purely physical acts. It will be useful to attempt to make the distinction between "freedom of expression" and "free expression". Freedom of expression is a legal principle which seeks to protect the ability of individuals to engage in a particular activity without interference on the part of the state. Free

---

[59] Part I of the *Constitution Act, 1982*, being Schedule B to the *Canada Act 1982* (U.K.), 1982, c. 11, s. 2(b) [hereinafter *Charter*].
[60] *R.W.D.S.U. v. Dolphin Delivery Ltd.*, [1986] 2 S.C.R. 573.

expression is the activity one engages in when one is exercising one's freedom of expression. Sumner made a similar distinction.[61]

The fourth phrase has little to do with the three previous ones. **Freedom of information** is a very different notion from freedom of speech, freedom of the press, or freedom of expression. Freedom of information is a phrase which was invented in the United States and which is misleading. It has to do with the ability of individuals to gain access to information in the possession of the state. Freedom of information legislation in the United States gives people a legal right of access to such information. The federal legislation in Canada is more accurately titled as the *Access to Information Act*.[62] This title does describe what the statute is about. Many people who do not understand what freedom of information means have, in recent years, confused freedom of information and freedom of speech and expression. The confusion is compounded by the fact that freedom of information is a phrase with little inherent meaning. In Canada, Provincial access to information statutes tend to be called Freedom of Information Acts.

In recent years, the phrase "right to information" has come to enjoy a degree of acceptance.[63] "Right to information" does have some inherent meaning and does, indeed, describe the phenomenon it refers to.

In this book we will consider primarily those limits on freedom of expression that are imposed by the state. We will not look at limits that arise from the structure of ownership of the mass media. By and large, the law does not deal with these matters. We will briefly address why this should be the case, but in order to do so, we have to note distinctions between the

---

[61] *The Hateful and the Obscene,* op. cit., p.9.

[62] R.S.C. 1985, c. A-1.

[63] The Commonwealth Human Rights Initiative, based in New Delhi, has been using the phrase "right to information". See *C.H.R.I. News,* vol. 9, no. 1, February 2002.

structures of the broadcasting media and the print media, and the proprietary rights of the owners of each.

The Electronic Media

The history of broadcasting regulation in Canada began, for practical purposes, in 1928, when the government of William Lyon Mackenzie King established a Royal Commission under the chairmanship of Sir John Aird, a prominent banker. The mandate of the Aird Commission was to consider what kind of system should be set up to regulate radio broadcasting in Canada. In the 1920s, broadcasting meant radio broadcasting, and commercial radio broadcasting was limited to what we would now describe as the AM frequency band.

Because only a limited range of broadcasting frequencies could be used commercially, the response in all countries was for the state to take over the regulation and, more important, the allocation of broadcasting frequencies. If the state had not done so, the result would have been chaos. This simple reality is often referred to as the *scarcity argument*. Given recent fundamental changes in the technology of broadcasting, this scarcity is either no longer with us or is about to disappear. In an era when everyone who has a telephone and a computer can be, arguably, engaged in broadcasting, scarcity has little significance. One reason that newspaper publishing has not for many years been subjected to state regulation is that there has never been scarcity in relation to newspapers. Anyone with a piece of paper and a pen can produce a newspaper. No one may read it, but that is a different question. There is no technological barrier, comparable to the one that existed in the early days of radio broadcasting, to anyone producing a newspaper. Thus, the most basic justification for state regulation of broadcasting may well have disappeared, or be in the course of doing so.

The Aird Commission's report, completed in nine months, was brief and straightforward. The commissioners claimed to have discovered "...unanimity on one fundamental question— Canadian radio listeners want Canadian broadcasting."

> *At present the majority of programs heard are from sources outside Canada [namely, the U.S.]. It has been emphasised to us that the continued reception of these has a tendency to mould the minds of the young people in the home to ideals and opinions that are not Canadian. In a country of the vast geographical dimensions of Canada, broadcasting will undoubtedly become a great force in fostering a national spirit and interpreting national citizenship.*[64]

The answer, clearly, was that broadcasting must be "...carried on in the interests of Canadian listeners and in the national interests of Canada." This would be achieved through "...some form of public ownership, operation and control behind which is the national power and prestige of the whole public of the Dominion of Canada." So not only was there to be state control of broadcasting, and direct state involvement in providing programming, but the Aird Commission recommended that there be no private broadcasting. This is important because, in the history of Canadian broadcasting, private broadcasting and American broadcasting have, in practice, meant very much the same thing.

The *Aird Commission Report* was, in fact, the high-water mark of the related ideas that broadcasting in Canada should be Canadian, national, and public. A confusing succession of official reports and

---

[64] *Royal Commission on Radio Broadcasting*, Report, Ottawa, King's Printer, 1929.

legislation followed.[65]

Few subjects have been studied officially as extensively as broadcasting in Canada. As well as the Aird Report, there were official studies in 1951, 1957, 1965, and 1986. Major national broadcasting legislation was enacted in 1932, 1936, 1958, 1968, 1976, and 1991. Indeed, one of the few constants of Canadian politics is that, with the exception of the short-lived Conservative Clark government of 1979, every time there has been a change in the party in power in Ottawa, there has been a change in the broadcasting legislation. Competing political perspectives have been essential in shaping broadcasting policy.

It will be argued that two threads run throughout the story. The position of private broadcasting has expanded and improved, while the public, or state, element has declined in importance. At the same time the emphasis, both rhetorically and in fact, on the Canadianness of Canadian broadcasting has been diminished.

The recommendations of the Aird Report were not implemented immediately, but, after intense lobbying by the Canadian Radio League, a group strongly committed to Canadian public broadcasting, legislation was enacted in 1932.[66] This legislation followed the Aird recommendations in broad outline, but with one important exception: provision was made for privately-owned radio stations.

The original legislation was not well thought out. A House of Commons Special Committee looked into the matter in 1936 and recommended certain changes. The Committee affirmed the "...principle of complete nationalization of radio broadcasting in Canada" and called for the physical extension of broadcasting

---

[65] The classic account remains Margaret Prang, *The Origins of Public Broadcasting in Canada* (1965), 46 Canadian Historical Review 1. A recent and valuable general history is Marc Raboy, *Missed Opportunities: The Story of Canada's Broadcasting Policy*, Montreal and Kingston: McGill-Queen's University Press, 1990.

[66] *Canadian Radio Broadcasting Act*, Statutes of Canada, 1932, c. 51.

coverage to ensure that the largest number of Canadians possible would receive programming.[67]

A fresh statute, the *Canadian Broadcasting Act*, was enacted in 1936.[68] This Act established a new body called the Canadian Broadcasting Corporation (CBC). The CBC was to perform a dual role. It was mandated to "carry on a national broadcasting service" and, at the same time, to issue regulations "to control the character of any and all programmes broadcast," and to make recommendations on all applications submitted for the licensing of private stations. In other words, it was to be both broadcaster and regulator.

In 1949 an archetypically Canadian project was launched— the Royal Commission on National Development in the Arts, Letters and Science.[69] Inevitably, the inquiry (known popularly as the Massey Commission after its Chair, the diplomat and public servant, Vincent Massey) turned its attention to broadcasting. The Commission's report observed drily, "We do not wish to suggest that our national system of broadcasting has fulfilled all the hopes of its founders and its supporters." But neither, apparently, had it failed, for the report went on to state that:

> *The national system, however, has constantly kept in view its three objectives for broadcasting in Canada: an adequate coverage of the entire population, opportunities for Canadian self-expression generally, and successful resistance to the absorption of Canada into the general cultural pattern of the United States.*

---

[67] Canada, House of Commons, *Special Committee to Inquire into the Administration of the Canadian Radio Broadcasting Act*, 1932, Report, Official Report of Debates of the House of Commons, volume III, Ottawa, 1936, p. 3077.

[68] Statutes of Canada, 1936, c. 24.

[69] See *Report*, King's Printer, Ottawa, 1951, pp. 38–41.

So, at least insofar as the Massey Commission was concerned, there was to be no retreat from the fundamental principles set out in the Aird Report.

However, the *Massey Report* was written just before the dawn of the television age. While it could be argued that, even by 1950, a reasonably distinctive Canadian approach to radio broadcasting was alive and thriving, the same argument cannot, I believe, be made today about television broadcasting.

Massey had recommended a new major study of broadcasting. In 1955 the Royal Commission on Broadcasting was launched. It became known as the Fowler Commission,[70] after its Chair, Robert M. Fowler, President of the Canadian Pulp and Paper Association.

The *Fowler Report*, and even more important, its legislative aftermath, the 1958 *Broadcasting Act*,[71] were turning points in Canadian broadcasting. First, private broadcasting acquired a status, which if not quite equal to that of public broadcasting, was close enough. Section 10 of the new Act spoke of a "national broadcasting system" which was to have both "public" and "private" elements. Private broadcasting had come a long way from the death sentence passed on it in the Aird Report. Second, the CBC, as had long been urged by private broadcasters, lost its regulatory authority. It was to continue to operate broadcasting facilities and to provide programming, but its authority over private broadcasters was taken away and given to a newly-created state agency, the Board of Broadcast Governors. The result was that Canada would henceforth have, in fact, two separate and distinct broadcasting systems—the CBC and the private broadcasters. Third, the new Act made the CBC financially dependent on annual appropriations by Parliament, thus allowing the government in power to restrict the money available to the

---

[70] Queen's Printer, Ottawa, 1957.
[71] Statutes of Canada, 1958, c. 22.

public broadcaster and, if the government so wished, force it to raise revenues through commercial advertising. Finally, the new Act qualified the national commitment to having broadcasting which was "Canadian." The Act spoke, ominously, of a "broadcasting service" which was to be "basically Canadian in content and character." The 1958 legislation laid the foundation for what has occurred since—the ascendancy of private broadcasting and the concomitant decline and commercialisation of public broadcasting.

In 1965 Robert Fowler was asked to look at Canadian broadcasting again, but this time as chair of a ministerial advisory committee, rather than of an independent royal commission.[72]

In retrospect the second *Fowler Report* can be seen as the last attempt to resuscitate the principle that broadcasting in Canada should be both "public" and "Canadian." It sought to argue that "private" broadcasters were really "public" in character in that they made use of a public asset—the airwaves—and were subject to public regulatory control. Fowler also saw the CBC as the "essential" element in the broadcasting system. He proposed the creation of an agency to regulate all broadcasting and, in the process, promote its Canadianness.

The new *Broadcasting Act* of 1968[73] created yet another regulatory authority, the Canadian Radio and Television Commission (CRTC).[74] This body replaced the Board of Broadcast Governors. The CBC and the private broadcasters were put on a formally equal footing, subject only to the convoluted and unclear proviso that:

---

[72] Canada, Advisory Committee on Broadcasting, *Report*, Ottawa, Queen's Printer, 1965.
[73] Statutes of Canada, 1967-68, c. 25.
[74] In 1975 the Commission's regulatory jurisdiction was expanded to include national telecommunications systems and its name was changed to the Canadian Radio-Television and Telecommunications Commission. See Statutes of Canada, 1974-75-76, c. 49.

Where any conflict arises between the objectives of the national broadcasting service [that is, the CBC] and the interests of the private element of the Canadian broadcasting system, it shall be resolved in the public interest, but paramount consideration shall be given to the objectives of the national broadcasting service.

The Act was also unusual for Canadian legislation in that it set out, in section 3, a broad, rambling, and wordy statement of "Broadcasting Policy for Canada." This affirmed that the airwaves were "public property" and that broadcasting should "safeguard, enrich and strengthen the cultural, political, social and economic fabric of Canada." There were also other, more overtly political, goals set out. Broadcasting was to contribute to "national unity." One Member of Parliament remarked at the time that this suggested a move from "public broadcasting" to "state broadcasting."

The new Act crowned the complete emancipation of private, commercial broadcasting in Canada. The Canadian broadcasting system had evolved into something vastly different from what Sir John Aird had hoped to create.[75]

It is likely that nothing has done more to transform Canadian broadcasting than a technological development which began to make itself felt in the 1960s. This was cable television.

Prior to the advent of cable, substantial numbers of Canadians were too far away from CBC or private transmitters to be able to receive television signals off-air. Cable transmission promised to remedy this. Nevertheless, far more urgent and important to millions of potential Canadian viewers, cable would also bring them American television, clearer and crisper and in greater profusion than would ever be available off-air. This was the real impetus behind the spread of cable television in Canada.

---

[75] Quoted in Raboy, above, note 65, at p. 178.

Cable was unregulated until 1968 when the new Act expanded the jurisdiction of the regulatory agency, the CRTC, to include "broadcasting receiving undertakings"—cable systems.[76] In the early days of cable television, subscribers could only be offered signals on the twelve channels available in the VHF range. The CRTC issued regulations, binding on all cable operators, to establish a system of priorities. The regulations required cable operators to make all local Canadian signals available before channels could be allocated to signals originating from the U.S. This had the result of limiting the number of US stations the ordinary cable subscriber could receive.

The cable operators responded by offering "augmented" service, providing customers with converters which would allow them to receive additional signals beyond those available in the VHF range. The result was that cable operators could provide the Canadian signals they were required to carry and give their customers all the U.S. signals customers wanted. Today, standard television receivers have built-in converters which create the potential for cable subscribers to receive a hundred, or more, different signals. The simple fact is that, in the case of cable television, technology allowed the cable operators more effectively to challenge the ability of the Canadian state to limit the amount of U.S. programming available directly to Canadian viewers.

Nonetheless, the dream of broadcasting which would be both public and Canadian was not completely dead. The first Chair of the newly-created CRTC, Pierre Juneau, came into office determined to reverse the direction of the previous decade. Juneau strengthened the "Canadian content" requirements which had first been introduced in 1959. The purpose of these was to require broadcasters to devote a fixed proportion of their broadcasting time to "Canadian" programming. In 1972

---

[76] See *Broadcasting Act*, 1968, S.C. 1967–68, c. 25, s. 3(d).

broadcasters were directed to devote sixty percent of the broadcasting day to Canadian content. But, as one commentator has noted, "the quotas are not as demanding as they appear."[77] The period during which the observance of the quotas is to be measured has steadily increased in length. Although there are separate quotas for "prime time" television programming, the regulations actually define prime time as 6 PM to midnight, a period which is conveniently wider than the actual peak viewing hours. Finally, the question of what constitutes "Canadian" programming has been interpreted in an exceedingly formal fashion. Thus, a Canadian network can produce a cop show which it hopes to market in the U.S., fly U.S. flags from all the buildings, dress its police in U.S.-style uniforms, and hire American actors for the leading roles, but, if the show is actually shot in Canada with Canadian crews and Canadian extras, it will qualify as "Canadian content."

Juneau was also determined the CBC should attempt to play the role originally intended for it. In 1974 the CRTC renewed the CBC's broadcasting licences. In its formal decision the Commission called the CBC "the cornerstone of the Canadian broadcasting system"[78] and noted its special responsibilities under the *Broadcasting Act*. However, the reality, the Commission said, was "...a lack of purpose, determination and vigour in implementing the objectives established by Parliament." The problem was that the CBC had become too much like a commercial broadcaster. It was too dependent on advertising revenues and had exhibited "...a preoccupation with mass audience concepts, stimulated by the contemporary North

---

[77] Bruce Feldthusen, *Awakening From the National Broadcasting Dream: Rethinking Television Regulation for National Cultural Goals*, in David H. Flaherty and Frank E. Manning, eds. *The Beaver Bites Back? American Popular Culture in Canada*, Montreal and Kingston: McGill-Queen's University Press, 1993, 42 at 60.

[78] Decision CRTC 74–70, Ottawa, 31 March 1974.

American marketing environment (that) is inappropriate for a publicly supported broadcasting service." As a condition of renewing its licence, the CRTC required that CBC television drastically reduce the amount of commercial advertising it carried and increase its Canadian content.

There is an inescapable reality about state-operated broadcasting, however. If such a broadcasting service is to operate entirely free of commercial constraints, it must be given full financial support. To the extent it is not given sufficient money to discharge its formal mandate, it is obliged to turn to commercial sources for financing. And the more it has to rely on advertising revenues, the more its programming will become indistinguishable from the fare offered by commercial broadcasters.

Pierre Juneau was not successful. The period since the mid-1970s has seen the unrelenting abandonment of the goals of the Aird Report. Indeed, the author of a recent history of Canadian broadcasting entitled his chapter on the 1980s, "The Eclipse of Public Broadcasting."[79] More concretely, this period was one of uncertainty and pessimism—uncertainty about what, if anything, "Canadian" broadcasting meant and pessimism whether there remained any real possibility of maintaining a broadcasting system which was both public and Canadian. A major reason for the abandonment of the goals of the Aird Report was the evaporation of the self-confidence which had originally underlain it. Two official reports are redolent of the confusion of the period.

Louis Applebaum and Jacques Hébert were co-chairs of something called the Federal Cultural Policy Review Committee,[80] which produced its report in 1982. The committee

---

[79] Raboy, above, note 65, at p. 267.

[80] *Report*, Ottawa, Supply and Services Canada, 1982. (The careful reader will have noted that the government publications office was no longer called the "Queen's Printer.")

asserted, without much vigour, that there was still a national broadcasting system, with a "privately-owned" and a "state-owned" component. It went on to note that the CBC was not playing the role envisaged for it. Indeed, "...we need a better, more vital, more courageous CBC." Finally, the CRTC had not in fact used its regulatory authority to require that private broadcasters comply with Canadian content rules.[81] The Committee was, if anything, too charitable in its assessment of the CRTC. It was widely apparent by the middle of the 1980s that the CRTC had largely abandoned the attempt to regulate what was being broadcast in Canada.

The last official enquiry to note is that of the Task Force on Broadcasting Policy of 1985-86.[82] This report is a testimony to the degree of confusion which has become endemic in current Canadian public discourse. It talked of "community" and provincial involvement in broadcasting, and repeated shibboleths about "Canadian" broadcasting, but the committee, in the end, clearly had no concrete idea how to address any of the manifold ills of the national broadcasting system.[83]

The final abandonment of the goals of Canadian broadcasting, as enunciated by Sir John Aird, occurred during the period, 1984–1993, when Brian Mulroney was Prime Minister.

---

[81] See John Meisel, *Stroking the Airwaves: The Regulation of Broadcasting by the CRTC* in Benjamin D. Singer, ed. Communications in Canadian Society, 3rd ed., Scarborough, Ontario, Nelson, 1991, p. 217.

[82] *Report*, Ottawa, Supply and Services Canada, 1986. By this time, changes in fashion had dictated that "ad hoc committees" should be styled "task forces."

[83] The current *Broadcasting Act*, Statutes of Canada, 1991, c. 11, states in s. 3(1)(b) that the Canadian broadcasting system now has three elements: the "public" (CBC and the French-language service, Radio Canada), the "private," and the "community." It is not at all clear what this means and was only mentioned in the Act, I suspect, in order to create the impression that the government had listened to the recommendations of the Task Force.

Mulroney, as I understand his time in office, had two broad policy goals. He sought closer integration of Canada with the United States and he wished to reduce the role of the state in Canadian society. The effects of these policy goals on broadcasting were, first, that the CRTC formally embraced the principle of "self-regulation" on the part of private broadcasters and, second, that funding for the CBC was cut drastically.[84]

The result is what exists today—a system where the average Canadian television viewer can watch dozens of U.S. signals, where "Canadian" private programming, in my opinion, is indistinguishable from American programming, and where CBC television is indistinguishable from private television. The one exception to this dismal picture is CBC radio, which still manages to be both Canadian and non-commercial.

One thread which, as I see it, runs through the story of the CBC is technological backwardness. The CBC did not initiate television broadcasting until 1952, even though the U.S. networks had been providing television programming since roughly the end of the Second World War. As a young boy in Toronto in the 1940s, I can recall that we had been watching Buffalo television stations for several years before CBC television appeared in 1952. Colour became commonplace on the U.S. networks in the 1950s. The CBC's first colour broadcast aired on 1 July 1967. As far as I am aware, the CBC was the last major television network in North America to broadcast in stereo sound.

By 2001 the CRTC seemed to have decided to micro-manage Canadian broadcasters. It did so in order to implement the Canadian sacred cow of multiculturalism. In renewing the broadcasting licence of the Global Television Network, the Commission ordered that, in its news-gathering and news-reporting, Global should:

---

[84] CRTC, *Annual Report*, 1986–87, Ottawa, Supply and Services Canada, 1987.

a.   ...use...people from minority groups as sources regardless of whether the issue being discussed is particularly related to a minority community;

b.   [ensure] that stories about ethnic communities do not appear solely within the context of coverage of cultural celebrations or reporting of negative stories;

c.   [ensure] that on-air personalities reflect the diversity of the community that the station serves; and

d.   [ensure] that reporters and journalists from minority communities are not assigned exclusively to covering stories of principal concern to cultural groups.[85]

That ruling, made by the CRTC in 2001, seems to me, if one is prepared to accept my suggestion (above) that Canada today can best be understood as a totalitarian theocracy, to be a fresh and unprecedented step in Canada's apparently relentless descent into totalitarianism.[86]

It might be regarded as an early manifestation, in Canada, of positive censorship. Since the distinction between positive censorship and negative censorship is, possibly, not widely understood, it will be useful to devote a sentence or two to explicating it. Negative censorship, which is the better known of the two, involves the state ordaining to its citizens, "You *may not* say A,B or C, and, if you do, you will be punished". Positive censorship, on the other hand, involves the state ordaining, "You *must* say X,Y and Z and, if you fail to do so, you will be punished".

This decision is problematic, particularly in two respects. First, the Commission appears to have attempted to take over Parliament's responsibility for making broadcasting policy and,

---

[85] *Licence renewals for the television stations controlled by Global* (2 August 2001), Broadcasting Decision, CRTC 2001-458.

[86] Arendt wrote of, "...the permanent domination of each single individual in each and every sphere of life", *Origins,* p. 326.

second, the conditions laid down are likely an infringement of the guarantee of freedom of expression in section 2(b) of the *Charter*. What the Commission decreed in this instance could probably be described as "broadcasting equity."[87] The regulations, made by the CRTC, which apply to all radio broadcasters in Canada, state, in part, that a licensee may not broadcast "any abusive comment...likely to expose an individual or a group or class of individuals to hatred or contempt on the basis of race, national or ethnic origin, colour, religion, sex, sexual orientation, age, mental or physical disability." It has been held that this prohibition may not be enforced directly against licensees, but only through the licensing process.[88]The CRTC recently refused to renew a licence because of repeated violations of this regulation.[89]

Some final thoughts on broadcasting follow. I do not believe the current position to have been inevitable. Many unimaginative Canadian commentators have suggested that the dream of Canadian broadcasting was always unattainable.[90] This is to misunderstand history. We got to where we are through a process, through conscious choices made at a number of key junctures. Had different choices been made, the outcome would also have been different. To take one obvious example, had the CBC been more generously funded over the last two decades, the programming it presents today would be very different.

Other countries confronting similar issues also have choices. The range of possible choices may be broad or it may be narrow, but there is always some opportunity to make choices.

With respect to creating a national broadcasting system, it must be remembered that what is involved is not a

---

[87] For a searching discussion of "equity" and similar concepts, see Martin Loney, *The Pursuit of Division: Race, Gender and Preferential Hiring in Canada*, Montreal: McGill-Queen's University Press, 1998.

[88] *R .v. Buffalo Broadcasting Ltd.* (1977) 36 C.P.R. (2d)170.

[89] *Re CHOI-FM, Broadcasting Decision CRTC 2004-271.*

[90] Feldthusen, above, note 77, is a typical expression of this perspective.

straightforward conflict between "us" (nationals) and "them" (foreigners). The goal of Canadian broadcasting was largely subverted, not by Americans, but by Canadians who were proponents of private broadcasting. The history of Canadian broadcasting is not a history of a united people struggling bravely to resist a hostile cultural invasion from the south. The fact is that substantial numbers of Canadians have for long seen that there was money to be made in supplying U.S. programming to their fellow Canadians and even more substantial numbers of Canadians have been eager to have as much of that American programming as possible.[91]

A major concern of the Aird Report in 1929 was the growing domination of commercial radio broadcasting in Canada by American broadcasters.[92] What should the Canadian response be? The Commission made a number of fundamental recommendations, many of which are still relevant.

First, it urged that the state should regulate broadcasting, not simply to allocate frequencies, but to ensure that there was a broadcasting system in Canada which reflected and promoted Canadian identity, Canadian values, and Canadian culture. The Commission's report said, as has been noted, it had discovered "unanimity on one fundamental question—Canadian radio listeners want Canadian broadcasting."

Further, the Aird Commission recommended not only that the state regulate broadcasting but that it provide broadcasting services. Indeed, the Commission recommended that the state have a monopoly on providing broadcasting services, as was the position of the British Broadcasting Corporation in the United Kingdom at the time. This crucial recommendation was not

---

[91] See Irvin Goldman and James Winter, *Mass Media and Canadian Identity, in Singer*, above, note 81, at p. 146.
[92] Royal Commission on Radio Broadcasting, *Report*, Ottawa: King's Printer, 1929.

adopted by the government of Canada and, from the outset, limited private radio broadcasting was permitted. Most important for present purposes, the Aird Commission recommended that the airwaves be regarded as public property, to be regulated by the state in the public interest. This principle, although it has been much watered down, continues in the current *Broadcasting Act*.[93]

How has the principle that broadcasting frequencies are public property worked in practice? First, no one may legally operate a broadcasting undertaking without a licence issued by the state through the agency of the Canadian Radio-Television and Telecommunications Commission. Second, the CRTC administers regulations that apply to all broadcasters. There are three sets of regulations: the *Radio Regulations*, the *Television Broadcasting Regulations*, and the *Cable Television Regulations*.[94]

Although the proprietary rights of the owners of the broadcasting media are limited through being subject to control and regulation by the state, the state or public role in Canadian broadcasting in recent years has become far more apparent than real. For many years private broadcasting was formally regarded as subordinate to the Canadian Broadcasting Corporation, the state-run broadcasting operation, but, during the Conservative Diefenbaker era, private broadcasting was given legal recognition as having the same status as the CBC. More recently, the CRTC has largely taken itself out of the business of directly regulating Canadian broadcasting. It no longer aggressively enforces the broadcasting regulations. Indeed, it has formally embraced the principle of "self-regulation" on the part of private broadcasters,[95] largely through encouraging the development of voluntary codes.

The CRTC has three levels of authority over licensees. First,

---

[93] S.C. 1991, c. 11.

[94] The *Radio Regulations* are SOR/86–982; the *Television Broadcasting Regulations* are SOR/87–49; and the *Cable Television Regulations* are SOR/86–831. All three have been much amended.

[95] See M. Raboy, above, note 65.

it can cancel a licence. Every broadcaster in Canada knows the CRTC has never cancelled a licence because of a breach of the applicable broadcasting regulations. Second, the CRTC can suspend a licence. It has suspended licences, not for any breach of the general broadcasting regulations, but usually for a breach of the specific terms of a particular licence. When an application is made for a licence, especially a radio licence, it is necessary to fill out a "promise of performance" form. The CRTC has established various program categories and, in the promise of performance, the applicant is obliged to set out the number of hours per week it intends to broadcast in different performance categories. What has happened many times in the history of radio licensing is that someone, especially in one of the larger urban markets, applies for a licence and promises to provide, say, X hours a week of innovative, Canadian-written and -produced radio drama, Y hours a week of uplifting talks, and Z hours a week of Canadian public affairs programming. The submission sounds ideal and the applicant gets a licence. Immediately, the station begins to broadcast twenty-four hours a day of Top Forty music. The CRTC has suspended licences for flagrant violations of the promise of performance.

Third, the CRTC can also refuse to renew a licence. Licences are granted for specific terms, usually five years. Even the CBC has to apply every five years for a new licence. Where there have been refusals to renew, they have usually arisen because of problems with the financial or technical elements of the regulations. The simple fact is that the CRTC plays a muted role in regulating the content of what is broadcast in Canada. As a result, the proprietors of the broadcasting media, rather than the state, determine what is broadcast in Canada.

In 2009 the CRTC began holding hearings on the question of whether it should exercise regulatory jurisdiction over the

Internet, ostensibly in order to make its content "more Canadian"[96]

In June of 2009 the CRTC issued a policy statement in which it consciously and deliberately eschewed exercising jurisdiction over the Internet.[97] The reasoning adopted by the Commission was compelling. The Commission characterised the *Broadcasting Act* as "an artefact of history" and urged that "the internet must be allowed to evolve."

The Commission went further, arguing that "...technological progress has undermined the assumptions on which the *Broadcasting Act* is based" and offered this strong conclusion:

> *The paradigm of broadcasting is bound in time by the technology which informed it. We are moving away from that technology and its limits and our laws should move to address problems appropriate to today and not those of 1958 or 1997.*

The Print Media

There would appear to be substantial distinctions between the authority of the owners of the broadcasting media and of the owners of the print media, although the significance of this ostensible distinction has been diminished in recent years. For the reasons noted above, in practice, there is little difference between owning a radio station or a television network and owning a newspaper. Yet while there is a seemingly elaborate system of broadcasting regulation, the print media are unregulated.

From the standpoint of the law, owning a newspaper is much the same as owning any other form of private property. The

---

[96] Grant Robertson and Matt Hartley, *CRTC New Media hearings, Globe and Mail,* 17 February 2009.

[97] Broadcasting Regulatory Policy, CRTC 2009-329.

proprietor of a newspaper stands in the same relation to her newspaper as the proprietor of a soap factory or a used car lot does to her property. Owners have, within provincial employment laws, absolute authority over hiring and firing. This authority includes the right to dismiss journalists who express uncongenial opinions in the pages of the newspaper or outside the workplace.[98] Owners have authority over all financial matters affecting their newspapers. They decide how much or how little money will be spent on hiring and keeping editorial staff and how newspaper profits will be disposed of. Will profits be reinvested in improving the newspaper or, as often happens where newspapers are part of conglomerate corporate empires, will they be used to finance other corporate ventures? Finally, owners have complete freedom to dispose of newspapers. They can sell them to whomsoever they choose or they can simply fold them.

Disputes over the authority wielded by owners arise periodically, because there are people who believe there are significant social differences between newspapers and detergent or used cars. Such beliefs are widely expressed only when something especially outrageous occurs.

Something outrageous happened in the summer of 1980. The Southam Corporation closed the Winnipeg *Tribune*, and the Thomson chain closed the Ottawa *Journal*.[99] Both Winnipeg and Ottawa were, as a result, left as one-newspaper towns. A degree of public concern was expressed and the Liberal Trudeau government responded by setting up a royal commission to look

---

[98] General questions relating to the extent of employer authority over journalist employees are discussed in *Cashin v. Canadian Broadcasting Corp.*, [1988] 3 F.C. 494 (C.A.), and *Canadian Broadcasting Corp. v. Canada (Labour Relations Board)*, [1995] 1 S.C.R. 157.

[99] These acts were made legally possible because of a Supreme Court of Canada decision which, in effect, told newspaper owners that the existing federal competition legislation did not apply to them. *R. v. K.C. Irving Ltd.*, [1978], 1 S.C.R. 408.

into newspapers. The commission was chaired by Tom Kent. Kent began his career as a journalist in the United Kingdom, then moved to Canada where, among other things, he headed Prime Minister Lester Pearson's war on poverty in the mid-1960s and, after the Royal Commission, became Dean of Management Studies at Dalhousie University. He had, despite the often critical views of some newspaper owners about him, an abiding faith in capitalism.[100]

The Kent Commission produced its report in 1981 and recommended certain limitations on the proprietary rights of newspaper owners.[101] In response, Kent was roundly vilified on editorial pages from sea to sea. The Commission's recommendations were portrayed as a monstrous scheme to destroy freedom of expression and freedom of the press in Canada. The reality was different. Kent proposed the enactment of a *Canada Newspapers Act* to inhibit further concentration of newspaper ownership and to reverse it in severe cases. The Act would have guaranteed a degree of independence for newspaper editors and journalists. Advisory committees would be set up across the country to permit members of the local community to express their views about local newspapers. Draft legislation was prepared, but as the hysteria of denunciations of Kent and all his works mounted, the government lost its nerve. The draft bill went nowhere and the report was quickly forgotten.

The only lasting significance of the Kent Commission lay in the impetus it gave to press councils. Newspaper owners apparently decided that, having torpedoed the Commission, they should make some symbolic concession to one of its recommendations. Perhaps they wished to give the appearance of

---

[100] See Tom Kent, *The Significance of Corporate Structure in the Media*, (1985) 23 The University of Western Ontario Law Review, no. 2, 151.
[101] Royal Commission on Newspapers, *Report*, Ottawa, Minister of Supply and Services, 1981.

limiting their ownership rights and of recognizing the legitimacy of a public interest in the content of newspapers. So they decided to join press councils. To what degree, if any, do these councils limit the proprietary authority of newspaper owners?

The Ontario Press Council, Canada's first, was formed in 1972, with eight newspapers as members: the Toronto *Star*, the London *Free Press*, and a number of Southam papers. Membership grew slowly, with only one daily and a few weeklies joining before 1981. But 1981 was, as the Council put it, a "record year for growth." One daily and nine weeklies joined. The *10th Annual Report* for 1982 stated, "Council membership booms." The number of dailies belonging to the Press Council increased from ten to thirty-two, and included the *Globe and Mail* and some other Thomson papers. Membership among weeklies jumped from fourteen to forty-nine. Eighteen more dailies joined the Council in 1983 and, by the beginning of 1985, all forty-two English-language daily newspapers in Ontario were members.[102]

The activity was not confined to Ontario. The Ontario Council stated in its 1982 *Report*: "The press council movement got into high gear across Canada in late 1982." By 2003 there were press councils in Quebec, Manitoba, Alberta, and British Columbia, in addition to the Atlantic Press Council.

The Ontario Press Council was based on the model provided by the UK Press Council. Its structure is bipartite, in that there are two parties—the newspapers and the public. The parties receive equal representation in all the committees and organs of the Council. The Atlantic Press Council and the press councils in Western Canada all follow the Ontario model. The Quebec Press Council is different, having a tripartite structure: the newspapers,

---

[102] Copies of Ontario Press Council *Annual Reports* and other documents can be obtained from the Council's Office at Ryerson University, 350 Victoria Street, Toronto, Ontario, M5B 2K3. See also Alti Rodal, *Press Councils in Canada*, Ottawa, 1983, unpublished.

the public, and the journalists. This tripartite structure would seem to reflect more accurately the nature of newspaper organizations. The problem with the Ontario Press Council structure is that it defines the interests of proprietors and reporters as being identical, something which, in the experience of anyone who has ever been a reporter, is questionable. The tripartite structure in Quebec not only allows members of the public to complain about newspapers but also allows journalists to complain about newspapers.

The most important function of press councils is to hear complaints. Normally, aggrieved persons must have exhausted all available legal remedies before a press council will entertain a complaint. When a council determines that a complaint has some substance, it will set up a committee to conduct a formal hearing into the complaint. This committee will reach a decision as to whether the newspaper's coverage of particular stories was proper or adequate, whether the photograph on page 1 was tasteless, and so on. In Ontario, the committee hearing a complaint reflects the bipartite structure of the Council. An equal number of representatives of the newspapers and of the public will be on the committee. The rules provide that where the decision is adverse to the newspaper, the offending newspaper is obliged to print the text of the decision. The problem with the Ontario Press Council is that there is no mechanism in its constitution for enforcing its decisions. The normal mechanism that all private or voluntary associations use for enforcing their rules is expulsion: if a member of a private club does not obey the rules, the member is thrown out. The Ontario Press Council's constitution contains no power to expel a member. So a newspaper can consistently refuse to print the text of adjudications that are critical of it. Press councils, in effect, do little to limit the proprietary authority of newspaper owners.

The problem, for people who are not enthusiastic about free expression, with press councils is that they do not have the authority to interfere directly with the content of newspapers or other publications. Throughout 2009, Barbara Hall, who chairs the Ontario Human Rights Commission has, as I interpret her actions, repeatedly demonstrated hostility to free expression. In a submission of 7 February 2009 to the Canadian Human Rights Commission, she called for the creation, by the state, of a national press council of which all media would be required to be members. This council would, as she saw it, have the authority to deal with complaints from persons who imagined themselves to have been "discriminated" against by the media.[103]

The proprietary authority of owners of newspapers and radio and television undertakings can be used to shape and define freedom of expression. The law simply does not directly address this matter. The law speaks only to limitations on freedom of expression that are imposed by the state. To take a leading illustration of this fact, the *Canadian Charter of Rights and Freedoms* creates rights only as against the state. The *Charter's* guarantee of freedom of expression cannot, thus, be enforced against media owners or managers.

The bulk of this book looks at freedom of expression in Canada. First, it addresses the issue in relation to the Constitution of Canada, and then focuses attention on the various and substantial limitations on freedom of expression that are found in our law. Because it is often difficult to dissociate general or abstract questions about freedom of expression from concrete issues that confront working journalists, a recurring theme throughout the book is the question whether the law should recognize any special rights or special status for journalists.

---

[103] Joseph Brean, *Human Rights Commission calls for Media Council*, National Post, 12 February 2009

FURTHER READING

A useful, if somewhat dated, survey of Canadian newspapers is found in the report of the Kent Commission: Royal Commission on Newspapers, *Report*, Ottawa, Minister of Supply and Services, 1981 (Chair: T. Kent). The fullest current survey of the regulation of broadcasting is M. Raboy, *Missed Opportunities: The Story of Canada's Broadcasting Policy*, Montreal, McGill-Queen's University Press, 1990.

For a detailed collection of primary materials on media law, see R. Martin and G.S. Adam, *A Sourcebook of Canadian Media Law*, (2d ed.), Ottawa, Carleton University Press, 1994. A useful practical guide is R.S. Bruser and B.M. Rogers, *Journalists and the Law: How to Get the Story without Getting Sued or Put in Jail*, Ottawa, Canadian Bar Foundation, 1985. An excellent source for keeping up with developments is "The Press and the Courts" service of the Canadian Newspaper Association, Suite 200, 890 Yonge Street, Toronto, Ontario, M4W 3P4, telephone (416) 923-3567; website www.can-acj.ca.

CHAPTER 1

Free Expression and the Constitution

WHAT EFFECT HAS Canada's federal structure had on freedom of expression? To answer this question it is necessary to examine the division of powers and responsibilities between the two levels of government and to see how this division has been interpreted by the courts in such a way as to provide a limited degree of constitutional protection for freedom of expression. Similarly, the *Canadian Charter of Rights and Freedoms* has created a substantive guarantee of freedom of expression[104].

The basic principle of constitutional government is that the state is subject to the law. The state and all its organs must act within the rules set out in the constitution. Section 52(1) of the Constitution Act, 1982[105], expresses this principle clearly by stating that "[t]he Constitution of Canada is the supreme law of Canada." Consequently, any act of the state which is not in accordance with the requirements of the Constitution is invalid. Thus, to the extent that the Constitution protects freedom of expression, state acts that interfere with free expression may be open to challenge before the courts and, if the challenge is successful, may be declared invalid.

---

[104] Part I of the *Constitution Act, 1982*, being Schedule B to the *Canada Act 1982* (U.K.), 1982, c. 11, s. 2(b) [hereinafter *Charter*].

[105] Being Schedule B to the *Canada Act 1982* (U.K.), 1982, c. 11, s. 52(1).

Federalism

General Considerations

For 115 years after Confederation, Canada's written Constitution consisted largely of the *British North America Act of 1867*.[106] Nowhere in the text of that Act is there reference to freedom of speech, freedom of expression, freedom of the press, or anything similar. The central purpose of the *BNA Act* was to create Canada's institutions of government. More specifically, it set out the basic elements of the federal system, dividing the authority to make laws between the Parliament of Canada and the provincial legislatures. The *BNA Act* did not contain any formal protection for rights. The limits it established on law-making authority were functional rather than substantive.

The task of interpreting the *BNA Act* and, more particularly, the way it apportioned law-making powers between Ottawa and the provinces was left to the courts. It is worth spending some time describing the federal structure set out in the Act and the way that structure was elaborated by the courts. The *BNA Act*, like all federal constitutions, is organized around lists of legislative subject-matters. Section 91 lists the areas in which Parliament, the federal legislature, has the authority to make laws. These areas tend to be national in scope and significance. Sections 92, 92A, and 93 list the areas in which the provincial legislatures may make laws, areas that are more local in scope. Section 95 sets out those areas—agriculture and immigration—where legislatures at both levels may make laws.

The judicial approach to dispute resolution, despite substantial oscillation over the years between preferences for either a centralized or a decentralized approach to Canadian federalism, is quite simple. When someone challenges the validity of a statute—

---

[106] (U.K.), 30 & 31 Vict., c. 3.

for example, a provincial statute—the court must determine whether that statute is within the powers of the provincial legislature to enact (*intra vires*, and, therefore, constitutional) or beyond the powers of the provincial legislature to enact (*ultra vires*, and, therefore, unconstitutional). The court will follow a two-stage approach. In the first stage, it will examine the impugned law to determine its subject-matter and to discover what that law is really all about. This stage is described as "characterizing" the law. Having determined the subject-matter of the law, the court will then go to the lists in the Constitution to see where this subject-matter is to be found. Since we are dealing hypothetically with a provincial law, if the court finds its subject-matter in the provincial list, the law is valid. But if the court finds the subject-matter of the law under scrutiny in the federal list, it is invalid, because it is a provincial enactment dealing with a subject-matter about which only Parliament may constitutionally make laws.

The "Implied Bill of Rights"

The Supreme Court of Canada was able to create a limited degree of constitutional protection for freedom of expression out of the division of powers. This protection originated in a decision called *Reference Re Alberta Legislation*[107]—the first major discussion of the significance of freedom of expression by the Court. It is noteworthy that such a crucial concern did not receive extensive judicial consideration until 1938.

The background to the decision is of interest.[108] In the 1930s Canada experienced a major economic depression, and the areas

---

[107] [1938] S.C.R. 100.

[108] The classic account is C.B. Macpherson, *Democracy in Alberta: Social Credit and the Party System*, 2d ed., Toronto, University of Toronto Press, 1962.

most hard hit were the three prairie provinces—Manitoba, Saskatchewan, and Alberta. Not only were these provinces devastated economically, but the effects of the depression were exacerbated by prolonged drought. The economies of the prairie provinces were, at the time, based on agriculture. Oil of a commercially exploitable quality and quantity was not discovered in Alberta until 1947.

These extreme economic conditions in western Canada, as in other places undergoing similar stresses at other times, led to extreme political responses. The response in Manitoba and Saskatchewan was the Cooperative Commonwealth Federation (CCF), founded in Regina in 1933; in contrast, the response in Alberta was Social Credit. In the 1935 Alberta election the world's first Social Credit government was voted into office. The new government was determined to bring about the Social Credit millennium in Alberta.

One of the many difficulties Social Credit experienced in Alberta was a lack of enthusiasm for it amongst the province's newspapers. The newspapers, and in particular the Edmonton *Journal*, were highly critical of Social Credit. The *Journal*, in fact, became the only Canadian newspaper ever to win a Pulitzer Prize, when it received an honorary award for some of its writing about Alberta politics. This criticism became increasingly annoying to Social Credit, and as part of its legislative package, it introduced a statute called *An Act to Ensure the Publication of Accurate News and Information*. When governments enact statutes with titles like this, their objectives are likely to be the opposite of what the words suggest.

For our purposes, the *Act to Ensure the Publication of Accurate News and Information* said three things. The first had to do with any story about a Social Credit policy or program which the authorities believed to be inaccurate or misleading. Social Credit did not believe in the institution of government, so it was in an embarrassing position when it found itself the government of

Alberta. It announced that it was not really the provincial government and passed legislation setting up the Social Credit Board, which was, in fact, the government of Alberta. The leader of Social Credit, William Aberhart, likewise did not want to call himself the premier of Alberta, so he took the title of chairman of the Social Credit Board. The legislation stipulated that the chairman of the Social Credit Board had the power, when he believed that a newspaper story was inaccurate or misleading, to order the offending newspaper to print a story setting out the official Social Credit position on the matter.

Is that censorship? The newspaper was free to print its inaccurate, biased, or distorted story. It did not have to take its story to the chairman of the Board to receive permission before being allowed to publish it. If censorship necessarily involves prior restraint, there does not appear to be any such restraint here. The power given to the chairman of the Social Credit Board could be said to be a prior restraint only to the extent that, by being required to use space to carry the official Social Credit story, the freedom of newspaper proprietors to choose what to put in their pages was limited. The implication in the Act was that the official Social Credit position should receive the same prominence as the inaccurate or misleading story. If the inaccurate and misleading story was on page 1, then, presumably, the official Social Credit story had to go on page 1.

It could be argued that the Social Credit Board demanded a kind of free advertising. The government had conferred on itself a power to secure free advertising. Formerly, in American broadcasting law, there was a doctrine known as the "fairness doctrine."[109] This doctrine was invented by the courts ostensibly

---

[109] *Red Lion Broadcasting Co. v. Federal Communications Commission*, 395 U.S. 367 at 368 (1969). The fairness doctrine obliged American broadcasters to present "both sides" of controversial issues. By the 1980s, the fairness doctrine had fallen into disrepute and disuse and,

to promote freedom of speech. The fairness doctrine said that, if a broadcaster presented one side of a controversial issue, that broadcaster had to afford time to those on the other side of the issue to present their point of view. This first provision in the Act to Ensure the Publication of Accurate News and Information was a sort of state-based fairness doctrine.

The second provision in the Alberta legislation was more ominous: it was a kind of anti-leak provision. If the chairman of the Social Credit Board was not happy with a story dealing with one of his party's policies, programs, or initiatives, he could require the proprietors of the offending newspaper to disclose their sources for the story.

The third element in the legislation was the most ominous: when the chairman of the Social Credit Board had either directed a newspaper to print a story giving the Social Credit version, or had required the newspaper to disclose its sources for a particular story, and the newspaper had refused or failed to do what had been demanded of it, he could order the newspaper to be closed. That, clearly, would be a prior restraint.

The Government of Canada, which was not sympathetic to Social Credit, took the extraordinary step of referring the entire package of legislation enacted under Social Credit directly to the Supreme Court of Canada for a determination of its constitutionality. What did the Court say about the *Act to Ensure the Publication of Accurate News and Information*, or, more colloquially, the Press Bill?

The problem with the Alberta Press Bill was that it seemed to place limits on freedom of expression. But since the phrase freedom of expression was not to be found in the text of the *BNA Act*, how could it be argued that there was a constitutional

---

practically speaking, was dead. Brian C. Anderson and Adam D. Thierer, *A Manifesto for Media Freedom*, New York, Encounter Books, 2008 is a vigorous argument against resurrecting the doctrine.

problem with this statute? The answer lies in the realm of judicial creativity. Chief Justice Lyman Duff, who gave the most important judgment, concluded that freedom of expression, which he defined as the "free public discussion of public affairs," was the essential precondition to the operation of democratic government. As he put it, "[F]ree public discussion of public affairs...is the breath of life for parliamentary institutions." Parliamentary institutions, and, therefore, democratic government, could not function without freedom of expression. Indeed, freedom of expression was fundamental to the Canadian constitutional system, transcended any provincial interest, and underlay the "peace, order and good government of Canada." The significance of this conclusion was that, under the *BNA Act*, only Parliament was given the authority to make laws that addressed the peace, order, and good government of Canada.

Put another way, Chief Justice Duff saw in the Press Bill a law that restricted the free public discussion of public affairs. What was the subject-matter of such a law? Chief Justice Duff concluded that the true subject-matter of a law that limited the free public discussion of public affairs was the peace, order, and good government of Canada. Only Parliament had the constitutional authority to make such a law; a province could not make a law about the peace, order, and good government of Canada. The Chief Justice decided that the Press Bill was an attempt on the part of a provincial legislature to enact a law dealing with a subject-matter that did not belong to it. Thus, the law was invalid.

Duff was able to create a degree of constitutional protection for freedom of expression out of a Constitution that nowhere referred to freedom of expression. When he talked about freedom of expression, it is clear that he was referring to political expression. He meant political expression when he talked about the free public discussion of public affairs. It would seem that, in 1938, Duff had a hierarchy of forms of expression in mind. Some forms were clearly more important than others, and most

57

important of all was political expression.

There was, further, no discussion of individual rights in Duff's judgment. Freedom of expression deserved protection, in his opinion, not because it was a right claimed by individuals, but because it was an essential precondition to democratic government. The basis for freedom of expression was not individual, but social.

There was also a concurring judgment by Mr. Justice Cannon. He added two further arguments in support of the conclusion that the statute was beyond the competence of a province. He looked historically and comparatively at legislation that sought to restrict or control political expression. He looked at the United Kingdom and concluded that laws which placed limits on political expression were historically part of that country's criminal law. He also looked at the existing *Criminal Code* of Canada and noted that there already was a provision creating the offence of sedition, which sought to define the limits of acceptable political discourse. He concluded that to attempt to set limits on political discussions was to make criminal law. But, in the division of powers between Ottawa and the provinces under the *BNA Act*, only Parliament had the constitutional authority to make criminal law. Once again, the legislature of a province had tried to enact legislation dealing with a subject-matter—criminal law—that belonged exclusively to Ottawa. Therefore, once again, the Press Bill was *ultra vires*.

Mr. Justice Cannon's second argument had to do with something he called "the status of Canadian citizen," odd terminology, given that the first citizenship legislation in Canada was not enacted until 1946. He said that both the incidents that flowed from the status of Canadian citizen and the status itself were matters relating to the peace, order, and good government of Canada. Only Parliament could place limits or conditions on the status of Canadian citizen. More particularly, he said that one of the incidents of possessing the status of a Canadian citizen was that a person was free to take part in political debate. To limit the ability of Canadians to take part in political debate, Cannon decided, was to place limits on the status of Canadian citizen. In enacting the Press Bill, Alberta had made a law about the peace, order, and good government of Canada—an area beyond the competence of a province. Again, the provincial legislation was invalid.

A number of general observations may be made about these decisions. First, Chief Justice Duff did not say that there was a discrete constitutional subject-matter called "newspapers" or that the legislative subject-matter of the press belonged entirely to Ottawa. As he said in his judgment, "Some degree of regulation of newspapers everyone would concede to the provinces." What aspects of newspapers could provinces regulate? Their jurisdiction would extend to the business aspects of newspapers, one obvious example being employment relations affecting newspapers. Also, as the Supreme Court of Canada decided in a number of cases over the following years, questions relating to advertising could be dealt with under provincial law[110]. The Court said that it was open to the provinces to regulate newspaper advertising, because to do so was to regulate a contractual relationship, an element of property and civil rights, a matter listed in section 92 as within provincial jurisdiction. In saying this, the Court was reinforcing the notion of a hierarchy of forms of expression. There was political expression and there was commercial expression, and they clearly stood on different footings.

Second, although the result of the Alberta Press Bill decision was the creation of a degree of constitutional protection for freedom of expression, it was protection only against limits imposed by a province. Canadian federalism has been viewed as an either/or system. Every conceivable subject is to be found somewhere in the division of powers between Ottawa and the

---

[110] The last such decision was *Canada, (A .G.) v. Law Society (British Columbia)* [1982] 2 S.C.R. 307.

provinces. If a particular matter is not one that can be regulated by the provinces, then, by definition, it must be one that can be regulated by Ottawa. The clear implication of the Press Bill decision is that, had this legislation been enacted by Parliament, it would have been valid. There was no absolute protection for freedom of expression arising out of this decision.

This decision is often referred to as the beginning of the "Implied Bill of Rights" theory: it gave a degree of constitutional protection to certain rights, but these rights are *implied* because they were not set out explicitly in the text of the Constitution.

The Implied Bill of Rights theory stayed around for a number of years. An important Supreme Court of Canada decision of the 1950s—*Switzman v. Elbling*[111]—addressed the constitutionality of a Quebec statute called *An Act to Protect the Province Against Communistic Propaganda*. The title of the Act made its purpose clear, but the operative section said:

> *It shall be illegal for any person, who possesses or occupies a house within the Province, to use it or allow any person to make use of it to propagate communism or bolshevism by any means whatsoever.*

This wording raises an obvious question. If Quebec wanted to protect itself against communist propaganda, why did it not just say: "It shall be illegal for any person to propagate communism or bolshevism by any means whatsoever." Why tie the prohibition to the use of a house? Why draft a statute in such an odd fashion? The answer is that the people who wrote this statute had obviously addressed the same concerns that underlay the Supreme Court's decision in the Press Bill case. They could see that if a statute said directly that it was unlawful to propagate communism or bolshevism in Quebec, such legislation would amount to a

---

[111] [1957] S.C.R. 285.

province attempting to place limits on the free public discussion of public affairs, something a province could not do. The drafters attached the statute to the use of houses because land use was clearly an element of property and civil rights in the province. There is no doubt that a province can say that a house may not be used as a brothel or a bar or a glue factory or a law office. That is land-use legislation. The argument advanced by Quebec was that a law saying you could not use a house to propagate communism or bolshevism was also a law about land use, which is to say, about property and civil rights and, thus, valid.

The teeth in this Act provided that if the attorney general of the province were satisfied that a house was being used to propagate communism or bolshevism; he could order that the house be locked up. The house could be closed without any requirement of a charge or a hearing. That is why this statute came to be known popularly as the *Padlock Act*.

A dispute arose between a landlord and a tenant in Montreal. The landlord sought to end the lease on the ground that the leased premises had been used unlawfully for the purpose of propagating communism. The tenant conceded this fact, but argued that the *Padlock Act* was unconstitutional and, therefore, of no relevance. The dispute ended up before the Supreme Court of Canada.

A majority of the judges in the Court reiterated the principles of the Alberta Press Bill decision. This was especially true in the judgment of Mr. Justice Ivan Rand. Mr. Justice Rand suggested that freedom of expression was as important to human beings as the ability to draw breath. More to the point, he held that free expression was an essential element in a democratic society. Thus, legislation which limited that freedom, as the *Padlock Act* clearly did, despite its transparent attempt to appear to address land use, was beyond the competence of a province. It was beyond the competence of a province because it dealt with the peace, order, and good government of Canada and because it dealt with matters properly belonging to the criminal law.

The judgment of Mr. Justice Douglas Abbott is interesting. His judgment was unique, even though most commentators agree that it is wrong. Mr. Justice Abbott concluded that not only was legislation of this kind beyond the competence of a province to enact, but it was also beyond the competence of Parliament. What was his basis for saying so? He relied on the Preamble to the *BNA Act*, which said that Canada is to have a constitution "similar in Principle" to that of the United Kingdom. Abbott focused on those words and said that one of the principles of the UK Constitution was the protection of free expression. He then said that the effect of the Preamble to the *BNA Act* was to place freedom of expression on a constitutional basis, making it impossible for either a province or Parliament to enact legislation to limit it. This point is wrong for a very simple reason. There is, or has traditionally seemed to be, only one principle in the Constitution of the United Kingdom: the absolute, unlimited, unqualified supremacy of Parliament. There are no legal limits on the law-making authority of the UK Parliament, so, if it had at any time wanted to enact legislation restricting or denying freedom of expression, it was constitutionally free to do so.

In the 1970s the Implied Bill of Rights theory began to fall into disfavour in the Supreme Court of Canada. This is exemplified in a decision called *McNeil v. Nova Scotia (Board of Censors)*.[112] Gerry McNeil was a journalist who was living at the time in Dartmouth and wanted to see the movie *Last Tango in Paris*. He went to the Court twice in his attempt to do so. Nova Scotia had a statute called the *Theatres and Amusements Act*. The Act created an Amusements Regulation Board, which was the province's movie censorship agency. There is a long-standing tradition in Canada of provinces censoring movies, although in recent years they have moved from censoring to classifying. McNeil questioned whether there was any constitutional basis for

---

[112] [1978] 2 S.C.R. 662.

this censorship.

Why do governments censor movies? What are they trying to accomplish? Nobody has ever censored movies because they are badly acted, poorly written, boring, abysmally directed, or totally lacking in originality. They are censored in order to remove the "naughty" bits and, more recently, violence. The problem that arises is that the underlying goal in creating such a system of censorship is the preservation of public morality. But when the state acts to uphold public morality, it is, arguably, making criminal law. This was the basis of McNeil's argument before the Supreme Court of Canada.

As with most of the division of powers cases, this one came down to a matter of characterization, to a determination of the true subject-matter of the legislation that was being challenged. What was the subject-matter of the censorship provisions in the Nova Scotia *Theatres and Amusements Act*? Was it the regulation of public morality, which would mean they were about criminal law, and, therefore, invalid, or was it the regulation of a particular business in the province, which would make them about property and civil rights in the province and, therefore, valid?

McNeil's argument seemed to be strengthened by the fact that the *Criminal Code* already contained express prohibitions against obscenity and against offering an immoral or indecent performance in public—and, by the fact that when the state censors movies, it is placing limits on free expression. In the end the judges of the Court split five to four. The majority decided the subject-matter of the legislation was the regulation of a business in the province.

Clearly, a provincial legislature can enact legislation regulating businesses. The mere fact that the statute might have incidental effects on matters such as criminal law that were within federal jurisdiction would not affect its validity.

Broadcasting

For obvious reasons, the original text of the *BNA Act*, which dates from 1867, made no reference to broadcasting. When commercial broadcasting began to develop in Canada in the 1920s, this omission immediately became an issue. Did Ottawa or the provinces have the necessary constitutional authority to regulate broadcasting? When the Aird Commission was set up in 1928, the assumption around Ottawa was that Ottawa had this authority. The matter was forced before the courts in 1929 when the Quebec legislature enacted a statute called the *Radio Act*, which purported to establish a mechanism for regulating broadcasting in that province. The case ended up before the Judicial Committee of the Privy Council, then the final court of appeal for Canada, in 1932.[113]

The Judicial Committee decided that broadcasting was a matter exclusively within federal jurisdiction. The judges reached this conclusion for three reasons. First, they saw broadcasting as a matter of such significance to the country as a whole that it went to the peace, order, and good government of Canada. Broadcasting transcended purely local or provincial interests and was of importance to the entire nation. Second, the court upheld federal jurisdiction over broadcasting under section 132 of the *BNA Act*. This section gave Parliament the jurisdiction to legislate so as to implement treaty obligations. By this time Canada was a party to treaties with the United States and Mexico allocating broadcasting frequencies amongst the three countries. The Judicial Committee said Parliament must have the law-making authority to implement these obligations. Finally, section 92(10) of the *BNA Act* deals with "Works and Undertakings." Section 92(10) talks about steamships, railways, canals, and telegraphs. The Judicial

---

[113] Radio Communications in Canada (Regulation and Control of), [1932] A.C. 304 (P.C.).

Committee thought that this provision had some application because it saw an analogy between broadcasting and telegraphs. "Work" here is meant in a nineteenth-century engineering sense—a bridge, a canal, a line of rail. An "undertaking" is a commercial enterprise that uses a "work." So, a railway company is an undertaking and the work it uses is the railway track. Section 92(10) says that local works or undertakings are within provincial jurisdiction. That meant, for example, that a railway which operated entirely within one province would be under provincial jurisdiction. On the other hand, section 92(10) went on to say that where a work or an undertaking extended beyond the boundaries of a province or connected one province with another, it would be within federal jurisdiction. This is why national railways are within federal jurisdiction.

A similar issue was argued in litigation for many years concerning jurisdiction over provincial or local telephone systems. The Supreme Court resolved it in 1989 by noting that although local telephone systems continued to exist, they were all connected together through the Telecom Canada system. This interconnected system extends beyond the boundaries of any province and is, thus, within federal jurisdiction.[114]

In understanding the Judicial Committee's decision on broadcasting, it is important to be clear on its definition of broadcasting. The Committee saw broadcasting as the transmission and reception through the air of Hertzian waves. If we think about broadcasting today, it clearly means a lot more than this. But, for the Judicial Committee, the deciding factor about broadcasting was that Hertzian waves, by their nature, did not respect provincial boundaries. Thus, broadcasting was a work or undertaking which extended beyond the boundaries of the

---

[114] Alberta Government Telephones v. Canada (Radio-Television & Telecommunications Commission) [1989] 2 S.C.R. 225.

province or which connected one province with another. It was, therefore, a matter within federal jurisdiction.

Subsequent decisions have gone further. In 1973 the Ontario Court of Appeal, in *C.F.R.B. v. Canada (A.G.) (No. 2)*, said broadcasting should now be regarded as if it were *de facto* one of the enumerated heads of section 91 of the *BNA Act*—that is, as if the section which gives jurisdiction to Parliament to make laws actually said "broadcasting."[115] Other decisions have held that federal jurisdiction over broadcasting includes not only its technical aspects, but the financial aspects and all matters related to content.[116] The general view taken by the courts has been that everything involved in broadcasting is subject to federal jurisdiction.

Certain difficulties have arisen over the years. Cable television is one. Cable television works by taking signals from a large antenna that receives them off-air—called the head end—and then feeding them out to subscribers along copper wires or, increasingly, fibre optics. From the head end to the subscriber there is no transmission or reception of Hertzian waves through the air. The argument was made in the 1960s that cable television systems were, as a result, not broadcasting, or at least not broadcasting as understood by the Judicial Committee of the Privy Council in 1932. The argument was made further that it was technically feasible to create a cable television system wholly situate within one province—that is, a local work or undertaking and, thus, within provincial jurisdiction. This issue was a matter of ongoing negotiation between Ottawa and several of the provinces for many years. *The Broadcasting Act* was amended by Parliament to say that broadcasting included the operation of a cable television

---

[115] [1973] 3 O.R. 819 (C.A.).

[116] Capital Cities Communication Inc. v. Canada (Radio-Television & Telecommunications Commission) [1978] 2 S.C.R. 141.

system.[117] The basis for the dispute, of course, was the enormous amounts of money involved.

Parliament, through the *Broadcasting Act*, had said that anyone who wanted to operate a cable television system anywhere in Canada had to have a federal licence. The province of Quebec then amended its *Public Service Board Act* to state that anyone who wanted to operate a cable television system anywhere in Quebec had to have a provincial licence. Both regulatory bodies, the CRTC and the Public Service Board of Quebec, operated in the same fashion. They issued licences that were geographically exclusive. There is little competition in the cable business in Canada. Anyone who receives a cable licence receives an exclusive licence to provide cable services within a defined geographical area.

Both Ottawa and the province of Quebec were demanding that cable operators be licensed by them. For many years all cable operators in the province of Quebec simply got two licences— one federal and one provincial. Unfortunately, something went wrong in the town of Rimouski: the CRTC gave one cable operator an exclusive federal licence to operate a cable system in the town, and the Public Service Board gave a different operator an exclusive provincial licence. The matter ended up being litigated. The provincial argument looked at cable systems from the head end to the subscriber and said these systems were undertakings wholly situate in the province and, therefore, within provincial jurisdiction. The majority of the judges in the Supreme Court of Canada said that although the signal which cable systems sent to the subscriber was carried over copper wire, these systems, nonetheless, relied on the reception of Hertzian waves off-air. The wire-based delivery system did not alter the fact that cable systems were part of the general broadcasting system. As a result, cable systems were broadcasting and within federal

---

[117] See S.C. 1967–68, c. 25, s. 3(d).

jurisdiction.[118]

Advertising

Until the late 1970s, broadcasting was treated by the courts as if it were a monolith. Anything involved in what could be characterized as broadcasting was within federal jurisdiction. Then a problem was created by a regulation made under the *Quebec Consumer Protection Act*.

Quebec had in the 1970s, and still has, probably the most extensive system of consumer protection legislation in Canada. A regulation dealing with advertising directed at children said, "No one shall prepare, use, publish or cause to be published in Quebec advertising intended for children which...employs cartoons." This regulation raised a number of questions. First, the Supreme Court of Canada had earlier decided that the provinces could regulate print advertising. But clearly, and this has never been open to doubt, Ottawa can regulate broadcasting advertising as part of its general jurisdiction over broadcasting. The drafting in the Quebec regulation was very careful. It did not purport to prohibit the broadcasting of advertising intended for children which employed cartoons. Such a regulation would have been invalid, as its subject-matter would clearly have been broadcasting. The wording, that no one should "prepare, use, publish or cause to be published," was consciously aimed at advertisers, not broadcasters. Another feature was concealed here, one that fooled the Court. When "cartoons" was used in the regulation, it did not mean newspaper cartoons, but moving cartoons. There is only one medium that can employ such cartoons in advertising directed at children, and that is television. The point about this regulation was that it could have meaning only in relation to television.

---

[118] Dionne v. Quebec (*Public Service Board*) [1978] 2 S.C.R. 191.

The majority of the judges in the Court held that the regulation was directed towards advertising—that is, towards a contractual relationship. This meant that its subject-matter was property and civil rights in the province and, as a result, the regulation was valid provincial legislation. Thus, by means of some careful drafting, the province of Quebec was able to control part of the content of what was broadcast on television.[119]

The next logical step is found in a more recent Supreme Court decision about freedom of expression and the division of powers: *Irwin Toy Ltd. v. Quebec (A.G.)*.[120] There had been a further amendment to the Quebec *Consumer Protection Act*, and this amendment, in sections 248 and 249, absolutely prohibited all commercial advertising directed at persons under the age of thirteen. Now, if you live in the real world and you want to advertise to persons under the age of thirteen, you put your advertising on television, which, of course, is why the challenge to the legislation came from the Irwin Toy Company. But the majority of the judges was baffled by the form of the legislation. It did not expressly address broadcasting—the word "television" was not used in the statute. The statute spoke only of advertising. Once again the Court held that to deal with advertising was to deal with a contractual relation; as a result, the subject-matter of the legislation was property and civil rights in the province—and, thus, the provincial statute was valid.

The issue of advertising and its regulation continues to be important in relation to the division of powers. In 1995 the Supreme Court released its decision as to the validity of a federal statute called the *Tobacco Products Control Act*.[121] This Act prohibited the advertising in any medium in Canada of any tobacco product. There should be no division of powers problem

---

[119] *Quebec (A.G.) v. Kellogg's Co.* [1978] 2 S.C.R. 211.

[120] [1989] 1 S.C.R. 927 [hereinafter *Irwin Toy*].

[121] RJR-MacDonald Inc. v. Canada (A.G.) [1995] 3 S.C.R. 199.

with Parliament enacting legislation that prohibits the advertising of tobacco products over radio or television, because such legislation would clearly be characterized as being in relation to broadcasting. The more difficult question was whether Parliament had the authority to prohibit tobacco advertising in newspapers and magazines, because print advertising has been held, as we have seen, to involve matters of property and civil rights in the province. Where did Parliament get the authority to do this? The Supreme Court of Canada decided that the prohibition on advertising could be upheld as an exercise of Parliament's exclusive authority to make criminal law, the majority being convinced that the protection of public health was a valid objective to be sought in the making of criminal law.

A brief digression to discuss certain other legal issues relating to advertising is in order. The central policy issue with respect to advertising has been the regulation of false and misleading advertising. What should the state do about it? Many people might say that all advertising is, by its nature, false and misleading. In the early days of mass consumer advertising the possibility was created briefly that false and misleading advertising could be regulated through the law of contract. An ad says, "Use our toothpaste and you will become enchanting, alluring, exciting." You faithfully use the toothpaste for several months, but remain the same dull, boring person you always were. Can you sue the advertiser for breach of contract, arguing that it promised that if you used its toothpaste all sorts of wonderful things would occur, but you did and nothing happened?

There was an interesting case along these lines before the English courts in the latter part of the nineteenth century. The Carbolic Smoke Ball Company marketed something called the Carbolic Smoke Ball. The user held the ball in her hand, removed the top, and fumes came out. These fumes, when inhaled, were supposed to cure a range of ailments. A newspaper advertisement had said: "[A hundred pound]…reward will be paid by the

Carbolic Smoke Ball Company to any person who contracts the increasing epidemic of influenza, colds, or any disease caused by taking cold, after having used the ball three times daily for two weeks according to the printed directions supplied with each ball." The company deposited £100 with a bank to show its sincerity. A Mrs. Carlill bought a Smoke Ball and followed the directions, inhaling the fumes three times a day for two weeks. Despite this routine, she got sick. She sued the company and won, the court holding that the advertising claims were a term of her contract with the company.[122] Quickly, however, the courts reversed their direction and, since then, have consistently held that advertising claims are "mere puffs." They are not contractual terms and cannot be treated as contractual terms. As a result, the law of contract has been rendered useless as a legal mechanism for regulating advertising. The approach employed in Canada has been to use direct state intervention. A host of both federal and provincial statutes purports to regulate false and misleading advertising directly.

A different, but related, question is comparative advertising. Comparative advertising involves an attempt to demonstrate the ways in which one's product is superior to those of one's competitors. Engaging in this sort of advertising carries the risk that one may get involved in an obscure civil proceeding known variously as the tort of slander of goods, injurious falsehood, or malicious falsehood. To succeed in this action, a plaintiff must establish that a statement about her product was false, that it was intended to disparage her product, and that it actually resulted in her suffering a loss of business. There are few recent Canadian cases.[123]

---

[122] Carlill v. Carbolic Smoke Ball Co. [1893] 1 Q.B. 256 (C.A.).

[123] See *Rust Chek Canada Inc. v. Young* (1988), 47 C.C.L.T. 279 (Ont. H.C.J.). Actual loss need not be proved in Ontario. A recent decision of the High Court of Australia contains a very full discussion of injurious

Conclusion

The division of powers in the Constitution has been at the heart of major litigation. This has raised questions concerning both the protection of freedom of expression and the regulation of the mass media.

In 1982 major changes were made to the Constitution of Canada. The *British North America Act* was renamed the *Constitution Act, 1867*. Although the Act's name was changed, its content remained much as it had been. At the same time, a major new element, the *Constitution Act, 1982*, was added to our Constitution. The most important part of the *Constitution Act, 1982*, was the *Canadian Charter of Rights and Freedoms*, to which we now turn.

THE CHARTER GUARANTEE OF FREEDOM OF EXPRESSION

General Considerations

The adoption of the *Charter* in 1982 in no way ended or transformed the federal division of powers. As a result, there could, since 1982, be two distinct challenges to any state act that appeared to limit free expression: the traditional challenge arising from the division of powers; and a direct, substantive challenge based on the guarantee of freedom of expression in the *Charter*. This dual challenge was precisely what happened in the *Tobacco Products Control Act* litigation before the Supreme Court. The statute was argued both to be *ultra vires* Parliament and to be an unjustifiable limit on freedom of expression.

With the adoption of the *Charter*, the Canadian Constitution,

---

falsehood. See *Palmer Bruyn and Parker Pty. Ltd. v. Parsons* [2002] 2 L.R.C. 674.

for the first time, expressly recognized the existence and protection of certain rights and freedoms. It would, however, be wrong to imagine that none of these had existed previously in Canada. Although the *Charter* gave formal constitutional recognition to freedom of expression, it would be incorrect and a serious misreading of Canadian legal and political history to think that freedom of expression was unknown before 1982. At this point in the analysis, we encounter what seems to me to be a paradox, which is this: before there was a formal, explicit guarantee of freedom of expression in our country's constitution, Canadians enjoyed free expression. Since the adoption of just such a guarantee, we have lost a substantial part of our free expression. How did this happen? The primary answer must be found in the unusual, if not perverse, way in which the courts have interpreted the *Charter*.[124] The *Canadian Charter of Rights and Freedoms,* to give it its full name, is often referred to popularly as The Charter of Rights. This is correct, since the judges, as I interpret their decisions, have consistently preferred the rights over the freedoms. More important, the "Equality Rights" guarantee in section 15 has effectively swallowed the rest of the *Charter.* Amongst its many deleterious effects on Canada, the *Charter* has spawned a plethora of bad books.[125] It is inaccurate to lay the blame for the eclipse of free expression solely at the door of the judges. There are other factors which are found in the Canadian psyche and in Canadian society.

Canadians appear to me to be generally unenthusiastic about freedom, often regarding it as indecent and unacceptably

---

[124] Robert Ivan Martin, *The Most Dangerous Branch: How the Supreme Court of Canada has undermined our Law and our Democracy*, Montreal and Kingston, McGill-Queens University Press, 2003.

[125] Easily the worst is Ian Greene, *The Charter of Rights*, Toronto, Lorimer, 1989. For an elaboration of my analysis, see Robert Martin, *Review*, (1992) 23:3 Interchange 327.

"American". Canadians tend to believe that decent folk should eschew freedom and entrust the management of their lives to the state. To the extent I am capable of grasping these matters; it does appear to me that many Canadians think the state should play a central role in the raising of children.[126] The central argument, as I understand it, of Kenneth Minogue's *The Servile Mind*[127] is that, throughout the West, the habits of autonomy and independence which once characterised the behaviour of free citizens in a democracy have been transformed into servility. Margaret Thatcher and Ronald Reagan did great services to their fellow citizens by freeing them from their attachment to the "nanny state". It does seem to me that the phrase "nanny state" fails to catch either the depth or the passion of Canadians' attachment to the state. In our case, "mommy state" would be a more useful phrase. Just about everything in Canada today has become profoundly and remorselessly politicised. Those who support free expression are thought to be of the "extreme right" and irredeemably nasty.

It seems to me that Canada today is best understood as a totalitarian theocracy—a country totally in the grip of a secular state religion of equality.

Canadians seem bent, today, on creating a society from which all risks have been eliminated, or, as speakers of the pastiche would probably have it, a "risk-free" society. The state, of course, has been chosen as the vehicle for realising this goal. There is one dismal, and easily observable, feature of Canadian society. It is this. Whenever, as I see it, anything bad happens, there will be widespread cries for the state to "do something" in order to ensure

---

[126] See, Margaret Wente, *Motherhood, the new oppression*, Globe and Mail, 25 June 2010.
[127] op. cit.

that the bad thing may never happen again.[128] A society from which all risks, including the risk of having one's "self esteem" injured, have been eliminated, will not be, even remotely, "free and democratic".[129] Since 1982 the belief has tended to grow that, unless something is formally recognized in a constitution, it simply does not exist. The guarantee of freedom of expression is found in section 2 of the *Charter*, which purports to guarantee "fundamental freedoms." Four fundamental freedoms are set out in this section. The one with which we are concerned is found in section 2(b), which guarantees freedom of "thought, belief, opinion and expression." At our current level of technological development, a guarantee of freedom of "thought, belief and opinion" does not mean much. No one else has any way of knowing what I think or believe or what my opinions are until such time as I actually express them.[130]

---

[128] Joseph Brean, *Canada's 'addiction to rule-making'* ", National Post, 7 August 2010.

[129] For an interesting and original analysis of some of the pitfalls in the attempt to create a "safe" society, see Margaret Wente, *The Menace of Free Speech*, Globe and Mail, 26 March 2010.

[130] There is a key Canadian book devoted exclusively to these issues: Richard Moon, *The Constitutional Protection of Freedom of Expression*, Toronto, University of Toronto Press, 2000. This is a disappointing book. Emphasizing the "social character" of freedom of expression, Moon appeared to be more concerned with the dangers that might arise from the exercise of freedom of expression than with freedom of expression itself. He stated "Expression can cause fear, it can harass, and it can undermine self-esteem." at p. 4. It is not encouraging to discover that a person teaching in a university might imagine that something as ephemeral and infantile as "self-esteem" could possibly be more significant than free expression. It is possible to take a more robust approach. "Freedom of expression is a universal human right...Freedom of expression is the primary freedom, an essential precondition to the exercise of other freedoms. It is the foundation upon which other rights

Section 2(b) of the *Charter* talks of "freedom of…expression, including freedom of the press and other media of communication." This sub-section appears to be saying that freedom of the press is part of freedom of expression, but that may be misleading. As we noted in the discussion of the *Gay Alliance* case, circumstances can arise where there may appear to be conflict between freedom of expression and freedom of the press.

The structure of the *Canadian Charter of Rights and Freedoms* is such that all litigation involving it has two separate and distinct stages. In the first stage, the court must determine whether there has been a denial or an infringement of a right or freedom guaranteed in the *Charter*. At this stage, it is up to the party relying on the *Charter* to prove that one of her rights or freedoms has been infringed. In technical terms, the burden of proof rests initially with the party relying on the *Charter*. Logically, in order to determine whether there has been an infringement of a *Charter* right, the court must first determine the boundaries or the definition of the *Charter* guarantee in question. This has been one of the major tasks confronting the courts in applying the *Charter*. For example, section 2 also guarantees freedom of association. Freedom of association is most directly relevant to political parties and trade unions. Clearly, freedom of association guarantees some sorts of rights with respect to trade unions, but what are they? Does freedom of association guarantee a constitutional right to strike? Does it guarantee a constitutional right to bargain collectively? Is there a right not to belong to a union? The point is that the wording of the *Charter* itself does not provide answers to these questions. The *Charter* simply says that freedom of association is guaranteed, but does not define its specifics. That

---

and freedoms arise." Robert Martin, *Speaking Freely: Expression and the Law in the Commonwealth*, Toronto, Irwin Law, 1999, p. 685.

task was left to the courts.[131]

Similarly, the task of defining the limits and the precise content of freedom of expression was left to the courts. A host of issues was litigated. The courts were asked, for example: Does freedom of expression include pure commercial advertising? Does freedom of expression include hate propaganda? Does it include obscenity or pornography? What about communications on the street between prostitutes and potential clients? Advertising by dentists? Sticking posters or handbills on telephone poles?[132]

These are some of the issues that had to be addressed in order to give shape and dimension to the guarantee of freedom of expression. Again, the point is that in order to determine whether freedom of expression has been limited, one must first set out a definition of freedom of expression itself.

The second stage in *Charter* litigation involves the application of section 1 of the *Charter*. Section 1 says:

> *The Canadian Charter of Rights and Freedoms guarantees the rights and freedoms set out in it subject only to such reasonable limits prescribed by law as can be demonstrably justified in a free and democratic society.*

As a general principle, section 1 makes clear that the state may impose limits on *Charter* rights. The various guarantees set out are not absolute. Indeed, a substantial motive underlying the adoption of section 1 was a desire to give considerable leeway to legislatures to enact limits on rights.

The courts have determined that, if the party relying on the

---

[131] See Reference Re *Public Service Employee Relations Act* (Alberta), [1987] 1 S.C.R. 313 and Lavigne v. O.P.S.E.U., [1991] 2 S.C.R. 211.

[132] In each instance the Supreme Court of Canada decided the activity was expression.

Charter is successful in proving that one of her rights has been limited, the burden shifts to the other party—usually the state— to satisfy the court that the particular limit can be justified in a free and democratic society. If the limit on the *Charter* guarantee is found to be justified, the particular state act that created it is constitutional; if the limit cannot be justified, the state act creating it is unconstitutional and will be declared invalid.

In *R. v. Oakes* the Supreme Court of Canada created a detailed methodology for applying section 1.[133] This methodology seeks to assess both the end that the state is seeking and the means it has chosen to achieve that end.

Rather than looking in detail at the general methodology to be followed in *Charter* litigation, we will now investigate the specific approach that is used in cases involving freedom of expression. This approach was set out by the Supreme Court of Canada in *Irwin Toy Ltd. v. Quebec (A.G.)*, a decision we have already looked at in relation to division of powers issues.[134] The *Irwin Toy* methodology seeks to define an approach to freedom of expression which all courts are supposed to follow. It is very complicated. The essential steps in this methodology are summarized in Figure 1.

---

[133] [1986] 1 S.C.R. 103.
[134] Above note 120.

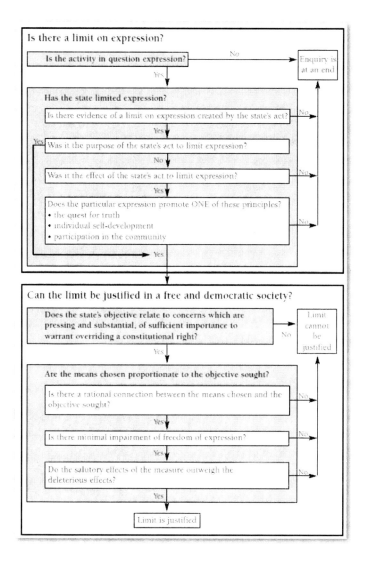

Figure 1: How to Apply the Guarantee of Freedom of Expression in Section 2(b) of the *Charter*

The Meaning of Expression

The first phase in the *Irwin Toy* analysis involves determining whether the freedom of expression of the party relying on the *Charter* has been limited. This simple question is broken down into a series of sub-questions. The first sub-question addresses the activity in question—that is, it seeks to discover whether what the party relying on the *Charter* was engaged in amounted to expression. The traditional Canadian approach was set out in the 1938 *Alberta Press Bill* case, discussed above. The Supreme Court, in that decision, saw the essence of expression as the "free public discussion of public affairs". It accepted that there was a hierarchy of forms of expression, with political expression at the summit of the hierarchy. In *Irwin Toy*, on the other hand, the Supreme Court consciously rejected any notion of a hierarchy of forms of expression. The Court said that if the activity in question had expressive content, if it sought to convey a meaning, then it qualified as expression and was constitutionally protected.

This is a broad definition. It excludes little from expression and, to reinforce the point, the Court accepted that even pure physical acts could qualify as expression. The Court chose the banal example of someone knowingly and intentionally parking a car in a restricted parking zone as a form of political protest. The Court said that such an act would qualify as constitutionally protected expression. Thus, everything from the free public discussion of public affairs to the way you park your car can be subsumed within expression. The only exception the Court was prepared to recognize in *Irwin Toy* was for pure physical acts of violence. These acts would not qualify as expression.[135] The

---

[135] In *R. v. Banks*, (2007) 84 O.R. (3d) 1, the Ontario Court of Appeal was prepared to hold that "squeegeeing" qualified as constitutionally protected expression. "Squeegeeing" denotes an activity whereby

Ontario Court of Appeal expatiated on this question in *R. v. Khawaja.*[136] The accused/appellants sought to question the constitutionality of the terrorism offences in the *Criminal Code.*[137] The constitutional argument focussed on the definition of "terrorist activity" in section 83.01(1)(b)(i)(A). That provision required the Crown to prove that the relevant act or omission was committed "in whole or in part for a political, religious or ideological purpose, objective or cause". The argument was raised that this provision with respect to motive could have a "chilling effect" on the expression of political or religious opinions and was, thus, a limit on freedom of expression. The court had little difficulty with these arguments, holding that the sort of violence proscribed in the offences related to terrorism did not advance any of the "values" underlying s. 2(b) and that the concerns about a "chilling effect" were purely speculative and that the appellants were obliged to adduce concrete evidence of the existence of such an effect.[138]

The implications of this approach to the definition of expression were made clear in subsequent cases. The *R. v. Keegstra* decision is a good illustration.[139] James Keegstra, the accused, was a school teacher, and the mayor, in the small town of Eckville, Alberta. In the course of his historical research he claimed to have discovered a Jewish plot to take over the world and believed that he was under an obligation to inform his students about this plot. He was eventually charged, under what is now section 319(2) of the *Criminal Code*, with wilfully promoting hatred against any group of people identifiable on the basis of their race, religion, or

---

adolescents armed with squeegee mops attack stopped cars, make a show of cleaning their windshields and demand payment.

[136] (2010) 103 O.R. (3d) 321.
[137] R.S.C. 1985, c.C- 46, s. 83.
[138] 103 O.R. (3d) at p. 360.
[139] [1990] 3 S.C.R. 697.

national origin. Keegstra claimed, among other things, that the existence of this offence was a limit on his constitutionally guaranteed freedom of expression. The first question the courts had to answer was whether the promotion of hatred qualified as constitutionally protected expression. One argument advanced by the Crown was that to promote hatred was to encourage violence, so that the promotion of hatred could be regarded as analogous to physical acts of violence and thus would not be constitutionally protected. The Supreme Court said no. It said there was a difference between threats of violence and acts of violence. Hate propaganda was, thus, expression.

A year later the Supreme Court heard the *R. v. Butler* case.[140] This case dealt with the constitutionality of section 163(8) of the *Criminal Code*, the section that proscribes obscenity, or, in more common usage, pornography. Butler ran a video shop in Winnipeg. The typical contemporary obscenity prosecution involves a video shop; there has not been a prosecution of a book for more than two decades. Butler was charged with possessing and selling obscene material. Like Keegstra, he argued that the section of the *Criminal Code* under which he was charged was a limit on his constitutionally guaranteed expression. Was obscenity expression? In the *Irwin Toy* case the Supreme Court had said that anything that attempted to convey a meaning qualified as expression. But in *Butler* the Manitoba Court of Appeal had concluded that pornographic videotapes were not an attempt to convey meaning because they contained nothing but a series of physical acts devoid of intellectual content. On appeal, the Supreme Court disagreed. It said pornographic videotapes did attempt to convey some sort of meaning. That meaning might be odious or distasteful to many, but nonetheless there was an attempt to convey meaning. Therefore, said the Court, obscenity, like hate propaganda, qualified as expression.

---

[140] [1992] 1 S.C.R. 452.

There is a problem here. At some stage in applying a constitutional document like the *Charter* the courts, whether they like it or not, are going to have to discriminate, to make choices. They are going to have to uphold some limits on constitutionally guaranteed rights and to strike other limits down. Some sort of ranking of different forms of expression is inescapable.

Unfortunately, pornography is the one form of expression that has consistently been protected by the courts, in particular, by the Supreme Court of Canada.[141] The approach taken to date has led, as we will see, to some serious inconsistencies in the judicial decisions on these matters.

The Supreme Court decided, in *Irwin Toy*, that just about anything qualified as expression. As a result of this approach, the first stage in *Charter* litigation, determining whether a guarantee in the *Charter* has been limited, is almost a given. Consequently, the heart of decisions involving the guarantee of freedom of expression lies in the section 1 analysis, which is to say, in the determination of whether the particular limit on expression can be justified in a free and democratic society. Since their core is usually found in the section 1 analysis, Supreme Court decisions on freedom of expression tell us little about the meaning or significance of free expression. Most of these decisions are ad hoc evaluations of the desirability of particular state policies. The Supreme Court's views about expression as set out in *Irwin Toy* were borrowed, without acknowledgment, from the American academic Thomas Emerson. Emerson thought free expression was important because it was the foundation for three essential social goals. These were:

  i)   seeking truth;
  ii) democratic government; and

---

[141] See, *R.* v. *Butler* [1992] 1 S.C.R. 452; *R.* v. *Sharpe* [2001] 1 S.C.R. 45 and *Little Sister's Book and Art Emporium* v. *Canada* [2000] 2 S.C.R. 1120.

iii) self-realisation.[142]

It was only in *R. v. Sharpe*,[143] the 2001 decision on child pornography, that a judge of the Supreme Court addressed the importance of free expression. Chief Justice McLachlin stated that free expression "...makes possible our liberty, our creativity and our democracy."[144] She added that freedom of expression also protects "...unpopular or even offensive expression."[145] The Chief Justice appeared to move away from the *Irwin Toy* notion that all forms of expression are equal, when she stated, "while some forms of expression, like political expression, lie closer to the core of the guarantee than others, all are vital to a free and democratic society."[146]

There is one other decision in which the Supreme Court discussed both the meaning and the significance of freedom of expression. That decision was *Libman v. A.G. Québec*,[147] in which the Court stated that:

> *political expression is at the very heart of the values sought to be protected by the freedom of expression*

---

[142] T. I. Emerson, *The System of Freedom of Expression*, New York, Random House, 1970.

[143] (2001) 194 D.L.R. (4th) 1 (S.C.C.). For more detailed analysis, see Robert Martin, *Case Comment, R. v. Sharpe*, (2001) 39, no. 2 Alberta Law Review 585. In *R. v. Katigbak* (2010) 100 O.R.(3d) 481, the Ontario Court of Appeal set out a history of the state's efforts to control child pornography, as well as both a gloss and a qualification on the Supreme Court of Canada's decision in *Sharpe*.

[144] (2001) 194 D.L.R. (4th) at pp. 22–24.

[145] *Ibid*, at p. 22.

[146] *Ibid*, at p. 23.

[147] [1997] 3 S.C.R. 569.

guaranteed by s. 2(b) of the Canadian Charter.[148]

If a court determines that the activity in which the party relying on the *Charter* is engaged is, indeed, expression, it must move to the second part of the first phase of the analysis. This part involves determining whether the state has acted in such a way as to limit expression.

Ordinarily, the *Charter* can only be invoked against the state. Unless the act complained of emanates from the legislative, executive, or administrative branches of the state, there is no basis for claiming any of the rights guaranteed in the *Charter*. Thus, a newspaper reporter could not raise a *Charter* claim against an editor who refused to print one of her stories.

This principle was qualified somewhat by the Supreme Court of Canada in two decisions from the 1990s—*Dagenais v. Canadian Broadcasting Corp.*[149] and *Hill v. Church of Scientology of Toronto.*[150] In these decisions it was suggested that the *Charter* might be relied on as a basis for shaping or altering rules of the common law even where there was no direct state act involved. Although *Charter* rights may still be invoked only against the state, the Court held that judges have the authority to alter the common law so as to make it consistent with what it described as *Charter* "values." The difficulty with this interpretation is that, since the word "value" does not appear anywhere in the text of the *Charter*, it is impossible to state with any degree of certainty what constitutes, or does not constitute, a *Charter* value.

The party relying on the *Charter* is obliged to prove, through evidence, that her expression is being limited. The courts have said that it is not enough simply to assert that one's expression has

---

[148] *Ibid.* at 591.
[149] [1994] 3 S.C.R. 835.
[150] [1995] 2 S.C.R. 1130 [hereinafter *Hill*].

been limited. Real proof is required.[151]

At this point, two possibilities arise. The first applies if the purpose underlying the state's act was to limit expression. The cases of *Keegstra* and *Butler* illustrate this situation. If the wilful promotion of hatred amounts to expression and the state makes it a crime to promote hatred, then clearly the state's purpose in so acting was to limit expression. Likewise, if the state says that no one may distribute obscene material, and obscenity is a constitutionally recognized form of expression, then, once more, the clear purpose of the state's act was to limit expression. In such a case there has been an infringement of freedom of expression and it becomes incumbent on the state to show that the particular infringement can be justified in a free and democratic society.

The other possibility is that the state might have acted in order to achieve some quite different purpose, but the effect of its act, perhaps an unintended effect, has been to create a limit on expression. This is what happened in *Committee for the Commonwealth of Canada* v. *Canada*.[152] The respondents wished to engage in political discourse with travellers in an airport owned by the government of Canada. Such activity was prohibited under the Government Airport Concession Operations Regulations, the clear purpose of which was to provide for the orderly operation of airports. The Court held that the public areas of airports could be analogized to traditional "public arenas" in which individuals were entitled to express themselves freely. It concluded that, whatever the state's purpose might have been, since the effect of its action was to limit free expression, there was an infringement of a *Charter* guarantee, which infringement would have to be justified under section 1. There is a qualification on this point, however. In *Irwin Toy* the Court said that where it is only the effect of the state's act, rather than its purpose, to limit expression, the party

---

[151] *MacKay v. Manitoba*, [1989] 2 S.C.R. 357.
[152] [1991] 1 S.C.R. 139.

relying on the *Charter* will also be required to show that the expression in question promoted one of the following principles or "values":

(1) seeking and attaining the truth is an inherently good activity;

(2) participation in social and political decision-making is to be fostered and encouraged; and

(3) the diversity in forms of individual self-fulfilment and human flourishing ought to be cultivated in an essentially tolerant, indeed welcoming, environment not only for the sake of those who convey a meaning, but also for the sake of those to whom it is conveyed.[153]

Why is such a distinction, which is not even suggested in the text of the *Charter,* warranted? If the state's *purpose* in acting is to restrict expression, then all forms of expression are protected; if it is merely the *effect* of the state's having acted that restricts expression, then only those types of expression which promote one of the three principles set out above are protected. There does not appear to be any basis for this distinction in the *Charter* text.

If a court decides that expression has indeed been limited by the state, it must move on to determine whether the limit can be justified under section 1.

Applying Section 1

There are two parts to the second phase of the *Irwin Toy* analysis. The first involves an assessment of ends; the second of means.

---

[153] *Irwin Toy*, above, note 120 at 976. This statement is an unnecessarily florid reformulation of Thomas Emerson's analysis.

In the first part, the state must persuade the court that the objective sought to be achieved through the creation of the limit on freedom of expression relates to concerns that are pressing and substantial in a free and democratic society, or which are, to use the phraseology of other cases, of sufficient importance to warrant overriding a constitutionally guaranteed right. In *Irwin Toy* the Court believed that the objective behind a prohibition against all commercial advertising directed at persons under thirteen was the protection of a group that was vulnerable to manipulation. This objective was held to meet the required standard. In *R. v. Keegstra*,[154] which, as we have noted, dealt with the *Criminal Code*'s ban on the wilful promotion of hatred, the state's objective was seen as two-fold—to prevent the pain suffered by persons who were the objects of hate propaganda and to reduce racial, ethnic, and religious tension and "perhaps even" violence in Canada.

The Supreme Court's decision in *Keegstra* can be seen as a clear example of double-think. In this decision the Court invented something it called "free expression values," despite the fact that neither section 2(b), nor the rest of the *Charter*, contains the word "values." The really important thing, or so the Court believed, was free expression values, rather than free expression itself. Thus, the state could legitimately suppress expression if it claimed to be doing so in the name of free expression values. This, I believe, is tantamount to saying that the way to protect free expression is to suppress it.[155] *R. v. Butler* dealt with the constitutionality of the *Criminal Code* offences directed against obscenity. The Supreme Court concluded that the state's objective was "the avoidance of harm to society." The harm was seen to lie in an enhanced propensity towards violence, degradation of women, and the reinforcement of "male-female

---

[154] Above, note 139.

[155] Terry Heinrichs, *Censorship as Free Speech: Free Expression Values and the Logic of Silencing*, (1998) 36 Alberta Law Review 835.

stereotypes" on the part of men who were exposed to obscene material.

In this stage of the analysis, the courts have often adopted, without acknowledging that this was what they were doing, the "harm" principle set out by J.S. Mill in his essay *On Liberty*.[156] As Mill saw it, the "harm" principle meant that the state could only legitimately interfere with the liberties of individuals in order to prevent objective social harm. A careful reading of Supreme Court decisions on expression suggests that, when the court is attempting to discover whether the goal the state was seeking to achieve when it created a limit on expression was "pressing and substantial," it is really assessing the seriousness of the "harm" the state was seeking to avoid. It does seem to me that, in *Keegstra*,[157] *Butler*,[158] and *Sharpe*,[159] substantial portions of the various judgments were devoted to assessing the seriousness of the "harm" the state was seeking to avoid. To look back at older Canadian jurisprudence on freedom of expression, a great deal of space in *R. v. Boucher*[160] was given over to a discussion of "harm." L.W. Sumner has provided a comprehensive elucidation and analysis of Mill's ideas and the role they have played in the development of a Canadian jurisprudence about freedom of expression in his *The Hateful and the Obscene: Studies in the Limits of Free Expression.*[161]

In recent years there has been a disturbing change of direction. Under the J.S. Mill approach, objective harm is the point at which the state may legitimately suppress expression. But that point has now shifted the point at which expression may be suppressed has become that of subjective offensiveness. The move

[156] Chicago, Henry Regnery Company, 1947.
[157] Above, note 139.
[158] Above, note 141.
[159] Above, note 143.
[160] [1950] 1 D.L.R. 657 (S.C.C.).
[161] Toronto, University of Toronto Press, 2004 at pp.18-23.

89

from a limit set at objective harm to one set at subjective offensiveness does not bode well for freedom of expression.

There is considerable subjectivity in the judicial approach to these matters. If protecting children from commercial manipulation is "pressing and substantial," why should not the protection of adults, many of whom are also credulous and gullible, be pressing and substantial? Although it would seem that preventing racial, religious, or ethnic violence is of sufficient importance to justify overriding a constitutional right, it is not self-evident that making sure people's feelings do not get hurt, which is what the first objective identified in *Keegstra* appears to amount to, is equally important. In *Butler* the Court conceded there was no solid evidence that obscenity actually caused any anti-social behaviour.

If the state's objective does not meet the required standard, the limit cannot be justified and the particular state act creating it will be struck down by the court. If, however, the objective sought by the state is acceptable, then the court must turn to an assessment of the means selected by the state in order to achieve its objective. The purpose of this assessment is to determine whether the means selected by the state are "proportionate" to the end it is seeking. Three separate inquiries are required here.

First, the court must ask whether there is a "rational connection" between the end sought and the means chosen. In practice, this comes down to a test of efficacy, with judges attempting to divine whether the means chosen will actually work and lead to the achievement of the end. In *Keegstra*, for example, three judges of the Supreme Court were not convinced there was a rational connection between criminalizing hate propaganda and successfully suppressing it. They were not persuaded that the offence in the *Criminal Code* was an "effective way of curbing hate-mongers." The stringency of this part of the assessment was much diluted in the *Butler* decision. There it was suggested that all that was necessary was a "sufficiently rational link between the criminal sanction [against obscenity]…and the objective." This assertion avoided a serious logical difficulty presented by the evidence in the case. If there was, indeed, no evidence that exposure to obscenity led to anti-social behaviour, it would have been impossible to accept that criminalizing obscenity could suppress or control such behaviour.

The state must next show that the means it has chosen will result in the "minimal impairment" of the right in question. Logically, of course, this is not possible, since it involves proving a negative. It cannot be proved that no conceivable means exists which might have resulted in a less serious infringement of the right than the one actually selected. A court is, at this stage, really being asked to determine whether the measure in question goes too far. Limitations on rights that are "overbroad" or "excessively vague" will likely be seen as going too far. In *Osborne v. Canada (Treasury Board)*[162] the Supreme Court struck down a prohibition which prohibited all federal civil servants "engag[ing] in work" for or against a political party on the ground that it was not "carefully designed to impair freedom of expression as little as reasonably possible" and went "beyond what is necessary to achieve the objective of an impartial and loyal civil service." Likewise, in *R. v. Zundel*,[163] a section of the *Criminal Code*, section 181, which made it an offence to publish false news that "causes or is likely to cause injury or mischief to a public interest" failed the minimal impairment requirement because the words "injury or mischief to a public interest" were "undefined and virtually unlimited," and, consequently, the section was held to be of no force or effect.

The third and final question with respect to the means adopted involves an analysis of any "deleterious effects" that may result from them. According to Chief Justice Antonio Lamer in

---

[162] [1991] 2 S.C.R. 69.
[163] [1992] 2 S.C.R. 731.

Dagenais v. Canadian Broadcasting Corp.,[164] "it is necessary to measure the actual salutary effects of impugned legislation against its deleterious effects." This statement appears to suggest that the judge, at the end of the day, must somehow balance the good likely to be achieved through the state act in question against the bad that may occur as a necessary by-product of it. It is difficult to see how judges can do this in a way which is consistent and which produces objective principles that can be generalized to other cases.

If the means chosen fail to meet any of these three standards, they are not proportionate to the objective and the limit on the *Charter* guarantee cannot be justified. The court will then declare the state act that has been challenged to be of "no force or effect"—that is to say, invalid. If the means chosen are proportionate to the objective sought, the limit is justified in a free and democratic society and the challenged state act is constitutionally valid.

Conclusion

Charter analysis has generally been seen to involve two stages, but, particularly in relation to cases involving freedom of expression, only one stage seems to matter. Since, as the Supreme Court decided in *Irwin Toy*, "if the activity conveys or attempts to convey a meaning," it qualifies as constitutionally protected expression, this stage of the analysis is largely without substance. It is a hurdle that is so low as to be virtually non-existent. The serious analysis, on which the validity of the state act will stand or fall, inevitably takes place in the second stage. Sumner appears to support this perspective, having asserted that, "...the really difficult issues will be faced in the course of the...section 1 analysis".[165]

---

[164] Above, note 149 at 888.

[165] *The Hateful and the Obscene*, op. cit., p.56.

The problem is that, having accorded equal constitutional protection to all forms of expression, by refusing to make any distinctions among them, the Supreme Court, in order to avoid striking down every existing limit on any form of expression, has had to make the process of justification under section 1 an easy one. In fact, having said at stage one that they would not discriminate amongst forms of expression, the judges have found it necessary to introduce precisely that sort of discrimination at stage two. So, we have the Supreme Court of Canada saying in *Butler* that obscenity "does not stand on equal footing with other kinds of expression which directly engage the 'core' of the freedom of expression values." This assertion appears directly to contradict the *Irwin Toy* approach of not discriminating amongst forms of expression.

It is difficult to suggest any general theory about the meaning of freedom of expression as guaranteed in the *Charter*. The main reason is that each of the Supreme Court's decisions on free expression and the *Charter* tends to stand alone. It is difficult to generalize about them. It could be argued that what we have in these cases is little more than a random collection of *ad hoc* policy analyses. This is where the Court's methodology has led it. When we read *Butler*, we discover what the Court thought about the virtue or desirability of a particular criminal prohibition against obscenity. When we read *Keegstra*, we discover what it thought of a similar prohibition against hate propaganda. The decisions do not tell us very much about freedom of expression, about what it means and why it matters, and, most important, why it should have received constitutional protection.

Chief Justice Duff, in his judgment in the Alberta Press Bill case, clearly understood the essential significance of freedom of expression in a democracy. And, in some of their judgments, judges of the contemporary Supreme Court have tried to adopt a principled approach to freedom of expression. In *Edmonton Journal v. Alberta (A.G.),*[166] Mr. Justice Peter Cory observed, "It is difficult to imagine a guaranteed right more important to a democratic society than freedom of expression." This approach has not been the norm. Madam Justice Bertha Wilson took a "contextual" approach to expression, deciding that it would mean one thing in one context and other things in other contexts.[167] The contextual approach makes a general theory of freedom of expression impossible. The "contextual approach", as I see it, involves the politicisation of adjudication. Thus, a judge who follows the "contextual approach" in dealing with a claim based on freedom of expression will ask herself two questions. First, does the person raising this claim belong to a social group which I tend to favour? And, second, do I agree with what this person is expressing? If the answer to both questions is "yes", the claim will be upheld.

The problem is that the *Irwin Toy* methodology is fundamentally flawed. It has frustrated the development of a useful jurisprudence. Legal decision making, particularly by the highest court of appeal, should lead to the creation of general, and generalisable, principles. The purpose of these principles is to provide a framework that will give direction to judges in resolving each new case that arises. The Supreme Court's decisions about freedom of expression do not provide such direction. As Professor Peter Hogg has concluded, the Court's approach to expression is "unprincipled and unpredictable."[168]

To summarize, the Canadian courts have given some guidance in one area. They have seen freedom of expression as involving a process. That process begins with the gathering of information. If freedom of expression is, in concrete terms, about the publication of information and opinions and we recognize that that

---

[166] [1989] 2 S.C.R. 1326 at 1336.

[167] *Ibid.* at 1354–56.

[168] P.W. Hogg, *Constitutional Law of Canada*, 3d ed., Toronto, Carswell, 1992, at 965.

information and those opinions have to come from somewhere, then the protection afforded by freedom of expression should also extend to the collection of the information. A Federal Court decision, *International Fund for Animal Welfare Inc. v. Canada (Minister of Fisheries & Oceans)*,[169] addressed the *Seal Hunting Regulations*. These regulations set up a permit system that was designed to limit the access of reporters to the Atlantic coast seal hunt. The court decided that the guarantee of freedom of expression would extend to protecting the ability of reporters to gather information. Going further, while freedom of expression clearly includes the publication of information, it must, in addition, as the Ontario Court of Appeal determined in *Information Retailers Assn. of Metropolitan Toronto v. Metropolitan Toronto (Municipality)*,[170] extend to the sale and distribution of information and opinions. Freedom of expression protected the ability of booksellers to operate bookshops and to sell and distribute books and periodicals. In a 2010 decision,[171] the Ontario Superior Court of Justice decided that freedom of expression might also include a right to anonymity, and that persons who made postings on a website assuming that they would remain anonymous had a "reasonable expectation of privacy".[172]

Finally, as the Federal Court held in *Luscher v. Deputy Minister of National Revenue (Customs & Excise)*,[173] freedom of expression includes the right to receive information. Luscher was a Canadian whose hobby was importing pornography from the United States. He challenged certain provisions of the Customs Tariff which limited his ability to do this. The court accepted that the receipt of information was a necessary part of expression and struck down

---

[169] [1987] 1 F.C. 244 (T.D.).

[170] (1985), 52 O.R. (2d) 449 (C.A.).

[171] *Warman* v. *Wilkins-Fournier et al.* (2010) 100 O.R. (3d) 648.

[172] *Ibid.*, at p.654.

[173] [1985] 1 F.C. 85 (C.A.).

the prohibition that was being challenged. The Supreme Court has recognized the same principle, stating in one decision that freedom of expression "protects listeners as well as speakers."[174] Expression is a process, then, that extends from gathering information to publishing information, to selling and distributing information, and finally to receiving information. All the stages in the process are protected under the guarantee of freedom of expression.[175]

As a final point, the courts have not interpreted section 2(b) as creating any special rights or special status in the mass media or in reporters.[176] Freedom of expression can be exercised by everyone—high school teachers, video shop owners, dentists, and cigarette manufacturers.

FURTHER READING

The leading, and the most comprehensive, work on Canada's Constitution is P.W. Hogg, *Constitutional Law of Canada*, 5th ed., two vols., Toronto, Carswell, 2007.

---

[174] *Ford v. Quebec (A.G.)*, [1988] 2 S.C.R. 712 at 767.

[175] Freedom of expression does not encompass a right to be listened to. *Native Women's Association of Canada v. Canada* [1987] 1 F.C. 244 (T.D.)

[176] See *Hill*, above note 150, and *Moysa v. Alberta (Labour Relations Board)*, [1989] 1 S.C.R. 1572.

CHAPTER 2

State Security and Public Order

Limitations on freedom of expression may be imposed by the state to achieve some purpose peculiar to the state. These limitations include emergency powers and the control of sensitive information.

Emergency Powers[177]

EMERGENCY POWERS ARE an anomalous phenomenon in any constitutional democracy. As we have seen, the basic principle of constitutional democracy is that the state is bound by the constitution. That is the rule-of-law principle. Just as each individual has no choice but to obey the law, so the state is obliged to act within the constitution. We have long since abandoned the idea that the state can do whatever it likes simply because it is the state. The very notion of emergency powers is anomalous because it posits that, in times of national crisis or national emergency, the state may step outside the constitution. The state may do things in a time of national emergency which it would not be permitted to do in normal times. The justification is that in extreme circumstances the state can take extreme measures to ensure its

---

[177] For a comprehensive review, see Robert Martin, *Notes on Emergency Powers in Canada*, (2005) 54 University of New Brunswick Law Journal 161.

own existence. There is a useful analogy between the notion of emergency powers as far as the state is concerned and the defence of self-defence in criminal law.

The ordinary rule of the criminal law is "Thou shall not kill." However, self-defence has always recognized an important exception to the rule that one person may not take another's life. That exception arises when one individual is directly threatening to kill another. To preserve her own life, that individual may lawfully kill the person who was threatening her life. Under extreme circumstances, then, an individual may lawfully do something that is prohibited under normal circumstances. The justification is, once again, found in the extreme circumstances.

What do states most commonly seek to do during states of emergency? First, they give themselves the power to arbitrarily arrest and detain people, to arrest people without charges and hold them without trial.

Second, they impose censorship.

The War Measures Act

In Canada, emergency powers were found for a long time in a federal statute called the *War Measures Act*.[178] The statute was first enacted in August 1914 to give the national government the powers it believed to be necessary to prosecute the war. The *War Measures Act*, although substantially amended after the First World War, remained part of Canadian law from 1914 to 1988. The important thing to remember about it, however, was that, unlike most statutes, the *War Measures Act* was not normally in operation. It was law throughout those years, but remained dormant in ordinary times. It came into operation only when it was invoked by a proclamation issued by the Governor General. The *Act* was invoked on three separate occasions: immediately after its passage

---

[178] S.C. 1915, c. 2.

in 1914; in 1939 on the outbreak of the Second World War; and once in peacetime by the government of Pierre Trudeau in October 1970.

What actually happened with the *War Measures Act?* The mechanism was a simple one. Once the *Act* had been proclaimed, plenary law-making authority was transferred from Parliament to the Governor in Council—that is, to the federal cabinet. Under the *Act,* Canada was transformed from a parliamentary democracy into an executive dictatorship. The Cabinet was given a power, which was practically limitless, to make regulations having the force of law.

The operative part of the *Act* was section 3 which, when stripped of its extra words, said: "The Governor in Council may do…such…things…as he may…deem necessary." The legal authority to do such things as are deemed necessary is an authority without limit. During both world wars Canada was largely ruled by orders in council made under the *War Measures Act.* There were literally thousands of them dealing with every aspect of Canadian life. Inevitably they included orders that provided for censorship.

Various publications were prohibited during the First World War. Many of these publications were, for obvious reasons, German language newspapers, but the list also included Irish nationalist publications and a number of left-wing publications. Many of the existing orders in council were brought together in the *Consolidated Orders Respecting Censorship* of 1918.[179] The chief censor was given broad authority to withhold from public consumption any material that commented unfavourably on the causes or operations of the war. Thus, criticism of the consistently abysmal leadership of the British Army on the Western Front, which was where most Canadians were killed, could lead one to run afoul of the censors.

In addition to the censorship regulations imposed under the

---

[179] P.C. 1918–1241, C. Gaz. 1918. 4376.

War Measures Act, extensive use was made of the *Criminal Code* offence of sedition. In 1916, in a case called *R. v. Trainor*,[180] a man was chatting with some people in a drugstore in a town in Alberta and said that he approved of the sinking of the *Lusitania*. He was charged with sedition and convicted. His appeal was allowed, and one of the judges observed:

> *There have been more prosecutions for seditious words in Alberta in the past two years than in all the history of England for over a hundred years and England has had numerous and critical wars in that time.*

A major change was made in the censorship regulations after the Russian Revolution of 1917. The timing seems unusual, given that Canada was at war with Germany, Austria, and their allies, not with Russia. The list of censored publications was extended to include a considerable range of pro-Bolshevik or communist-oriented publications.

Also subject to being suppressed during the First World War were publications that advocated temperance. Somehow, promoting temperance was seen as interfering with the war effort. In addition, many organizations were declared to be unlawful under the *War Measures Act*, so that membership in any of them was subject to sanctions.

The *War Measures Act*, once invoked, stayed in operation until its proclamation was revoked by the Governor in Council. Hostilities ended in November 1918, but the *Act* remained in operation until 1920. It was next invoked in 1939, and, immediately, regulations were adopted for the defence of Canada. These regulations imposed limitations on expression and created offences with respect to the expression of opinion and the communication of information. Regulation 39A(c) said:

---

[180] (1917), 10 Alta. L.R. 164 (C.A.).

No person shall print, circulate or distribute any book...card, letter, writing, print, publication or document of any kind containing any material, report or statement...which would or might be prejudicial to the safety of the State or the efficient prosecution of the war.[181]

That is about as broad a censorship regulation as one could find anywhere. In one case a high school teacher was prosecuted for breaching this regulation because, during a discussion in his classroom, he had encouraged the presentation of pacifist opinions. He was convicted. The court that convicted him said:

The whole intention [of the regulations] is to compel individuals to maintain silence or speak in the unconquerable spirit by which troops in action must be moved if they are to win.[182]

Any expression of another opinion would, presumably, have been an offence under the *Defence of Canada Regulations*. Various organizations were proscribed. In addition, a range of publications was prohibited, including for a period, left-wing publications. Given that the war was being fought against Nazi Germany, this censorship seems strange.

There was little criticism of the aggressive suppression of opinion and basic rights under the *War Measures Act*, although the leader of the Cooperative Commonwealth Federation (CCF), M.J. Coldwell, did speak out about the *Defence of Canada Regulations*. In May 1940 he said in the House of Commons:

We are prepared to support the struggle against

---

[181] P.C. 1939–2891, C. Gaz. 1939. 1126.
[182] *R. v. Coffin*, [1940] 2 W.W.R. 592 at 602 (Alta. Prov. Ct.).

> *aggression and for the preservation of democratic*
> *institutions, but we insist that democratic institutions*
> *shall be respected and safeguarded in our own*
> *country.... Ever since the outbreak of war we have been*
> *governed by decree...largely in secrecy.*[183]

Once again, while the fighting in Europe ended in May 1945 and in the Pacific in September 1945, the *War Measures Act* stayed in effect until 1947. There was no legal mechanism in the *Act* by which the government could have been compelled to revoke the proclamation.

The *Emergencies Act*

In 1988 Parliament repealed the *War Measures Act* and replaced it with a new statute called the *Emergencies Act*.[184] The *Emergencies Act* is in many respects an improvement on the *War Measures Act*. The first problem with the *War Measures Act* was its all or nothing nature. Taking the case of the invocation of the *Act* in October 1970, let us assume that on the island of Montreal, or even in the province of Quebec, there existed a serious and substantial threat to the security of the state. Once the *War Measures Act* was proclaimed in October 1970, however, it applied throughout Canada, not just in Montreal or Quebec. In October 1970 Vancouver was not a hotbed of extreme Québécois nationalism. Nonetheless, the city authorities there were having considerable problems with what they regarded as undesirable elements on the streets—drug dealers, panhandlers, petty criminals, transients, prostitutes, and so on. Under the *Public Order Regulations*,[185] which had been made pursuant to the *War Measures Act*, there was a

---

[183] House of Commons, *Debates*, 20 May 1940, at 51.
[184] S.C. 1988, c. 29.
[185] SOR/70–444.

generally unlimited power to arrest people and detain them for ninety days. The streets of Vancouver were cleaned up for a while by arresting all the undesirables under the *War Measures Act*.[186] It was not possible to have a state of emergency in one province or in one defined locality.

Second, the proclamation of the *War Measures Act* created a full-scale national emergency. There was no gradation or levels of emergency. Nor, third, was there any requirement that the government of Canada consult with provincial governments before invoking the *Act*. Finally, there was only limited opportunity for involvement by Parliament in determining whether a real state of emergency existed or how long the emergency should continue.

The *Emergencies Act* addressed a number of these concerns. It made it possible for states of emergency to be declared either in a province or in a limited area; it provided for consultation with provincial governments; and it substantially increased the oversight role of Parliament in the emergency process. It provided for finite limits on the duration of states of emergency and also for different levels of emergency.

There are four levels of emergency in the *Act*: public welfare emergency, public order emergency, international emergency, and war emergency. Various levels of power are given to the authorities in each specific level of emergency. The one worth talking about for present purposes is a war emergency, because this is the only level of emergency under the *Act* during which the imposition of censorship is permitted. A war emergency is the big one, the all-out state of emergency. In fact, the powers available to the state during a war emergency are as broad as the powers that were available under the *War Measures Act*. Section 38 of the *Emergencies Act* says:

---

[186] R. Haggart and A.E. Golden, *Rumours of War*, 2d ed., Toronto, New Press, 1979 at 111.

> *When the Governor in Council believes, on reasonable grounds, that a war emergency exists and necessitates the taking of special temporary measures for dealing with the emergency, the Governor in Council...may, by proclamation, so declare.*

Section 40 goes on:

> *While a declaration of war emergency is in effect, the Governor in Council may make such orders or regulations as the Governor in Council believes, on reasonable grounds, are necessary or advisable for dealing with the emergency.*

The Governor in Council may do whatever he or she believes is necessary to deal with the war emergency. The authority created clearly would include the power to impose various forms of censorship.

An important question has to do with the status of the *Charter* guarantee of freedom of expression during a war emergency. There are two possibilities. One involves the use of section 33, the notwithstanding clause in the *Charter*. Section 33 allows either Parliament or a provincial legislature to declare that a particular statute is to operate notwithstanding many of the guarantees, including freedom of expression, set out in the *Charter*.[187] The federal *Emergencies Act* would be an obvious candidate for a section 33 clause. The *Canadian Bill of Rights*,[188] a statute introduced under the Diefenbaker government, gave to Parliament the power to declare that any federal statute was to operate notwithstanding the

---

[187] *Canadian Charter of Rights and Freedoms*, Part I of the *Constitution Act, 1982*, being Schedule B to the *Canada Act 1982* (U.K.), 1982, c. 11, s. 33 [hereinafter *Charter*].

[188] S.C. 1960, c. 44, reprinted in R.S.C. 1985, App. III.

Bill of Rights. That power was used only once—in the *War Measures Act.* Parliament, however, has not exercised its authority under section 33 of the *Charter,* although two provincial legislatures have, but there is nothing to prevent it doing so in the future. The second possibility is that, since section 33 has not been relied on, it would be open to individuals who were subject to any regulations made under a war emergency declared pursuant to the *Emergencies Act* to challenge those regulations on the basis of the *Charter.* The courts would then have to decide, on a case-by-case basis, whether those limitations—for example, a regime of censorship imposed on the mass media—could be justified in a free and democratic society.

State Information

Official Secrets

What about confidential information in the possession of the state? The *Official Secrets Act,*[189] a federal statute, was based on legislation first enacted in the United Kingdom in 1889. The original purpose of the UK *Official Secrets Act* was to address espionage. An embarrassing situation arose in the United Kingdom when a number of individuals were arrested on the ground that they had been spying on behalf of a foreign power and, to considerable official consternation, it was discovered that this activity was not against the law.

Canada's *Security of Information Act* also addresses espionage and creates offences in respect of it. It is difficult to question the legitimacy of any state making it an offence to spy against it on behalf of a foreign state, so there is little that can usefully be said about the espionage provisions in the *Act.* However, other parts of

---

[189] R.S.C. 1985, c. O-5. In 2001 the *Act* was renamed the *Security of Information Act:* See *Anti-Terrorism Act,* S.C. 2001, c. 41, s. 25(1).

the *Act* relate to the communication of certain kinds of information that are in the possession of the state. These parts are problematic and worth discussing. Indeed, on the face of it, the *Security of Information Act* is unacceptably oppressive legislation.[190]

The first and most basic difficulty with the *Act* is that it is not at all clear to what it applies. For example, section 4(3) makes it an offence to receive any "secret official code word, password, sketch, plan, model, article, note, document or information." There is a simple, but fundamental, problem with that wording. The list set out begins with two adjectives, "secret official," and following them is a series of nouns, "code word, password, sketch, plan, model, article, note, document or information."

Do the two adjectives "secret official" modify only the immediately following nouns "code word," or do they modify all the subsequent nouns in the series? That is to say, does this statute apply only to *secret official information*—presumably, the real state secret security information—or does it apply to *any* information? The distinction matters because if this section applies to any information, it is possible that offences could be committed under the *Security of Information Act* by a journalist simply having in her possession some sort of information that the government of Canada did not want her to have.

The second difficulty has to do with this odd offence of receiving information. Section 4(3) makes it clear that one commits the offence by the very act of receiving any information to which the *Act* applies. Strictly speaking, then, as soon as a plain brown envelope filled with photocopied documents arrives at someone's desk in a newsroom, an offence has been committed.

Furthermore, as a third difficulty, section 4 contains a reverse onus provision. The state does not have to prove the guilt of the

---

[190] For background, see W.S. Tarnopolsky, *Freedom of the Press* in Newspapers and the Law, Ottawa, Minister of Supply & Services, 1981, at 19–21.

accused person; rather, the accused has to prove her innocence. An accused person is deemed to be guilty of an offence by the very act of receiving information unless she can prove that the communication to her of the code word, password, sketch, plan, model, article, note, document, or information was "contrary to his desire." How would a reporter prove that it was contrary to her desire that an envelope had landed on her desk?

The fourth difficulty is that the *Act* creates a practically unlimited power of arrest. Under Canadian law there are two ways a person may lawfully be arrested: either with a warrant— that is, pursuant to a formal authorization issued by a judicial officer—or without a warrant.

Our law says that police officers can arrest persons without a warrant only when they have reasonable and probable cause to believe that an offence has been committed. Without going in detail into a complicated area of law, it can be said that reasonable and probable cause is substantially more than suspicion. This provision is an important protection for basic liberties. Section 10 of the *Security of Information Act*, however, says that an individual can be arrested without a warrant if she is found committing an offence, or if she is reasonably suspected of having committed or having attempted to commit or *being about to* commit an offence under the *Act*. Thus, if a police officer reasonably suspects that a plain brown envelope containing documents to which this *Act* applies is about to land on a reporter's desk, that reporter can be arrested.

Fifth, this statute is the only one in effect today which allows police officers to authorize searches. Under the *Criminal Code*, search warrants can be issued only by a judicial officer. If the police cannot get a judicial officer to issue a search warrant under the *Criminal Code*, they cannot legally conduct a non-consensual search. The *Security of Information Act* is unique in that it gives to RCMP officers of the rank of superintendent or above the power to authorize searches.

Sixth, in section 14, the *Act* makes express provision for secret trials. Such trials, again, are contrary to fundamental principles of the Canadian legal system.

The final difficulty is found in section 15, which states that the maximum penalty that can be imposed in respect of an offence under the *Act* is fourteen years. The next most serious punishment available in our criminal justice system is life imprisonment.

The former Law Reform Commission of Canada described the *Official Secrets Act* in 1986 as "one of the poorest examples of legislative drafting in the statute books."[191]

I agree.

Many of the deficiencies in the *Act* were dealt with in *O'Neill v. Canada (Attorney General)*[192]. O'Neill was a reporter with the Ottawa *Citizen*. She had written a series of articles based on information she had received through an unauthorized "leak". The R.C.M.P. commenced an investigation into suspected breaches of the *Security of Information Act*. As part of this investigation the R.C.M. Police was granted warrants to search O'Neill's residence and office. O'Neill sought to have the warrants quashed.

Ratushny, J. granted O'Neill's application. The judge was critical of s.4 of the *Act*, finding a number of infringements of the *Charter*. She found the section to be vague and "overbroad" and was concerned at the apparent absence of *mens rea* with respect to a serious criminal offence. She was particularly concerned that the *Act* failed to define key terms such as "secret" and "secret official". Ratushny, J. accurately and fully identified the many flaws in the *Security of Information Act*.

How was the *Official Secrets Act* applied in practice? Its most extensive use stemmed from the Gouzenko affair. In 1945, Igor

---

[191] Law Reform Commission of Canada, *Crimes against the State* (Working Paper 49), Ottawa, The Commission, (1986) at 30 [hereinafter, *Crimes against the State*].

[192] (2007) 82 O.R. (3d) 241 (S.C.J.).

Gouzenko, a cipher clerk at the Soviet Embassy in Ottawa, went to the RCMP and claimed that a spy ring was operating out of the embassy. The official response to Gouzenko's claims was extraordinary. The *War Measures Act* was pressed into service.

As we have already noted, even though the Second World War was over, the *Act* was still in operation. A large number of people were rounded up under regulations made pursuant to the *War Measures Act*. They were arbitrarily arrested, not brought before a court, held incommunicado, and forced to appear without legal representation before a royal commission composed of two Supreme Court of Canada judges. It should be a matter of some concern that two Supreme Court judges were prepared to take part in this investigation.

The detainees were required to give evidence against themselves before the royal commission. This evidence was then used as the basis for laying charges. Some persons were charged with actual breaches of the *Official Secrets Act*, but in fact more were charged with *conspiring* to breach the *Act*. Conspiracy is a strange criminal offence. Its essence is an agreement to commit an unlawful act, not necessarily a criminal act, but *any* unlawful act. The crime of conspiracy is perfected when the agreement to commit the unlawful act is made.

The unlawful act itself does not have to be committed. By relying on the offence of conspiracy in the Gouzenko affair, the Crown did not have to prove that a particular accused person had actually breached the *Official Secrets Act*, just that he had agreed with someone else to do so. One of the many people eventually convicted was a Member of Parliament, Fred Rose.[193]

In recent years there have been few prosecutions, and these few have dealt mainly with the espionage sections of the *Act*. One non-espionage prosecution was the *R. v. Treu* case. It involved a

---

[193] See *R. v. Mazerall*, [1946] O.R. 762 (C.A.) and *Rose v. R.*, [1947] 3 D.L.R. 618 (Que. C.A.).

civil servant who took some files home which, he said, he forgot about. He later left the government, went into business, and just happened to use some of those files.[194]

Besides *O'Neill*, the only recent prosecution involving a journalist or the media was that of Peter Worthington in 1979, when he was the publisher of the Toronto *Sun*. He and the *Sun* had become convinced there was a Soviet spy network operating in Canada and that the government was not doing anything about it. Worthington claimed to have top secret documents that outlined Soviet espionage activities.

To seek to prove his point, he published one of these documents in the pages of the *Sun*. As a result, he was charged under section 4 of the *Official Secrets Act*. He went to trial before an Ontario provincial court judge who acquitted him on the ground that the document in question, which the judge clearly accepted had once been subject to the *Official Secrets Act*, no longer was. The reason, according to the judge, was that disclosures had brought the document, "now 'shopworn' and no longer secret, into the public domain."

Surely this reasoning is wrong. It suggests that the way to avoid conviction under the *Official Secrets Act* was simply to publish any secret documents one had in one's possession. The Crown did not appeal Worthington's acquittal because the matter had by this point become quite embarrassing to the government of Canada.[195]

Canadians can take a certain amount of comfort in the Doug Small prosecution. What happened to Small suggests that the *Official Secrets Act* did indeed apply only to actual security information, and not simply to any information in the possession of the government of Canada.

In 1989, Small, a reporter for Global Television, was leaked a

---

[194] (1979), 104 D.L.R. (3d) 524.

[195] *R. v. Toronto Sun Publishing Ltd.* (1979), 24 O.R. (2d) 621 (Prov. Ct.).

copy of a summary of the federal budget in advance of its announcement by the minister of finance. This leak annoyed the government. Small was prosecuted, but the important point is that he was not prosecuted under the *Official Secrets Act*. Presumably, the opinion of the government of Canada's lawyers must have been that the *Official Secrets Act* did not apply to budget documents. These documents were clearly "information," but one must assume the advice was that they were not "secret official information."

To repeat, the fact that Small was not prosecuted under the *Official Secrets Act* strongly suggests that the official view of the *Act* is that it applies only to actual security information. Small was prosecuted for theft, but the difficulty faced by the prosecution was the principle that information as such cannot be stolen. You can misappropriate information that is presented in a particular form—which is what copyright law is all about—but there cannot be property in the information itself.

Small was acquitted. He was acquitted because the document he had in his possession was in fact a photocopy of the budget document. He had nothing that was the property, or could be proven to be the property, of the government of Canada. The implication was that, if he had had an actual budget document, he probably could have been convicted of theft for stealing those specific pieces of paper. One simple lesson to be learned from this case is that when journalists receive leaked documents, they should make sure they are photocopies.

Access to Information

The federal *Access to Information Act*[196] serves as a balance to legislation like the *Security of Information Act*. The purpose of the *Access to Information Act* is not to maintain the tradition of

---

[196] R.S.C. 1985, c. A–1.

governmental secrecy as exemplified in the *Security of Information Act*, but to change it substantially, if not end it completely.

The *Access to Information Act*, passed in 1983, sets out its objective and its limitations in section 2(1):

> *The purpose of this Act is to extend the present laws of Canada to provide a right of access to information in records under the control of a government institution in accordance with the principles that government information should be available to the public, that necessary exceptions to the right of access should be limited and specific and that decisions on the disclosure of government information should be reviewed independently of government.*

We will analyse the *Act* according to the structure set out in this provision: the right of access; limits; and review.

The Right of Access

The Supreme Court of Canada has recognized access to information as an essential element in democratic government, first, because it encourages, and makes possible, the participation of citizens and second, because it makes government accountable.[197] In a recent decision,[198] interpreting Ontario's freedom of information legislation concerning municipalities, the Ontario Court of Appeal affirmed the approach taken in *Dagg* and held that the underlying principle was "presumptive access". In the specifics of the case, it was held that problems involved in readjusting computer programmes could not be used to justify a

---

[197] Dagg v. Canada (Minister of Finance) [1997] 2 S.C.R. 403.

[198] Toronto Police Services Board v. Information and Privacy Commissioners (2009) 93 O.R. (3d) 563.

denial of access.

The general right of access created by the federal *Act* is not so broad as might appear. First, "government institution" does not, in fact, mean *any* government institution; it means only those institutions that are listed in the Schedule to the *Act*. Any institution not mentioned in this appendix, such as, for example, the Canadian Judicial Council, the Court Challenges Program, the National Judicial Institute, the Supreme Court of Canada or the CBC, is not subject to the *Act*.

It is not clear why these institutions which are central elements of our judicial system should have been shielded from public scrutiny by excluding them from the ambit of the Act.

Second, while the right of access is granted to "all individuals present in Canada,"[199] it does not appear to extend to corporations. Since, however, an application may be made by an agent acting for a corporation, this is not a substantial obstacle. Third, and perhaps most important, finding something, whether as a general matter or under the *Access to Information Act*, is very much a matter of knowing what you are looking for. The request for information must be sufficiently full and detailed for an experienced government employee familiar with the subject-matter to locate the record requested with a reasonable effort. If this condition is not met, there is no obligation to provide the information.

To make the task easier, however, the *Act* requires the government to produce an annual *Access Register*. This publication describes in detail what each department or agency of the government of Canada does and the types of records it controls. Furthermore, each department or agency has an access coordinator, whose job is to assist persons applying for information. Any reporter whose responsibilities cover particular federal departments or agencies would do well to establish good

---

[199] Privacy Act Extension Order, No. 2, SOR/89–206.

working relations with the appropriate access coordinators. Fourth, there is provision in the *Act* for fees to be charged. There is a basic application fee of $5, as well as charges for photocopying and any time in excess of five hours spent searching for the records sought. Applicants may ask for a waiver of all fees and should do so as a matter of course.

Finally, the *Act* makes no reference to the purpose behind an application. As a result, at no stage of the process is the applicant required to establish that she wishes the information for some useful or legitimate purpose, nor, indeed, should the applicant even be asked why she wants the information.

Limits

Various categories of information are exempt from disclosure under the *Act*. Access legislation will apply to the courts and to the judiciary, except where its application might compromise the independence of the judiciary.[200] The federal *Act* provides for both mandatory exemptions and discretionary exemptions.

Mandatory Exemptions

Under the *Act*, the head of the government institution "*shall* refuse to disclose" [emphasis added] information that falls into any of the following categories:

• Any personal information as defined in the *Privacy Act*. The *Privacy Act* was enacted at the same time as the *Access to Information Act*. Its purpose is to protect the confidentiality of personal information about individuals which is in the possession of the government of Canada. This exemption prevents applicants

---

[200] Ministry of the Attorney General v. Information and Privacy Commissioner et al. (2011) 104 O.R. (3d) 588.

having access to personal information about other people.

- Any information being sought in a business context which contains trade secrets or other confidential commercial information. The *Act* is not intended to provide a competitive edge for any business enterprise. This is not to say that the *Act* cannot be used to further purely commercial ends. There are businesses, for example, which have used the *Act* to gain access to rulings and decisions made under the *Income Tax Act*. This material has then been published commercially.

- Any documents prepared for the work of the Cabinet, or Cabinet confidences. The traditional principle of Cabinet secrecy is maintained.

- Any information obtained by the government of Canada in confidence from a foreign government, an organization of states, a provincial government, or a municipal government.

- Information obtained or prepared by the RCMP while performing contractual policing services for a province or municipality, where there has been a prior agreement not to disclose such information.

- Any information that may not be disclosed pursuant to some other statute.

Discretionary Exemptions

The head of a government institution *may* refuse to disclose any record from a long list of categories of information. These categories include:

- Information that could reasonably be expected to be injurious to the conduct of federal-provincial affairs, or the conduct of international affairs and the defence of Canada, or of any state allied with Canada, or the "detection, prevention or suppression of subversive or hostile activities."

- Information relating to law enforcement, including the detection, prevention, and suppression of crime.
- Information that could reasonably be expected to facilitate the commission of a crime. As examples, the *Act* includes in this category technical information relating to weapons or potential weapons or information on the "vulnerability" of particular buildings.
- Information that could reasonably be expected to threaten the safety of individuals.
- A great deal of information of an essentially economic nature. This includes information injurious to the "financial interests" of the government of Canada or the ability of the government to "manage" the country's economy, such as information about contemplated changes in the bank rate, or tariffs or taxes. It further includes government trade secrets and scientific or technical information obtained through government research.
- Any information subject to solicitor-client privilege.
- Information the government was already planning to release within ninety days of the request being made. Additional time may be allowed for the translation and publication of such information.

Even if a reporter is unable to gain access to certain information following the rules laid down in the *Act*, it may well be that she is still able to get the information through other means. Assuming that the information is not subject to the *Security of Information Act*, no offence will be committed through the publication of such information. A denial of access does not amount to a prohibition against publication.

Review

The person applying for information is supposed to receive an answer within thirty days of making the request, although the government agency has the ability to extend this period for a further thirty days or, sometimes, even longer. The applicant should either get the information sought or, if disclosure is not to be granted, written reasons for the refusal. These reasons must either indicate the section of the *Act* under which access is being refused or state that the record being sought does not exist.

If the record sought belongs to a class to which access is not permitted, there is no obligation to inform the applicant whether the particular record exists. Within a year of the refusal to grant access to the information sought, a complaint can be taken to the information commissioner. The commissioner can also address issues concerning fees and delays. The procedure followed by the commissioner is closer to an investigation than to a hearing, but the applicant, the relevant government institution, and any third party opposing the release of information about itself are all allowed to present arguments to the commissioner.

Once the information commissioner has reached a decision, that decision is communicated to the government agency in question. The agency is not bound to follow the information commissioner's decision. If the agency still refuses to grant access, either the applicant or the information commissioner may have the agency's refusal reviewed by the Federal Court of Canada. It is the refusal of access that is to be reviewed, not the decision of the information commissioner.[201]

The Federal Court has shown a general inclination in favour of disclosing information rather than withholding it. In a 1986 decision, *Canada (Information Commissioner) v. Canada (Minister of Employment & Immigration)*,[202] the court said: "[T]he purpose of the *Access to Information Act* is to codify the right of access to information held by the government. It is not to codify the government's right of refusal. Access should be the normal

---

[201] Dagg v. Canada (Minister of Finance), [1995] 3 F.C. 199 (C.A.).
[202] [1986] 3 F.C. 63 at 69. (T.D.).

course. Exemptions should be exceptional and must be confined to those specifically set out in the statute."

All the provinces except Prince Edward Island have access legislation. The majority of these statutes use the misleading phrase "freedom of information". All the statutes follow the broad path of the federal legislation in setting out a general right of access to information, qualifying that with specific exemptions, and, at the same time, seeking to protect the privacy of individuals. In five provinces—Alberta, British Columbia, Ontario, Quebec, and Saskatchewan—the access legislation also applies to municipal governments.[203]

An acceptable regime of access to information should include all, or most, of the following:

i) constitutional or statutory recognition of a right of access to information which is in the possession of the state;

ii) a right of access which is broadly defined and which extends to all organs, agencies, or departments of the state;

iii) a narrow definition, in precise and specific language, of permitted exemptions to the right of access;

iv) statutory language which makes clear that access is to be the norm and that exemptions are to be resorted to only in exceptional cases;

v) speedy processing and disposition of requests for access;

vi) independent review of any denial of access;

vii) minimal or no fees or other charges for the processing of requests for access;

viii) the creation and training of a cadre of officials to assist persons in the making of requests for access; and

ix) wide publicity about the right of access and explanation of

---

[203] Municipal Councils are generally obligated to hold public meetings. By-laws enacted at a closed meeting may, for that reason, be quashed. *Corporation of the City of London* v. *RSJ Holdings Inc.* [2007] 2 S.C.R. 588.

the procedures to be followed.[204]

What, exactly, is the juridical basis for access to information in Canada? Some have suggested that the guarantee of freedom of expression and freedom of the press in s.2(b) of the *Charter* should be interpreted so as to include a right to information. The Ontario Court of Appeal addressed this question in *Criminal Lawyers' Association* v. *Ministry of Public Safety and Security*.[205] Juriansz, J. A. concluded, "The right of (access to government information) is statutory and not constitutional."[206]

This matter was appealed to the Supreme Court of Canada, which released its decision[207] on 17 June 2010. A bench of seven judges rendered a unanimous decision, concluding, as a general principle, that, "Section 2(b) of the *Charter* guarantees freedom of expression, but it does not guarantee access to *all* documents in government hands." The judges did suggest that a claim to access might be founded on section 2(b) where three conditions were met:

a. access is shown to be a necessary precondition of meaningful expression;

b. access does not encroach on protected privileges, i.e. solicitor-client privilege; and

c. access is compatible with the function of the institution concerned.

A claimant would be obliged to establish that "…access is necessary for the meaningful exercise of free expression on matters of public or political interest."

---

[204] Robert Martin and Estelle Feldman, *Access to Information in Developing Countries*, Berlin, Transparency International, 1998 at 74.

[205] (2007) 86 O.R. (3d) 259 (C.A.).

[206] *Ibid.*, at 296.

[207] *Ministry of Public Safety and Security* v. *Criminal Lawyers' Association* [2010] 1 S.C.R. 815. The parties were joined by a host of interveners.

CRIMINAL LIBEL

There are two broad categories of libel in Canada: civil libel and criminal libel. Civil libel is the mechanism whereby individuals may seek to protect their reputations (see chapter 4). The broad purpose of criminal libel is to preserve public order. Criminal libel punishes certain forms of expression largely because they are seen as creating threats to public order. There are three forms of criminal libel in the *Criminal Code*: seditious libel, defamatory libel, and blasphemous libel.

Seditious Libel

Seditious libel is the crime that has traditionally been used to prosecute unacceptable political speech. The *Criminal Code* deals with sedition in sections 59 to 62. These sections are exceedingly unsatisfactory. Section 59(1) says, "[s]editious words are words that express a seditious intention," and goes on in subsection 2 to note that a "seditious libel is a libel that expresses a seditious intention."[208]

Unfortunately, the *Code* does not tell us exactly what is meant by a seditious intention. It does, however, set outer limits. It tells us that it is seditious to advocate the use of force as a means of accomplishing a governmental change within Canada. At the other extreme, section 60 provides that certain things are not seditious.

For example, it is not seditious, to use the classic formulation, to say or argue in good faith that "Her Majesty has been misled or mistaken in her measures." It is not sedition to engage in reasonable criticism of the government of the day. Nor is it sedition to criticize in good faith the Constitution of Canada or of a province, or to criticize the Parliament of Canada or the

---

[208] *Criminal Code of Canada*, R.S.C. 1985, c. C–46, s. 59 [hereinafter *Criminal Code*].

legislature of a province, or the administration of justice. At the one extreme, then, advocating the overthrow of the government of Canada by force is seditious, but, at the other, engaging in normal political discourse is not. What conduct falls in the middle?

There has not been a prosecution for sedition since the 1940s. The last prosecution arose out of the ongoing struggle in Quebec between the Jehovah's Witnesses and the government of Maurice Duplessis. It focused, in particular, on a tract circulated in Quebec by the Witnesses. The tract was in French, but its title translated into English was "Quebec's Burning Hate for God and Christ and Freedom Is the Shame of All Canada."

In the kind of society that existed at the time in Quebec, and especially rural Quebec, those words were inflammatory. The persons who had been circulating this pamphlet were prosecuted for sedition. The case, *Boucher v. R.*,[209] went to the Supreme Court of Canada, where the judges divided five to four. The nature of their division is important, and has been important, in ensuring a substantial degree of freedom of political expression.

All the judges agreed that in order for there to be a conviction, the Crown would have to prove that the words used by the accused, whether in a speech, a book, a pamphlet, or whatever, were seditious in and of themselves. What does that mean? The Court looked to older case law, especially older English case law, and suggested that words are seditious if they tend "to create discontent or disaffection among His Majesty's subjects or ill-will or hostility between groups of them." On that definition, a great many utterances could be regarded as seditious—and this is where the key distinction between the majority and the minority in the Court in *Boucher* lay. The minority judges were prepared to say that an accused person could

---

[209] [1951] S.C.R. 265.

be convicted on the basis of words alone.[210]

If the words that the accused published were seditious in and of themselves, then, said four of the nine judges, that is enough, she is guilty. Five of the nine judges, however, said that there must be another element. They decided that not only does the Crown have to show that the statements made were seditious in and of themselves, but it must show in addition that when the accused uttered the seditious words she did so with the intention of inciting riot, tumult, or disorder. The point is simple, but important: five of the nine judges were saying the purpose of the offence of sedition is not to punish expression pure and simple.

The purpose of the offence, rather, is to punish people who would seek to undermine public order. Sedition exists not to protect society against unpleasant words, but against real threats to social peace. The point to be derived from *Boucher* is that the Crown must prove that the accused uttered seditious words with a seditious intent.

The result of this decision has been to make it extremely difficult to convict someone of sedition. How is the Crown to prove that the accused actually intended to incite riot, tumult, or disorder? This is undoubtedly the main reason there has not been a prosecution for sedition since *Boucher*.

The former Law Reform Commission of Canada described the offence of sedition as an "outdated and unprincipled" law, and

---

[210] The judges who took this view relied on *Wallace-Johnson* v. *The King* [1940] AC 231, a Judicial Committee decision interpreting the criminal law of the colonial Gold Coast. In 1961, in *D.P.P.* v. *Obi* [1961] All N.L.R. 186, the Federal Supreme Court of Nigeria expressly rejected *Wallace-Johnson*. As recently as 1993, the Malawi Court of Appeal attempted to breathe some life back into *Wallace-Johnson,* describing it as an "impregnable" precedent. *Chihana* v. *Republic of Malawi.* [1996] 1 L.R.C. 1. For background, see, Shola Adenekan, *Chakufwa Chihana*, The Guardian, 13 July 2006.

further in 1984, took the view that, as a result of the *Boucher* case, it was so narrowly circumscribed as no longer to have any practical utility. The Commission recommended that it be removed from the *Criminal Code*, but it is still there, even though there have been no prosecutions for fifty years.[211]

Defamatory Libel

Defamatory libel is the most prolix offence in the *Criminal Code*, its definition occupying sections 297 to 316. In these sections, the offence sounds very similar to civil libel, but there are some distinctions. Mere insults exchanged between two people can amount to defamatory libel, for example, whereas with civil libel, publication to a third person is required (see chapter 4, section A(1)(c)).

What is defamatory libel all about, and what is the point of it? There are few prosecutions, but, as the Law Reform Commission of Canada noted in a 1984 study, some prosecutions still take place.[212]

An interesting one occurred in Vancouver in 1969 when the *Georgia Straight*, one of the better known of the underground publications of the 1960s, was prosecuted.[213] The *Georgia Straight* did not like a particular magistrate in Vancouver, Lawrence Eckhardt, and was highly critical of him. It also conferred a number of awards upon him. On one occasion it gave him the Order of Abundant Flatulence, and on another awarded him the Pontius Pilate Certificate of Justice. In the citation for this certificate the paper said:

---

[211] *Crimes against the State*, above note 14 at 35–36.

[212] Law Reform Commission of Canada, *Defamatory Libel* (Working Paper 35), Ottawa, Minister of Supply and Services, (1984).

[213] *R. v. Georgia Straight Publishing Ltd.* (1969), 4 D.L.R. (3d) 383 (B.C. Co. Ct.).

> *To Lawrence Eckhardt, who, by closing his mind to*
> *justice, his eyes to fairness, and his ears to equality, has*
> *encouraged the belief that the law is not only blind, but*
> *also deaf, dumb and stupid. Let history judge your*
> *actions—then appeal.*

The trial court was not at all clear what the crime of defamatory libel was about. It did refer to perhaps the best-known Canadian prosecution, which occurred in Alberta in the 1930s.[214] Unwin, the accused in this case, had circulated a pamphlet showing on one side the names of nine prominent citizens of Edmonton, all under the heading "Bankers' Toadies." On the other side were the words:

> *God Made Bankers' Toadies, just as He made snakes,*
> *slugs, snails and other creepy-crawly, treacherous and*
> *poisonous things. NEVER therefore, abuse them—just*
> *exterminate them!*

He was charged with defamatory libel and convicted. The court said that the distinction between civil libel and criminal libel was that civil libel was a private matter between individuals. If you say insulting and untrue things about someone which tend to harm that person's reputation, then she can sue you civilly and be awarded compensation. By way of contrast, a defamatory libel prosecution is a public matter between the state and the accused. In *Unwin*, the court suggested that the purpose of such a prosecution was not so much for the redress of a private wrong, as it was to punish the accused for the wrong done to the public. The theory appears to be that some statements can be so extreme that they cease to be a purely private matter between individuals and become a public matter engaging the attention of the state.

---

[214] *R. v. Unwin*, [1938] 1 D.L.R. 529 (Alta. C.A.).

That is all very well until we look into the history of the offence of defamatory libel in England. The offence was created by the Court of Star Chamber in the seventeenth century as an anti-duelling measure. The theory was that if A made extreme and insulting statements to B, B might be so offended that he would feel obliged to challenge A to a duel. And A or B would probably end up dead. The point of the crime was to discourage A from making the outrageous statements about B which would lead B to challenge A to a duel. This might have made a great deal of sense in seventeenth-century England, but duelling is not a widespread phenomenon in twenty-first century Canada.

Despite that, we continue to have this anti-duelling measure in our *Criminal Code*. The Law Reform Commission of Canada said there was simply no justification whatsoever for having this offence and recommended that it be removed.[215] As of this writing, that was twenty-eight years ago, and the offence is still in the *Criminal Code* and people are still being prosecuted. Once again, it must be noted that the purpose of the offence, at least in the seventeenth century, was to maintain public order by punishing expression that would tend to undermine it.

Strangely enough, there have, in recent years, been a few reported cases dealing with defamatory libel. Each of these has involved a constitutional challenge to the offence of defamatory libel, especially on the basis of the guarantee of freedom of expression in section 2(b) of the *Charter*. The judicial response to these challenges has not been entirely satisfactory. In *Lucas v. Saskatchewan*[216] two persons stood outside a police station carrying signs containing a scurrilous attack on a senior police officer. *R. v. Gill*[217] was similar in that it involved people carrying posters which

---

[215] Law Reform Commission of Canada, *Working Paper 35: Defamatory Libel*, Ottawa, 1984.

[216] (1995) 31 C.R.R. (2d) 92 (Sask. Q.B.).

[217] (1996) 29 O.R. (3d) 250.

were viciously critical of guards at Kingston Penitentiary. In *Lucas* the court determined that the objective underlying the offence of defamatory libel was "...the protection of individuals from false defamatory attacks on their privacy and reputation."[218]

In *Gill* the court believed that the purpose of defamatory libel was "...the protection of an individual's rights, namely prohibiting an individual from being defamed."[219] These observations suggest that defamatory libel belongs more to tort law than to criminal law. From this perspective, it would appear that the true subject matter of the defamatory libel provisions in the *Criminal Code* is "property and civil rights in the province."

Thus, the offence of defamatory libel could be seen as an attempt by Parliament to legislate about a subject-matter reserved exclusively to the provincial legislatures. The judges who held this opinion about defamatory libel should have found the *Criminal Code* provisions to be *ultra vires* and, therefore, invalid. The Manitoba Court of Appeal fell into the same error in *R. v. Stevens*,[220] holding that Parliament's objective in creating this offence was "the protection of reputation."

At this point it must be remembered that there are two separate and distinct bases upon which the constitutionality of a law may be questioned. First, there is the traditional division of powers basis. Here, the party challenging the law argues that it is *ultra vires* the legislature which enacted it. Second, it may be alleged that the law is an unjustifiable infringement of one of the guarantees in the *Charter*. The offence of defamatory libel is open to both challenges.

In *Lucas* the court held that section 300 of the *Criminal Code* was a justifiable limit on freedom of expression. The court also

---

[218] Above, note 37 at 102.
[219] Above, note 38 at 255.
[220] [1995] 4 W.W.R. 153.

held that section 301 did not meet the minimal impairment standard and could not, therefore, be justified.

The Court held that the state's objective in enacting section 300 related to concerns which were pressing and substantial.[221] It also held that there was a rational connection between the objective being sought and the means chosen to achieve the objective and the offense created only a minimal impairment of freedom of expression.[222]

The Court held that, because the Crown was not obliged under section 301 to prove that the accused knew that the statements which she uttered were false, the limit on freedom of expression created in section 301 did not meet the minimal impairment standard and could not be justified under section 1 of the *Charter*.[223] In *Gill*, the Court reached a similar conclusion about section 301 and declared it to be of no force or effect.

The reasoning of the court in *Gill* was similar to the reasoning of the court in *Lucas*. It was also held that, because the Crown was not required to prove that the accused knew the statements which she had uttered to be false, section 301 could not be justified as creating only a minimal impairment of freedom of expression.[224]

In *Lucas* the court held that section 300[225] of the *Criminal Code* was a justifiable limit on freedom of expression. The court also held that section 301[226] did not meet the minimal impairment

---

[221] Above note 216 at 104.

[222] *Ibid*.

[223] Above note 216 at 108.

[224] (1996) 29 O.R. (3d) 250 at 256.

[225] Section 300 states: "Everyone who publishes a defamatory libel that he knows is false is guilty of an indictable offence and is liable to imprisonment for five years."

[226] Section 301 states: "Every one who publishes a defamatory libel is guilty of an indictable offence and is liable to imprisonment for two years."

standard and could not, therefore, be justified. In *Gill*, the Court reached a similar conclusion about section 301 and declared it to be of no force or effect.

Blasphemous Libel

Blasphemous libel is the third and final form of criminal libel. Once again, it would seem that the justification for the offence is that extreme statements made about the religious beliefs of individuals can lead to a breakdown in public order.[227] For this reason, the uttering of such statements may properly be limited by the state.

Section 296 of the *Criminal Code* deals with blasphemy. As is the case with sedition, the Code does not define blasphemy. It simply states that:

> It is a question of fact whether or not any matter that is
> published is a blasphemous libel.

One qualification provides that it is not blasphemous to express "an opinion upon a religious subject" as long as such opinion is expressed in "good faith" and "decent language.

There are two significant problems with this offence. First, it has been held that in order for there to be a conviction, the Crown does not have to prove that the accused intended to blaspheme; it is enough to prove that the accused intentionally uttered statements that were found to be blasphemous.[228] Second, while the matter has not been the subject of a judicial decision in Canada, an English court has decided that the offence of blasphemy applies only to the Christian religion. Statements made

---

[227] *R. v. Rahard* (1935), 65 C.C.C. 344 (Que. S.C.).
[228] *R. v. Gay News Ltd.*, [1979] 1 All E.R. 898 (H.L.).

about other religions, no matter how extreme, could not, by definition, result in a conviction for blasphemy.[229]

As with defamatory libel, although there are few prosecutions for blasphemous libel, they do occur from time to time.

The *Charter*

What about these three offences and the *Charter*? Since there have been no recent sedition prosecutions, there has been no opportunity to question the constitutionality of the offence.

All three offences seem to be questionable limits on freedom of expression. Furthermore, in the case of blasphemous libel, if the offence were to be held to apply in Canada only to statements made about Christianity, this would seem to conflict with the equality guarantee in section 15 of the *Charter* and the affirmation of "multicultural[ism]" in section 27.

FURTHER READING

No single work deals specifically and in detail with the matters addressed in this chapter. An essay by W.S. Tarnopolsky, *Freedom of the Press*, in a volume prepared by the Royal Commission on Newspapers, Newspapers and the Law, Ottawa, Minister of Supply & Services, (1981), 1, is helpful. A compendious source on access to information and related issues, which is regularly updated, is C.H. McNairn and C.D. Woodbury, *Government Information: Access and Privacy*, Toronto: Carswell, (1992).

---

[229] *R. v. Chief Metropolitan Stipendiary Magistrate; ex parte Choudhury*, [1991] 1 Q.B. 429.

CHAPTER 3

Free Expression and the Judicial Process

What is the law on reporting about the legal system and about access to the courts? Detailed rules govern what may and may not be reported concerning proceedings that are either pending or actually before the courts. There are also difficulties that can arise for journalists who get caught up with the legal system.

The Openness Principle

IN OUR SYSTEM the courts are public institutions. The courtroom is a public place, and what takes place there is public business. Thus, what happens in the courtroom should, as a matter of principle, be open to the public and, more to the point, to reporters and to the media. This principle of the openness and the public nature of the judicial system had been recognized even prior to the adoption of the *Charter*.

It does not seem that all Canadian judges understand this principle. In the summer of 2002 an oppressive cloak of secrecy shielded a trial held in St. Thomas, Ontario from public view— this proceeding involved a matter which had attracted considerable attention and been widely reported in the local media. The trial judge, Eleanor Schnall, did not close the court to the public or to reporters, but did impose sweeping, and questionable, restrictions on what might be reported about it. The judge claimed that these orders were intended to protect the children whose family was at the centre of the hearing from public scrutiny. The banning orders made by the judge were so broad as to effectively prohibit reporting about the proceeding. One commentator suggested that, initially, the proceeding was conducted "in virtual secrecy."[230]

Another judge did lift these bans, but not before the trial judge herself gave an interview to a television reporter in which she gave out information in a fashion which was probably a breach of her own orders.[231]

It should be emphasised that the ban imposed by Justice Schnall went far beyond those found in section 45(8) of the Ontario *Child Protection Act*.[232] Interestingly enough, while the existing prohibitions in the *Act* seek to protect the identities of the child and the parents involved in a hearing, the parents whose conduct had precipitated the St. Thomas hearing were opposed to the ban made by Justice Schnall.[233]

The clearest source for the openness principle is a 1981 decision of the Supreme Court of Canada, *Nova Scotia (A.G.) v. MacIntyre*.[234] Linden MacIntyre, a CBC reporter, went to a courthouse in Halifax and asked both to inspect some search warrants and to be allowed to see whatever had been discovered as a result of the search. A justice of the peace was not sympathetic to the request and told MacIntyre it was impossible.

---

[230] Christie Blatchford, *A Thin Line between Abuse and Discipline*, National Post, 11 July 2002. See also, Oliver Moore, *Ontario Judge Lifts Veil on Spanking Trial*, The Globe and Mail, 29 June 2002.

[231] Christie Blatchford, *Judge Who Demands Silence Speaks Out*, National Post, 2 July 2002.

[232] R.S.O. 1990, c. C.11.

[233] Christie Blatchford, *Parents Urge Media Ban Be Lifted*, National Post, 12 June 2002.

[234] [1982] 1 S.C.R. 175.

MacIntyre disagreed and litigation ensued. The litigation was initially between MacIntyre and the attorney general of Nova Scotia, but that official was joined by the attorney general of Canada and the attorneys general of six other provinces, all of whom were opposed to allowing MacIntyre to see this material.

In his judgment, Mr. Justice Brian Dickson [as he then was] laid down some important principles, although perhaps it is more accurate to say, affirmed them, because it was his view that they had always been part of the Canadian legal system. He said that the basic principle governing judicial proceedings was their openness. Openness was to be the rule; covertness the exception. He said further that what must be sought was maximum public accessibility: "At every stage the rule should be one of public accessibility and concomitant judicial accountability."[235]

In other decisions Canadian courts have emphasised the importance of the openness principle, stating, for example, that the openness of the courts is "…one of the hallmarks of a democratic society"[236] and that the principle is "the very soul of justice"[237] and, to underscore the point, "Courts are and have, since time immemorial, been public arenas."[238] The principle enunciated in *MacIntyre* was affirmed and, to a degree, circumscribed in *Vichery v. Nova Scotia Supreme Court.*[239] In this case, a man (Nugent) was convicted of second degree murder largely on the basis of evidence contained on certain audiotapes and videotapes. He appealed against the conviction and the appellate court held that the various tapes should not have been

---

[235] *Ibid.*, at p. 186.

[236] *Re Southam Inc. and the Queen (No. 1)* (1983) 41 O.R. (2d) 113 (C.A.).

[237] *Canadian Broadcasting Corporation v. A.G. New Brunswick*, [1996] 3 S.C.R. 480 at 495.

[238] *Ibid.* at 499.

[239] [1991] 1 S.C.R. 671.

admitted as evidence and overturned the conviction. A journalist tried to obtain the tapes and the matter ended up before the Supreme Court of Canada. The Court added a gloss to *MacIntyre*, "Criminal appeals, like criminal trials, should be as open as possible", but qualified that somewhat, "N's privacy interests as a person acquitted of a crime outweigh the public right of access to exhibits judicially determined to be inadmissible against him."

The Court pronounced against media excesses.[240]

> *Nugent cannot escape from proceedings in which he was involved, nor from the fair and accurate reporting of them, but the courts must be careful not to become unwitting parties to his harassment by facilitating the broadcasting of material which was found to have been obtained in violation of his fundamental rights.*

In recent years, Canadian judges have not always understood the openness principle as clearly as Justice Dickson did. Since the 1980s, Canadian courts, led by the Supreme Court of Canada, have gradually made sexual assault trials an exception to the openness principle. In this respect the courts were largely following the lead of Parliament. In 1983 Parliament, ostensibly to address the "under-reporting" of sexual offences, made substantial amendments to the *Criminal Code* provisions dealing with sexual assault.[241] These legislative changes limited the public nature of sexual assault proceedings. Section 486(3) of the *Criminal Code* gave the judge presiding over a sexual assault prosecution the authority to prohibit the publication of any information that could disclose the identity of the complainant. The constitutionality of this provision was upheld in *Canadian*

---

[240] *Ibid.*, at p. 685.
[241] See Robert Martin, *Bill C-49: A Victory for Interest Group Politics*, (1993) 42 University of New Brunswick Law Journal 357.

Newspapers Co. v. A.G. Canada.[242] Section 486(1) of the *Criminal Code* authorizes a judge to exclude the public from all or part of a sexual assault trial. In one instance a trial judge excluded the public and the media from the part of a sexual assault proceeding which involved the sentencing of an accused person who had pleaded guilty. The Supreme Court of Canada upheld both the judge's order and the constitutionality of section 486(1).[243] The trial judge offered this explanation for his order:

> *I say some of the facts I knew beforehand or some I had some idea. I don't know exactly what the facts were thus the order.*[244]

In an extreme manifestation of this tendency, a judge conducting a sexual assault trial in Ottawa at the end of 2000 made an order prohibiting the publication of any details about the trial including his own name and the verdict.[245]

Any limit on openness, any limit on the access of the public to the courts, has to be justified as an exception to the openness principle. Justice Dickson formulated his approach in the following words: "[C]urtailment of public accessibility can only be justified where there is present the need to protect social values of superordinate importance."[246] Although it is not clear what he meant by "social values of superordinate importance," Mr. Justice Dickson obviously had in mind something substantial.

By way of illustration, Dickson gave two examples of social

---

[242] [1988] 2 S.C.R. 122. A judge may not rescind a publication ban made pursuant to s. 486(3) without the assent of the complainant. (*R. v. Adams*, [1995] 4 S.C.R. 707.)

[243] *C.B.C. v. New Brunswick* (A.G.) [1996] S.C.R. 480.

[244] *Ibid.* at 521.

[245] Mark Bowrrie, *Judge Flip-Flops on Publication Ban*, Law Times, 27 November 2000.

[246] [1982] 1 S.C.R. at p. 186.

values of superordinate importance which, he believed, would justify limiting the principle of openness. He put them in the context of access to search warrants and to the material discovered as a result of a search. Since a search warrant is a court document and since material discovered as a result of a search comes into the possession of the court, the openness principle would generally require that members of the public be entitled to see search warrants and any material that had been discovered during their execution.

What social values could justify limiting access in such a situation? First, the administration of justice was a value of superordinate importance. This meant that members of the public could not see search warrants before they had been executed. Clearly, a major part of the value of search warrants as tools in law enforcement is the element of surprise. Thus, the administration of justice would justify limiting the openness principle to this extent.

The second social value of superordinate importance was the protection of the privacy of the innocent. What did that mean? Mr. Justice Dickson said that where a search warrant had been executed but nothing was found, it would be justifiable to limit access to that warrant. That does not seem as clear-cut and as self-evident as the first instance. If, for example, I claimed to a reporter that I was being harassed by police searches of my home or office, one of the things I would want to do to substantiate my claim would be to produce the warrants authorizing the searches I claimed to have taken place. Dickson's second social value might make this impossible.

Judges have expanded the openness principle by holding that section 2(b) of the *Charter*,[247] the guarantee of freedom of

---

[247] *Canadian Charter of Rights and Freedoms*, Part I of the *Constitution Act, 1982*, being Schedule B to the *Canada Act 1982* (U.K.), 1982, c. 11, s. 2(b) [hereinafter *Charter*].

expression, has the effect of putting the openness principle on a constitutional basis. To what extent can an individual reporter challenge either legislation or a judicial order which limits her ability to report about a particular proceeding or which denies access to the courts? The legal question at issue here is called "standing."

To what extent does a reporter have the necessary standing to mount a legal challenge to such restrictions? Here we want to look at the earliest litigation in which a media organization attempted to rely on the *Charter*; the decision of the Ontario Court of Appeal in *Reference Re s. 12(1) of Juvenile Delinquents Act (Canada)*.[248]

The Southam Corporation has been aggressive in using the Charter as a means of expanding what it sees as the legal and constitutional rights of journalists. Is litigation a useful means of improving journalism? Has the litigation the Southam Corporation has been involved in actually made a concrete contribution to enhancing the legal status of journalists? Furthermore, one can question whether paying the lawyers who conduct this litigation is a useful or desirable means of investing the funds of a media corporation.

A federal statute, the *Juvenile Delinquents Act*,[249] previously dealt with trials of young persons and was replaced in 1983 by the *Young Offenders Act*.[250] Section 12 of the earlier *Act* said that the trials of juveniles were to take place "without publicity." Towards the end of 1981, the Supreme Court of Canada decided that this phrase meant that during the trial of a juvenile the courtroom was to be closed.[251] Nobody was to get in, except, of course, lawyers, social workers, psychologists, police, parents, and so on. But no reporters.

---

[248] (1983), 41 O.R. (2d) 113 (C.A.).

[249] R.S.C. 1970, c. J-3.

[250] R.S.C. 1985, c. Y-1 [hereinafter *YOA*].

[251] *B.(C.) v. R.*, [1981] 2 S.C.R. 480.

In the spring of 1982 the *Charter* became part of the Canadian Constitution and, shortly after that, the Ottawa *Citizen* decided to use it as the basis for challenging the constitutionality of section 12 of the *Juvenile Delinquents Act*. The *Citizen* sent a reporter to the court-house in Ottawa to attend the trial of a juvenile and, when she was turned away, the newspaper instituted its challenge.

Further comment on "standing" is necessary here. Standing addresses the important question of who is entitled to raise issues before the courts and, more particularly, who is entitled to challenge the constitutionality of legislation. By way of illustration, standing was a central issue in the attempts of both Henry Morgentaler and Joe Borowski to change the law about abortion.[252] Borowski was challenging section 251 of the *Criminal Code* because it permitted abortions under certain circumstances, and Morgentaler was challenging the same section because it did not give women complete freedom of choice.

They were both relying on section 7 of the *Charter* for their challenges, but from different perspectives. Borowski said that by permitting abortions at all, the state was infringing the right to life of foetuses, a right he argued was guaranteed in that section. Morgentaler claimed that by placing restrictions on access to abortion, the state was infringing the liberty and security of the person of women, also guaranteed by section 7. The major procedural difference between the two cases was that Morgentaler, when he raised these challenges, was actually in court accused of violating section 251 of the *Criminal Code* by performing abortions other than in accordance with the procedure laid down in that section.[253] He had run concretely and directly up against the section. Since he was directly affected by the law, he

---

[252] As general background, see F.L. Morton, *Morgentaler v. Borowski: Abortion, the Charter, and the Courts*, Toronto, McClelland & Stewart, (1992).

[253] *R. v. Morgentaler*, [1988] 1 S.C.R. 30.

thereby had the necessary standing to challenge its constitutionality.

But Borowski's situation was different. He had not run up against section 251 in the course of actual litigation; he simply did not agree with it. As a result, there was controversy before the courts as to whether Borowski should be granted the necessary standing to challenge the law,[254] although, in the end, the Supreme Court concluded that he could be heard. It should be added that being granted standing simply means that a court has agreed to hear an individual's case. It in no way guarantees that the court will actually decide the case in that person's favour.

There is a deeper problem here. If we broaden the notion of standing, we come very close to the point of allowing people to raise constitutional challenges to laws solely on the basis that they do not like them. This has the obvious effect of politicizing the role of the courts. If I can challenge the constitutionality of a law for no reason other than my distaste for it, it would seem that I am attempting to use the courts as a political, rather than a legal, forum.

The issue of standing arose at once in the Ottawa *Citizen*'s challenge to section 12 of the *Juvenile Delinquents Act*. The *Citizen* reporter was seeking to raise an issue in the course of a proceeding to which she was not a party. The proceeding was entirely a matter between the Crown and a particular juvenile. Now along comes someone who is an outsider to this proceeding, yet wants to raise legal arguments relevant to it. How can she do this? On what basis did the *Citizen* have the standing to challenge the constitutional validity of section 12 of the *Juvenile Delinquents Act*, when it was not a party to any proceeding involving that section?

Take another example, one that has happened from time to time. While conducting a trial a judge orders, "I do not want this

---

[254] *Canada (Minister of Justice)* v. *Borowski*, [1981] 2 S.C.R. 575. See also *Borowski* v. *Canada (A.G.)*, [1989] 1 S.C.R. 342.

witness identified by name in the mass media." A reporter might stand up and assert to the judge, politely, "I think that order is an infringement of rights guaranteed under section 2(b) of the *Charter* and I think you should reconsider it." Where does that reporter get the standing to raise this issue when, once again, she is not a party to the proceeding actually before the court?

For a long time the generally held view was that the necessary standing was provided by section 24(1) of the *Charter*. That section says:

> *Anyone whose rights or freedoms, as guaranteed by this Charter, have been infringed or denied may apply to a court of competent jurisdiction…[for a] remedy….*

Now the section cannot mean what it says literally. No one can know for sure whether her rights or freedoms have been infringed or denied until a court decides they have been. What the section has to mean, and can only mean, is that anyone who *claims* that her rights or freedoms have been infringed or denied may apply to a court for a remedy. It had been assumed until December 1994 that this was the basis on which journalists claimed standing to challenge rulings made during proceedings to which they were not parties. But the Supreme Court of Canada in its *Dagenais v. Canadian Broadcasting Corp.*[255] decision complicated the issue as to how exactly journalists might bring these challenges before the courts.

The *Dagenais* decision casts doubt on the idea that section 24(1) gives journalists, or other third parties, the necessary standing. *Dagenais* says that when a judge makes an order that results in imposing an unjustifiable limitation on freedom of expression, that judge has made "an error of law." The process of challenging an error of law is more complex than simply getting

---

[255] [1994] 3 S.C.R. 835.

up in court and suggesting that a particular ruling was incorrect. If the ruling was made by a judge of an inferior court, an application might be made to have it reviewed by a judge of a superior court. The decision of that superior court judge may then be appealed to the provincial court of appeal and, thence, where appropriate, to the Supreme Court of Canada. If, however, the original order was made by a superior court judge, it may be, according to *Dagenais*, appealed directly to the Supreme Court of Canada.

To return to the *Reference Re s. 12(1) of Juvenile Delinquents Act (Canada)* case, the court accepted that the requirements of standing were met. The substantive question raised by the *Citizen* was whether the guarantee of freedom of expression in section 2(b) should be interpreted as including a constitutional guarantee of the openness of the courts. The Ontario Court of Appeal said it should.

The reasoning adopted by the court in reaching this conclusion is not clear. To begin with, it is not immediately apparent that the phrase "freedom of expression" necessarily includes a guarantee of the openness of the courts. The judges in the *Reference Re S. 12(1) of Juvenile Delinquents Act (Canada)* case talked about the Constitution as a "living tree." Whenever judges talk like this, they are really saying that the constitutional text does not actually authorize them to do what they want to do, but, if they call the Constitution a living tree, they can feel free to put a broader interpretation on it. The court referred to a number of American decisions that had reached similar conclusions. The court further recognized that access to the courts was not specifically enumerated in the fundamental freedoms part of the *Charter*, but said that, having regard to the historic origin and necessary purpose of public access, it was reasonable to regard public access to the courts as an integral part of the fundamental freedom of expression. The argument is that freedom of expression includes both a right to gather information and a right to comment publically about the operations of fundamental state institutions. Obviously, however, no one can either gather information or comment publically about the way these institutions operate unless she can get into them. Since the courts are clearly key state institutions, the guarantee of freedom of expression is, thus, interpreted as including a right of access to them.

This approach to interpreting section 2(b) of the *Charter* has been affirmed by the Supreme Court of Canada. Giving judgment in *Edmonton Journal v. Alberta (A.G.)*,[256] Mr. Justice Cory asserted:

> *There can be no doubt that the courts play an important role in any democratic society. They are the forum not only for the resolution of disputes between citizens, but for the resolution of disputes between the citizens and the state in all its manifestations. The more complex society becomes, the more important becomes the function of the courts. As a result of their significance, the courts must be open to public scrutiny and to public criticism of their operation by the public.*[257]

In recognizing that the openness principle had a constitutional basis, Mr. Justice Cory also recognized an essential practical corollary to the principle. This is the special role of the mass media in making the principle concrete. He said:

> *...as listeners and readers, members of the public have a right to information pertaining to public institutions and particularly the courts. Here the press plays a fundamentally important role. It is exceedingly difficult for many, if not most, people to attend a court trial.*

---

[256] [1989] 2 S.C.R. 1326.

[257] *Ibid.*, at p. 1337.

> *Neither working couples nor mothers or fathers house-*
> *bound with young children, would find it possible to*
> *attend court. Those who cannot attend rely in large*
> *measure upon the press to inform them about court*
> *proceedings—the nature of the evidence that was*
> *called, the arguments presented, the comments made by*
> *the trial judge—in order to know not only what rights*
> *they may have, but how their problems might be dealt*
> *with in court. It is only through the press that most*
> *individuals can really learn of what is transpiring in*
> *the courts. They as "listeners" or readers have a right to*
> *receive this information. Only then can they make an*
> *assessment of the institution. Discussion of court cases*
> *and constructive criticism of court proceedings is*
> *dependent upon the receipt by the public of information*
> *as to what transpired in court. Practically speaking,*
> *this information can only be obtained from the*
> *newspapers or other media.*[258]

Indeed, to take another illustration, Madam Justice Boland of the Ontario High Court advanced the matter a step further in *R. v. Robinson.*[259] She suggested that the mass media have a duty, not necessarily legal, but certainly moral or professional, to inform the public of what is happening in our courts. She stated:

> *Openness prevents abuse of the judicial system and*
> *fosters public confidence in the fairness and integrity of*
> *our system of justice. The press is a positive influence in*
> *assuring a fair trial.*

Not only are judicial proceedings themselves public, but the

---

[258] *Ibid.*, at p. 1339.
[259] (1983), 41 O.R. (2d) 764 (H.C.J.).

documents that form a part of a proceeding are also public. Every such document is a public document and, following the principle laid down in the *MacIntyre* case, should be subject to public access. The problem is that if a court official refuses to give a reporter access to a document, that reporter may have to litigate to have the refusal overturned. In most such situations, however, the threat of litigation should be sufficient to overcome official or judicial recalcitrance.

It is not the business of court officials to decide what is proper reporting about judicial proceedings. The law of contempt of court and the law of libel, as we shall see, already address that issue. If a reporter makes a bad job of reporting a particular trial, she may commit the offence of contempt of court. Alternatively, if she gets what is asserted in a particular document all wrong she may libel somebody. The law already has mechanisms to deal with errors or failings that may occur in reporting. There is no need and no place for administrative officials, or even judges, to attempt to add new ones.

This issue became a matter of controversy in Prince Edward Island in 1995. The province's superior court introduced a rule that prevented members of the public, including reporters, from seeing statements of claim filed by plaintiffs in civil suits. In February 1996 this policy was reversed by a new provincial chief justice. All documents filed with the courts in civil proceedings would thenceforth be available to the public, subject to a residual authority in judges to seal confidential documents. This process was entirely a matter of administrative decision making by the province's judges. There was no litigation to test the legality of such action.

Cameras and Other Tools

Two specific issues arise in relation to the openness principle. The first has to do with the use of cameras, video recorders, and audio recorders in the courtroom. This has become a vexed issue of late. A standard provision dealing with these matters is found in section 136 of the Ontario *Courts of Justice Act*.[260] Section 136 prohibits taking, or attempting to take, a photograph, motion picture, audio recording, or other record capable of producing visual or oral representations by electronic means or otherwise at a court hearing, during the course of a trial, or of any person entering or leaving a courtroom or of any person inside a court-house who is there for the purpose of taking part in a judicial proceeding. There is an exception to this blanket prohibition, one that it took some time to achieve. Reporters may use audio recorders in courtrooms as a means of taking notes, but not to record material to be broadcast. The clear policy and tradition of the Canadian legal system has been against allowing the use of cameras, audio recorders, or video recorders in the courtroom.

There are some interesting manifestations of this tradition, one being the unusual 1976 case of *R. v. Rowbotham (No. 3)*.[261] Rowbotham was an American who had been in and out of Canadian courts and in and out of jail regularly. In this instance he had been arrested at Toronto International Airport trying to import a considerable amount of cannabis, and he was put on trial for offences under the *Narcotic Control Act*. An American publication called *High Times* sent a reporter to cover the trial. The simplest way to describe *High Times* is to say that it takes an approach to drugs roughly similar to the approach *Penthouse* takes to sex. It features the High of the Month and so on.

The *High Times* reporter, to the horror of the presiding judge, actually went to where the judge's car was parked outside the court-house and tried to photograph him. The judge was having none of it, and made an order that no "person shall take, or attempt to take any photograph, motion picture, or other record

---

[260] R.S.O. 1990, c. 43.
[261] (1976), 2 C.R. (3d) 241 (Ont. G.S.P.).

capable of producing visual representations by electronic means or otherwise, of any person in any way involved in the case of Regina and…Rowbotham…either inside the Peel County Court House, or outside the Peel County Court House."

Strictly speaking, that meant no one could take a photograph of a witness in the case walking down Yonge Street in Toronto. The reporter for *High Times* became disgusted with the Canadian judicial system and left Peel County, vowing never to return.

A more illuminating case was the prosecution in 1992 of CBC reporter Cathy Squires for photographing something going on inside a courthouse.[262] Squires did not deny having taken the photograph, but based her defence on the *Charter* guarantee of freedom of expression. That guarantee has been interpreted, as we have seen, to mean that the courtroom is open to the public, including reporters.

Since reporters have a constitutional right to be inside the courtroom, she argued that there was no justification for imposing limits on the means or tools that reporters might use while there. If the reporter has a right to be in the courtroom, she should have a constitutional right to be there with an audio recorder or a video recorder. Squires was convicted at trial, and the matter eventually went to the Ontario Court of Appeal. Five judges heard the appeal. Three decided that what is now section 136 of the Ontario *Courts of Justice Act* was constitutional, and two decided it was not. All the judges agreed that the section created a limit on the *Charter* guarantee of freedom of expression.

> *If television journalists are unable to photograph persons entering or leaving a courtroom, their freedom of expression is curtailed.*

The majority in the court, nonetheless, found this limit to be

---

[262] *R. v. Squires* (1992), 11 O.R. (3d) 385 (C.A.).

justified in a free and democratic society. The state's objectives in creating this limit were seen as three-fold:

i)   maintaining order and decorum in the courtroom;
ii) guaranteeing unimpeded access to the courtroom; and
iii) guaranteeing reasonable expectations of privacy.[263]

The means chosen to achieve these objectives were held to be proportionate to them. The general direction of the majority's reasoning was summed up in the judgment of Mr. Justice Houlden:

> *The fair and impartial administration of justice requires a calm, dignified atmosphere. If photographing and televising is permitted of persons entering or leaving the courtroom, that atmosphere will, I believe, be disrupted.*

In the result, Squires's conviction and the $500 fine imposed on her were upheld. The Supreme Court denied her leave to appeal. Litigation based on the *Charter* will not, then, succeed in opening Canadian courtrooms to television cameras.

These issues were revisited in British Columbia in *R. v. Pilarinos*[264] in 2001. In this case, Glen Clark, a former Premier of British Columbia, was being tried on criminal charges. Given the identity of the accused, there was considerable media interest in the proceeding, and several stations and networks wished to televise it. This was prohibited, but not pursuant to a statute, rather pursuant to something called "Supreme Court Policy on Television in the Courtroom."[265] The policy prohibited:

---

[263] *Ibid.*, at p. 393.
[264] (2001) 158 C.C.C. (3d) 1 (B.C.S.C.).
[265] *Ibid.* at 11.

> ...broadcasting, televising, recording or taking of
> photographs in the courtroom, or areas immediately
> adjacent thereto...without the consent of the parties to
> a proceeding and without the permission of the
> presiding judge.

There were several questions before the court in relation to this policy. The first was, did the judges possess the authority necessary to make and seek to impose such a policy? There was no doubt that such power existed. Part of the inherent jurisdiction of a superior court was the power of a court to control its own process, including the "...power to make any order in relation to the publicity of the proceedings."[266] Second, was the Policy a limit on the freedom of expression guaranteed in section 2(b) of the *Charter?* No, it was not.

> Excluding cameras and tape recorders from the
> courtroom does not prevent the gathering of
> information, as the courts are open to everyone. It only
> limits the technical manner in which information is
> gathered. I conclude that the latter is not a
> constitutionally protected right.[267]

In this regard, the Court affirmed the principle that "...the media have no greater rights regarding freedom of expression than any other citizen."[268]

Since there was no infringement of a *Charter* right, there was no need for the Court to have recourse to section 1. Nonetheless, the Court did vary the Policy by qualifying it in this fashion:

---

[266] *Ibid.* at 16–17.

[267] *Ibid.* at 25.

[268] *Ibid.* at 26.

> *...reporters may bring audio recording devices into the courtroom for the sole purpose of providing verification of their notes.*[269]

This issue remains the oldest and hardiest of the old chestnuts of Canadian media law, which is to say, should television cameras be allowed into Canadian courtrooms?

A distinction is growing between the actual practice today in trial courts and in appellate courts. The Federal Court of Appeal now regularly allows videotape recordings of its proceedings, and the Supreme Court has allowed them on a number of occasions. The Ontario Court of Appeal appears ready to adopt a similar practice. Nobody seems to care seriously about whether journalists record proceedings before appellate courts, largely because these proceedings are not very interesting. The reason, of course, is that there are no ordinary people there, no witnesses. All that happens before appellate courts is lawyers arguing points of law.

Should video recorders be allowed in trial courts? My own view has changed substantially since I watched the 1995 O.J. Simpson proceedings in California. I was once convinced that it was simply a matter of time until we had television in Canadian courtrooms, but watching the circus surrounding the O.J. Simpson trial made me rethink the matter. The real issue may not be simply the question of guaranteeing a fair trial or decorum and dignity inside the courtroom. It may be a matter of maintaining the integrity of the judicial process, of ensuring that the judicial process is not swallowed by the entertainment industry. What was often lost sight of during the O.J. Simpson proceeding was that it was a real trial of a real person who was charged with murdering two other real people. The whole business was not staged as yet another means of providing titillation for television

---

[269] *Ibid.* at 59.

viewers.

Any serious proposals that have been put forward for allowing television into Canadian courtrooms have been based on an understanding that there will not be scrums in the courtroom, but fixed cameras that will provide videotape on a pool basis equally to all news agencies. It has never been seriously suggested that individual reporters be allowed to bring video cameras into the courtroom.

How would television affect judicial proceedings? Many have suggested that since television has not destroyed our legislatures, it will not destroy our courts. But there are many significant differences between televising what goes on in the legislature and what goes on in the courtroom. One is that members of legislatures are elected, and one of the ways they got elected was by creating a certain image. A crucial thing in the life of a politician today is to be a good television personality and to establish a good public image, primarily through television. Considerations like this are not only foreign to judicial proceedings, but are subversive of them. There will be no benefit to the legal system from encouraging lawyers, and above all judges, to become media stars.

A paper produced by the Law Reform Commission of Canada in 1987 makes at least one sound assertion—that there is little empirical information about these matters.[270] I am not sure how one would get such information, however. There is empirical information that allowing reporters to use audio recorders as a means of taking notes in the courtroom has substantially increased the accuracy of court reporting.[271] In other words, there is

---

[270] Law Reform Commission of Canada, *Public and Media Access to the Criminal Process* (Working Paper 56), Ottawa, The Commission, (1987).

[271] Peter Calamai, "Discrepancies in News Quotes from the Colin Thatcher Trial", in N. Russell, ed., *Trials and Tribulations, an Examination of News Coverage given Three Prominent Canadian Trials*,

evidence that the use of contemporary technology will improve reporting, but there is no information about the effect that allowing video recorders into Canadian courtrooms would have on the integrity of the judicial process.

It may be inevitable that we will have television coverage of judicial proceedings. Once the foot in the door of video coverage of appellate proceedings has been accepted, it becomes more difficult to argue in favour of restricting video coverage of trial court proceedings. The current practice is hard to justify. Reporters are permitted to use video recorders to cover the dull proceedings; they may not use them to cover the interesting ones.

The entire question was reviewed extensively by the Supreme Court of British Columbia in *R. v. Cho*.[272] The court accepted that the situation in B.C. was different from that in Ontario as canvassed in the *Squires* decision, in that, in Ontario, the prohibition against television cameras in the courtroom was statutory, whereas, in British Columbia, it arose under common law. The B.C. court was cautious in dealing with the question, taking the general view that, "...subject to the overriding duty and right of the individual trial judge to control his or her process, the time has now arrived to permit the introduction of equipment designed to more accurately depict public events." The judge concluded:

> However, given my view of the state of the law and particularly the absence of any cogent reasons in support of the existing common law ban, I am prepared to permit the introduction of the video and still cameras to record counsels' submissions to the jury and my instructions...there will be no filming of the accused

Regina, School of Journalism and Communication, University of Regina, (1986), p.1.
[272] (2000) 189 D.L.R. (4th) 180.

*and no filming of the jurors. In this trial, the
experiment will be restricted to filming the submissions
at the close of the trial, should the media wish to avail
themselves of the opportunity.* [273]

Preventing Embarrassment

To what extent can limitations on the openness of the courts be
justified in order to protect parties from embarrassment? *R. v. An
Unnamed Person*[274] is an example. In this case a seventeen-year-old
woman was charged with infanticide, and the trial judge had
issued an order prohibiting publication of her identity.

The judge did so to spare her public embarrassment. As Mr.
Justice Zuber of the Ontario Court of Appeal made clear, there is
no basis whatsoever for such orders. The power of judges to place
limits on the openness of the courts or on public access to the
courts has to do solely with protecting the process of the courts,
with guaranteeing the due administration of justice. It has nothing
to do with avoiding embarrassment. There is no authority for
limiting publicity surrounding any judicial proceeding solely in
order to protect anyone from embarrassment.

Legislative Proceedings

Discussion of the openness principle includes media coverage of
the proceedings of Parliament of a provincial legislature. Quite
different considerations apply.

Although the courts have decided that section 2(b) of the
Charter creates a broad right of public and media access to judicial
proceedings, this has not been the result in the case of legislative
proceedings. The Supreme Court of Canada dealt with this

---

[273] *Ibid.*, at p. 191.
[274] (1985), 22 C.C.C. (3d) 284 (Ont. C.A.).

question in *New Brunswick Broadcasting Co. v. Nova Scotia (Speaker of the House of Assembly).*[275] The Nova Scotia House of Assembly had prohibited television coverage of its proceedings. A number of media organizations sought a judicial order to the effect that this prohibition was an unjustifiable limit on freedom of expression. The Court rejected this claim.

It held that Canadian legislatures possessed such inherent privileges as are necessary to ensure their proper functioning. Legislative privilege was, further, a part of the unwritten constitutional law of Canada. The Court went on to say that no one principle of the constitution could be applied so as to negate any other principle. More specifically, the judges decided that the manner in which a particular legislature chose to exercise its privileges, which clearly included the authority to exclude "strangers"—that is, anyone who was not a member of the legislature—could not be subject to judicial review. Thus, if the legislature of Nova Scotia wished to prohibit television coverage of its proceedings, that was entirely up to the legislature of Nova Scotia.

Contempt of Court

The most significant limitations on the openness principle are found in the law of contempt of court. There is civil contempt of court and there is criminal contempt of court.[276] We will say nothing about civil contempt, as it is of no particular relevance to the mass media. The Canadian law of criminal contempt of court is a strange, anomalous, and, most important of all, unclear element of our criminal law.

A useful place to begin is in contrasting how reporters and

---

[275] [1993] 1 S.C.R. 319.

[276] The distinctions between civil contempt and criminal contempt were elaborated in *Chiang* v. *Chiang* (2009) 930. O.R. (3d) 483 (C.A.).

editors should look at contempt of court with the way lawyers tend to look at it. Lawyers are told from the start of their careers that their primary responsibility is to keep their clients out of trouble. One form of trouble lawyers are especially concerned to protect their clients from is criminal prosecution. Contempt of court is a crime. Lawyers, by their deepest instincts, want to advise their clients not to commit crimes. Thus, they are going to be careful and attempt to steer clients who are journalists away from committing, or running the risk of committing, contempt of court.

Journalists, in contrast, should put contempt in perspective. One way to do that is to realize that there are different levels of crimes. To be convicted of contempt of court is not the same thing as being convicted of molesting children. Contempt does not carry with it the moral opprobrium that attaches to many other crimes.

The most common punishment awarded upon conviction for contempt of court is a fine. Seldom is a reporter sent to jail for contempt of court. And where a journalist has committed a contempt of court in good faith and in the course of her work, it is overwhelmingly likely that her employer will pay her fine. A person who has been convicted of contempt of court will have, in popular language, a "criminal record." Once again, it is important to be clear that there are criminal records and there are criminal records. Having a criminal record for contempt of court is not like having a criminal record for fraud. A contempt conviction is not going to prevent someone being bonded. It is not going to prevent someone travelling outside Canada.

I am not suggesting that journalists be carefree about committing the offence of contempt of court. I am simply saying that lawyers often take a more cataclysmic view of these matters than is always justified.

There is a further problem with contempt of court in Canada, one that makes lawyers even more cautious. Contempt is the only crime that is not defined in the *Criminal Code*. Our criminal law was inherited from and is based on English criminal law.

In England the criminal law is part of the amorphous common law. There are statutes that define particular crimes, but England has no general criminal code. One of the reasons we adopted a *Criminal Code* in 1892 was a feeling that the English approach was not adequate.[277] Criminal law has serious consequences for individuals. You can go to jail, you can be fined, your life can be ruined, and, of course, in 1892 you could be hanged. The view was that if the state was going to impose serious consequences like these on individuals who breached the criminal law and, at the same time, was going to reject any defence based on not knowing the law, the state was under an obligation to make the criminal law as knowable as possible. This is the main argument in favour of having a *Criminal Code*. Of course, the average Canadian does not spend much time reading the *Criminal Code* and, even if she did, it is, by and large, incomprehensible to anyone who is not a lawyer.

One logical result of the adoption of the *Criminal Code* was that the whole common law of crimes was abolished in Canada. The *Criminal Code* says, in section 8, that it is a complete statement of the criminal law of Canada. The *Charter*, in section 11, reinforces this stand by providing that persons can only be punished for offences that already exist in law. However, section 9 of the *Criminal Code* exempts the law of contempt of court from this basic principle. Contempt of court is thus preserved as the one common law crime still enforced in Canada.[278]

The major result is that nobody knows for sure what the law

---

[277] See D.H. Brown, *The Genesis of the Criminal Code of 1892*, Toronto, University of Toronto Press, 1989.

[278] The Ontario Court of Appeal has held that the existing law of contempt of court meets the standards required by the *Charter*. See, *R. v. Cohn* (1984) 48 O.R. (2d) 65 (C.A.).

of contempt of court is. Lawyers will admit that they do not know its precise boundaries. The vagueness and uncertainty compound the problems with contempt of court by reinforcing the caution of lawyers.

The final point to address is the likely effect on a journalist's career of a conviction for contempt of court. If, in good faith and in the course of serious professional reporting, someone ends up writing or broadcasting something that leads to her being convicted of contempt of court, it is unlikely that this conviction will result in her career being ruined. It might well make her reputation.

Defining Contempt

Turning to the substance of the matter, the first question to ask and to which we cannot find an answer in the *Criminal Code* is, What is contempt of court? If someone asks what is theft, a lawyer can point to the sections in the *Criminal Code* which define it. But not with contempt of court.

So what, in a general sense, is involved? Useful guidance can be found in a 1979 decision of the UK House of Lords, *A.G. v. Leveller Magazine Ltd.*[279] This case, as is true of a fair amount of English media law, emerged from one of the periodic spy scandals that were once such an entertaining feature of English life. There had been a prosecution under the UK *Official Secrets Act* during which the judicial officer presiding had to deal with two witnesses who were serving officers in the British Army and who did not want their identities made public. The judge directed that in the course of these proceedings the one officer was to be referred to as Colonel A and the other as Colonel B. However, while giving evidence, Colonel B revealed two facts.

First, he gave the name of the army unit to which he belonged

---

[279] [1979] A.C. 440 (H.L.).

and, second, he mentioned that information about his posting to that unit was to be found in a particular issue of an army publication. A reporter did not have to be an investigative genius to figure out that all she had to do was get that issue, look up information about a colonel being posted to the unit named, and she would have Colonel B's real name. A number of publications did so and published the name. The judge presiding at the original proceeding was mightily offended by this outcome. Contempt of court proceedings were instituted. The question that the House of Lords had to address was whether the publication of Colonel B's identity amounted to a contempt of court. The order made by the judicial officer at the trial was to the effect that *during the course of the proceeding* this person should be referred to as Colonel B. The judge's ego was bruised, the judge's feelings were hurt, the judge was angry, but was this a contempt of court?

The House of Lords said that criminal contempts of court share a common characteristic. They all involve interference with the due administration of justice. The reason the offence exists, the House of Lords emphasized, is to provide a legal mechanism to prevent interference with the administration of justice. Thus, contempt addresses behaviour, actions, and, more to the point, publications that interfere with, or create a real risk of interfering with, the due administration of justice.

What is meant by interference?

It is something that will frustrate the operation of the courts, something that will make it impossible, either generally or in a particular case, for the judicial system to operate the way it is supposed to. Contempt is not, then, a matter of the egos or the whims of judges. Its purpose is to ensure that the judicial system operates the way it was intended to. Thus, it is only when behaviour amounts to an interference with the due administration of justice that it becomes a contempt of court.

Contempt of court has to be balanced with the openness principle. Justice and the due administration of justice both require that the courts operate in public. As a result, fair and accurate reports of what happens in the courtroom are an integral part of the due administration of justice. Contempt of court deals with other kinds of behaviour, acts that interfere with, rather than complement, the due administration of justice.

Figure 2 sketches out a general structure for understanding contempt of court. It is an attempt to give some order and coherence to the law. From the outset, a distinction is made between two broad categories of criminal contempt. The distinction is expressed in Latin: there are contempts that are committed *ex facie*—outside the courtroom; and there are contempts that are committed *in facie*—inside the courtroom.

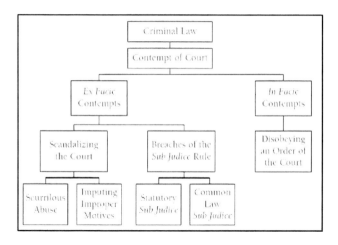

Figure 2: The Law of Contempt of Court

Ex Facie Contempts

We will focus on two forms of *ex facie* contempt: first, scandalizing the court, and second, breaches of the *sub judice* rule.

Scandalizing the Court

Scandalizing the court is a long-winded way of describing contempts committed through saying nasty things in public about judges. This is odd. If you say mean, hurtful, horrible things about me in public, I may well be able to sue you civilly for libel, but that is a matter between you and me. But judges, and only judges, have enjoyed this special protection that, under certain circumstances, it can be a crime to be publically critical of them. Scandalizing the court derives, as does our entire law of contempt, from English law. There have, over the last few decades, been prosecutions in England for scandalizing the court, but no one has been convicted since 1930.[280] In Canada, there were convictions until well into the 1980s.

Scurrilous Abuse

There are said to be two sub-branches of scandalizing the court. The first is described as directing scurrilous abuse at a judge. It is difficult to define what is meant by scurrilous abuse, but some examples can be found in Canadian cases: describing a judge and a jury at a murder trial as themselves murderers and adding that the judge was a torturer;[281] saying that a judicial decision was silly and could not have been made by a sane judge;[282] saying that a court was a mockery of justice;[283] writing of a particular trial that the "whole thing stinks from the word go";[284] accusing a court of

---

[280] See *R. v. Commissioner of Police of the Metropolis; ex parte Blackburn* (No. 2), [1968] 2 Q.B. 150 (C.A.).

[281] *R. v. Vancouver Province*, [1954] 3 D.L.R. 690 (B.C.S.C.).

[282] *Re Ouellet (Nos. 1 & 2)* (1976), 72 D.L.R. (3d) 95 (Que. C.A.).

[283] *R. v. Murphy* (1969), 1 N.B.R. (2d) 297 (C.A.).

[284] *Re Landers* (1980), 31 N.B.R. (2d) 113 at 115 (Q.B.).

intimidation and "iron curtain" tactics;[285] and, finally, saying of a particular magistrate, "If that bastard hears the case I will see to it that he is defrocked and debarred."[286]

So, what exactly is scurrilous abuse? It is using language about a judge or the judiciary which is vulgar, abusive and threatening. In the 1980s a court in New Brunswick said that any criticism that was "ungentlemanly" amounted to scandalizing the court.[287]

Imputing Improper Motives

The other branch of scandalizing the court, which is called imputing improper motives, is easier to define. Imputing improper motives means alleging that a judge takes bribes. It embraces any allegation that a judge is biased, that a judge is partial.[288]

The astonishing thing about the law of scandalizing the court as it was applied in Canada is that the truth was no defence. Even if you had a videotape of an intimidating-looking individual dressed in a pinstriped suit handing an attaché case full of money to a judge, you could not introduce that in your defence. The offence consisted solely in saying publicly that the judge took bribes. The truth or falsity of that statement was irrelevant.

The most famous Canadian case involving scandalizing the court was a 1954 prosecution from British Columbia, *R. v. Vancouver Province*.[289] Eric Nicol was a well-known journalist who wrote for the Vancouver *Province*. The story in question involved a

---

[285] R. v. *Western Printing & Publishing Ltd.* (1954), 111 C.C.C. 122 at 123 (Nfld. T.D.).

[286] *Anger* v. *Borowski*, [1971] 3 W.W.R. 434 at 437 (Man. Q.B.).

[287] *Re Landers*, above note 284 at 116.

[288] *Re Duncan*, [1958] S.C.R. 41.

[289] Above note 281.

particularly tragic murder prosecution. The accused was a young man called William Gash. He was nineteen years old, married, and had one child. He and his wife and child were living with his parents because he was out of work. In order to get money, Gash was persuaded to take part in the robbery of a shop. In the course of the robbery the proprietor of the shop was murdered. Gash was charged with murder and convicted. At that time, a trial judge had no discretion as to sentence when someone was convicted of murder. The judge was obliged to sentence the convicted person to death. Gash was sentenced to death by hanging.

Nicol's story was an allegorical fantasy. In it, Nicol had died and now stood before the eternal judgment seat, accounting for his life on earth. William Gash had been hanged, and Nicol was accused of murder. Because Nicol was a Canadian citizen and Gash had been put to death by the Canadian state, Nicol was responsible for Gash's death. Nicol attempted to defend himself in the following words:

> Although I did not myself spring the trap that caused my complainant to be strangled in cold blood, I admit that the man who put the rope around his neck was in my employ. Also serving me were the 12 people who planned the murder, and the judge who chose the time and place and caused the complainant to suffer the exquisite torture of anticipation.

Thus, he described the members of the jury and the judge as murderers, and added that the judge was a torturer.

It is important to grasp that these assertions about the judge and the members of the jury amounted to civil defamation. A number of members of the jury did sue Nicol and the *Province* civilly for libel and won.[290] But the issue before the court in this

---

[290]   *MacKay v. Southam Co.* (1955), 1 D.L.R. (2d) 1 (B.C.C.A.).

case was whether, in addition, Nicol's comments amounted to a crime. The British Columbia Supreme Court held that it was necessary, in order to ensure the due administration of justice, to punish people who made assertions like this about the courts and the process of the courts. The judge said:

> *No wrong is committed by anyone who criticises the Courts or a Judge in good faith, but it is of vital importance to the public that the authority and dignity of the Courts should be maintained.... To refer to the jurors in this case as criminals and to describe the Judge as causing exquisite torture is calculated to lower the dignity of the Court and destroy public confidence in the administration of justice.*

Nicol and the *Province* were convicted. Nicol was fined $250, and the paper $2500.

The most significant recent prosecution for scandalizing the court is the case of *R. v. Kopyto*.[291] Harry Kopyto used to be a lawyer in Toronto. In this instance he had been representing a person named Ross Dowson. In the 1960s and 1970s Dowson had been involved with the League for Socialist Action, a Trotskyite group in Toronto. Dowson claimed to have been the object of RCMP dirty tricks, and, in the 1970s, he began an attempt to gain legal redress against the police. He tried civil actions, private prosecutions, and a variety of legal remedies. They all failed. His last attempt ran out in December 1985 and there were no further legal avenues open to him. As Dowson's lawyer, Kopyto made a public statement about this last proceeding which was subsequently reported in the *Globe and Mail*. Kopyto said:

> *This decision is a mockery of justice. It stinks to high*

---

[291] (1987), 62 O.R. (2d) 449 (C.A.).

> *hell. It says it is okay to break the law and you are immune so long as someone above you said to do it. Mr. Dowson and I have lost faith in the judicial system to render justice. We're wondering what is the point of appealing and continuing this charade of the courts in this country which are warped in favour of protecting the police. The courts and the RCMP are sticking so close together you'd think they were put together with Krazy Glue.*[292]

Kopyto was convicted of scandalizing the court. The *Globe and Mail* might well also have been convicted for publishing Kopyto's remarks, but no proceeding was instituted against it. Kopyto appealed to the Ontario Court of Appeal. The court had no doubt that under the existing law of scandalizing the court, Kopyto had committed the offence.

But the crucial issue before it was whether the existing offence of scandalizing was a justifiable limit on the freedom of expression guaranteed in the *Charter*. The court held that comment by citizens about the courts must come within the protection of section 2(b) of the *Charter*.

> *As a result of their importance the courts are bound to be the subject of comment and criticism. Not all will be sweetly reasoned. An unsuccessful litigant may well make comments after the decision is rendered that are not felicitously worded. Some criticism may be well founded, some suggestions for change worth adopting. But the courts are not fragile flowers that will wither in the hot heat of controversy.*[293]

---

[292] *Ibid.*, at 455.
[293] *Ibid.*, at p. 463.

This approach is similar to the attitude the English courts have adopted towards scandalizing the court for the last forty years. In one English prosecution where the accused was acquitted, the judge said:

> [I]f a judge is going to be affected by what is written or said, he is not fit to be a judge.[294]

The majority in the Court of Appeal took the view that the existing offence of scandalizing the court limited freedom of expression and that, further, this was a limit which could not be justified in a free and democratic society. In its view, the existing offence of scandalizing was too broad and infringed freedom of expression far more than was necessary to protect the administration of justice.[295]

Five judges heard the *Kopyto* appeal. Three of them decided that the offence of scandalizing the court could not be justified in a free and democratic society, and two decided that it could. The decision, strictly speaking, is only a precedent in Ontario. But since this decision was released in 1988 and since there do not appear to have been any further prosecutions in Canada, I think that we can take it that scandalizing the court is effectively dead in Canada. Its demise was long overdue. Judges have always had exactly the same right as anybody else to sue civilly for defamation. The additional protection of the criminal law was

---

[294] See U.K., *Report of the Committee on Contempt of Court*, 1974, Cmnd. 5794 at 98.

[295] A very full discussion of the history and purpose of scandalizing the court can be found in a decision of the Constitutional Court of South Africa, *S. v. Mamabolo*, [2001] 1 L.R.C. 32. The Court observed that, "...robust and informed public debate about judicial affairs promotes peace and stability" (*Ibid.* at 52) and, "It is particularly important that, as the ultimate guardian of free speech, the judiciary show the greatest tolerance to criticism of its own functioning" (*Ibid.* at 69).

unnecessary.

Breaching the *Sub Judice* Rule

We will now look at another kind of *ex facie* contempt, one that involves breaches of the *sub judice* rule. The *sub judice* rule is that branch of the law of contempt of court which does not seek to *prohibit* the publication of information, but merely to *delay* its publication until such time as there is no longer a risk of prejudicing the outcome of proceedings before the courts. The implicit major premise underlying the *sub judice* rule is that there is certain information which, if published while judicial proceedings are pending or actually before a court, could have the effect of prejudicing the outcome of those proceedings. It is useful to subject some of the elements of, and some of the assumptions underlying, the *sub judice* rule to analysis.

First, while a lawyer would describe the *sub judice* rule as delaying, rather than prohibiting the publication of information, that distinction is substantially less meaningful to a journalist. The newsworthiness of information is very often a function of its timeliness, and to delay the publication of information can amount in practice to prohibiting its publication.

The purpose of the *sub judice* rule, as with the law of contempt of court generally, is to protect the integrity of the judicial process. Freedom of expression is, as a general principle, to be respected, but the *sub judice* rule limits that freedom whenever a real risk of prejudice to the administration of justice arises.

But what effect does the *sub judice* rule actually have on the media? The following is a completely fictional story written a number of years ago by an English journalist. The point of the story is to show how the *sub judice* rule distorts reporting. The *sub judice* rule is much stricter in England, but the story gives a clear idea of the flavour of these things and how the *sub judice* rule often operates to distort news stories.

164

Stout balding Mr John Jones, cashier to a firm of textile converters, was missing yesterday from his home in Cemetery Avenue, Openshaw.

Round the corner in Funeral Street, Mr Henry Brown said he had not seen his blonde attractive wife Mamie since the week-end.

A director of the firm which employs Mr Jones said yesterday that the firm's books would have been due for audit next week. Mr Jones was also treasurer of the local Working Men's Holiday Fund.

Neighbours described Mrs Brown as a gay girl. It is understood that she and Mr Jones were close friends.

At a flat in Southpool, stout balding Mr Arthur Smith said he had never heard of Mr Jones of Openshaw. Blonde attractive Mrs Dolly Smith said she had never been known as Mamie Brown. Early yesterday police were seeking to interview a stout, bald-headed man whom they believed could be of assistance to them in their inquiries into a case of fraudulent conversion.

A man accompanied police to Southpool police station. Blows were exchanged in Southpool's High Street after a man ran at high speed along the street. Police ran at high speed along the street after a man. Later a man was detained. A man will appear in court today.[296]

That example is much exaggerated, but it is designed to highlight some of the effects of the *sub judice* rule. In England the media still do not actually report that somebody has been arrested. Someone is simply said to be "assisting police with their inquiries."

---

[296] J. Townsend, quoted in Australia, Law Reform Commission, *Reform of Contempt Law* (Issues Paper No. 4), Sydney, The Commission, (1984) at 14–15.

Everyone, of course, knows exactly what that means, but it is done to avoid publishing anything that might, even conceivably, create a risk of prejudicing subsequent proceedings.

The serious difficulty with the *sub judice* rule, as is the case with much of the law of contempt of court, is that there is little empirical foundation for it. There is no factual basis for saying that certain information, or indeed any information, will actually prejudice the outcome of proceedings. It is difficult to imagine how anyone would test such a thing. In this context it is useful to quote two statements made by Canadian judges about two highly publicized judicial proceedings.

The first was the *Keegstra* trial. The James Keegstra affair received an enormous amount of publicity, especially in Alberta. One of the things Keegstra's lawyer argued before the courts was that the whole proceeding should be adjourned *sine die*—that is, indefinitely. He argued there had been so much publicity that it would be impossible for James Keegstra to receive a fair trial anywhere in Alberta. The trial judge said:

> *You know, I do not buy that argument. I do not buy the argument that people in high places, or the newspapers or television necessarily have the influence you readily give them. As a matter of fact, you know, there is another school of thought that they used to teach us when I was younger, that you only believed about ten percent of what you read.*[297]

Implicit in the *sub judice* rule are the assumptions, first, that people believe everything they see on television or hear on the radio or read in the newspapers and, second, that they are going to be influenced by what they see or hear or read. I suspect that jurors

---

[297] Transcript of unreported pre-trial hearing (*R. v. Keegstra*) (10 October 1994), (Alta. Q.B.).

are far more capable of putting extraneous influences out of their minds than the Canadian legal system has often given them credit for.

The second example has to do with a murder prosecution in Winnipeg in the 1980s. Somebody came into a small shop on the outskirts of the city and murdered the person working there. It was a particularly nasty murder and there was a tremendous public clamour to arrest someone and put that individual on trial. A young man called Sophonow was arrested and charged with the murder.

He went on trial, and everything that happened at this trial was reported in great detail. At the end of the trial Sophonow was convicted of murder. He appealed to the Manitoba Court of Appeal. The Manitoba Court of Appeal ordered a new trial. The second trial was reported as extensively as the first and, at the end of this trial, Sophonow was again convicted of murder. He appealed again to the Manitoba Court of Appeal and that court ordered a new trial, a third trial. By this time there could not have been a man, woman, or child in the province of Manitoba who was not intimately familiar with every detail of the whole business. Nonetheless, a jury was assembled for the third trial. This time, Sophonow was acquitted. The Crown appealed to the Manitoba Court of Appeal, but that court decided enough was enough. Before the second trial was to take place, an application had been made for an indefinite adjournment on the ground that there had been so much publicity, so much reporting about the first trial, that it would be impossible to assemble an unbiased jury for the second trial. The Chief Justice of Manitoba said in response to this argument:

> *The mere fact that a previous trial...has been reported at length in the media should not ordinarily provide a case of probable bias or prejudice on the part of the jurors at the second trial for the same offence. It is most*

167

unfair to prospective jurors and contrary to the jury
system to assume that since these prospective jurors may
have some prior knowledge of the case by virtue of the
media they are probably biased or prejudiced.[298]

The interesting thing about that statement, if it is accurate, is that it undercuts much of the basis for the *sub judice* rule. The rule, as we have noted, is based on the assumption that certain kinds of information can have the effect of prejudicing the minds of potential jurors and, more generally, prejudicing the entire community. The Chief Justice seemed to dismiss those possibilities.

We will now look in detail at the *sub judice* rule under two headings. We will look, first, at statutory examples and then at the common law of *sub judice*. While, as has been noted, the major parts of the law of contempt of court remain uncodified, some elements have been put in statutory form.

Statutory Sub Judice

This section deals, more precisely, with statutory limits on what may be reported concerning judicial proceedings.

Sexual Offences

A discussion of the way sexual assault trials have been turned into non-public proceedings was found earlier in this text in *The Openness Principle* section.

---

[298] The Chief Justice was in dissent. See *R. v. Sophonow* (1984), 11 D.L.R. (4th) 24 at 56 (Man. C.A.). As an example of a case where it was held that publicity had destroyed the possibility of a fair trial, see *R. v. Vermette*, [1988] 1 S.C.R. 985.

We begin the discussion of statutory *sub judice* by looking at what the *Criminal Code* says about sexual offences. In 1983 and in 1992, major reforms were made to the *Criminal Code* provisions dealing with sexual offences.[299] The 1983 reforms did a number of things. First, they removed the offence of rape from the *Criminal Code* and substituted for it two new offences—sexual assault and aggravated sexual assault. Strangely, the *Code* did not define sexual assault.

One objective of the reforms was to abandon certain limitations found in the offence of rape—in particular, that rape could only be committed by a man against a woman, that a husband could not rape his wife, and that nothing short of non-consensual intercourse could constitute the offence. The 1983 amendments made it clear that sexual assault could be committed by a person of either sex against a person of either sex, that a husband could, as a matter of law, sexually assault his wife, and that various forms of conduct short of intercourse might constitute the offence. The details were left to be worked out by the courts, which have broadly defined sexual assault as any assault of a sexual nature.

Second, procedural changes were also made to provisions dealing with sexual offences in 1983. These changes were designed to address what was seen to be a major problem in the application of the law dealing with sexual offences: underreporting by complainants. Sexual offences were thought to be occurring in greater numbers than were actually being reported to the police. The 1983 reforms aimed to remove two legal obstacles to the reporting of sexual assaults by complainants. The first obstacle was that since the trial of a sexual offence

---

[299] For general background, see Robert Martin, *Bill C—49: A Victory for Interest Group Politics* (1993) 42 U.N.B.L.J. 357, and J.V. Roberts & R.M. Mohr, eds. *Confronting Sexual Assualt: A Decade of Legal and Social Change*, Toronto, University of Toronto Press, 1994.

took place in open court, the name of the complainant could be published in the mass media. One of the factors that was identified as inhibiting the reporting of sexual assaults was the knowledge on the part of the complainant that her name could be made public. It was believed that limiting the ability of the media to report the complainant's identity would remove one legal obstacle to the reporting of the offence.

The second obstacle had to do with the nature of rape trials. It was perceived that they often turned into a trial of the woman who was the complainant rather than of the man who was the accused. How did this happen? In most sexual offence proceedings the key witness for the Crown is the complainant herself. She, clearly, must have the most substantial, most direct, evidence concerning the commission of the offence.

Prior to 1983, and consistent with the general procedure in all criminal prosecutions, counsel for the accused was free fully to cross-examine all the Crown's witnesses. One of the matters with respect to which the accused's counsel could cross-examine the complainant in a rape prosecution was her previous sexual history. At the time, the law was based on the view that previous sexual history went to the credibility of the complainant as a witness. The implicit assumption was that the more sexual experience a woman had had throughout her life, the less likely it was that she would tell the truth. That assumption was both sexist and illogical. More to the point, a woman who reported a rape could be subjected to a humiliating and, of course, public cross-examination. There was a general sense that many complainants in sexual assaults were not reporting them in order to avoid this experience. As a result, the second procedural element in the 1983 reforms substantially limited the ability of the accused to cross-examine the complainant about her previous sexual history.

Turning to the specifics of the law, we begin with the question of identifying the complainant. The relevant provision is section 486(3) of the *Criminal Code*. It provides that where the accused is charged with a sexual offence—sexual assault, aggravated sexual assault, and some other offences—the presiding judge has the authority to make an order banning publication of the identity of the complainant. The subsection says that if either the Crown or, more important, the complainant applies for the banning order, the trial judge *must* make it. The judge has no discretion.

Alternatively, if neither the Crown nor the complainant applies for an order, the trial judge *may* make such an order on her own initiative. Section 486(3) achieves one of the important aims of the 1983 reforms, which was to give to the complainant herself the power to determine whether her identity would be made public.

If an order is made, it does not simply prohibit the publication of the name of the complainant. It is an order, to use the words of the *Criminal Code*, banning the publication *of any information that could disclose the identity of the complainant*. This can mean serious constraints on reporting about sexual offences. Take one example that has actually arisen on a number of occasions. As has been noted, by definition, a husband could not rape his wife, but it is now legally possible for a husband to sexually assault his wife. Thus, in a case where a husband was charged with sexually assaulting his wife, a publication ban would make it impossible to name the accused. In the circumstances of such a case, the accused's name would clearly be information that *could* disclose the identity of the complainant. The same would also likely be true if the accused happened to be a relative of the complainant, especially if they had the same surname.

What makes this provision problematic is that it does not simply prohibit the publication of any information that *does* disclose the identity of the complainant, but any information that *could* disclose her identity. This means that, in difficult cases, reporters and editors would have to consider such factors as the precise relation between the complainant and the accused, any institutional connection between them, the size of the community in question, and the particular details of the offence.

The *Criminal Code* does not contain a specific offence of breaching an order made under section 486(3). Any breach would, then, be dealt with as a contempt of court. There have, in fact, been few prosecutions for breaches of this provision. One reason is that the very existence of the section has occasioned considerable caution on the part of reporters and editors. Another is that there has been a general reluctance, except in the most blatant of cases, to prosecute. If it were to be clear from a story that the reporter was simply trying to provide as much information about the accused as possible without actually identifying her, then I think it is unlikely there would be a prosecution.

R.(L.) v. Nyp[300] is one of the few reported examples of a breach of such an order. An undercover police officer had been sexually assaulted. A ban under section 486(3) was made on 12 May 1992 at the trial of her assailant. Despite this ban, the Kitchener-Waterloo *Record* three days later published an article that described the assault and identified the police officer by name. The reporter who wrote the article had been present in court when the publication ban was made by the trial judge. The reporter, Gary Nyp, was brought before the same judge in a contempt proceeding. He was acquitted on the ground that the breach of the publication ban was "inadvertent." In one instance, a reporter was convicted of breaching such an order even though he had not been aware of its existence. The conviction was overturned on appeal.[301] Subsequently, however, the police officer sued Nyp and the owner of the *Record*, Southam Inc., civilly for negligence. The court held that the conduct of the reporter in publishing the plaintiff's name had not met the

---

[300] (1995), 25 C.C.L.T. (2d) 309 (Ont. Gen. Div.).
[301] *R. v. Helsdon* (2007) 84 O.R. (3d) 544.

standard expected of a "reasonably prudent reporter." The court awarded general damages of $12,000 each against Nyp and Southam. A further $5000 in punitive damages was awarded against Southam for "contemptuous disregard of the plaintiff's rights."

The banning order does not operate retrospectively. It acquires legal force only from the moment that it is made. If no publication ban is made, there is no legal obstacle to the identification of the complainant.

In 1988 the Thomson chain challenged what is now section 486(3) of the *Criminal Code* as an infringement of the *Charter* guarantee of freedom of expression.[302] Clearly, it is a limit. If the state says you cannot report certain information about a judicial proceeding, the state has beyond doubt limited freedom of expression. But is this a limit that can be justified in a free and democratic society? What was the state's objective? The Supreme Court said it was to encourage the reporting of sexual assaults. Was that objective pressing and substantial? Did it seek to uphold social values of superordinate importance? Beyond any doubt, said the Court. Was there a rational connection between limiting publication of the identity of the complainant and encouraging the reporting of sexual assaults? Yes, said the Court. The real problem before the Court was the issue of minimal impairment.[303] The argument was made that the minimal impairment standard required that some degree of discretion be retained in the trial judge to decide in the context of each case whether or not to impose a ban. The Court disagreed and said that under the special circumstances of sexual assault the total absence of discretion in the trial judge was justifiable. Section 486(3) was upheld in its entirety.

While we are dealing with section 486, mention should also

---

[302] *Canadian Newspapers Co. v. Canada (A.G.)*, [1988] 2 S.C.R. 122.
[303] See Chapter 1, section B(3), for a discussion of minimal impairment.

be made of subsection (1). It gives the judge presiding at a sexual offence trial a broad authority to:

> ...*exclude all or any members of the public from the courtroom for all or part of the proceedings...*

when she is of the opinion that it is in the interest of "public morals, the maintenance of order or the proper administration of justice" to do so. This provision is clearly a substantial limitation on the openness principle and on freedom of expression.

Nonetheless, the Supreme Court of Canada held in 1996 that it was constitutional.[304] The Court delayed the release of its reasons, but since it upheld a decision by the New Brunswick Court of Appeal, some instruction can be gained from the judgments of that court. The sexual assaults in this case involved young female complainants. The court concluded that the need to protect these complainants was sufficient to justify the limit on freedom of expression. This reasoning appears to miss the point. The issue is not whether the particular way the trial judge exercised the discretion created by section 486(1) can be justified, but whether section 486(1) itself can be justified.

Turning to the second procedural element of the 1983 reforms, not only were limits placed on the ability of the accused to cross-examine the complainant about her previous sexual history but the freedom of the mass media to report on such matters was also limited. Before addressing these matters in detail, it must be noted that further changes were made in the *Criminal Code* provisions dealing with sexual assault in 1992.

There was concern that the 1983 reforms were a substantial interference with the right of accused persons to defend

---

[304] *Canadian Broadcasting Corp. v. New Brunswick (A.G.)*, [1996], 3 S.C.R. 480. The decision of the New Brunswick Court of Appeal is reported at (1994), 148 N.B.R. (2d) 161 (C.A.).

themselves fully. This issue went before the Supreme Court in 1991 in a case called *R. v. Seaboyer*.[305] Seaboyer argued that his Charter right to a fair trial had been infringed because he was limited in his ability to cross-examine the complainant. The Court accepted his argument and struck down the then existing provisions in the *Criminal Code*. So, from 1991 to 1992, there was a hiatus during which there were no statutory rules on the question. Then, in 1992, further amendments to the *Criminal Code* created a new set of limitations—sections 276.1 to 276.4—on the ability of accused persons to cross-examine complainants about their previous sexual history.[306] What does the *Criminal Code* now say about reporting on such matters?

The *Code* sets out a procedure that the accused must follow before he will be permitted to exercise his still limited right to cross-examine the complainant about her previous sexual history. He must make an application in writing to the trial judge to be allowed to do so. The application must set out the purpose of the proposed cross-examination and its relevance to whatever defence is being raised. The judge will then hold a hearing in her chambers. The judge, the prosecutor, and counsel for the accused will be present at this hearing. The judge will decide whether to permit the limited cross-examination. If the judge decides to allow it, the cross-examination takes place in open court and can be fully reported—subject, of course, to any ban that might have been made on disclosing the identity of the complainant.

The other possibility is that the judge will refuse to allow the cross-examination. If this happens, the *Criminal Code* prohibits any reporting whatsoever about the whole business. It may not be reported that the accused applied to be allowed to cross-examine the complainant. No one may report any of the evidence or

---

[305] [1991] 2 S.C.R. 577.

[306] *An Act to amend the Criminal Code (sexual assault)*, S.C. 1992, c. 38, amending R.S.C. 1985, c. 46.

arguments that the accused presented, nor that there was a hearing in the judge's chambers, nor anything that might have happened at that hearing. If the judge says there is to be no cross-examination of the complainant about her previous sexual history, then not a word may be published about the whole matter.

As a final point, a provision of this nature is often referred to journalistically as a "rape shield law." This phrase suggests that it is a law that exists to shield rapists. The phrase is misleading and should be abandoned.

Young Persons

The governing legislation is a statute from 2003 called the *Youth Criminal Justice Act*.[307] This act repealed and replaced the *Young Offenders Act*. Both these statutes limited the openness principle with respect to the trials of young persons who had, allegedly, committed crimes.

We will begin by discussing the two statutes—the *Juvenile Delinquents Act* and the *Young Offenders Act*—which preceded the *Youth Criminal Justice Act*. The purpose underlying the discussion of these statutes is to elaborate and elucidate the ways in which each placed limitations on the principle of the openness of the courts.

The Canadian legal system, like all legal systems, recognizes that, below a certain age, persons should not be held criminally responsible for their acts. There is room for debate in any society as to what that precise age should be. In our system it is twelve. We make a distinction between persons over twelve and persons under twelve. Persons over twelve are criminally responsible, persons under twelve are not.

Having made that distinction, we go on to make a further distinction. We have created two subclasses of persons who are

---

[307] For detailed analysis, see Nicholas Bala and Sanjeev Anand, *Youth Criminal Justice Law,* 2nd ed., Toronto, Irwin Law, 2009.

criminally responsible for their acts. One is persons between twelve and eighteen, and the other is persons over eighteen. Persons over eighteen are regarded as fully responsible for their acts and are dealt with through the normal court system. Persons between twelve and eighteen stand in a grey area. They are criminally responsible for their acts, but not as responsible as persons over eighteen. Thus, as a general principle, persons between twelve and eighteen are dealt with in different courts and according to different rules from persons over eighteen. These matters were the subject of a much-criticized federal statute called the *Young Offenders Act*.[308]

The important parts of the *Young Offenders Act* for reporting purposes were sections 38 and 39. The *Act* stated that these sections dealt with the protection of the privacy of young persons. Section 38 set out a prohibition on the publication of certain information. Before looking at this prohibition in detail, it is important to understand the distinction between section 38 of the *Young Offenders Act* and section 486(3) of the *Criminal Code*, the section dealing with the publication of the identity of complainants in sexual assault trials. Section 486(3) gives a judge the authority to make an order banning the publication of certain information. That was not the case with section 38 of the *Young Offenders Act*. Under the *Young Offenders Act*, a judge did not have to do anything. The publication ban was imposed directly by the statute itself.

Section 38 prohibited the publication of any report in which there was any information serving to identify a young offender— the person charged with an offence. But the section went further and prohibited the publication of any information that would serve to identify a young *complainant* or a young *witness*. Much like section 486(3) of the *Criminal Code*, the prohibition was not just on naming, but on identifying. The section itself provided that it was

---

[308] *YOA*, above note 18.

an offence to breach the prohibition it imposed.

The *Juvenile Delinquents Act*, the predecessor to the *Young Offenders Act*, contained a similar prohibition against identifying the juvenile delinquent, but the *Young Offenders Act* added two further classes of persons who might not be identified. If it is considered legitimate to take special steps to protect the identity or the privacy of young offenders, what is the justification for creating similar protection with respect to young complainants or even young witnesses? If a young person—a person under eighteen—is the complainant in an offence committed by an adult, there is no special protection for that individual's identity, nor is there any special protection for the identity of any young person who appears as a witness before an adult court.

Section 39 was a further and substantial compromise of the principle of the openness of the courts. Section 39 gave a judge hearing a young offender proceeding a broad discretion either to close the courtroom or to exclude particular persons from the courtroom. If the trial judge thought that evidence or information presented would be seriously injurious or seriously prejudicial to the young offender, a young witness, or a young complainant, or if it would be in the interest of public morals or the maintenance of order, she might exclude the public generally, or any section of the public, from the proceedings. This seems odd, because in any criminal proceeding, most of the evidence presented by the Crown is going to be prejudicial to the accused.

Sections 38 and 39 were the objects of a constitutional challenge by Southam Inc., once again through the Ottawa *Citizen*.[309] In 1984 the Ontario High Court upheld the constitutionality of the two sections. It must be obvious that both sections limit freedom of expression. The question, therefore, is whether these limits can be justified in a free and democratic society. What was the state's objective in creating them?

---

[309] *Southam Inc. v. R.* (1984), 48 O.R. (2d) 678 (H.C.J.).

According to the Court, it was to promote the rehabilitation of young offenders. As the means to achieve that objective, the state chose to protect young offenders from the harmful effects of publicity.

This concern raises a problem, however, one that the court did not address. Even if the state's objective and the means it has chosen can be justified—promoting the rehabilitation of young *offenders* by protecting them from the harmful effects of publicity—what has either of these got to do with protecting young *witnesses* and young *complainants*? There is no need to rehabilitate, at least in the sense in which the court used the word, a witness or a complainant.

These matters were addressed in 2001 by the Alberta Court of Queen's Bench.[310] This case involved an analysis of the constitutionality of section 38(1), which prohibited publishing the identity of a young person who had been the object of an offence allegedly committed by a young person. The court was not impressed with section 38(1). It believed there was no "empirical research" to the effect that the section addressed a "real problem." It said that:

> *Using the age of the perpetrator as the sole criterion in creating a prohibition on identifying the victim is clearly inconsistent, confusing and is not rationally connected to achieving the apparent objectives of the legislation.*[311]

The court concluded that the limit on freedom of expression could not be justified and ordered that the words "a child or a young person who is a victim of the offence" in section 38(1) be struck down. One can only assume that an analysis of the

---

[310] *R v. Thompson* (2001), 48 C.R. (5th) 267.
[311] *Ibid.* at 280.

prohibition against identifying a young witness would have led to a similar conclusion.

There must also be some question about the matter of promoting the rehabilitation of young offenders by protecting them from the harmful effects of publicity. Does society not have an equal interest in promoting the rehabilitation of adult offenders? If the rehabilitation of young offenders is prejudiced by the harmful effects of publicity, why should we not create a similar protection for adult offenders? Are not adult offenders going to be affected by publicity?

What is lacking in the *Southam* judgment is any empirical foundation. The reasons given by the court must stand or fall on a comparison of the recidivism rates for young offenders with the recidivism rates for adult offenders. If it turned out that the recidivism rate for young offenders was substantially lower than that for adult offenders, it could be concluded that the *Young Offenders Act* was indeed working and, presumably, the limits it imposed on expression could be justified in a free and democratic society. But if there was no difference in the two rates, there would be no basis for upholding the *Act*. Unfortunately, the comprehensive statistics that would make such a comparison possible do not exist.

Section 38 appeared to say that the mass media could not ever publish any information serving to identify the young offender. In its own terms, section 38(1) applied forever. However, once a young offender had passed the age of eighteen and had, in addition, been charged with a subsequent offence that was being heard before an adult court, there would have been little danger of being prosecuted for breaching section 38 if one had published a report about the earlier proceeding under the *Young Offenders Act*.

To avoid any problems, it would have been preferable to report that "a person is being prosecuted under the *Young Offenders Act*," rather than "a young offender is being prosecuted." The individual being prosecuted is not, strictly speaking, a young offender until conviction.

Amendments were made to the *Act* in 1986 after tremendous public, and especially police, outcry.[312] Subsections 38(1.1) to (1.4) allowed a police officer to apply to a youth court for an order allowing publication of the identity of the young offender, if there was reason to believe that the young person would be dangerous to others and that the publication of the report would assist in apprehending her. This publication was to be used solely for police purposes. The order permitting publication was effective only for two days.

In an analogous vein, a child protection hearing held under Ontario's *Child Protection Act*[313] is not a public proceeding. The usual procedure contemplated under the *Act* is that, "a hearing shall be held in the absence of the public."[314] It is clear that a public hearing is an exception to this approach. Even if a hearing is held in public, the *Act* contains restrictions on what may be reported. Section 45(8) prohibits the publication of information that:

> ...has the effect of identifying...a child who is a witness at or a participant in a hearing or the subject of a proceeding, or the child's parent or foster parent or a member of the child's family.

Which social values of superordinate importance are being upheld by this cloak of secrecy?

In 2003 the *Young Offenders Act* was replaced by a fresh statute

---

[312] *An Act to Amend the Young Offenders Act, the Criminal Code, the Penitentiary Act and the Prisons and Reformatories Act*, R.S.C. 1985 (2d Supp.), c. 24, amending R.S.C. 1985, c. Y-1.

[313] R.S.O. 1990, c. C.11.

[314] *Ibid.*, s. 45(4).

called the *Youth Criminal Justice Act*.[315] The new *Act* placed as many limitations on the openness principle and on freedom of expression as did its predecessor. Section 110 of the new Act largely reproduces section 38 of the old one, while section 132 of the new *Act* reaffirms the preference for secret trials found in section 39 of the old one. Section 111 of the new *Act* repeats the prohibitions, found in section 38 of the old *Act*, on identifying young complainants and young witnesses.

Given that the Alberta Court of Queen's Bench invalidated section 38(1) of the *Young Offenders Act*, which had prohibited identifying a young complainant,[316] it is difficult to grasp why Parliament would re-enact the identical words in section 111(1) of the new *Act*. There is one slight improvement over the *Young Offenders Act*. As noted above, the prohibitions in section 38 of the *Young Offenders Act* appeared to apply forever. Under section 110(3) of the new *Act*, the offender may decide to make her identity public after she has reached the age of eighteen. Likewise, section 111 of the new *Act* states that a young witness or young victim (the *Act* actually uses the question-begging word "victim") may decide, after reaching eighteen, to make his or her identity public. Would a reporter covering a particular proceeding under the *Youth Criminal Justice Act* encounter any difficulties, if she discovered the birth dates of a young offender, young victim, or young witness and contacted each after she had turned eighteen in order to ask each to be permitted to reveal her identity? Since this action in no way represents an attempt to circumvent the law, I would not imagine that the reporter could face any legal consequences.

---

[315] S.C. 2002, c. 1, in force 1 April 2003.
[316] *R. v. Thompson* (2001), 48 C.R (5th) 267.

Preliminary Inquiries

The *Criminal Code* contains two broad categories of offences. This feature is derived from the old distinction in English law between felonies and misdemeanours. Felonies were the more serious offences; misdemeanours were the less serious. The distinction was important, because, when English criminal law was at its most barbaric, there was only one punishment possible on conviction of a felony and that was death. A felony trial was a serious business and, thus, a special procedure was adopted to precede the trial itself. The point was to determine whether there was sufficient evidence against the person accused of a felony to justify putting her on trial.

Even though we no longer have the death penalty, we maintain this distinction between less serious offences and more serious offences, except that we now call the more serious ones "indictable" offences and the less serious ones "summary conviction" offences. In fact, we have three categories of offences. We also have something called "hybrid" offences. These can be either indictable or summary conviction offences.

If someone is charged with a summary conviction offence, that person goes straight to trial. If, however, someone is charged with an indictable offence, there must be a preliminary inquiry before a trial can be held. The purpose of the preliminary inquiry is, once again, not to determine whether this individual is guilty or innocent. It is to determine whether there is sufficient evidence against her to justify holding a trial. A preliminary inquiry is normally conducted by a justice of the peace. For present purposes, the point about a preliminary inquiry is that some of the evidence introduced may never be introduced at the trial or may be held to be inadmissible. Publication of this evidence might prejudice the outcome of the subsequent trial.

The preliminary inquiry takes place in open court. Reporters are entitled to be there and are entitled to take notes. There are, however, certain limitations on what may be published about a preliminary inquiry. Section 539 of the *Criminal Code* provides that prior to the preliminary inquiry actually beginning, the prosecution, or the accused, or any one of the accused if there is more than one, may ask for a publication ban. If the prosecution asks for a ban, the justice *may* make it. If an accused person asks for the ban, the justice *must* make it.

What is the result of an order banning publication? It is that the evidence given at the preliminary inquiry may not be published until such time as it is no longer possible to prejudice the outcome of the subsequent trial. When is that? At the end of a preliminary inquiry there are two possibilities. The justice holding the inquiry may discharge the accused on the ground that there is not sufficient evidence to justify holding a trial. If there is not going to be a trial, clearly its outcome cannot be prejudiced. Thus, if the accused is discharged at the end of the preliminary inquiry, the publication ban is spent. The other alternative is that the justice may commit the accused for trial. If the accused is committed for trial, it is still possible to prejudice the outcome of the trial. When will it no longer be possible to prejudice the outcome of the trial? Obviously, when the trial is completed. At that point, once again, the ban is spent. Whether there is subsequently an appeal is irrelevant.

A number of points about a publication ban made at a preliminary inquiry should be noted. First, it is a ban on publication. It is not a ban on reporters being present in the courtroom, nor is it a ban on their taking notes. There is a significant practical point in this distinction. A number of reporters who have written books about well-publicized criminal trials have used the preliminary inquiry as the basis for their books. They have written the book from their notes taken at the preliminary inquiry and had the manuscript ready in proof form. When the actual trial began, they checked the proofs each day against what happened at the trial. Thus, the instant the trial was completed, the book could be printed. Taking notes at the preliminary inquiry, even though these notes may not be published at that time, can also be useful for other reasons, such as checking the evidence that is subsequently given at the trial. To repeat, once the trial is completed, information from the preliminary inquiry may be published.

The application for the publication ban must be made before the taking of evidence at the preliminary inquiry starts. Once the preliminary inquiry is under way the opportunity to apply for the ban has passed. If the accused is not represented by counsel, the presiding justice must inform the accused of her right to apply for a publication ban.

Nonetheless, if the commencement of the inquiry passes without an application for a ban being made, it is too late. Here again one can make a comparison with section 486(3) of the *Criminal Code*, the section that deals with an order banning publication of the identity of the complainant in a sexual offence proceeding. An application under section 486(3) can be made at any time during the proceeding.

Section 539(3) makes it an offence to fail to comply with a publication ban. A reporter covering a preliminary inquiry should assume, until the contrary is established beyond any doubt, that the publication ban has been made.

There is no rule in the *Criminal Code* about the form of a publication ban and it is sufficient for the justice to say:

> *I hereby order that none of the evidence to be given at*
> *this preliminary inquiry shall be published.*

The onus is on a reporter to find out whether a ban has been made.

The constitutionality of publication bans at preliminary inquiries has been challenged. Such a ban is obviously a limit on freedom of expression, so is it a limit that can be justified in a free and democratic society? What is the state's objective? It is, obviously, to ensure that the accused receives a fair trial, something that is, itself, guaranteed in section 11 of the *Charter*. The only decision on this ban is from the New Brunswick Court of Queen's Bench in 1983.[317] The court upheld the constitutionality of section 539 of the *Criminal Code*.

The basis for its decision was the traditional Canadian approach that, whenever there is an apparent conflict between an accused person's right to a fair trial and freedom of expression, freedom of expression must give way and the accuseds' right to a fair trial must take precedence. However, in 1994, in *Dagenais v. Canadian Broadcasting Corp.*,[318] the Supreme Court gave notice that it would not continue to follow this approach. The Court said that judges should attempt to "balance" the right to a fair trial and free expression, with neither taking precedence over the other. One of the results of the *Dagenais* decision is that the constitutionality of section 539 of the *Criminal Code* must now be open to doubt.

Whether a publication ban is made or not, section 552 of the *Criminal Code* creates an absolute prohibition against publishing anything about the fact that the prosecution might have sought to have a confession entered into evidence during a preliminary inquiry. The obvious point of this rule is that information that the accused might have confessed is, in and of itself, highly prejudicial. Further, even if the preliminary inquiry accepts the admissibility of a confession, it is perfectly conceivable that the trial court will not. This is an absolute statutory ban and it operates regardless of whether a publication ban has been made under section 539. Once again, this prohibition lapses at the point at which it is no longer possible to prejudice the outcome of the trial—either when the accused is discharged or, if the accused is

---

[317] *R. v. Banville* (1983), 45 N.B.R. (2d) 134 (Q.B.)
[318] Above note 149.

committed for trial, when the trial is completed.

Bail Hearings

Under the *Criminal Code* and under section 11 of the *Charter*, a person who is simply charged with an offence is an innocent person, a constitutionally innocent person. Such a person has a basic right to liberty—to move about freely, undisturbed and unimpeded by the state. There is no constitutional or theoretical problem with locking up someone who has actually been convicted of a crime by a court. But it is difficult in principle to justify locking up a constitutionally innocent person. Our criminal law recognizes that a person accused of a crime should *prima facie* be at liberty until such time as she may be convicted.

However, the *Criminal Code* also recognizes that there can be exceptional circumstances where an accused person should, nonetheless, be held in custody until her trial. In order to allow these issues to be addressed, section 515 of the *Criminal Code* makes provision for bail hearings to be held before a justice of the peace. At this hearing the Crown may argue in favour of having the accused remanded in custody. Section 515 sets out a *primary* and a *secondary* ground on which the justice's decision to do so may be based. The primary ground is that the detention of this accused is necessary in order to ensure her attendance at trial. Clearly the state has an overriding interest in ensuring that someone accused of a crime does show up for her trial. The secondary ground set out is that the detention of this accused is necessary for the protection or safety of the public. The section also allowed for detention that was necessary in "the public interest," but in 1992 the Supreme Court found that this phrase was a vague and, therefore, unjustifiable limit on the freedom of the individual.[319]

---

[319] *R. v. Morales*, [1992] 3 S.C.R. 711.

The point is that a bail hearing is held for the sole reason of determining whether an exception should be made in a particular case and a still-innocent person be locked up. The eventual question of guilt or innocence is not in issue at a bail hearing. It must be obvious that the Crown, in order to persuade the justice conducting the bail hearing to remand someone in custody, may introduce all sorts of highly prejudicial information. The accused's previous record and the accused's propensity to violence are among the sorts of things that might be introduced. They are probably not relevant to the question of guilt or innocence and would likely be inadmissible at the trial.

Section 517 allows a publication ban to be made at a bail hearing. The specific rules are very similar to those concerning publication bans at a preliminary inquiry. If the Crown asks for a publication ban, the justice *may* make it; if the accused asks for a publication ban, the justice *must* make it. The application for a ban, in contrast to the rule about preliminary inquiries, can be made at any time during the bail hearing.

If the ban is made, there is a complete prohibition on publishing any information or any evidence presented at the bail hearing. Not even the reasons given by the justice for her decision may be published. Nonetheless, the bail hearing takes place in open court, so reporters can be there and take notes, but nothing can be published while the ban remains in effect. As with the ban issued at a preliminary inquiry, the bail hearing ban stays in operation until it is no longer possible to prejudice the outcome of a subsequent trial. If the accused is charged with an indictable offence and is discharged at the preliminary inquiry, there will be no trial to be prejudiced and the ban is spent. Alternatively, if the accused goes to trial, whether it is a summary conviction offence or an indictable offence, the publication ban is spent at the end of the trial—at the point at which it is no longer possible to prejudice the outcome of the trial.

Section 517(2) makes it an offence not to comply with an order made under section 517(1). The constitutionality of this section has been challenged on the basis of the *Charter*. Once again, a clear limit on freedom of expression has been created.

In 1984 a Canadian woman called Kathy Smith was charged in California with the murder of John Belushi. The United States applied for her extradition to be tried on this charge. She was remanded in custody pending the outcome of the extradition proceedings and a banning order was made in connection with the bail hearing. The Ontario Court of Appeal held that the state's purpose in limiting expression was to guarantee the accuseds' right to a fair trial. It further held that whenever there is a conflict between the accuseds' right to a fair trial and freedom of expression, freedom of expression must give way.[320] This decision was also made before the Supreme Court's decision in *Dagenais*, so there may be doubt today as to the constitutionality of section 517.

The question of the constitutionality of s.517 was addressed in 2007 by both the Ontario Superior Court and the Alberta Court of Queen's Bench. The Ontario decision was *Toronto Star Newspapers Ltd.* v. *The Queen.*[321] The Court decided that it was bound by the decision of the Ontario Court of Appeal in the *Global Communications* decision.[322] that s. 517 infringed the guarantee of freedom of expression in s. 2(b) of the *Charter*, but declined to revisit the section one analysis. The Alberta Court conducted a very full analysis of s. 517 in *R. v. White.*[323] It concluded that s. 517 infringed the guarantee in s.2 (b) and, further, that the infringement could not be justified under section

---

[320] *Global Communications Ltd.* v. *Canada (A.G.)* (1984), 44 O.R. (2d) 609 (C.A.).

[321] (2007) 84 O.R. (3d) 766.

[322] Note 320, above.

[323] *R. v. White* (2007) 221 C.C.C. (3d) 393.

1 because it failed to meet both the "rational connection" and the "minimal impairment" criteria. The Court redrafted s. 517, employing the techniques of "severance" and "reading in". The Court removed the words "...and shall on application by the accused" and added the words "where a jury trial is possible" at the beginning of the section. Thus, the justice of the peace conducting a bail hearing *may* make a publication ban if the accused applies for one and only if it is possible that the accused will be tried by a jury. The result of the two decisions was that s. 517 meant one thing in Alberta and another in Ontario.

The two decisions discussed in the previous paragraph were both appealed to the respective provincial courts of appeal. Strangely enough, the courts of appeal seem to have traded positions. In its decision[324], the Ontario Court of Appeal largely adopted the position taken by the Alberta Court of Queen's Bench in *White*[325]. The Ontario Court of Appeal expressly overruled its earlier decision in *Global Communications*[326]. The decision is an example of the solipsistic prolixity often found in Canadian judicial decisions. The Court was of the view that, in its existing form, s.517 created a limit on freedom of expression and, further, after a careful and exhaustive analysis, that this was a limit which could not be justified in a free and democratic society. In the result, the Court redrafted s. 517 along much the same lines as the Alberta court had done in *White*. The result is that the justice conducting a bail hearing in Ontario *may* make a banning order if the Crown applies for it and *shall* make the order if the accused applies, *where and for so long as the charge(s) may be tried by a jury*.

It does seem, with respect, that Madam Justice Feldman did not fully grasp the distinctions amongst the judicial techniques of "severance", "reading in" and "reading down". The Alberta Court

---

[324] *Toronto Star Newspapers Ltd* v. *Canada* (2009) 302 D.L.R.(4th) 385.
[325] Note 323, above.
[326] Note 320, above.

of Appeal's decision[327] reached the conclusion that, while s.517 did create a limit on freedom of expression, this was a limit which could be justified in a free and democratic society. The court seems to have reached that conclusion because s.517 did not restrict access to the courtroom, nor did it prevent the media gathering information about the proceeding, nor did it prohibit publication of information about the proceeding, merely "delaying" it until the completion of the trial.

Two appellate court decisions had not changed the position that s.517 of the *Criminal Code of Canada* meant one thing in Alberta and another in Ontario. This position might have been expected to have changed and the contradiction resolved in the first half of 2010. The Supreme Court of Canada heard appeals in both cases and, on 17 November 2009, it reserved judgment. Thus, one might have expected that the Court's judgments would be rendered during 2010. The Supreme Court of Canada dealt with both appeals in one judgment[328] which was released on 10 June 2010.

In the result, the constitutionality of s. 517 in its original form was upheld. The Court appeared to have returned, to a degree, to the more traditional Canadian position of seeming to favour an accused person's right to a fair trial and the integrity of the judicial process over freedom of expression. As a general principle it was asserted that, "Trial fairness and liberty interests must not clash with freedom of expression. They can be reconciled." From the outset, the Court accepted that an order made under s. 517 would limit freedom of expression, so the central question was whether this was a limit which could be justified in a free and democratic society.

The Court wrote about "...the accused's and society's interest in a fair trial." The argument that a discretionary

---

[327] *R.v. White* (2008) 298 D.L.R. (4th) 659.
[328] *Toronto Star Newspapers Ltd.* v. *Canada* [2010] 1 S.C.R. 721.

publication ban would be preferable to a mandatory ban was dealt with simply and directly. "A discretionary ban would entail additional issues and adjournments and would result in longer hearings." The Court's conclusion was simple, direct and practical. The mandatory ban in s. 517 operated so as to "...guarantee as much as possible trial fairness and fair access to bail. Although not a perfect outcome, the mandatory ban represents a reasonable compromise."

Eight judges of the Supreme Court concurred in this result. There was, nonetheless, a dissent from Madam Justice Abella. The basis for her dissent was the mandatory nature of the ban as set out in s. 517. She was convinced that the deleterious effects of the mandatory ban outweighed its salutary effects and that the limit on freedom of expression could not, therefore, be justified. She would have redrafted s. 517 in such a way as to create a discretion in the justice of the peace conducting the bail hearing Thus, after a great deal of time, and litigation before several different courts, section 517 of the *Criminal Code* has survived in its original form and now means, one presumes, the same thing in every province.

Jury Trials

A jury in a criminal trial can be directed in one of two ways when it is not actually sitting in the courtroom hearing evidence or deliberating—that is, when the court is not in session. One is that the jury may be given permission to separate: the jurors may go home and live their normal lives and, most important for our purposes, read newspapers, watch television, listen to the radio, and so on. The other is that the jury may be sequestered: members, when they are not sitting in court, are, in effect, imprisoned in a hotel. The television and the telephone are taken out of their rooms, they cannot get newspapers and the sheriff provides their food from a local restaurant. This is an unreasonable burden to inflict on citizens who are already undergoing considerable inconvenience in order to perform a public duty. One of the strengths of the Canadian legal system is that juries are seldom sequestered, something that is common in the United States. This difference is one of the benefits of Canada's more restrictive rules about reporting judicial proceedings. The more controlled position for juries in the United States results from its laxer reporting rules.

Section 648 of the *Criminal Code* addresses the issue of reporting about things that happen during the course of a criminal trial when the jury is not in the courtroom. A variety of proceedings may go on during a criminal trial which require that the jury be sent out of the courtroom. The most common has to do with the admissibility of a confession. The Crown wants to introduce a confession, ostensibly made by the accused, into evidence. At that point the jury is sent out of the room and a hearing called a *voir dire* is held to determine whether or not the confession was made voluntarily.

If the judge decides the confession was made voluntarily, then the confession may be admitted. The jury is called back and its members get to know about the confession. If the judge decides the confession was not made voluntarily, it is not admissible. The jury is called back and nothing more is said about the confession. The *Criminal Code* provides that if the members of the jury have been sequestered, reporters are free to report about things that happened in the courtroom when the jurors were not there; there is obviously no way jurors are going to find these things out. But if the jury has been given permission to separate, no one may report on anything that happened when the jurors were out of the courtroom. Subsection (2) of section 648 makes it an offence to breach this prohibition.

A serious drawback to the Supreme Court's decision in *Dagenais* is that the Chief Justice actually recommended sequestering juries. He said there were many means short of publication bans which could be used to guarantee the fairness of a trial. One of them was sequestering juries. It is not clear on reading the judgment that the Chief Justice understood that sequestration seldom happens in Canada, or, more important, that it would be a major imposition on jurors.

Section 649 makes it an offence for a juror, except in an investigation of possible jury tampering or perjury offences, to disclose to anyone any information about what went on in the jury room. What is interesting about this offence is that it can only be committed by the juror or ex-juror who makes the disclosure. It is not specifically stated that a reporter commits an offence if she asks a juror to tell her what happened in the jury room. While a reporter should not be running a risk by *asking*, she should avoid encouraging, cajoling, or browbeating. Nonetheless, if the juror is foolish enough to tell the reporter, no offence would be committed by publishing that information. However, in the real world, no juror is likely to tell a reporter anything, because the last thing judges do with jurors at the end of a trial, before they discharge them, is give them a lecture and put the fear of God into them. They suggest to jurors that if they ever breathe a syllable about anything specific that happened in the jury room, or during any of their deliberations, they could face severe penalties.

It may be possible to ask jurors very general and non-specific questions—about their feelings, for example. "Did you find it difficult? Were there psychological strains?" A juror would probably not be committing an offence by answering questions like that.

Common Law *Sub Judice*

We turn now to the common law of *sub judice*, the undefined, vague, amorphous parts of *sub judice*. The aim is to try to extract from the cases some principles that can be followed or that can operate as guidelines in dealing with these issues.

We begin with a 1973 decision of the English House of Lords in what is undoubtedly the most famous decision on *sub judice*: *A.G. v. Times Newspapers Ltd.*[329] We will discuss only the judgments given in the House of Lords. Although that body's decision was overruled by the European Court of Human Rights in 1979, it is the reasoning of the House of Lords which has consistently been cited in Canadian courts.

In 1958 a drug called thalidomide was developed and marketed in a number of countries. At the time, thalidomide was prescribed to women in the early stages of pregnancy and was supposed to be effective in controlling some of the difficulties experienced in those months—morning sickness, general debilitation, and so on. The drug was apparently effective at doing this. Unfortunately, it had an unexpected, but tragic, side effect. Many of the children of women who had taken thalidomide were born without limbs. They had hands and feet, but in many cases, either their hands or their feet, or in some cases both, were attached directly to their torsos.

Thalidomide was immediately withdrawn from circulation. It had been marketed in the United Kingdom by a subsidiary of the Seagram's empire, a corporation called Distillers (Biochemicals) Limited. The families of these children obviously wanted compensation, and sought it from Distillers. As a legal matter, the families of the thalidomide children sued Distillers for negligence.

The litigation, therefore, involved the law of torts—the law of civil wrongs, or non-criminal injuries. In English law each tort has its own special rules and its own special peculiarities. To understand what happened in this case, it is necessary to know something about the tort of negligence.

A plaintiff in a negligence action cannot ordinarily ask a court to infer negligence from results. Thus, a woman who had taken thalidomide could not simply point to her armless or legless child

---

[329] [1973] 3 All E.R. 54 (H.L.).

195

and say that the people who marketed this drug must have been negligent. The plaintiff has to prove actual negligence on the part of the defendant. In this case, that meant requiring the plaintiffs to show that somewhere in the process of research, development, testing, manufacture, and marketing of thalidomide, somewhere in that complicated series of events, there had been actual negligence on the part of Distillers.

This was the difficulty facing these families in their lawsuits. They had to identify the specific points at which Distillers had been negligent and, further, show that this negligence had caused their children's deformities. These difficulties were compounded by the fact that Distillers was a wealthy multinational and could afford the best lawyers available. Although these lawyers did not do anything unlawful or unethical, they certainly raised every possible defence or legal obstacle that Distillers had available in resisting the claims against it. Offers to settle were made to the families, but these offers were generally regarded as inadequate.

We now move forward to 1972. The thalidomide children were not babies any more. Some of them were teenagers, but there was still no compensation from Distillers. The various lawsuits were inching their way along, but little had happened for fourteen years. Along came the *Sunday Times*. It had an Insight Team—a permanent group of investigative reporters which was given the resources and the time to work on complicated and difficult stories. The *Sunday Times* Insight Team was assigned to work on the thalidomide story and the litigation with Distillers.

Two stories were eventually prepared. The first was a history of the litigation between the families of the thalidomide children and Distillers. It talked about the foot-dragging that Distillers' lawyers had engaged in and was critical of both Distillers and its lawyers. At the end of the piece, the *Sunday Times* urged Distillers to do the right thing and make a fair, indeed generous, offer of settlement to these families. The first piece was actually published. This story made reference to the second piece, which was to come later and was promised to be a review of the research, development, testing, manufacturing, and marketing of thalidomide. It was going to explain how the whole tragedy happened. That piece had not actually been published when the litigation began.

The response to the publication of the first story was that the attorney general moved to have the *Sunday Times* cited for contempt of court. The attorney general further sought an order prohibiting the publication of the second piece on the ground that its publication would amount to a contempt. The matter eventually ended up before the House of Lords. In its judgment the court dealt with the two articles separately.

With respect to the first piece, the judges said there was no contempt of court in commenting critically, but in fair and temperate language, on the conduct of litigation. It was not contempt to comment critically, nor was it contempt to urge specific courses of action on litigants. The metaphor used was that it would not be a contempt of court to suggest to Shylock that he forego his pound of flesh.

There is little critical writing in the Canadian media about the way people conduct themselves in litigation and the behaviour of parties and their lawyers. The judgment in the *Sunday Times* case made it clear that as long as the parties to litigation are not subjected to public ridicule or public contempt, there is no contempt in commenting on their conduct.

The second article, however, led to a different result. The court said that what must be avoided in this area of contempt of court was what it described as trial by newspaper. On this basis, the judges concluded that the second piece would amount to a contempt of court and, thus, could not be published.

Why?

Because, said the House of Lords, the *Sunday Times* had taken it upon itself to resolve precisely the issue that would be before the court when, if ever, this matter actually went to trial. The issue before the court would be, was Distillers negligent? That was exactly the question the *Sunday Times* addressed in the second article. Whenever the media purport to resolve an issue that will be before the courts, they are acting in breach of the *sub judice* rule. The essence of the breach in this case lay in *prejudging* an issue that would eventually have to be resolved by the courts.

The House of Lords said:

> *The law on this subject is and must be founded entirely on public policy. It is not there to protect the private rights of parties to a litigation or prosecution. It is there to prevent interference with the administration of justice and it should in my judgment be limited to what is reasonably necessary for that purpose. Public policy generally requires a balancing of interests which may conflict. Freedom of speech should not be limited to any greater extent than is necessary but it cannot be allowed where there would be real prejudice to the administration of justice.*

The court went on, however, to conclude that it would find a breach of the *sub judice* rule only when a particular publication created a real risk of prejudice to the administration of justice, as opposed to a remote possibility. It also held that there must be strong evidence to satisfy a court that a particular publication would indeed create a real risk of prejudice. In the end, the House of Lords upheld an order prohibiting publication of the second article. This has been a much criticized decision, but it is a decision that has been quoted over and over in Canadian courts.

The House of Lords asserted that the *sub judice* rule did not prevent publication, but merely postponed it. The implication was that the second piece could be published sometime in the future after the eventual trial had ended. The interesting result of this litigation and the attention that was focused on it was that the

Distillers Corporation made a more generous offer to the families of the thalidomide children and settlements were reached.

Having a general sense of the scope of the *sub judice* rule, we can turn to specific concerns that arise in its application. The first one has to do with prejudicing the outcome of a trial and can be exemplified by the case of one-time corporal Denis Lortie. In 1984 he was a member of the Canadian Armed Forces stationed at Valcartier. He took an automatic weapon to the National Assembly in Quebec City. Once inside the legislative building, he began shooting indiscriminately, killing a number of people and wounding others. Given the place he picked to go on his rampage, not only were there permanent videotaping facilities in the building, but there were many reporters around. The result was that many media agencies had videotape of Lortie firing his weapon—that is to say, actually committing some of these murders. There was much debate as to whether these tapes could be aired. The worry was that airing them might amount to a breach of the *sub judice* rule.

When we reflect concretely on the notion of creating a real risk of prejudice to the outcome of a pending trial, it must mean creating a real risk of prejudicing the resolution of a specific issue that will actually be before the court. Lortie was charged with murder. If we think about his trial, it must be clear what would be in issue and what would not be. It is evident, given the circumstances of this crime, that identity could not be an issue. It was inconceivable that Lortie could go before the court and deny that he committed the killings or attempt to argue that the police had arrested the wrong person. The point here is simple, but requires some judgment. It is not a matter of editors or news directors deciding that nothing can be published about a particular pending trial. It is a matter of familiarizing oneself with the specific circumstances of the trial and attempting to determine, in consultation with lawyers if necessary, what will be the specific issues the trial court is going to have to address and resolve. There should have been no risk in airing those videotapes. It must be clear that sanity, not identity, would have been the only issue before the court. If something is not in issue, then, by definition, the media cannot prejudice its resolution.[330]

The second question about the application of the *sub judice* rule concerns the time at which it begins to operate. There is little in the way of clear direction or guidance that can be given here because of the vagueness and uncertainty of the law. In Ontario a decision in a civil libel action called *Bielek v. Ristimaki* points up this uncertainly.[331] The *sub judice* rule does not apply only to criminal matters, but to civil ones as well. In this case, both the plaintiff and the defendant were members of the municipal council in Timmins, Ontario, and were involved in a perfectly straightforward civil libel action. One of the documents a plaintiff files with a court in order to commence a civil action is a statement of claim; here she sets out what she is upset about, how the defendant has wronged her, and how much money she wants. The plaintiff in this case had filed a statement of claim asking for half a million dollars in damages.

As a court document, the statement of claim was a public document, and reporters were entitled to look at it and write stories about it. The *Timmins Daily Press*, the local paper, had done a story about this litigation. The newspaper had not only printed what the action was all about, but also how much money the plaintiff was asking for in the statement of claim. The article appeared in the paper and there were no legal problems. Time passed and about a year later the trial was set to begin.

One of the peculiarities of civil libel actions is that they are the last refuge of the civil jury. This was to be a jury trial. The

---

[330] The Quebec Court of Appeal differed with the analysis presented here. See *Lortie v. R.*, [1985] C.A. 451 (Que.) [hereinafter *Lortie*].
[331] (21 June 1979), (Ont. H.C.J.) [unreported]. See S.M. Robertson, *Courts and the Media,* Toronto, Butterworths, 1981 at 287–92.

jury had been picked and the trial was set to begin. Because the trial was starting that day, the *Timmins Daily Press* did another story about it and repeated the fact that the plaintiff was asking for half a million dollars. This time the reporter and the paper were brought before the court on contempt citations and convicted.

A year previously the identical information had been published and there was no problem, but to publish it the day the trial began was to commit a contempt of court. But when, exactly, did the *sub judice* rule begin to operate? All the trial judge could say on the issue was:

> ...*it's a question of timing.*

The closer you get to the date of the trial, the greater the risk. The reason the newspaper could publish the amount the plaintiff wanted when the statement of claim was first issued is that at that point no one could be certain there would ever be a trial at all. And even if there was going to be a trial, it would happen at some time in the future. A newspaper or broadcaster can be confident about publishing this information when a statement of claim is first issued, but as the trial draws closer one has to be more cautious.

We must note here a basic practical difference between civil proceedings and criminal proceedings. With civil proceedings, in the majority of cases where a statement of claim is issued, there is probably not going to be a trial. Equally, in most cases where criminal charges are laid, there is likely going to be a trial.

The third point about the *sub judice* rule is that the rigour with which it is applied varies according to the court dealing with the particular case. Built into the *sub judice* rule is a certain distrust of juries and an assumption that juries, which are made up, not of lawyers, but of ordinary human beings, are fickle and much influenced by what they read in the newspapers or see on television. The *sub judice* rule is applied with the greatest rigour in dealing with a trial that is to be held with a jury. It is applied with less rigour when the trial is to be conducted by a judge alone.

Fourth, at what point does the *sub judice* rule cease to apply? It seems that its application ends when the trial ends, when it is no longer possible to prejudice the outcome of the trial. The general view in Canada is that there is no *sub judice* rule with respect to appellate proceedings. There are two reasons. First, there are ordinarily no factual issues in dispute before appellate courts; they accept the findings of fact reached by trial courts and they deal only with legal issues. Second, appellate courts are always composed exclusively of judges and tend to operate in a much more rarefied and abstract atmosphere than do trial courts.[332]

A fifth, and crucial, point about *sub judice*, and about contempt generally, is that culpability may depend on the language and tone used in a particular story. This can be seen in *Zehr v. McIsaac*,[333] a case that involved a dangerous offender proceeding before a single judge in Toronto. On the day the proceeding was actually under way before that judge, the *Globe and Mail* published, on page 5, a piece with the heading, *Fed Up With Deciding on Confining Criminals Indefinitely, MD Says*. There was no reference in the heading to the actual person who was the subject of the dangerous offender application. The story began with:

> *A director at the Penetanguishene Mental Health Centre says he is fed up with being asked to decide whether criminals should be designated dangerous offenders and thus incarcerated indefinitely. The courts should stop foisting the question on psychiatrists and instead make the dangerous offender designation*

---

[332] *Bellitti v. Canadian Broadcasting Corp.* (1973), 2 O.R. (2d) 232 (H.C.J.). *Lortie*, above note 330, takes a different view.

[333] (1982), 39 O.R. (2d) 237 (H.C.J.).

automatic if a crime is repeated a certain number of times, said Russell Fleming, director of the centre's forensic science unit.

The story continued in this vein until the bottom third of the article, where it read: "Dr. Fleming's remarks came after he testified in the Supreme Court of Ontario concerning a Crown application to have a convicted rapist designated a dangerous offender." The story was saying that this person had a criminal record. It went on:

A 24-year-old man with a long record of breaking and entering was convicted in December of raping a woman while holding a knife to her throat. He had one previous conviction, but the Ontario Court of Appeal ordered another trial at which the man was found not guilty. "We and the police are satisfied he has done it twice anyway," John McIsaac, the Crown attorney handling the case, said.

Contempt of court proceedings were instituted, but both the paper and the writer were acquitted. Why? First, the judge made reference to the "type and tenor" of the article. Clearly the subject-matter of the article was not this particular alleged dangerous offender, but dangerous offender proceedings generally. As far as the tenor was concerned, the story was written in straightforward and dispassionate language. The position of the article in the newspaper, on page 5, was also significant. The absence of the offender's name from the article was important. There was material that tended to identify the individual in question, but his name was not included. There was no sensationalism. This piece came as close as possible to breaching the *sub judice* rule, but the way it was written, the way it was placed in the paper, the head, the lead, and everything about it was such that the judge was induced to acquit. This decision can be seen as illustrating the general principle that the *way* you do something may be just as important as *whether* you do it.

The sixth point about *sub judice* has to do with *mens rea*. In order for someone to be convicted of a crime, the Crown must first establish that she has committed the *actus reus*—the guilty act constituting the particular offence. Not only does the Crown have to show that the accused performed the guilty act, but that, in addition, the accused did so with the required *mens rea*—with the necessary degree of mental culpability. The basic difference between murder and manslaughter has to do with *mens rea*. The *actus reus*, causing another person's death, is the same for both offences, but it is the mental element that makes murder 1 different from murder 2 and murder 2 different from manslaughter.

Turning to contempt of court, the *actus reus* involved in breaching the *sub judice* rule is the publication of material that creates a real risk of prejudice to the outcome of proceedings before a court. What is the *mens rea*? The crucial question here is whether the Crown has to establish that the accused published the material in question with the intention of either prejudicing or creating a risk of prejudicing the outcome of a matter before the courts or, simply, that the accused published the material intentionally. In *R. v. CHEK TV Ltd.*,[334] a television station in Victoria aired some videotape about a person who was at the time on trial for murder. The videotape came from a story the station had broadcast a year earlier when there had been a hostage incident and a riot at a British Columbia penitentiary. It showed an artist's impression of this same person who was now standing trial for murder holding a knife to the throat of a prison guard. This was, of course, highly prejudicial, since it not only suggested that he was a violent individual, but made clear that he had a

---

[334] (1985), 23 C.C.C. (3d) 395 (B.C.S.C.).

criminal record.

The station's defence was that airing this tape had been a mistake, that it had been done by a junior and inexperienced employee, and that there had been no intention of prejudicing the outcome of proceedings before the court. The court said that the *mens rea* required was not an actual intention to interfere with proceedings before the court, but simply an intention to publish material that had that tendency. The only question, then, was whether the station had intentionally aired the tape. Since the answer to that question was clearly yes, the station was found to have committed contempt.

The Ontario Court of Appeal addressed the question of *mens rea* in *R. v. Helsdon*.[335] The accused, a reporter, was charged with breaching a publication ban made under s. 486 (3) of the *Criminal Code*. He claimed not to have been aware that the publication ban had been made. The Court held that it was not necessary to establish that the accused had subjective knowledge of the ban, merely that he intentionally published the offending information.

The last issue to deal with in relation to *sub judice* is that of publication bans. When a general publication ban is made, as in the thalidomide case, the court is issuing an injunction. An injunction is an order made by a court with the purpose of preventing the commission of an unlawful act. The unlawful act the court is concerned with preventing in these cases is a breach of the *sub judice* rule. Now, generally speaking, individuals are free to choose whether they will obey the law or not. Anyone is free to break the law as long as she is prepared to accept the consequences of so doing. An injunction should only be issued to restrain a breach of the law when the injury to someone which would result from that breach would be irreparable. The injury that would result from a breach of the *sub judice* rule is the prejudicing of a proceeding that is pending or before the court.

---

[335] (2007) 84 O.R. (3d) 544.

That injury is seen as irreparable. Thus, the point of the injunction, of the publication ban, is to prevent that injury occurring.

The leading case on publication bans is *Dagenais v. Canadian Broadcasting Corp.*[336] The CBC, together with the National Film Board, prepared a so-called docudrama entitled *The Boys of St. Vincent*. This purported to be a fictional account of the abuse of boys at a Roman Catholic-run institution. It was to air in December 1992. At that time, however, there were several real trials pending or before the courts of real men charged with real abuse of real boys in real institutions. A number of these men, Dagenais being one of them, applied for an order to delay the broadcasting of *The Boys of St. Vincent* until such time as their trials had been completed. Clearly, once the trials were completed, there could be no possibility of prejudicing their outcome.

An application for an injunction was made to a single judge of the Ontario Court of Justice without giving notice to the CBC. One of the peculiarities of these injunctions was that they could be made *ex parte*, without both sides being present at the hearing. The judge made an order that the docudrama not be aired anywhere in Canada and that no information about the injunction itself be broadcast. The very next day the CBC appealed this order to the Ontario Court of Appeal. That court amended the original order to say that the ban would apply only in Ontario and to a particular television station in Montreal. The basis for generally sustaining the injunction was the court's conclusion that the airing of this docudrama would create a real and substantial risk of prejudice to criminal trials that were pending or under way before the courts. The CBC and the National Film Board appealed further to the Supreme Court of Canada.

The Supreme Court's judgment may indicate a significant

---

[336] Above, note 149. For more detailed analysis, see Robert Martin, *Case Comment*, (1995) 74 Canadian Bar Review, 500.

change in direction in Canadian law in the whole area of reporting about judicial proceedings. Chief Justice Antonio Lamer asserted, as we have seen, that the traditional notion that the right to a fair trial must always take precedence over free expression should be abandoned. He said further that there was no hierarchy of rights in the *Charter*, so that no single right was to be preferred over any other right.

Instead of freedom of expression giving way to the right to a fair trial, the two, he said, must be "balanced." He also said that the American approach—called the "clash model"—of free press versus fair trial must be abandoned, because the two are not necessarily always in conflict. A judge hearing an application for a publication ban must attempt to balance the two rights and should issue a ban only when she is satisfied that:

(a) the publication in question will create a real and substantial risk of prejudice to judicial proceedings; and

(b) there is no reasonable alternative means of preventing that risk.

What did the Chief Justice mean by reasonable alternative means? He talked of sequestering juries. He talked about adjourning proceedings. He also spoke about change of venue—changing the location of a trial. He referred to challenges for cause during jury selection. And, finally, he said that when the judge charges the jury at the end of the trial, or possibly even during a trial, she should give strong directions to the jurors to put certain things out of their minds.

The problem with this analysis lies in the notion of "balancing." How is it possible in an adversarial system to *balance* competing claims? At the end of the day the judge has to make a choice. In the final instance the judge must choose either freedom of expression or the right to a fair trial. The Chief Justice's judgment in *Dagenais* suggests that the judge can somehow simultaneously choose both.

Another problem with the *Dagenais* decision is that it casts doubt on a great deal of existing case law. Many of the issues discussed in this chapter had once appeared to be resolved, but they may now have to be revisited, case by case. In *R. v. Mentuck*[337], the Supreme Court of Canada reaffirmed and added a major gloss to *Dagenais*.

The Manitoba Court of Queen's Bench was hearing a trial on a charge of second degree murder. Certain questions arose concerning police undercover operations. Two specific issues were addressed, first, whether the court could lawfully make an order prohibiting the publication of information concerning the methods employed by the police in undercover operations and, second, whether an order prohibiting the publication of the identities of police officers involved in undercover operations could be made.

The Court accepted that, while the publication ban in *Dagenais* had been made in order to protect the rights to a fair trial of persons accused of crimes, there might be other circumstances that could justify a publication ban. The Supreme Court reformulated the general principle as follows:

A publication ban should only be ordered when:

a. such an order is necessary in order to prevent a serious risk to the proper administration of justice because reasonable alternative measures will not prevent the risk; and

b. the salutary effects of the publication ban outweigh the deleterious effects on the rights and interests of the parties and the public, including the effects on the right to free expression, the right of the accused to a fair and public trial and the efficacy of the administration of justice.[338]

---

[337] [2001] 3 S.C.R. 442.

[338] *Ibid.*, at p. 462.

> *The burden of proof was placed on the party seeking the publication ban, "...because the presumption that courts should be open and reporting of their proceedings should be uncensored is so strong and so highly valued in our society that the judge must have a convincing evidentiary basis for issuing the ban."*[339]

In the result, the Court decided that a ban on publishing the identities of police officers involved in undercover operations might be acceptable, while a ban on publishing information about the methods they used would not.

In Facie Contempts

As clear an example as one could possibly ask for of contempt committed *in facie* can be found in *B.K.* v. *R.*[340] The appellant was subpoenaed as a witness at a preliminary enquiry. When the presiding judge attempted to have him sworn as a witness, B.K. refused to be sworn, saying, *inter alia*, to the judge:

> *I ain't testifying man. Fucking charge me. Whatever you fucking want, man. I ain't testifying.*[341]

The judge convicted the accused summarily and sentenced him to six months imprisonment. After sentence was passed, B.K. said to the judge, "Fuck you, you goof." The sentence of six months imprisonment is probably the most severe ever imposed by a Canadian court for contempt. The contempt may well be the most extreme ever committed in a Canadian court.[342]

---

[339] *Ibid.*, at p. 465.
[340] [1995] 4 S.C.R. 186.
[341] *Ibid.* at 190.
[342] *Ibid.* at 191.

The Supreme Court of Canada noted that the power to punish summarily for contempt is extraordinary and should be used only with "scrupulous care."[343]

The one form of *in facie* contempt which can be committed by journalists is disobeying an order of a court. *In facie* contempts are most often committed by lawyers. Lawyers may show up late for court, they do not show up, they show up drunk or they engage in abusive arguments with the judge. The one time that a journalist can commit this form of contempt occurs when she is called as a witness and is asked either to reveal the identity of a source or to reveal information received in confidence from a source. If the journalist refuses to be sworn as a witness or, having been sworn, refuses to answer a question properly put to her, she commits a contempt of court. This is an issue that looms far larger in movies and television dramas than in real life. Nonetheless, it is an issue of some interest.

What we are talking about, in legal terminology, is the question of whether there exists, or should exist, a privilege in journalists—a legal right in journalists—to refuse to disclose certain information to courts. A privilege, in this context, means a legal right to say:

> *I do not want to tell you that and, more to the point, I am under no legal obligation to tell you. I have a right to refuse to disclose that information.*

Does Canadian law recognize any privilege in journalists to refuse to disclose information received in confidence from a source, including the identity of the source? The simple answer is no, but it is necessary to investigate how that answer has been reached.[344]

---

[343] *Ibid.* at 200.

[344] A very full survey of the entire question is found in S.N. Lederman, P. O'Kelly, & M. Grottenthaler, *Confidentiality of News Sources* in P.

The older approach that Canadian courts took to the question of privilege was described as the class or category approach. There were certain fixed classes or categories of relations that were recognized as giving rise to privilege in respect of communications made during the course of those relations. Their number was limited and included the solicitor-client relation, the relation of husband and wife, communications with and among high officers of state, and jury deliberations.

The law was quite mechanical. If you were party to one of those relations, communications made within it were privileged. If you were not, you had no basis for claiming privilege. If a solicitor had received information from a client during the course of the solicitor-client relationship, the solicitor could claim a privilege to refuse to divulge that information. But since the journalist-source relation did not fit within any of the recognized categories, no basis existed for such a claim by a journalist.

In recent years Canadian courts have moved away from the category approach and have adopted a more flexible approach that is not confined to categories, but is based on a step-by-step analysis of the relation in question. This analysis is borrowed from an American writer called Wigmore, who wrote an eleven-volume treatise on the law of evidence.[345] Wigmore laid out four criteria which he said should be applied, and which Canadian courts have adopted,[346] in order to determine whether a particular relation gives rise to privilege. I will set out Wigmore's criteria and then determine whether any of them is satisfied with respect to the journalist-source relation.

Wigmore's first criterion was that the communications must

Anisman & A.M. Linden, eds., *The Media, The Courts, and The Charter*, Toronto, Carswell, (1986), 227.

[345] See J.H. Wigmore, *Evidence in Trials at Common Law*, vol. 8, 3d ed., rev. by J.T. McNaughton, Boston, Little, Brown, 1961.

[346] The first case was *Slavutych v. Baker*, [1976] 1 S.C.R. 254.

originate in a confidence that they will not be disclosed. Certainly the journalist-source relation satisfies that criterion. When a source discloses confidential information to a journalist, the expectation is that at least one important part of that information—the source's identity—will not be disclosed.

Wigmore's language is somewhat archaic and stultified, so I will set out what he said and then try to put it in ordinary words. He formulated his second criterion:

> *The element of confidentiality must be essential to the full and satisfactory maintenance of the relation between the parties.*

He was saying that not only must the relation originate in confidence, but it must continue on that basis. Confidentiality must be essential to the continuation of the relation. Here, again, the journalist-source relation passes muster.

Turning to Wigmore's third criterion, he stated that the relation must be one "which in the opinion of the community ought to be sedulously fostered." This statement simply means that it is a socially legitimate and valuable relation and, generally speaking, although not always, Canadian courts have accepted that the journalist-source relation satisfies the third criterion.

When it comes to Wigmore's fourth criterion, however, the journalist-source relation generally, in the past, failed to measure up. "The *injury* that would inure to the relation by the disclosure of the communications must be *greater than the benefit* thereby gained for the correct disposal of litigation."

He is saying is that a court weighing this question must do a balancing act. What is the benefit gained in resolving the case before the court of getting the information, as weighed against the injury to the relation that would result from forcing its disclosure? Which is more valuable—getting the information before the court or harming the relation through the forced disclosure of that information? Canadian courts have generally said that the nature of the journalist-source relation is such that it will not satisfy Wigmore's fourth criterion. Judges have agreed that disclosure will result in injury to the relation between the journalist and the source, but the benefit of getting the information before the court has consistently been taken to outweigh that injury.

In the era of the *Charter* it has been argued that the guarantee of freedom of expression in section 2(b) should be interpreted as creating a degree of journalistic privilege. It has been asserted that freedom of expression, or freedom of the press, demands recognition of such a privilege. This is not an assertion all Canadian journalists would necessarily agree with. The issue was litigated before the Supreme Court in 1989 in *Moysa v. Alberta (Labour Relations Board)*.[347] It was an unusual case.

Moysa was a reporter with the *Edmonton Journal*. She did a story about some employees of Hudson's Bay Company outlets in Edmonton trying to organize themselves into unions. One of the largest unorganized sectors in the Canadian economy is retail distribution, and for a long time the labour movement has been trying to do something about this and failing.

The precise facts, at least what one can glean of them from the Supreme Court judgment, are not clear, but, allowing for a certain amount of surmise, it seems that roughly the following happened. Moysa, in preparing her story, talked to some of the employees at one Hudson's Bay outlet who were active in the organizing drive. She also talked to management. A reasonable inference is that Moysa, whether advertently or not, communicated the names of these employees to someone in management. Management then sacked six employees, presumably the ones whose names it got from Moysa.

The now former employees of the Bay filed complaints before the Alberta Labour Relations Board that they had been fired for

---

[347] [1989] 1 S.C.R. 1572.

trying to organize a union. The Bay denied this. Since the employees had brought the complaints, they had the burden of proving that they were true. They called Moysa as a witness. She was subpoenaed and appeared before the Labour Relations Board; she was asked whether she had spoken with management. She responded that she could not reveal that information and claimed journalistic privilege.

In this case the issue was backwards. Moysa was not claiming a privilege in respect of information she had *received* from a source. She was trying to claim a privilege in respect of information that, insofar as I understand the facts, she *gave* to a source. This definitely was not the case to take to the Supreme Court to argue in favour of journalistic privilege. The issue of privilege did not even arise on these facts.

The Court denied the claim to privilege. The judges said, further, although not very strongly, that there might be some basis in section 2(b) of the *Charter* for a claim to journalistic privilege, but that the Court could decide that only when it got a real case. In my opinion, however, you do not have to read far between the lines to conclude that the Court did not hold out much hope that, even in a proper case, it would find in favour of a privilege. In my view, the correct conclusion is that in Canadian law there is no privilege as such.

The broad issue was dealt with recently by the Ontario Court of Appeal in *St. Elizabeth Home Society (Hamilton, Ontario)* v. *The Corporation of the City of Hamilton.*[348] The best word to describe this decision is *tantalising* in that, while the Court did not quite come right out and say there *is* journalistic privilege, neither did it say there *isn't*.

A reporter for the Hamilton *Spectator* wrote a series of articles about a local nursing home. A major basis for these articles was documents he had received from a confidential source. The

[348] (2008) 89 O.R. (3d) 81.

articles sparked litigation. The reporter was subpoenaed to testify as a witness during this litigation. He refused to answer questions that would have revealed the identity of his source. The trial judge went to considerable lengths to accommodate the reporter, the confidential source identified himself to the court, but the reporter persisted in his refusal to testify and was found to be in contempt.

The bulk of the decision of the Court of Appeal was devoted to an analysis of whether the reporter should have been found to be in contempt. The Court laid down four principles to be followed by a judge adjudicating a claim to privilege. First, the traditional class/category approach should no longer be regarded as determinative and, second, each such claim should be resolved on a case by case basis through the application of the Wigmore analysis, third, that "...judges should resort to citations for contempt in the face of the court only as a last resort",[349] and that the claim to privilege should be resolved before the judge addressed the question of contempt.

The Court of Appeal concluded that the trial judge erred in initiating contempt proceedings himself and overturned the reporter's conviction. It did not make a ruling on the question whether the reporter had raised a valid claim to privilege.

An important question underlying these decisions is whether the *Charter*'s guarantee of freedom of expression and freedom of the press can be regarded as creating any special legal status for journalists. The Supreme Court's decision in *Moysa* suggests that it cannot.

These decisions, however, are not the end of the matter for a journalist called as a witness. We turn to an English decision called *A.G. v. Mulholland*.[350] It arose out of a spy scandal. Two reporters for the *Daily Telegraph* wrote a story about Soviet spies

---

[349] *Ibid.*, at 94.
[350] [1963] 2 Q.B. 477 (C.A.).

in the British Admiralty. As a result, a tribunal of inquiry was set up to look into the question. Inevitably, the reporters who wrote the story that led to the tribunal being established were the first witnesses called before it. They were asked to tell the tribunal the sources for their story, but they refused. They were cited for contempt of court, convicted, and then appealed to the Court of Appeal.

The court accepted that there was no such thing as a privilege in law, but it did not say that journalists could be subpoenaed and questioned at will or whimsically. The court said that journalism was an "honourable" profession and that the confidences members of honourable professions receive in the course of their work should be respected.

As a result, a journalist who was called as a witness should not be subjected to a fishing expedition. Practically speaking, it was held that a journalist witness should be required to reveal information received in confidence from a source only when the party seeking that information is able to satisfy the court as to two matters. First, it must be shown that the information sought is relevant, that it bears directly on the resolution of an issue actually before the court. It is not, then, simply a matter of a party saying I would like to know this, or I think it is interesting, or I would like to find out. Second, it must also be shown that the information sought is *necessary*. Necessary here means that the issue that is before the court cannot be resolved unless the court has this information.

The decision in *Mulholland* has been accepted in Canadian courts, so that before a journalist can be required to reveal information received in confidence, the court must be satisfied that the information sought is both relevant and necessary. And only when the court is so satisfied can the journalist who is a witness be required to disclose that information.

But even at this point all is not lost. Even if the court decides that the information sought is relevant and necessary, the journalist witness, or her lawyer, may ask the judge to use the "moral authority" of the court to suggest to counsel asking the question that the question "not be pressed."[351] This is what has happened traditionally in the cases of priests and penitents, physicians and patients, and so on. None of these relations gives rise to a legal privilege to refuse to disclose information received during its course, but at the end of the day counsel would say to the trial judge, "I ask you to use the moral authority of the court to suggest that the question not be pressed," and the judge would say to the lawyer posing the question, "I ask you not to press the question." A wise lawyer would know the right response.

So, summing up, what is the practical position? There is no privilege to allow a journalist legally to refuse to divulge information. If a journalist is subpoenaed, she is surely going to know why. That journalist should go to court with a lawyer and, when she goes into the witness box and is sworn, remembering that it is an offence under the *Criminal Code* to refuse to be sworn,[352] and the fateful question is asked, the lawyer representing her will stand up and request that counsel asking the question be required to satisfy the court that the information sought is both relevant and necessary. If counsel is not successful in both endeavours, the journalist should not be required to answer the question. If, however, the court is satisfied that the information sought is relevant and necessary, then the lawyer representing the journalist should ask the court to use its moral authority to suggest that the question not be pressed. The court may accede to that request. If, however, the judge declines to exercise the moral authority of the court, the journalist is on her own. If she refuses to answer the question, by that refusal she has

---

[351] *Reference Re Legislative Privilege* (1978), 18 O.R. (2d) 529 at 540 (C.A.).
[352] See *Criminal Code of Canada*, R.S.C. 1985, c. 46, s. 545 [hereinafter *Criminal Code*].

committed a contempt of court.

One of the unfortunate things about contempt of court is that in a superior court, at any rate, the trial judge can punish summarily—right there and then. The judge can say, "I find you guilty of contempt of court and I sentence you to three days in jail." After the journalist has had a chance to reflect on things for three days, she can be brought back to the court and asked the question again, and, if she refuses to answer, she would commit a fresh offence and could be punished summarily again. This, in theory, could go on forever. It has never happened to a journalist in a Canadian courtroom and, in the unlikely case that it did, everybody involved would probably go to extraordinary lengths to find some way out of what would be an embarrassing situation. It is worth noting that, because contempt of court is a common law crime, the maximum punishment that may be awarded is nowhere specified, but is at the discretion of the judge.

The final point on the issue of privilege has to do with something called the *newspaper rule*. This rule is of limited application as it arises only in civil libel proceedings and only at the pre-trial stage of examination for discovery. The newspaper rule says that a media defendant in a libel action cannot be required at discovery to reveal the source of the allegedly libellous statements. Why would the plaintiff's lawyer want to know where the defendant got the allegedly libellous material from? Presumably, because it would give that lawyer a much better idea of how strong a defence the defendant might be able to mount. The newspaper rule has been upheld in Ontario,[353] but rejected in other provinces.[354] The question of privilege is discussed further later.

---

[353] See *McInnis* v. *University Students' Council of the University of Western Ontario* (1984), 48 O.R. (2d) 542 (H.C.J.).
[354] See, for example, *Baxter* v. *Canadian Broadcasting Corp.* (1978), 22 N.B.R. (2d) 307 (Q.B.).

Conclusion

Before leaving our discussion of contempt of court, it is worthwhile to stress again the unsatisfactory state of Canadian law on the subject. Reform and codification of the law are both long overdue.

In 1982 the then Law Reform Commission of Canada produced proposals for codifying the law of contempt.[355] Although the idea of reducing the uncertain common law of contempt to a statutory form was desirable, the substance of what was proposed was a disaster. It would have made an unnecessarily restrictive offence even more restrictive. The report died.

In 1984 an omnibus Criminal Law Reform Bill[356] was introduced in Parliament. Part of this bill would have codified much of the law of contempt. The bill was not enacted. Nothing has happened since. It would seem that much of the existing law of contempt of court denies a number of the rights set out in the *Charter*. Despite this restriction, there has not been a systematic challenge, based on the *Charter*, to the existing law. One of the difficulties in the way of such a challenge has been uncertainty about whether the *Charter* can apply to purely judicial acts, such as the judge-created, non-statutory law of contempt. The Supreme Court's decision in *Dagenais*[357] may have made it procedurally easier to make such a challenge.

It is noteworthy that the Ontario Court of Appeal in *Kopyto*[358] was able effectively to jettison scandalizing the court. But in an

---

[355] Law Reform Commission of Canada, Contempt of Court, (Report 17), Ottawa, Minister of Supply & Services, 1982.

[356] Bill C-19, 2d Sess., 32d Parl., 1984.

[357] Above note 149.

[358] Above note 291.

earlier decision, *R. v. Cohn*[359] in 1984, the Court of Appeal found no contradictions between the *Charter* and the essentials of the law of contempt of court. There is a further respect in which contempt is different from other crimes. The contemnor may have an opportunity to make amends for, or "purge", the contempt. If she complies with the order, the breach of which led to her being cited, and/or apologies to the judge involved, the contempt may be expunged.[360]

DEALING WITH MATERIAL THAT MIGHT BECOME EVIDENCE IN A LEGAL PROCEEDING

General Considerations

What are the legal responsibilities of journalists who have in their possession information that they know, or ought reasonably to know, might be sought to be used as evidence in a subsequent proceeding before the courts?

The law is really quite simple and consists of two principles. They are best understood as two poles. The first is that no one is under any legal obligation to assist the police or other authorities in the investigation of any matter. Even if someone were an eye-witness to an absolutely horrifying murder, that person is under no legal obligation to tell anybody about it. That is one pole. The other is that no one may in any way obstruct the police or other authorities in carrying out their duties, including the gathering of evidence during an investigation. It is an indictable offence to obstruct, pervert, or defeat the course of justice.[361]

---

[359] Above note 278. The Supreme Court of Canada refused leave to appeal, suggesting that, at this time, it agreed with the Ontario Court of Appeal.

[360] *Chiang v. Chiang* (2009) 93 O.R. (3d) 483.

[361] *Criminal Code*, s. 139.

Let us make this example as concrete as possible. Someone who has a videotape that clearly shows the commission of a serious criminal offence is under no obligation to bring the existence or contents of that videotape to anyone's attention. If, however, that person destroys the videotape in order to prevent it being used as evidence in a subsequent proceeding, she has committed the offence of obstructing the course of justice.

This issue arises in a number of contexts. One that occurs with some regularity has to do with the use of video outtakes. No legal question can arise with respect to videotape that has been aired, since it thereby enters the public domain. But outtakes, by definition, are not aired.

We could, of course, just as easily be talking about material on audiotapes which is not aired; or photographs, either negatives or contact sheets, which are not actually printed in a newspaper or magazine; or material in notebooks which does not form part of a published story; or obviously, and more and more commonly, information stored in computers which has not been used in stories.

What are a journalist's obligations with respect to all these types of material? To repeat, there is no obligation to inform anybody or bring such matters to anyone's attention. But what must be avoided is destroying or erasing such material under circumstances where it could be alleged that this was done with the purpose of preventing it becoming evidence in a judicial proceeding. How can problems be avoided? The simple answer is to have a standard course of conduct. A standard operating procedure must be established, always followed, and never deviated from. Thus, one would keep video outtakes for a specified period of time and erase them or reuse the tape. If there is a standard course of conduct and it is well known and everybody follows it, then, whenever a question is raised about why a videotape was erased, the answer will be: that is the way it is always done. The management of any media organization should establish clear rules and clear procedures and make sure all employees follow them.

It is worth raising a question about the moral and social, and not simply legal, obligations of journalists. Something that Global Television did in Toronto in 1979 is of interest. There was a demonstration at the headquarters of the Workers' Compensation Board organized by a group called the Union of Injured Workers. For one reason or another the demonstration got out of hand. It turned into a riot and many people were arrested and charged with assaulting police, obstructing police, and so on.

A Global cameraperson shot the riot and, while a fair amount of videotape was aired, a lot of outtakes remained. The network was not clear what to do with them. What it finally decided to do, after much soul-searching and discussion, was organize a public screening. It let this fact be known to everyone who had an interest in the matter, both the police and the accused. People in the media are often reluctant to make material like outtakes generally available because they do not want to be seen as agents of the police, as a part of the investigative apparatus of the state. The interesting thing in the Global case was that, by and large, the video outtakes were more useful to the accused as a means of establishing their innocence than they were to the police.

Searches of Newsrooms

The police can ask permission to search a newsroom and, if someone with the necessary authority agrees to allow them to do so, that is fine.

If, however, an organization or an individual is not prepared to assist the police by consenting to a search, the police can apply for a search warrant. Although searches may be authorized for specific purposes under certain federal and provincial statutes, as a general principle in the investigation of a criminal offence, a non-consensual search by the police of business or residential premises may only be conducted under the authority of a search warrant.[362] A warrant is a document issued by a judicial officer—a justice of the peace—authorizing the search of named premises. It is to be issued only when the justice is satisfied by information given by police on oath that there is in those premises material that is directly relevant to the investigation of an offence.[363]

There is considerable case law that repeats the phrase that search warrants are not to be issued to permit "fishing expeditions." It is definitely not sufficient for the police to go before a justice and say, "We don't really know what is in there, but we would like to go inside and have a look around."

What are the rights and duties of someone working in a newsroom when the police arrive with a search warrant? When executing a warrant to search business premises, the police should initially request entry. If entry is denied, they may force their way in. It is a convention that searches of residential premises should ordinarily be conducted in daylight. However, in the case of a newsroom that operates twenty-four hours a day, it probably does not matter whether the search is conducted in daylight or otherwise.

The person who greets the police officers at the door is entitled to ask to see the search warrant and it should be produced. It is permissible to check the warrant for any obvious defects, such as, for example, the police being at the wrong premises. If, however, there are no patent defects and it appears to be a valid search warrant, there is a legal obligation to get out of the way and let the police proceed with their search. Any attempt after that to oppose or interfere in any way with the officers conducting the search may amount to obstructing. As with

---

[362] See *Canada (Director of Investigation & Research, Combines Investigation Branch)* v. *Southam Inc.*, [1984] 2 S.C.R. 145, and J.A. Fontana, The Law of Search and Seizure in Canada, 3d ed., Toronto, Butterworths, 1992.
[363] *Criminal Code*, s. 487.

the general rule already noted, no one is under any obligation whatsoever to assist the police with their search; but it is unlawful to obstruct them.

A number of suggestions may be made about searches. If it is a television newsroom that is being searched, someone should videotape the search. Whoever is doing this taping should stay physically as far away from the police officers as possible, to avoid any possibility of being charged with assault or obstruction. If the police tell the person videotaping the search to turn the camera off, she is not obliged to comply, so long as she is in no way physically obstructing the search. In the case of a newspaper, it is going to be difficult to videotape a search, but there should be people with cameras around. Somebody should take photographs of the search, again staying as far away from the police officers as possible.

Problems can arise when the police ask for assistance during the course of a search. The first example is a bit dated, but makes the point. The police come to a locked filing cabinet and ask someone to open it. No one is obliged to produce a key and unlock the cabinet. However, the police are entitled, as a general rule, to use reasonable force in executing the search warrant. In these circumstances, that would mean using a crowbar to break open the filing cabinet.

To take another example, there may be a room where video outtakes are kept and the police might ask to see the outtakes from, say, the demonstration that occurred outside the minister's office yesterday. If no one helps the police, they are entitled to use reasonable force to find those outtakes and, if the room ends up trashed, so be it. A more vexed issue, one that has not yet been litigated, could arise if the police were searching for information stored in a computer. Let us say they ask a particular reporter for her access code. Once again she is not obliged to assist. But if the reporter refuses to divulge her access code, the police would be entitled to take the computer with them to allow their technical experts to attempt to figure out the code.

This is the core of the problem. How much inconvenience are principles worth?

What about the constitutionality of searches of newsrooms? One of the effects of the *Charter* has been to turn almost everything into a constitutional issue. In 1991 the Supreme Court decided a case about searches of newsrooms called *Canadian Broadcasting Corp. v. New Brunswick (A.G.).*[364]

The CBC argued two things about such searches, both based on section 2(b) of the *Charter* and its constitutional protection of freedom of the press. The first, and more extreme, position was that newsrooms should be regarded from the perspective of police searches as constitutional no-go areas. Logically, the CBC was arguing that there should be certain premises that are beyond the authority of the state, that the newsroom be regarded as the equivalent of the sanctuary of the medieval church. The Court said no. It is hard to imagine how it could have said anything else. How can any territory in Canada be beyond the jurisdiction of the Canadian state?

The second and more plausible argument the CBC made was based on the 1977 decision of the British Columbia Supreme Court in *Pacific Press Ltd. v. R.*[365]

Pacific Press is the organization that publishes both the Vancouver *Sun* and the Vancouver *Province*. A warrant had been issued authorizing a search of its premises. Lawyers for Pacific Press subsequently challenged the warrant before a court and, as a result, the court laid down two principles about searches of newsrooms. The first was that before a warrant is to be issued authorizing the search of a newsroom, the justice of the peace should be satisfied that there is no reasonable alternative source

[364] [1991] 3 S.C.R. 459.
[365] [1977] 5 W.W.R. 507 (B.C.S.C.).

from which the police might discover the information being sought. This meant that the justice is supposed to be satisfied that the newsroom has to be searched because it is the only place where this particular evidence can be found.

The second principle was that if there was an alternative source, an attempt must already have been made to obtain the information from that source and that attempt must have failed. The apparent result of this decision was that a warrant to search a newsroom would only be issued as a last recourse. But the *Pacific Press* decision was a decision of a trial court. It had been followed occasionally by other courts, and in *Canadian Broadcasting Corp. v. New Brunswick (A.G.)* the Supreme Court was asked to decide that it should be the general rule throughout Canada. The Court declined to do so. The judges said that, while a search of a newsroom gave "rise to special concerns," a newsroom was, at the end of the day, as amenable to a lawful search as any other workplace or, for that matter, residence in Canada.

The Ontario Court of Appeal revisited this question in 2008 in a matter[366] that raised questions both of searches and of journalistic privilege. In 2001 a reporter with the *National Post* received a document that purported to be the authorisation of a loan from the Business Development Bank of Canada to an undertaking in which then Prime Minister Jean Chretien was said to have an interest. The document became the subject of a police investigation both because of what it was claimed to reveal about the Prime Minister's financial dealings and because the Business Development Bank of Canada asserted that it was a forgery.

The reporter took the sensible course of action of placing the document in a secure location away from the newspaper's office. The subsequent litigation raised a host of issues. The question of special rules governing searches of newsrooms was dismissed

---

[366] *R. v. National Post* (2008) 89 O.R. (3d) 1.

quickly and briefly, the Court noting that the guarantee of freedom expression in s. 2(b) of the Charter:

> ...does not mean that press organisations or journalists are immune from valid searches under s.8 of the Charter.[367]

The Court expressly declined to rule on the existence, or otherwise, of journalistic privilege. The National Post appealed this decision to the Supreme Court of Canada. The Supreme Court released its decision[368] on 7 May 2010. The decision was very careful and very Canadian. As is often the case with Supreme Court decisions, there was a substantial number of intervenants. The judges affirmed that "...in appropriate circumstances, courts will respect a promise of confidentiality given to a secret source by a journalist" and that "...The public interest in being informed must be balanced against other important public interests, including the investigation of crime".

The court confirmed the equivocal jurisprudence that has recently been developing concerning journalistic privilege and searches of media premises. Concerning the question of privilege, the judges seemed to prefer the adoption of a middle ground between recognising a broad privilege and compelling disclosure, concluding that:

> A judicial order to compel disclosure of a secret source will not necessarily violate s. 2(b).

In addition, while there was no class privilege with respect to journalists, such claims should be dealt with on a case by case basis through the application of Wigmore's four criteria. The journalist

---

[367] Ibid., at p.19.
[368] R. v. National Post [2010] 1 S.C.R. 477.

claiming privilege would have the burden of proving that all four criteria had been met in her case.

As a general matter, the judges were convinced that:

> No journalist may give a secret source an absolute assurance of confidentiality.

Madam Justice Abella dissented, holding that:

> ...use of confidential sources can be an integral part of the responsible gathering of the news and the communication of matters of public interest.

On the question of searches, the Court believed that:

> ...the issuance of a warrant to search media premises was 'a particularly serious intrusion'.

While the issuance of warrants for such searches was permissible, the Court was concerned about issuing them *ex parte,* cautioning that an *ex parte* hearing could only be justified where there were "urgent circumstances". The judges were convinced that the media should be given the time and the opportunity to challenge warrants. The position that emerges from the Supreme Court's decision is deeply equivocal:[369] there may or there may not be journalistic privilege; and, while warrants may be issued for the search of media premises, some special considerations may apply. Turning to the specifics of the proceeding, the warrant for the search of the premises of the *National Post* and the assistance order made against it were both upheld.

The Supreme Court of Canada revisited the question of

---

[369] The National Post, itself, was both aware of, and concerned about the equivocal nature of the decision. See, editorial, *A bittersweet day for Press Freedom*, National Post, 8 May 2010.

journalistic privilege in October of 2010.[370] The litigation arose out of what had come to be known as the "sponsorship scandal" involving the government of Prime Minister Jean Chretien. A *Globe and Mail* reporter, Leblanc, had written articles, based on leaked information, about the matter.

During the course of litigation an attempt was made to require Leblanc to reveal details about this information. He claimed journalist-source privilege and the question wound up before the Supreme Court of Canada. The Court found that such a privilege could not be grounded in the guarantee of freedom of expression in s.2(b) of the *Charter*, nor was it willing to expand the category approach to embrace the journalist-source relation.

Under the analysis formulated by the Court, the party seeking the disclosure of such information would be required, initially, to satisfy the court that the information being sought was both relevant and necessary. At this point, a judge would turn to the Wigmore analysis, the "crucial" part of which was the fourth criterion which required "balancing the importance of disclosure to the administration of justice against the public interesting maintaining journalist-source confidentiality". In attempting to achieve this balance, a judge was to look at five factors:

the stage of the proceeding at which the claim to privilege was raised;

the centrality of the issue to the dispute;

whether the journalist is a party to the dispute, or simply a witness;

whether the facts, information or testimony are available by any other means; and

the degree of public importance of the journalist's story and whether the story has been published and is already in the public

---

[370] *Globe and Mail* v. *Canada (Attorney General)* (2010) 325 D.L.R.(4th) 193.

domain.

Lebel, J. elaborated further, noting that the burden of proving that a particular case is one for the application of journalist-source privilege rests with journalist claiming it, who must satisfy the court that:

> she was performing the work of a journalist;
> the source requested anonymity and she agreed to protect the source's identity;
> the protection has not been waived;
> the questions put to the journalist, if answered, would disclose the identity of the source; and
> the prejudice thereby caused to freedom of the press would outweigh any prejudice to the fairness of the trial.

The law concerning both publication bans and journalistic privilege is now to be found in two sets of conjoined Supreme Court of Canada decisions: *Dagenais / Mentuck* and *National Post / Globe and Mail.*

The *Criminal Code* was recently amended to allow for the issuance of what is called a tele-warrant.[371] This means that the police do not have to be physically present before the justice of the peace for a warrant to be issued. They can telephone a justice and tell her the basis on which they are seeking a warrant. Furthermore, since the justice is not able physically to issue the warrant, what results is not a traditional warrant signed and sealed by the justice, but something called a *facsimile* warrant. People working in newsrooms are entitled to ask to see the warrant, but what they are shown may be a facsimile warrant. That is still a real warrant.

Tele-warrants were devised to deal with organized crime and

---

[371] *Criminal Code*, ss. 487.1 and 487.2, as am. by S.C. 1995, c. 44.

with drug trafficking, when it is a matter of every second counting, when the police know that if they have to wait two hours to get into a certain place, the evidence they are looking for might be destroyed. It seems difficult to imagine those considerations applying to the search of a newsroom. An attempt might be made to litigate whether or not newsrooms can properly be searched on the basis of tele-warrants.

Taking Photographs or Videotapes against the Instructions of the Police

Section 129(a) of the *Criminal Code* makes it an offence wilfully to obstruct "a public officer or peace officer in the execution of his duty or any person lawfully acting in aid of such an officer." For someone to be convicted of this offence, the Crown must show that there was an obstruction that to some degree interfered with a police officer in carrying out the task she was engaged in and, further, that the accused did the obstructing intentionally.

Persons taking photographs for the media have been convicted of this offence for refusing to obey police instructions. In one case the conviction seems to have been based largely on the fact that the photographer entered an area from which the public had been excluded as a security measure during the visit of the leader of another state.[372]

In another, the police asked a photographer to stop taking pictures of a psychiatric patient they were moving to hospital. He continued taking photographs. He was convicted of obstructing largely because his presence was causing the patient to become agitated, thereby making the task of the police more difficult.[373]

These cases suggest that some degree of direct or indirect physical interference with the police will be necessary before a

---

[372] *Knowlton v. R.*, [1974] S.C.R. 443.
[373] *R. v. Kalnins* (1978), 41 C.C.C. (2d) 524 (Ont. Co. Ct.).

conviction can result. The obvious answer for photographers in such situations is to stay physically well away from the police.

FURTHER READING

No Canadian monograph deals exclusively and systematically with contempt of court. Two useful works that provide general background are S. M. Robertson, *Courts and the Media,* Toronto, Butterworths, 1981, and P. Anisman and A. M. Linden, eds, *The Media, the Courts, and the Charter,* Toronto, Carswell, 1986. Both are somewhat dated, particularly the Robertson book, which was published before the *Charter* became part of the Constitution.

CHAPTER 4

Free Expression and Private Rights

SO FAR WE have looked at limitations on freedom of
expression which are imposed by the state in order to further
some state purpose. In this chapter we change the focus, at least
somewhat. Although the limitations we will look at arise out of
the law of the state, they operate as means whereby individuals
may enforce private rights against other individuals.

The difficult task confronting the courts in civil libel actions is
to find an appropriate and socially acceptable means of balancing
the competing interests of freedom of expression and the
protection of the reputations of individuals. Frederick Schauer, a
leading U.S. commentator on libel, put the matter this way:

> *The law of defamation in a society reflects...the
> assumptions of that society respecting the relative
> importance of an untarnished reputation, on the one
> hand, and an uninhibited press on the other.* [374]

We will spend the bulk of the chapter investigating the law of civil

---

[374] F. Schauer, *Social Foundations of the Law of Defamation: A Comparative
Analysis*, (1980) 1 (3) Journal of Media Law and Practice 19. For a
Canadian view of these matters see Denis W. Boivin, *Accommodating
Freedom of Expression and Reputation in the Common Law of Defamation*,
(1996) 22 Queen's Law Journal 229.

libel and then analyse the extent, if any, to which an individual right to privacy is recognized.

CIVIL LIBEL

In the Canadian legal system there is both civil libel and criminal libel. We have already noted the three forms of criminal libel (see chapter 2, section C). The law of civil libel is part of the law of torts[375]. Torts addresses civil wrongs, or, to put it slightly differently, non-criminal injuries. By and large, the law of torts consists of legal mechanisms whereby people can seek redress for losses they have suffered as a result of the unlawful conduct of others. In a practical sense, the law of torts today is very much the law of car accidents.

The English law of torts is called torts in the plural for a reason. There is a series of different torts, each of which has different rules and its own complexities. This is especially true of libel, which is a complicated business and often difficult to understand. It is also a matter about which most lawyers do not know a great deal, for the simple reason that libel actions are not common.

What are the effects on individual journalists of being involved in a libel action? Many lawyers would regard publishing a contempt of court as a far more serious matter than publishing a libel, but from the perspective of an individual reporter or editor

---

[375] The law of torts belongs, for division of powers purposes, to the subject matter "property and civil rights in the province" and is, thus, a matter within provincial jurisdiction. Consequently, the law of civil libel may vary from one province to another. The province of Quebec does not have specific provisions concerning defamation and, thus, such matters are to be dealt with according to the general principles governing delictual liability. *Prud'homme* v. *Prud'homme* [2002] 4 S.C.R. 663.

the opposite may be true. Few things can do more to ruin a journalist's reputation than to write stories that lead to libel actions, especially libel actions that employers lose. The journalist gets a reputation as someone who is not thorough, but is sloppy, inaccurate, and so on. Libel can have exceedingly serious consequences for the career of a journalist.

Traditionally, the broad tort we are dealing with has been called defamation. Defamation is an unusual and unique tort. It is unique in that the behaviour of the tortfeasor, exercising freedom of expression, is both socially desirable and constitutionally protected.[376]

It should be stressed that, despite widespread popular belief in its existence, there is no such thing as "defamation of character."

Defamation was subdivided into two further categories called slander and libel. In the traditional definition, slander consisted of purely spoken words—words that emerged from someone's mouth, but were never reduced to any other form; libel, in contrast, was said to consist of written or printed words. That distinction has been overtaken by technological change. Although slander still means purely spoken words, libel embraces words or images that have been reduced to a permanent or potentially permanent form. Permanent or potentially permanent form includes not only written or printed words but material on film (both movie film and still film), audiotape, videotape, computer disks, and hard drives.[377] Quite different rules govern libel actions and slander actions. We will say nothing more about slander as such, because anyone can slander anyone else and the tort is thus

---

[376] This idea comes from discussions with a former student, John Simpson.

[377] In Roger D. McConchie and David A. Potts, *Canadian Libel and Slander Actions*, Toronto, Irwin Law, 2004, the authors have based the distinction on the word "transitory": "libel" takes on a "non-transitory" form, while "slander" is "transitory". (p. 9).

of no particular interest to journalists.

Some of the common law provinces—Manitoba, for example—have abolished the distinction between libel and slander and simply have one tort called defamation. Other common law provinces, such as Ontario, maintain the distinction. Henceforth, we will deal purely with libel, although the words "libel" and "defamation," or "libellous" and "defamatory", may be used as if they were interchangeable.

Two broad introductory points must be made about libel law. The first is that it applies to everything that a newspaper or broadcaster publishes, publish being used in the widest possible sense. With newspapers for example, the law of libel applies not only to news stories or editorial columns, but to literally everything that is in the newspaper. It applies to letters to the editor, to editorial cartoons and to classified advertisements. It applies to material that comes from sources outside the paper—wire stories, syndicated columns, and syndicated features. The law of libel can even apply to the way a newspaper is laid out. If someone puts the wrong cut line on a photograph, she may thereby have created a libel. You might have a story that is perfectly harmless and a head that is also perfectly accurate and harmless, but the way the page is laid out may create a libellous impression.

Let us say there is a story on page one about a pillar of the community, loved, honoured, and respected and, in particular, the retirement dinner held to honour this noble human being. There is an accompanying photograph of this person. On the same page, with a much bigger head, there is a story about a convicted child molester. The page is, unfortunately, laid out so that the huge head about the child molester looks as if it refers to the photograph depicting the pillar of the community. That is a libel. Even though each constituent element on the page, viewed independently of every other element, may be fine, the way the whole page has been put together can create an impression that is libellous. The same principle, slightly amended, applies to television. The words in a script may be absolutely innocent and no libellous imputation would be conveyed to anyone who read those words to herself. But the announcer who actually reads the script over the air may deliver it in a tone of voice that creates a libel. The visuals, or the music that is used, or the background, or the way different parts of a television story have been edited together may, nonetheless, create a libellous impression. Whether one is talking about broadcasting or newspapers, every single element of what has been published or any combination of those elements can become the subject of a libel action.

The court in *Myers v. C.B.C.*[378] engaged in a lengthy discussion of the factors to be considered in determining whether a television program was defamatory. The Court observed:

> *Because of the audio-visual nature of the television medium, the entire thrust and effect of the program— that is to say, the overall impression—in addition to the accuracy of the statements, is relevant,*[379]

and continued,

> *...simply because there are both visual and auditory aspects to television does not mean that one does not still look to the actual words used.*

Indeed, if

> *...the content of these words is not distorted by the audio-visual aspects of the broadcast, they should be deemed the primary conveyor of a programme's*

---

[378] (1999) 47 C.C.L.T. (2d) 272 (Ont. Sup. Ct.).
[379] *Ibid.* at 289.

meaning.[380]

Amongst the factors a court should look to are: "voice intonation, visual background, facial expression, gestures, background effects, scenery, music or images."[381] The court also recognised that:

> ...*although innocent words are used, a person [may be] held up to the most flagrant ridicule and contempt.*[382]

The second important general point to be noted is that, regardless of the source of a piece of information or an opinion, whoever publishes it is responsible for it. A radio station is responsible for everything that is aired by that station. A newspaper is responsible for everything that appears in its pages. Let us say that there is a libel in a wire story supplied by a news service. It may well be that the person who claims to have been libelled could sue the news service, but that is not the point. Any newspaper that publishes the story is responsible for it. The same is true for letters to the editor. The newspaper that publishes the letter can be held accountable in a libel action. A plaintiff may have choices about whom to sue, but that is not relevant now. The simple point is that anyone who publishes libellous material is legally responsible for it.

How would a libel action actually unfold? The first actor in a libel action, as indeed in any civil action, is the plaintiff. In civil actions the plaintiff not only instigates the proceeding, but has the burden of proof—the obligation of proving the case. In that sense, civil actions are analogous to criminal actions, though in criminal actions it is the Crown that initiates the proceedings and has the burden of proving that the accused is guilty. In libel cases, the

---

[380] *Ibid.* at 290.

[381] *Ibid.*

[382] *Ibid.*

plaintiff, the person who claims to have been libelled, initiates the action and has the burden of proving that she was indeed libelled.

The Plaintiff's Case

As was stated in *Hodgson v. Canadian Newspapers Co.*,[383] "...the plaintiff must prove three elements:

    i)   that the words complained of were published;

    ii) that the words complained of refer to the plaintiff;

    iii) that the words complained of, in their natural and ordinary meaning, or in some pleaded extended meaning, are defamatory of the plaintiff."[384]

We will look at each element in turn, although not quite in this order.

Defamatory

The first thing the plaintiff has to prove is that the material in question—the novel, the classified ad, the letter to the editor, the news story—was defamatory. What does that mean? I will quickly run through four definitions that are found in the cases, suggest that these definitions are not really helpful, and set out what I think is a more useful practical definition.

Material is said, first, to be defamatory if it would tend to lower the plaintiff in the estimation of right-thinking people generally. In determining whether a particular statement is defamatory:

> ...the statement is judged by the standard of an

---

[383] (1998) 39 O.R. (3d) 235.

[384] *Ibid.* at 248.

ordinary right-thinking member of society...the standard of what constitutes a reasonable or ordinary member of the public is difficult to articulate. It should not be so low as to stifle free expression unduly, nor so high as to imperil the ability to protect the integrity of a person's reputation. The impressions about the content of any broadcast—or written statement— should be assessed from the perspective of someone reasonable, that is, a person who is reasonably thoughtful and informed, rather than someone with an overly fragile sensibility. A degree of common sense must be attributed to viewers [and readers]. [385]

Second, material is said to be defamatory if it would tend to cause the plaintiff to be shunned or avoided.

Material is, on the third definition, defamatory if it would tend to expose the plaintiff to hatred, ridicule, or contempt. Notice the use of the verb "tend" in all those definitions. This points up an integral feature of libel actions—the plaintiff is not required to prove any actual injury. The plaintiff does not have to prove she was *actually* lowered in the estimation of right-thinking people generally, which would, presumably, involve getting a host of right-thinking people and bringing them into the courtroom as witnesses to say: "I saw that piece and it lowered the plaintiff in my estimation."

The plaintiff is required only to establish that the material at the basis of the action had that *tendency*. This is a remarkable feature of libel actions, as compared with other tort actions, where the plaintiff is required to prove injury. Once it is established that the material is libellous, injury to the plaintiff is assumed.

---

[385] *Color Your World Corp. v. C.B.C.* (1998) 156 D.L.R. (4th) 27 (Ont. C.A.).

The fourth definition, which takes a different tack, is that a libel is a false statement about a person to that person's discredit. It is not merely that a statement about someone is untrue, but that it is untrue *and* to that person's discredit.

All these definitions are far too abstract. I want to suggest a more practical approach, practical in the sense that it can be helpful in alerting working journalists early on that there might be a problem with a particular story. With this approach, a libel is simply something you would not like to see said in public about yourself. If a journalist is going to say something in print or over the air about somebody else that she would not like to have said about herself, then the first early warning bell should go off. This warning says there is a need to be careful with this story, to devote special care or attention to it.

We now turn to some decided cases that may assist in giving a better sense of when material is defamatory and when it is not. The first of these is *Brannigan v. S.I.U.*,[386] a case from British Columbia. One of the many interesting points about Canadian libel law is that the bulk of the reported cases come from British Columbia, which appears to be the country's libel capital.

In the 1950s, Canada still had an ocean-going merchant marine. Canadian vessels carried Canadian flags as they sailed the seas. The sailors who sailed in these ships belonged to a union called the Canadian Seamen's Union, a radical union with ties to the Labour Progressive Party, the communist party of the day. The government of Canada decided to smash this union and invited an American gangster, Hal Banks, to come to Canada to carry out the task. He arrived in Canada ostensibly to promote his own union, the Seafarers' International Union. A struggle between the SIU and CSU ensued. There was a great deal of violence and unpleasantness, but by the early 1960s it was over. The Canadian Seamen's Union was crushed, the SIU was

---

[386] (1963), 42 D.L.R. (2d) 249 (B.C.S.C.).

dominant, and in the process the Canadian merchant marine largely disappeared. *Brannigan* is a minor footnote to the whole business. The Seafarers' International Union published a magazine called *Canadian Sailor*. Brannigan, the plaintiff, belonged not to the CSU, but to a union with close ties to it, and itself a radical union, the Canadian Brotherhood of Railway, Transport, and General Workers. In the August 1961 edition of *Canadian Sailor* there was a piece about Brannigan. The sting of the piece was that Brannigan was a communist. He sued the SIU for libel. The key issue was whether it was libellous to call Brannigan a communist. The difficulty in answering this question arises out of the fact that there have been times and places where not only was it not libellous to call a trade unionist a communist, but it was positively complimentary. So how does one resolve the issue?

The court said that the question must not be addressed in the air, in the abstract. It must be addressed concretely. The court looked at the time, the place, and the circumstances under which these statements were published to determine whether they were defamatory or not. The context had to be looked at. What was the context in which these statements were made about Brannigan? It was Canada in 1961 when the Cold War was raging. More particularly, there was a battle going on between two hostile trade unions. The court concluded, looking at the time, the place, and the circumstances, that it was libellous to call Brannigan a communist. To put the same issue in a contemporary perspective, would it be libellous in 2012 to say that someone was gay or lesbian?[387]

Libel is said to be a tort of strict liability. The defendant's intention as to whether the statements complained of were to be interpreted as defamatory or not is irrelevant. It is absolutely beside the point for the defendant to argue that she did not intend

---

[387] This issue is discussed in Bruce MacDougall, *Outing: The Law Reacts to Speech about Homosexuality*, (1996) 21 Queen's Law Journal 79.

the statements to be defamatory. This is illustrated in another case from British Columbia, *Murphy v. LaMarsh.*[388]

Judy LaMarsh was a minister in various Pearson governments throughout the 1960s. In 1968 she published a book of political reminiscences, *Memoirs of a Bird in a Gilded Cage.* In her book she made certain references to Ed Murphy, a journalist whom she obviously did not like. The assertion that led to the libel action was the following:

> *[a] brash young radio reporter, named Ed Murphy (heartily detested by most of the Press Gallery and the members)."*

At the material time Murphy was a member of the Parliamentary Press Gallery in Ottawa. LaMarsh was asserting that he was "heartily detested" by most of the reporters with whom he worked in the Gallery and by the members of Parliament. Murphy sued. The court decided that it was not libellous to call someone "brash". The central issue was whether it was libellous to say that Murphy was "heartily detested" by most of the Press Gallery and the MPs.

LaMarsh was crafty and called as expert witnesses at the trial two well-known Canadian journalists of the time, Charles Lynch and Jack Webster. Each testified that neither of these assertions was libellous and, in fact, that both were complimentary. Why was Murphy heartily detested by most of the reporters with whom he worked in the Press Gallery? Well, obviously, because they spent all their time drinking in the Press Club and schmoozing with politicians. They were not doing their work, but Murphy was constantly out getting the good stories and so his fellow reporters were jealous of him. Likewise, MPs heartily

---

[388] (1970), 13 D.L.R. (3d) 484 (B.C.S.C.), aff'd [1971] 18 D.L.R. (3d) 208 (B.C.C.A.).

detested Murphy because they knew that he was always producing the great stories, finding the skeletons in the closets, and so on. Both expert witnesses said that whatever they might look like on the surface, neither statement was libellous of Murphy.

The court disagreed. The court said the proper perspective to adopt was not that of the defendant. In fact, what the defendant might have intended was quite beside the point. Equally, the standpoint was not that of someone like Lynch or Webster, with specialized or inside knowledge. The standard by which to measure whether these assertions were defamatory was that of the ordinary reader. The court said the question to be asked was:

> What would an ordinary person, reading that Ed Murphy was heartily detested by most of his fellow workers and the people about whom he wrote, think of Ed Murphy?

Phrased that way, the answer to the question is obvious. The ordinary reader would think there was something wrong with him. It is not the intention of the defendant that determines whether statements are defamatory or not, it is the way the ordinary listener, ordinary viewer or reader would interpret them.

Thomas v. Canadian Broadcasting Corp.[389] had to do with an investigative report aired on CBC Radio. The background was that Dome Petroleum had been exploring for oil in the Arctic under the Beaufort Sea. Exploring for oil under the seabed was, and is, a complicated and expensive business. First, in order to be permitted to carry out exploration, Dome Petroleum had to have a licence from what was then the Department of Indian Affairs and Northern Development. The licence was quite specific and, in particular, it dealt with what was called "[s]ecuring the [drill]

_____

[389] (1981), 27 A.R. 547 (N.W.T.S.C.).

casing." Exploring for oil in this fashion did not simply involve sticking the drill bit into the seabed and making a hole. It was necessary to secure the sides of the hole in order to give it stability. Dome's initial licence said that it had to secure the hole by creating a concrete sleeve around it down to a depth of 10,000 feet below the seabed. Obviously, that would have been extremely expensive, and after Dome had begun drilling it applied for an amendment to its original licence so that it would be required to secure the casing down only to 4000 feet. The amendment was approved. Sometime later there was an explosion at the site and, as a result, one worker was killed. Those are the basic facts. CBC Radio did some investigation and produced a piece. The point of this piece, and what the case addressed, is that the CBC strongly suspected that the villain in the whole affair was a civil servant working for the Department of Indian Affairs and Northern Development, Maurice Thomas, but it did not quite have proof. In the report, the CBC hinted at certain conclusions about Thomas, without coming out and saying them directly.

In its script the CBC set out the basic background to the story and then, with regard to the amendment to the drilling authority, said that it was approved "without any long examination." It is interesting to think about those words. What exactly does the phrase "without any long examination" mean? It does not mean anything, in fact, but seems to carry a sinister implication. The script continued. Reference was made to the explosion:

> Securing the casing with cement all the way down to 10,000 feet would also likely have prevented the gas problems which led to the explosion that killed data engineer, George Ross MacKay.

And a bit further on the script noted that there had been an inquest into the whole matter, but stated, "None of these facts were presented to the inquest jury last month." Then the script quoted somebody from an organization called the Committee for Original Peoples Entitlement saying, "[T]he government is not able to regulate Dome."

If you take those four statements—approved "without any long examination," "would also likely have prevented the gas problems," "none of these facts were presented to the inquest," "the government is not able to regulate Dome"—none of them directly asserts anything libellous about Maurice Thomas.

But what was being implied was that Thomas was at best incompetent and more likely on the payroll of Dome Petroleum while he was supposed to be working for the government of Canada. His corruption or incompetence was the direct cause of the explosion that led to someone's death, and he then tried to cover the whole thing up. Though unpleasant implications about Thomas are suggested, nowhere does the script actually say anything bad about him. In libel, implications of this kind are called innuendo—beating around the bush, hinting at things.

The simple point, which this case makes clear, is that hinting at something is just as culpable as coming right out and saying it. Journalists should never waste their time beating around the bush or coyly suggesting conclusions. If a reporter does not have all the details of the story verified, she should not try to make up for the gaps in it by hinting at things. Either have the story and say it straight out, or stick to the material that is actually available.

Reference to the Plaintiff

The second element in the plaintiff's case is that she must prove that the allegedly defamatory material refers to her. Libel is said to be a personal action. A plaintiff sues because her personal reputation has been attacked. The plaintiff is thus legally obliged to establish that the libel specifically identifies her. We will look now at some of the complications that can arise.

We begin with a charming old English case, *E. Hulton & Co. v. Jones*,[390] from 1910. This had to do with a provincial newspaper, the *Sunday Chronicle*, which did a piece about the scandalous behaviour of English tourists holidaying at Dieppe. This is what the paper said about the behaviour of some of these tourists.

> *Upon the terrace marches the world, attracted by the motor races—a world immensely pleased with itself, and minded to draw a wealth of inspiration—and, incidentally, of golden cocktails—from any scheme to speed the passing hour.... 'Whist! there is Artemus Jones with a woman who is not his wife, who must be, you know—the other thing!' whispers a fair neighbour of mine excitedly into her bosom friend's ear. Really, is it not surprising how certain of our fellow-countrymen behave when they come abroad? Who would suppose, by his goings on, that he was a churchwarden at Peckham?*

The clear suggestion in the story is that Artemus Jones is a fictitious name, but, unfortunately for the paper, a real person called Artemus Jones came along and sued it. (In 2012 in Canada it would probably not be regarded as libellous to say these things about someone, but clearly in England in 1910 it was libellous.)

The paper's response was to say to the plaintiff, "We were not talking about you. We did not mean to refer to you." But the defendant ran into the problem of libel being a tort of strict liability. The defendant could not argue that it did not mean to refer to this plaintiff. The question was not the intention of the defendant, but rather whether readers of the *Sunday Chronicle* who knew Artemus Jones could reasonably conclude that he was the one being referred to in this article. The court took the view that, since there were not many people called Artemus Jones, people

---

[390] [1910] A.C. 22 (H.L.).

who did know the real Artemus Jones could reasonably conclude that he was the one being referred to.

There is a standard disclaimer regularly seen in movies and novels—"All characters and events depicted in this novel (or film) are fictitious, no reference to any person living or dead is intended," and so on. This disclaimer is meaningless. It is an attempt on the part of publishers of novels and producers of movies unilaterally to absolve themselves of any liability.

In 1932 M.G.M. released a movie called *Rasputin and the Empress*. The movie is memorable for two reasons, first, because it gave rise to the litigation known as *Youssoupoff* v. *Metro-Goldwyn-Mayer Pictures Ltd.*[391] and, second, because it was the one time Ethel, John and Lionel Barrymore appeared on-screen together.

The movie purported to be about an ostensibly fictional kingdom that existed in Eastern Europe before and during the First World War. In this fictional kingdom there was a fictional royal family that lived in a fictional palace. The fictional queen had a fictional son who suffered from haemophilia. The queen spent an inordinate amount of time worrying about the survival of her son and tried all sorts of devices and remedies to cure him of this disease.

She became a bit crazy as a result and, at one point, a fictional mad monk appeared and moved into the royal family's palace, claiming he could cure the son. While he was living in the palace, this mad monk spent an evening in the company of a fictional princess to whom he fed large amounts of alcohol and whom he eventually seduced and, perhaps, more accurately, raped. A real prince who had been a member of a real royal family in a real kingdom in Eastern Europe and who was married to the real princess just referred to, saw the movie and sued MGM. It is an interesting comment on society in the U.K. in the 1930s that a man could claim he had been libelled because a movie suggested

---

[391] (1934), 50 T.L.R. 581 (C.A.).

his wife had been seduced by another man many years previously, before they were married. MGM said the movie was just a work of fiction, a fairytale. The English court, however, said that what MGM might have intended was beside the point. Persons who knew the real princess could reasonably conclude that she was the one being depicted. Thus, she had been sufficiently identified and her current husband could maintain a libel action.

This question of reference to the plaintiff reinforces the notion that defamation is a tort of strict liability. It is, as a result, not open to a defendant to say, "I had no intention of referring to the plaintiff. It is no defence to show that the defendant did not intend to defame the plaintiff."[392] The court in *Yousoupoff* elaborated further on this point, saying:

> ...though the person who writes and publishes the libel may not intend to libel a particular person and, indeed, has never heard of that particular person, the plaintiff, yet, if evidence is produced that reasonable people knowing some of the circumstances, not necessarily all, would take the libel complained of to refer to the plaintiff, an action for libel will lie.[393]

Furthermore, it is not necessary that the defendant specifically identify the plaintiff. The court in *Youssoupoff* added:

> Although the defendants did not use the name of the plaintiff, they used a description of her that could apply to no-one but the plaintiff.[394] (It would be useful to substitute "plaintiff's wife" for "plaintiff" in most of the preceding passages.)

---

[392] *Ibid.* at 582.
[393] *Ibid.* at 583.
[394] *Ibid.* at 585.

An interesting question of social and legal policy which arises here involves the extent to which Canadian law does and should recognize group defamation. If you assert that all lawyers are thieves and scoundrels, can I, as a lawyer, sue you? Does your assertion identify me to a sufficient degree to permit me to maintain a libel action against you? The answer is no. Simply belonging to a group about which defamatory statements have been made is not sufficient to entitle any individual member of that group to maintain an action. The plaintiff must be personally identified. If you say that all Fantasians are horse-thieves, the mere fact that I happen to be a Fantasian is not enough. The obvious question, then, is what degree of identification is required?

A case from British Columbia illustrates the point nicely.[395] In the early 1980s BCTV did a public affairs piece about street crime in Vancouver. As part of this piece there were various interviews with people on the streets—"streeters" in the jargon of the trade. In one of these interviews, reporters talked to someone whom they identified as a prostitute and asked her about police corruption. The key question put to her was whether she could name police officers actually involved in corruption. Her response, which was aired, was:

> Oh I could—yeah—but I'm not gonna name them— cause that would just get me up a creek without a paddle—but there is, I'd say three on the Morality Squad that are quite high for payoffs and I know two on the Narc Squad that are high up—right up on top that take payoffs, and there's a few other ones on—like Traffic—you know they're special squads that take some.

---

[395] *Booth v. British Columbia Television Broadcasting System* (1983), 139 D.L.R. (3d) 88 (B.C.C.A.).

These words led to a libel action. In order to understand what happened, we have to know the organization of the narcotics squad of the Vancouver police force. The squad was organized into two groups, one called the "undercover subgroup" and the other the "trafficking subgroup." Each group was headed by a senior police officer, and then within it were various ordinary police officers.

Eleven members of the narcotics squad of the Vancouver police force sued BCTV. Of these, one was the head of the undercover street group, one was the head of the trafficking group, and the other nine plaintiffs were ordinary police officers. The court dismissed the actions of these nine ordinary officers on the ground that none of them had been sufficiently identified as an individual, but upheld the actions of the head of the undercover group and the head of the trafficking group. Why?—because of the words: "I know two on the Narc Squad that are high up—right up on top." The court said these words were sufficient to identify these two plaintiffs as individuals; that reasonable persons who knew them could conclude that they were the ones being referred to.

Thirty years ago a libel action was started at the Carleton University Journalism School. A group of female journalism students held a press conference and said that male professors in the journalism school were sexually harassing female students. There were at the time about a dozen male professors in the school. Three of them launched a libel action. It was eventually settled, but, had it gone to trial, the issue would have been whether the assertion that male journalism professors sexually harassed female students sufficiently identified any individual plaintiff. One of the crucial factors with this question is going to be the size of the group referred to. If there had been only three male journalism professors at Carleton and all three had sued, they would probably have succeeded, but, on the facts of this case, the group was likely too large and there was insufficient identification of any individual for him to be able to maintain an action. The larger the group being referred to, the less likely it is that any individual member of that group will have been sufficiently identified.

A useful structure for analysing this question is set out in *Butler* v. *Southam Inc.*[396]

The largest group, the members of which have been permitted to maintain a libel action, is twelve. In *R. v. Vancouver Province*[397] a writer was convicted of scandalising the court in respect of a highly critical piece he had written about a murder trial. The piece contained extreme criticism of both the judge and the jury at the trial. Members of the jury, none of whom was identified by name in the piece, successfully sued the paper for libel.[398]

Canada today is, as I see it, a country much afflicted by what, or so it seems to me, can only be characterised as pseudo-history. Before beginning an analysis of pseudo-history, it will be useful to quote Orwell's famous dictum from his novel, *1984*:

> *Who controls the past controls the future. Who controls
> the present controls the past.*

An important characteristic of pseudo-history is the subordination of history to propaganda.[399] The eminent Canadian historian, Margaret MacMillan, has been critical of history in the service of

---

[396] (2001) 197 N.S.R. (2 d) 97 (C.A.).

[397] [1954] 3 D.L.R. 690 (B.C.S.C.). See chapter 3, section B(a)(i).

[398] *MacKay v. Southam Co.* (1955) 1 D.L.R. (2d) 1 (B.C.C.A.).

[399] See Robert Martin, *The Meteoric Rise and Precipitous Fall of Clara Brett Martin: Thoughts on the Misuse of History*, (1995) 4 Inroads 182. Martin Loney described much of what is taught in our universities under the rubric "history" as a "caricatured view of Canada". *The Pursuit of Division,* Montreal and Kingston, McGill-Queen's University Press, 1998 at p. 289.

ideology, noting that:

> ...the story they tell is at once breathtakingly simple
> and all-encompassing. Every event is fitted into the
> grand account and all is explained.[400]

The Australian, Keith Windschuttle is a leading critic of pseudo-history in that country. In his book, *The Fabrication of Aboriginal History, Volume Three, The Stolen Generations 1881-2008*[401], he wrote of:

> ...creative interpretations of selected evidence taken out
> of context by politically motivated historians.[402]

That assertion appears to me to present a solid, practical definition of the technique of pseudo-history. Judging the past by the standards of the present is both a defining characteristic and the primary methodological error of pseudo-history.[403] A discussion of pseudo-history in Canada is important and relevant, since, as I understand these matters, pseudo-history constitutes a significant part of the foundation upon which much of the apparatus of

---

[400] Margaret MacMillan, *The Uses and Abuses of History*, Toronto, Viking Canada, 2008, p. 64.

[401] Paddington, NSW, Macleay Press, 2009. For interesting commentary on this book, see Roger Sandall, *Aboriginal Sin?*, (2010) 28 The New Criterion, no.10, 75.

[402] Windschuttle, *op. cit.* p.1.

[403] Kathryn Blaze Carlson, *What happens when the heroes of the past meet the standards of today?*, National Post, 14 May 2011. L.P. Hartley's well-known dictum is highly relevant at this point. "The past is a foreign country: they do things differently there." *The Go-Between*, New York, New York Review Books, 2002. Although Hartley was a novelist rather than an historian, it would be well for historians to bear his assertion in mind.

repression, discussed in Chapter 5, has been constructed and is, often, justified.

Pascal Bruckner's powerful work *The Tyranny of Guilt: An Essay on Western Masochism*[404] may be viewed as a sustained and systematic attack on pseudo-history. The work might be characterised as a scathing indictment of the way in which an entire civilisation has come close to destroying itself by accepting, as he sees it, a grossly distorted caricature of its own history.

Bruckner noted:

> *From existentialism to deconstructionism, all of modern thought can be reduced to a mechanical denunciation of the West, emphasizing the latter's hypocrisy, violence and abomination.*[405]

He continued on Europe:

> *Ruminating on its past abominations—wars, religious persecutions, slavery, imperialism, fascism, communism—it views its history as nothing more than a series of massacres and sackings that led to two world wars...*[406]

and concluded:

> *Our past crimes command us to keep our mouths closed. Our only right is to remain silent.*[407]

> *The 1966 Report of the Cohen Committee (Special*

---

[404] Princeton, New Jersey, Princeton University Press, 2010.

[405] *Ibid.,* at p.2.

[406] *Ibid.,* at p.6

[407] *Ibid.,* at p.3

[408] Footnote entered in error.

Committee on Hate Propaganda) was a watershed in Canadian history. The Committee was chaired by Maxwell Cohen, then the Dean of the Faculty of Law at McGill University.[410] The Cohen Committee found a disturbing level of hate propaganda and recommended that Parliament amend the Criminal Code in an effort to deal with it.[411]

The Cohen Committee and its Report raise a historiographical question of fundamental importance: was the hate propaganda identified by the Committee merely the work of a marginal extremist fringe or did it reflect structures and attitudes that were deeply engrained in Canadian society and history?[412] Stefan Braun appears to share my perspective on the way in which these assumptions serve to justify the maintenance by the state of an apparatus of thought control. Braun wrote:

There is a latent cauldron of potentially monstrous hate waiting to boil over at some time in the future. Left legally unchecked to chance, social intolerance cannot be prevented from growing, expanding, and, ultimately, consuming all of society. All society must therefore be

---

[409] Footnote entered in error.

[410] For description, elaboration and analysis of the Report, see Robert Martin, "Group Defamation in Canada" in Freedman and Freedman, eds., *Group Defamation and Freedom of Speech,* Westport, Connecticut, Greenwood Press, 1995, pp. 191- 217.

[411] See p. 361.

[412] S. Anand, *Expressions of Racial Hatred and Racism in Canada: An Historical Perspective*, (1998) 77 Canadian Bar Review 181. This perspective would, of course, justify the sorts of measures recommended by the Cohen Committee.

preventively protected from hate with censorship.[413]

The way in which I see pseudo-history being used to justify the current thought police role of the state is as follows—the central postulate of pseudo-history[414] is that Canadian history, prior to 1968, is an uninterrupted litany of outrageous abuses of human rights.[415] It does seem that historians struggle with each other to portray Canada's past in the worst possible light, as in, "I'll see your treatment of Japanese-Canadians during the Second World War and raise you racial segregation in Dresden, Ontario". In April of 2010 John F Conway, a Professor of Sociology at the University of Regina, published a newspaper article which can, in my view, be seen as a distillation of the essence of pseudo-history.[416] Professor Conway appeared to understand Canadian history as an endless struggle between ordinary people and the

---

[413] *Democracy off Balance, op. cit.,* p.79.

[414] Brooke Jeffrey and Philip Rosen, *The Protection of Human Rights in Canada*, (1979) 2 Canadian Parliamentary Review, no.3, p.37, might well have a value which its authors, who were, at the time, researchers with the Library of Parliament, could neither have expected, nor imagined. It could be regarded as providing a definition of pseudo-history.

[415] Theodore Dalrymple has recently described this approach to history as a "…kind of historiography, which traces a current discontent or complaint backwards and then claims it to be the whole of history…". Theodore Dalrymple, *The New Vichy Syndrome: Why European Intellectuals Surrender to Barbarism*, New York and London, Encounter Books, 2010, p. xi. He continued, "A belief that one's history contains nothing good or worthwhile leads either to utopian dreams of a new beginning, or a failure to resist those utopian dreams: in other words to fanaticism or apathy. Fanaticism is resentment in search of power; consumerism is apathy in search of happiness." (*Ibid*).

[416] John F Conway, *Regina 16 say common folk won freedoms*, Calgary Herald 6 April 2010.

military. Conway's take on this history was replete with fairytale instances, such as the Metis at Batoche struggling against Gatling guns (assuming that Professor Conway understands what a Gatling gun was in 1885), workers in Winnipeg in 1919 facing the military "…in machine gun nests and armoured cars" and anti-conscription protestors during the Great War being "…shot down by the military on the streets of Quebec city".

To gain the benefit of the views of a real historian, we should note that Margaret MacMillan has observed, "It is all too easy to rummage through the past and find nothing but a list of grievances…"[417] Theodore Dalrymple has suggested that the current era might be described as an "Age of Resentment". He also believes that "Resentment Studies" constitute the stock in trade of the contemporary university.[418] Returning to Professor Conway, it appears from his biography on the Sociology website of the University of Regina that he might have had some less than completely satisfactory experiences with the military. He is said to have entered the Royal Roads Military College in 1961, but seems, for some reason, not to have graduated.

It might be helpful for me to describe a personal encounter with a proponent of pseudo-history. In 1996, Anthony A. Peacock published a book called, *Rethinking the Constitution: Perspectives on Canadian Constitutional Reform, Interpretation and Theory.*[419] This volume was a collection of essays, two of which were written by me. Broadly speaking, the volume sought to promote a revisionist approach to the study of the Canadian constitution and to argue that the history of constitutional government in Canada up until 1982 was worthwhile and valuable and had contained elements worth preserving. David Schneiderman, who now teaches in the

---

[417] Note 400, p.71.
[418] *It's all Your Fault*, New English Review, September 2010.
[419] Don Mills, Ontario, Oxford University Press.

Faculty of Law of the University of Toronto, wrote a review[420] of the book. He was not impressed. I believe "sneering contempt" to be the fairest and most accurate phrase that might be used to describe the tone of Schneiderman's review, which he concluded by dismissing the notion that Canada was once "an entirely decent country".[421] To be fair to Schneiderman, it should be noted that he did not indulge himself in the obvious and well-used device of denouncing all the contributors to the volume with whose views he did not agree as "racist", "sexist" and "homophobic". There were, nonetheless, certain dark hints scattered throughout his review.[422]

The necessary corollary to what I have described as the central postulate of pseudo-history is that, absent the guidance of the state's thought police, Canada would return to its accustomed slough. On 4 February 2010 law students at the University of Toronto organised the 3rd Biennial Conference on the subject: "Combatting Hatred in the 21st Century: Legal Remedies".

Reading through the conference schedule and the various explanatory papers prepared for it, as I interpret them, one message emerges clearly, which is that the gathering was, largely, premised on an assumption that Canada is seething with anti-Semitism and racism and that these vicious currents are kept in check only because of the diligent and dedicated efforts of all the people working in the state's thought control apparatus.[423]

These are evidently matters which are viewed with great concern at the University of Toronto, since the 2010 gathering was the third to address them. Because I am a graduate of the University of Toronto, I receive its propaganda organ, *U of T*

---

[420] *Book Review*, (1997) 22 Queen's Law Journal 531-538.

[421] *Ibid.,* at p. 538.

[422] *Ibid.,* at pp. 532-533.

[423] Joseph Brean, *Tales from the Hate Crime Underworld*, National Post 5 February 2010.

Magazine. A recent issue praised another graduate and current Toronto police chief, Bill Blair. He was being praised for attempting both to bring about "change" and to overcome the reprehensible past of yet another Canadian institution.[424] A major function of what many have described as the racism industry,[425] and the primary means by which it seeks to justify its continued existence, is maintaining the perception of massive and vicious racism lurking just below the surface of Canadian society.[426]

I have difficulty avoiding the impression that the racism industry is committed to promoting division and hostility amongst Canadians. I do find that hardly a day goes by that I do not come across a media report of the racism industry working to heighten division and hostility.[427] Two newspaper columns, published in April of 2010, were effective in elucidating the two elements which are at the core, as I understand it, of the racism industry: first, its intellectual corruption[428] and, second, its viciousness.[429]

Pseudo-history raises concerns which go beyond the abstract and the aesthetic. In November of 2010, Canada's Minister of Immigration, Jason Kenney, warned that to continue to teach Canada's history as a story of "oppression and injustice" was to

---

[424] John Loring, *Force for CHANGE: Toronto Police Chief Bill Blair breaks from (sic) the past*, (2010) 37 U of T Magazine, no.3, 35.

[425] Martin Loney has provided a full, original and valuable critical exposition of the racism industry in his *The Pursuit of Division*, Montreal and Kingston, McGill-Queen's University Press, 1998.

[426] See, Editorial, *Much ado about racism*, National Post, 19 March 2010.

[427] See, Joseph Brean, *Sumo suits instruments of 'oppression': Queen's student govt*, National Post, 29 March 2010 and Barbara Kay, "One punch, one MOWP = more campus outrage", *National Post*, 2 April 2010.

[428] Robert Fulford, *The latest from the anti-racism industry*, National Post, 3 April 2010.

[429] Jonathan Kay, *White and guilty*, National Post, 3 April 2010.

raise the risk of "social unrest".[430]

The authors of what I would describe as a leading work of pseudo-history attempted, in the first edition of their work, to explain the Conscription Crisis of 1917 on this basis: "Despite the eagerness of some women to serve overseas, they were unwelcome on the front lines."[431] No reference to support that assertion was provided, nor did the authors bother to name even one of the eager women. A prominent Canadian historian described this work as "grossly misinterpreting history."[432]

Before proceeding, I must declare a personal interest. My own father, who was a fine man, was a Major in the Canadian Army.[433] In August of 1944 he was killed in action in France. Consequently, I have substantial feelings of hostility towards those who disregard or denigrate the sacrifices of Canadians.[434]

---

[430] Brian Lilley, *Lack of historical knowledge threatens Canada's future: Minister*, Toronto Sun, 18 November 2010.

[431] Margaret Conrad and Alvin Finkel, with Veronica Strong-Boag, *History of the Canadian Peoples*, two vols., Mississauga, Copp Clark, Pitman, 1993, vol. 2, p. 299. This work has sold well and is now, as of 2008, in its fifth edition. These facts should, in no way, be regarded as affecting its characterization as pseudo-history. The success which the book has enjoyed might be regarded as an illustration of the principle that, in the land of the members of the visually-challenged community, the one-eyed person is dominant.

[432] J. L. Granatstein, *Who killed Canadian History?*, Toronto, Harper, Collins, 1998, p. 121. See also, Joyce Appleby, Lynn Hunt and Margaret Jacob, *Telling the Truth about History*, New York, Norton, 1994 and Gertrude Himmelfarb, *Where Have all the Footnotes Gone?* in On Looking into the Abyss: Untimely Thoughts on Culture and Society, New York, Knopf, 1995, p. 122.

[433] J. L. Granatstein, *Canada's Army: Waging War and Keeping the Peace*, Toronto, University of Toronto Press, 2002, pp. 275-276.

[434] See, Robert Martin, *How I lost my father—twice*, Globe and Mail, 11 November 1991.

In 1992, the CBC. aired a "docu-drama" called *The Valour and the Horror*. This effort, prepared by the brothers McKenna of Montreal, purported to present the stories of three different Second World War operations involving the Canadian Army and the Royal Canadian Air Force. A message which, as I recall the series, emerged very clearly was that the soldiers of the Canadian Army were incompetent and the Canadians who flew with 6 Bomber Group, Royal Canadian Air Force were war criminals.

To put the matter at its most basic, *The Valour and the Horror* was a calumny of the tens of thousands of Canadians who fought and died in a noble cause.[435] Canadian veterans who had fought against Nazism were outraged at the CBC for suggesting they were war criminals.[436] A group, led by a man named Elliott, who had been a navigator in the Royal Canadian Air Force, sued the CBC for libel. The matter ended up before the Ontario Court of Appeal. As I interpret that court's judgment, the judges were satisfied that the material which had been broadcast was, indeed, libellous. In her judgment, Abella, J.A., as she then was, spoke of:

> ...*the misplaced emphases, the caricaturish portrayals of some of the strategists, the inaccuracy of some of the detail and the omission of some of the countervailing considerations in the film.*"[437]

The libel action against the CBC was dismissed, largely on the ground that the group referred to was far too large to permit the

---

[435] J. L. Granatstein, *The Last Good War*, Vancouver, Douglas and McIntyre, 2005. For the views of real historians on *The Valour and the Horror*, see David A. Bercuson and S.F. Wise (eds.), *The Valour and the Horror Revisited*, Montreal and Kingston, McGill-Queen's University Press, 1994.

[436] To be fair to the CBC, it did make a commitment to the veterans' groups not to re-air the series. See MacMillan, *op. cit.,* note 27, p.137.

[437] *Elliott* v. *C.B.C.* (1995) 125 D.L.R. (4th) 534 at 538.

identification of any individual plaintiff. Knowing something of libel law, and cognizant of my responsibilities as a scholar, I shall refrain from expressing fully my opinions about the McKennas.

The reference above to 1968 is intended to focus on what I would describe as the year of Salvation. In that year, Pierre Trudeau became Prime Minister of Canada, the religion of equality was revealed to him and he began the process of transforming Canada into an acceptable country. At this point we must note another CBC effort, one which, I believe, must be regarded as a significant work of pseudo-history.[438] The period beginning in the 1950s with the start of CBC television was described in this volume as "The Awakening". The Chapter titled "The Awakening" has a title page with the slogan, "All Canadians are equal".[439]

What is the position with respect to libels directed at organizations? There are, in law, two kinds of persons—real persons and artificial persons. Corporations, artificial persons, have many of the legal attributes of human beings. One result is that a corporation has roughly the same rights to its reputation as does an individual. Thus, a corporation can sue for a libel just as an individual can. But an unincorporated organization cannot, because it does not have legal personality. *The Corporation of the Town of Halton Hills* v. *Kerouac*[440] is a very important recent libel judgment. Corbett, J. decided that neither the state, nor any of its agencies, could initiate libel actions. In the course of a full and

---

[438] Don Gillmor, Achille Michaud and Pierre Turgeon, *Canada: A People's History*, Toronto, McClelland and Stewart, 2001. For a listing of some of the many errors, both factual and of interpretation, in this work, see Robert Martin, *The Great War and Canadian Memory, Part 2*, Canadian Military History, (Summer 2005), Book Review Supplement, Issue 18, p. 1.

[439] Gillmor, Michaud and Turgeon, *op. cit.*, note 436, vol. 2, p.237.

[440] (2006) 80 O.R. (3d) 577.

learned judgment she enunciated a clear understanding of the significance of free expression:

> *Without free speech, there is no free press. Without a free press, there is no free political debate. Without free political debate, there cannot be true democracy. Freedom of speech, writ large, is a pillar of democracy.*[441]

She continued, observing that, "In a democracy, it is essential that the government be in the public domain, and be available for criticism of all kinds."[442] To permit defamation actions by the state would be to "chill" this essential element of free expression. She was clear that both public officials and public servants retained the right, as individuals, to institute defamation actions in order to vindicate their personal reputations.[443]

The trick in doing stories about organizations is to avoid identifying any of their individual members or officers or directors. The law is clear that a libellous statement about an organization is not in and of itself a libel about any member of that organization, unless, of course, that member is identified as an individual.

The last point to note is that it is not possible to libel a dead person. Since libel is a personal action, it may only be maintained by the person who claims to have been libelled. If a plaintiff were to drop dead an hour before judgment was to be given in her favour, that would be the end of the libel action. If, on the other hand, judgment had already been given, that judgment would become part of the dead person's estate. But an estate cannot proceed with a libel action. The important thing to remember is

---

[441] *Ibid.*, at p. 583.
[442] *Ibid.*, at p. 585.
[443] *Ibid.*, at p. 583.

that, while anyone can say anything she likes about a dead person, a degree of caution must be exercised so that in the course of making critical statements about a dead person one does not also libel a living person, as in: "X was a lunatic and has no doubt passed on those defective genes to her two children."

Publication

The third, and final, element in the plaintiff's case requires her to establish that the defamatory statements about her were published—that is, communicated to a third party. Strictly speaking, even one third party will do. If there are two people alone in a room and one calls the other all sorts of names or questions her ancestry and intelligence, there is no libel. The statements must be communicated to a third party. Insults or abuse as such are not libellous.

Legislation in every province makes the third element easier for the plaintiff. All the legislation deems that material which has been printed in a newspaper or broadcast over radio or television has been published.[444] It is reasonable to assume that, for example, somebody must read the London *Free Press*. It used to be the case in libel actions that the plaintiff would have to bring to court a parade of witnesses who would say, "Yes, I read the London *Free Press* last Saturday and I read that story" or "I watched the CBC prime time news and I saw the libellous assertions about the plaintiff." That, surely, is silly and a waste of time and money. The legislation makes it unnecessary.

The Ontario legislation defines broadcasting as follows:

> *"Broadcasting" means the dissemination of writing, signs, signals, pictures and sounds of all kinds, intended*

---

[444] See, for example, the Ontario *Libel and Slander Act*, R.S.O. 1990, c. L.12, s. 2 [hereinafter *LSA*].

> to be received by the public either directly or through
> the medium of relay stations, by means of, (a) any form
> of wireless radioelectric communication utilising
> Hertzian waves, (b) including radiotelegraph and
> radio-telephone, or cables, wires, fibre-optic linkages or
> laser beams.[445]

That definition, I assume, would be broad enough to cover libellous material disseminated through on-line computer services.

If the statements were not contained in a newspaper or broadcast over radio or television, the plaintiff will have to prove that they had actually been published.

An interesting issue, and one which has yet to be addressed by a Canadian court, concerns liability for defamatory statements published on the Internet. Who should be liable for such statements: the person who wrote and posted them or the Internet service provider? (I.S.P.) The best answer to this question is that, so far, there is no complete answer to it. The important issue seems to be whether the I.S.P. is simply a conduit through which information passes or the publisher of the information. The resolution of this issue will turn on the degree to which the I.S.P. filters or edits material.[446]

The greater the degree of control the I.S.P. exercises over the content of material, the greater the likelihood of its being found to be the publisher.[447] The United States has dealt with this question

---

[445] *Ibid.* s. 1(1).

[446] See, Ryan Savage, *Between A Rock and a Hard Place: Defamation and I.S.P.s* (2002) Asper Review of International Business and Trade Law, no. 2, 107.

[447] *Godfrey* v. *Demon Internet* [1999] 4 All E.R. 342 (Q.B .). See also, Andrew Bernstein and Rima Ramchandani, *Don't Shoot the Messenger: A*

by legislating it out of existence. The *Communications Decency Act* of 1996 gives I.S.P.s a statutory defence against libel actions. Canada has yet to produce either a judicial or a statutory response to the general question. In 2009, the British Columbia Court of Appeal dealt with the question whether the provision, on one website, of hyperlinks to other websites which contained defamatory material amounted to publication of that material by the website which provided the hyperlinks.[448] The BC court held that the mere provision of hyperlinks did not constitute publication.[449] On 1 April 2010 the Supreme Court of Canada granted leave to appeal the decision of the Court of Appeal.[450] The Supreme Court of Canada, in a judgment released on 19 October 2011, affirmed the view that the provision of hyperlinks to websites containing defamatory material did not amount to publication of the defamatory material.[451]

There is a significant conflict of laws question in this area. When defamatory material is published on the Internet, in what jurisdiction does publication occur?[452]

The question was dealt with indirectly in May of 2002 in *Socan v. Canadian Association of Internet Providers*. The Federal Court of Appeal decided that I.S.P.s are not generally liable for

---

Discussion of I.S.P. Liability, (2002) 1 Canadian Journal of Law and Technology, no. 2, 77 at p. 78.

[448] *Crookes v. Newton,* (2009) 311 D.L.R. (4th) 647.

[449] *Ibid.*

[450] Janice Tibbetts, *Court wades into Internet speech debate with hyperlinks case*, National Post, 1 April 2010.

[451] *Crookes* v. *Newton* (2011) 337 D.L.R. (4th) 1.

[452] See Randy A. Pepper, *Internet Defamation: Canadian vs. American Perspectives*, (2002) 25 Advocates Quarterly 190 at p. 193. The Ontario Court of Appeal addressed a number of questions concerning conflict of laws and libel in *Black* v. *Breeden et al.* (2010) 102 O.R. (3d) 748.

infringements of copyright committed by their users.[453]

This decision only suggests an answer to the question about liability. My surmise is that a libel published on the Internet might be treated in a fashion similar to that of a libel published as a letter to the editor in a newspaper.

Both the letter-writer and the newspaper could be held liable in such a situation.[454] Likewise, it might make sense to recognize the joint and several liability of the writer and the I.S.P. in a case where a libel was published on the Internet. Insofar as the plaintiff's case is concerned, it is sufficient that the libel has been published to one other person. How many people in fact saw or read the libel may be relevant to the question of damages, but not to the basic issue of liability. The analogy which I have suggested is clearly inapt. The editors of a newspaper review and edit all letters to the editor before they are published, a function which goes far beyond the minimal and, generally, non-existent filtering imposed by an I.S.P.

The final point to look at is the question of republication. If I am the initial publisher of a libel, to what extent and under what circumstances can I be held responsible for subsequent republications of that libel by other persons or organizations? As a general matter, any republication is a fresh libel and the original publisher cannot be held liable.

There is only one circumstance under which the initial publisher might be held liable for subsequent republication, and that is when the republication is a natural and probable

---

[453] *Society of Composers, Authors, and Music Publishers of Canada (Socan) v. Canadian Association of Internet Providers*, [2002] 4 F.C. 3. See also Alan Gahtan, *I.S.P.s Protected from Liability*, Law Times, 15 July 2002.

[454] See Robert Martin, *Libel and Letters to the Editor*, (1983) 9 Queen's Law Journal 188.

consequence of the initial publication.[455] This circumstance could arise with a news service. The news service publishes material by putting stories out on the wire. It does this so that subscribers will pick the stories up and republish them. Clearly, for example, any republication of a Canadian Press story by a CP subscriber is a natural and probable consequence of the initial publication by CP, assuming, of course, that the subscriber had republished the story exactly as it came over the wire and without making any changes to it. The simple point is that if a plaintiff is suing a news service for having published a libel, it might be able to hold the news service responsible not simply for what went out on the wire, but for subsequent republications by its subscribers.

What about the phenomenon known as "rip and read," in which it is alleged that some radio stations simply take stories from newspapers and read them over the air? A newspaper should not be liable in respect of what the radio station broadcasts, since "rip and read" would not be regarded as a natural and probable consequence of the initial publication.

Defamation, identification and publication are the three elements that the plaintiff has to prove. Proof of actual injury is not part of the plaintiff's case. As has been noted, if the plaintiff can establish the three elements required, injury to reputation is assumed.

If the plaintiff is successful in proving these elements, the plaintiff is said to have established a *prima facie* case. Having done that, the plaintiff will win if the defendant does nothing—that is, unless the defendant attempts to raise a defence. Alternatively, if the plaintiff does not establish a *prima facie* case, the defendant can move the court to have the action dismissed on the ground that there is no case to answer. The plaintiff has not discharged the basic burden that rests with her.

---

[455] *Basse v. Toronto Star Newspapers Ltd.* (1983), 44 O.R. (2d) 164 (H.C.J.).

The Defendant's Case

We turn now to the defendant's case, to the defences available to a libel action. The law recognizes six defences, and we will deal with each in turn. There are now six defences. The newest defence, public interest/responsible journalism, is dealt with later. The defendant is in no way required to look the six possible defences over, select one, and reject the other five. She could, in an appropriate case, plead all six.

In civil actions, there is no general principle that prevents a defendant from pleading a multiplicity of defences, from pleading overlapping defences, or, even, under certain circumstances, from pleading contradictory defences. It may be useful, at this point, to repeat a charming anecdote about the lawyer's child who was called into the office of the principal of her school in connection with the principal's effort to investigate a broken window in one of the school's buildings. On being asked about the broken window, the lawyer's child replied: "There is no window in that building and, if there is, it isn't broken and, if it is broken, I didn't do it and, if I did do it, it was an accident."

Although we address the various defences primarily as legal phenomena, underlying this approach is a commitment to the notion that, in a practical journalistic sense, the best defences to a libel action are good reporting and good editing.

Justification

The first defence is called justification. In ordinary language that means truth. A number of observations may be made about this defence. The first is that the law presumes defamatory statements to be false and, thus, requires the defendant to prove their truth. The plaintiff is not obliged to prove that the defamatory assertions are false.

This approach has occasioned a certain degree of concern about "libel chill". It has been argued that requiring the defendant to prove the truth of defamatory statements amounts to creating a "reverse onus". This is misleading, because the notion of reverse onus belongs exclusively to the criminal law. The lawyers who argue this, as I see it, are either not telling the truth or do not know what they are talking about.

The plaintiff in a libel action, as in all torts actions, has the burden of proof. The plaintiff, as we have seen, has to prove the three elements that make up a *prima facie* case. Only when the plaintiff has satisfactorily established those three elements is any obligation cast upon the defendant. Turning to the general policy question of whether the plaintiff should have to prove that the defamatory assertions are false or whether the defendant should have to prove they are true, there are a number of significant considerations that argue in favour of requiring the defendant to do so.

The first is the problem that anyone who has done an undergraduate course in philosophy or logic will be familiar with: It is impossible to prove a negative. If the defamatory statement is that I molest little children, I cannot prove that I have never molested a child. I can prove that I have not molested *this* child, or *that* child, or some other named child. I can prove that I did not molest a child last Wednesday, but, as a matter of logic, I cannot prove that I have never on any occasion molested any child.

But more to the point, the requirement that the defendant prove the truth of the statements in question is entirely consistent with the demands of good journalism. If a newspaper or broadcaster is going to publish damaging statements about someone, then before it actually does so, it should have sufficient factual underpinning for those statements to satisfy itself that they are true. And if it did not have sufficient factual underpinning to satisfy itself that the assertions were true, then it should not have published them.

Knowledge of the truth or falsity of statements that have been published is, and should be, peculiarly the province of the media. Who else is going to know better whether statements are true or false than the newspaper or broadcaster that published them? Indeed, in a 1995 decision, the Supreme Court of Canada not only rejected the notion of "libel chill", but expressly accepted the legitimacy of the current position:

> Surely it is not requiring too much of individuals that they ascertain the truth of the allegations they publish. [456]

It is important, in understanding the requirement of proving the truth of the allegedly defamatory statements, to grasp some of the distinctions between civil and criminal proceedings. Two different, but related, phrases are used in law—"burden of proof" and "standard of proof". "Burden of proof" addresses the question, "Who has to prove what?" We have seen that the plaintiff in a libel action initially bears the burden of proof. "Standard of proof" addresses the question of how well a party has to prove the things it is obliged to prove.

In criminal cases, the Crown has the burden of proving that the accused is guilty. How well does the Crown have to prove the accused's guilt? Beyond a reasonable doubt. Beyond a reasonable doubt does not mean absolute certainty, but if we were to put it in arithmetical terms, we would be talking about something around eighty percent certainty.

The standard of proof in civil proceedings is "on a balance of probabilities". That means that a fact is taken to have been proved if the court accepts that it is *more likely than not*. Arithmetically, more likely than not means fifty-one percent. The simple point is

---

[456] Hill v. Church of Scientology of Toronto, [1995] 2 S.C.R. 1130 at 1187.

that it is far less demanding to have to prove something in a civil proceeding than it is in a criminal proceeding. There is another important distinction. Libel actions are the last bastion of the jury in civil proceedings in Canada. But the way civil juries work is different from the way criminal juries work. Criminal juries operate on the basis of unanimity. If an accused person is to be convicted, twelve jurors out of twelve must be persuaded beyond a reasonable doubt that she is guilty.

Civil juries, in contrast, act on the basis of majorities. In Ontario a civil jury consists of six people. Five out of six members of a civil jury is sufficient to reach a verdict. In Saskatchewan a civil jury consists of twelve people, and ten out of twelve is sufficient to reach a verdict. Thus, for a defendant to prove that ostensibly libellous assertions are true, all she has to do, in Ontario, is persuade five jurors out of six that the assertions are more likely to be true than not.[457]

The normal method of proving facts in Canadian courtrooms is through the evidence of witnesses. There is scope for the use of documentary evidence, but litigants rely primarily on the oral testimony of live witnesses to prove facts. This practice leads to some important considerations about raising the defence of truth, considerations that have to do with sources. A crucial matter in libel actions has to do with a feature of the law of evidence called the "hearsay rule". This rule, or at least the exceptions to it, is exceedingly complicated, but its basic principle is easy to state: the only person who can testify as to the existence of a fact is someone who has direct knowledge of that fact through her own senses. That means, most commonly, someone who can say, "I saw it happen." The hearsay rule means a witness cannot seek to prove the truth of something by saying that someone else told her it happened. The response would be that, if somebody told you it

---

[457] See, Ontario, *Juries Act*, R.S.O. 1990, c. J.3, and Saskatchewan, *The Jury Act*, 1981, S.S. 1980–81, c. J-4.1.

happened, get that somebody here as a witness. Thus, if a defendant wants to establish the truth of ostensibly libellous assertions, she must have a witness or witnesses who can give direct personal evidence as to their truth. Using journalistic terminology, these witnesses are usually called "sources".

We now address four issues that can arise in relation to sources. The first is generally referred to as the problem of the disappearing source. A defendant is very much at the mercy of its sources in a libel action. The defendant is going to have to rely on a source going into the witness box, taking an oath, and saying in open court the same things that that person said to a reporter some time ago, possibly in confidence. Once the source steps into the witness box and starts giving evidence, the defendant has no control over what is being said. A crucial thing about sources that a reporter has to address and an editor may have to address and, eventually, a lawyer, is making a judgment whether this source, if it comes to it, will truthfully recount her information in court under oath. That judgment is crucial, because if a reporter has only one source, and her judgment and an editor's judgment is that they are not confident this person will tell the truth in court, then the story may have to be recast. The only means of eventually proving the truth of a particular assertion in the story may prove not to be reliable. This is one of the reasons reporters should try to have more than one source. The great virtue of having a multiplicity of sources is that, if source A proves unreliable, the defendant will have source B and source C to fall back on.

The second, and related, problem with sources has to do with their credibility. The point of raising the defence of truth is not to argue that, in some abstract philosophical or moral sense, a story is true. The concrete point is to prove to the satisfaction of a court that it is true. A crucial element in doing this, of course, is to persuade the court to believe the defendant's witnesses—that is, the sources.

The issue here is not whether the source is telling the truth, but whether the court believes that the source is telling the truth. A good example of this problem is a Newfoundland case, *Drost v. Sunday Herald Ltd.*[458] The facts were simple. A man was driving along a road outside St John's. Two RCMP constables allegedly came along, pulled him over to the side of the road, dragged him out of his car, and beat him up. The man went to a newspaper reporter and told him what had happened. Obviously, the reporter believed the man because his story appeared in the newspaper. One of the police officers sued the paper for libel. The paper's defence was truth, but, of course, its only witness was the man who claimed he had been beaten up. It turned out that this man had an impressive criminal record and was a well-known ne'er-do-well. What happened at the trial? Two sterling members of the RCMP said none of this ever happened, and one man who had a criminal record said it did. Who did the court believe? The paper lost the libel action.

Judgments will have to be made as to whether the sources for the story will be credible witnesses. Once again, if the conclusion is that the source or sources are unlikely to be credible witnesses, then it may be necessary to recast the story. This is another reason for trying to have more than one source. If a particular source is not going to be a credible witness, perhaps others will be.

These judgments about the reliability and credibility of sources cannot be made solely by the reporter who is working on the story. They should also be made by editors and, if necessary, by lawyers. That means that, in certain cases, an editor and the newspaper or the station's lawyer will have to interview the sources and reach conclusions about their reliability and credibility.

The third problem with sources is the unfortunate fact that they may often have their own agendas. Sources do not speak to

---

[458] (1976), 11 Nfld. & P.E.I.R. 342 (Nfld. T.D.).

journalists only because they are motivated by a commitment to truth. A source can have her own purposes and seek to manipulate a reporter or an editor in order to further those purposes.

A classic case is *Vogel v. Canadian Broadcasting Corp.*[459] The CBC in Vancouver had hired a young journalist and given him the official title of investigative reporter. It appears from the cases that formally to describe someone as an "investigative reporter" is a sure-fire way to destroy that individual's judgment. This person was sitting in the newsroom with his new title, all ready for the investigative pieces he was bound to do, when he received an anonymous phone call. The caller would not give his name, but said he had a great story. The story was about someone called Richard Vogel, who happened to be the deputy attorney general of British Columbia. The caller, although the reporter did not know it at the time, was actually a lawyer who worked in the Attorney General's Department and did not like Richard Vogel. More to the point, the caller wanted to get Vogel and had figured out that a good way to do so would be to induce CBC television to do a critical story about Vogel. The story was appealing to the investigative reporter because the caller claimed to know of three instances where the deputy attorney general had interfered with cases actually before the courts, i.e. interfered with the due administration of justice, in order to benefit his friends. This was a wonderful story, except for the fact that it wasn't true. The source's stories were not complete fabrications. There was a grain of truth in each, enough certainly to provide a sufficient basis for persuading a credulous reporter. The source also embellished his stories with certain theatrical flourishes that had the effect of further persuading the reporter. The source put out the bait. The reporter rose to it and was then skilfully played and landed. The reporter did make some effort to confirm the stories. There had indeed been three cases before the courts. And there were facts

---

[459] [1982] 3 W.W.R. 97 (B.C.S.C.) [*Vogel*].

about them which the source had accurately recounted and which the reporter confirmed. But the fundamental fact—that Richard Vogel had interfered in all three cases in order to help his friends out—was just not there.

The CBC went to air with this story in 1981 and eventually paid Vogel $125,000 in damages.

Reporters must approach sources, especially ones who are telling spectacular stories, with a certain amount of scepticism. There should be documents that back up what a particular source is saying. It would be useful for a reporter to ask herself why a source is giving her this information. What are the source's motives? Reporters should never forget the fundamental stricture that you do not believe everything people tell you. Everyone, in some way or other, has an axe to grind. Finally, the traditional reluctance of reporters to rely on material from sources who refuse to let their names be used in a story should be revived. If a source says she does not want her name used in a story, that fact must raise questions about the source's motives and, most important, about whether she is telling the truth.

The fourth and final problem in relation to sources arises when there aren't any—when reporters simply fabricate stories. This is precisely what happened in one of the more spectacular Canadian libel cases, *Munro v. Toronto Sun Publishing Corp.*[460] John Munro was a Member of Parliament from Hamilton, Ontario, and a minister in several Trudeau governments. The Toronto *Sun* hired someone and made the same mistake as had been made by the CBC in Vancouver, of calling him an investigative reporter. In fact it compounded its error and called two people investigative reporters. It took a young reporter who was eager to get his career going and teamed him with an older reporter whose career had not been doing much for about twenty years. This was a fatal combination.

---

[460] (1982) 39 O.R. (2d) 100 (H.C.J.) [*Munro*].

In the 1970s, PetroCanada, which originally was started as a state oil holding company, got into the service station business. PetroCanada acquired all the service stations in Canada, first, of PetroFina, then, of British Petroleum, and turned them into PetroCanada stations. In order to do this, a range of corporate regalia had to be designed and manufactured—colours for the pumps, flags, uniforms for the people working in the service stations, credit cards, and so on.

The supposed story was that John Munro had used his position as a federal minister to ensure that the PetroCanada contract went to a company in which he had an interest. He was, thus, accused of serious corruption. The problem with the story was that it had been made up. The younger reporter made it up and then sold it to his partner. It was easy to do so because the older reporter wanted to believe the story, just as the CBC reporter in *Vogel* had wanted to believe what the source was telling him. But the older reporter did have some residual skepticism and suggested he should talk to the younger reporter's sources. There ensued a great deal of cloak and daggerish to-ing and fro-ing, with the predictable result that the older reporter never quite managed to speak to any of the sources.

There was a certain amount of concern about this story in the *Sun* newsroom, especially since the plan was to run it on page 1. The reporters had a meeting with the editor, the publisher, and a lawyer to talk about the story. During the course of this meeting someone asked the younger reporter if he had any documents to support the story. The reporter said he once had the original documents, but had somehow lost them. He told the others not to worry and held up a microfiche saying, of the documents, "They are all here." No one at that meeting asked to look at the microfiche. The *Sun* published the story.

John Munro sued immediately. The *Sun* did a bit of further investigation, discovered the story was a fabrication, and issued a belated apology.

The trial judge made a number of observations about avoiding libel actions. These observations are nothing more than a lawyer's way of formulating some of the basic rules of good reporting and good editing.

> ...there must be a separation of functions between the reporter and the editor, it being the responsibility of the editor to confirm the accuracy of the contents of a story before publication.... [T]here must be constant supervision maintained by the editor over the reporter, with a regular reporting requirement.... [I]t is the editor's responsibility to know in detail before publication, the documentation to support the story and the reliability of the sources and so ensure its accuracy.[461]

If a reporter says to an editor, "I cannot tell you the identity of my source," the only reply the editor can make is, "In that case we cannot run the story." If the reporter says, "Trust me on this one," an editor's response and what an editor is paid to say is: "It's nothing personal, but it's not my job to trust you. I want to know who your sources are and I want to talk to the sources myself and in fact I think I want to arrange for our lawyer to talk to the sources." If the reporter refuses to divulge the identity of the sources, then the only course open to someone in an editorial position is to refuse to publish the story. The main reason the story in *Munro v. Toronto Sun Publishing Corp.* was printed is that when the editor asked the reporters who their sources were, they replied, "You're going to have to trust us on this one." And the editor made the mistake of agreeing.

If a reporter files copy that says that a federal minister is guilty of gross corruption or that the deputy attorney general of a

---

[461] *Ibid.*, at p. 118.

province has on three separate occasions interfered with cases actually before the courts in order to help his friends, then an editor is under a clear obligation to review every detail of such a story carefully. There cannot be any other course of action.

Reporters should never give their word to sources that they will under no circumstances reveal their identity. Reporters should be honest with sources. They should say to sources, "I will do my very best to protect your identity, but you have to understand some things about the way this business operates. I cannot give you an absolute guarantee." If necessary, the reporter should explain why she cannot give an absolute guarantee. To say anything else is to mislead the source. It is also important to remember what should be the response of the lawyer if it is decided that a particular story should be lawyered before being published. Whatever the editor says to the reporter, the lawyer must make clear to the editor and the reporter that she has to know who the sources are. If a lawyer were to review a story like the one in *Munro v. Toronto Sun Publishing Corp.*, the very first question she should ask would be the identity of the sources. If the reporter refused to divulge this information, the only advice the lawyer could give her client, the newspaper or broadcaster, would be not to run the story.

Other points in the judgment in *Munro* are worth noting—and it is remarkable that a judge would have to feel it necessary to say these things to people who work for a large urban daily newspaper. The judge added, "[W]here important documentation has been obtained it is good practice to put it in a safe place and to thereafter work from a copy." The idea that there could be an editor who, on asking a reporter to produce the documentation a story was based on, would accept the statement that the reporter had lost it and would further accept an assurance that it was on microfiche, but not demand actually to look at that microfiche, is also astonishing.

The final point the judge made may be controversial. "[W]hen the story is prepared—and the paper has the "goods" on the person targeted in the story it is basic and necessary that that person be confronted with the story so that his reaction be obtained." It seems clear that had the *Sun* contacted John Munro and told him the nature of the story it was planning to publish, Munro's reaction might have led to some rethinking. Some newspapers and broadcasters are reluctant to do this check as a matter of principle. I do not agree with this approach. I believe there is a professional obligation to apprise the person targeted of the story and, more to the point, it can help avoid a great deal of trouble.

What *Vogel* and *Munro* make clear above all is the value of good reporting and good editing as practical defences to a libel action. If there has been good reporting and good editing, you may still get sued, because there is, of course, no way to control such action. But, even if you are sued, if there has been good reporting and good editing, you are going to win. And where there has been bad reporting or bad editing, or both, you stand a good chance of losing.

Good reporting and good editing are directly relevant to other concerns that can arise when truth is raised as a defence. First, when the defence of justification is argued, a court may demand that the defendant prove the truth of precisely what was published. The court may give a strict interpretation to the allegedly defamatory words and then require the defendant to prove the literal truth of that interpretation. This is what happened in *Baxter v. Canadian Broadcasting Corp.*[462]

This case had to do with a report broadcast on *The Fifth Estate* in April 1977 about certain activities of John Baxter, a former minister of justice in New Brunswick. Rumours had been circulating in the province about kickbacks being made to a secret

---

[462] (1980), 30 N.B.R. (2d) 102 (C.A.).

Conservative Party fund. The RCMP began an investigation, but, according to the CBC, was ordered by Baxter to desist. The crucial words from the script were:

> In an internal police memo written in September, 1973, an RCMP sergeant reported that a man under investigation for another matter makes many references to kickbacks to a Conservative Party fund. The police wanted to follow that lead, but then a week later they were stopped by the then Minister of Justice, John Baxter, and their own superiors.

So the CBC said that Baxter, as minister of justice, had stopped an RCMP investigation into *kickbacks* made to his own party. Baxter sued. The CBC relied on the defence of justification. It lost.

The New Brunswick Court of Appeal concluded that the RCMP had been directed to stop its investigation of *political contributions* to the Conservative Party. Political contributions, the judges said, are not the same thing as kickbacks. The CBC's story was not, therefore, strictly true and the defence of justification failed.

A moment's reflection reveals the flaw in the court's reasoning. Political parties do not keep separate accounts for kickbacks; special receipts marked "kickback" are not given. A kickback is, on its face, a lawful political contribution. It is only after investigation that an ostensibly lawful contribution may be revealed to be a kickback. Thus, an order to stop investigating lawful political contributions would necessarily have the effect of frustrating the investigation of kickbacks.

The point is that the statement broadcast by the CBC expressed the logical and inevitable result of the order which Baxter, it was conceded, actually gave to the police. But because the matter was not stated with absolute precision, the defence of justification failed. One further sentence added to the script

281

would probably have allowed the CBC to avoid liability. The practical result is that stories, and especially stories that make serious allegations of corruption or impropriety, must be reviewed meticulously. The question to be asked of each sentence, each phrase, indeed, each word is: Can we prove precisely what this is saying? If the answer is not an immediate "Yes", the story may need more work.

The case of *Brannigan v. S.I.U.*,[463] dealing, as we have seen, with a bitter struggle between two unions, raises the question of circumstantial evidence. The defendant, it will be recalled, had asserted that Brannigan, the plaintiff, was a communist. The defendant sought to prove the truth of this assertion. It introduced evidence that Brannigan had belonged to a communist-dominated union, that he had friends who were communists, and that he had marched in May Day parades. It asked the court to infer from these facts that Brannigan was a communist. The court, correctly, refused. Evidence of surrounding circumstances will only be taken as proof of a particular inference if that inference is the only one that can reasonably be drawn from the evidence. Good journalism would suggest that negative conclusions should not be asserted about individuals on the basis of circumstantial evidence alone.

As with all useful things in life, there is a risk involved in raising justification as a defence. If a defendant relies on the defence of truth and sticks to it right to the bitter end and loses, then, unfortunately, that defendant is going to pay even more in damages. The theory is that, by maintaining to the bitter end that your nasty little story was true, you have worsened the injury to the plaintiff. A defendant must be confident of success when raising the defence of truth.

Commentators on libel law often note that the defence of truth is seldom raised in actual libel actions. This is correct—and for a very good reason. If the story is true, no one is going to sue.

---

[463] Above note 386.

If we reflect on what happens in a libel action, it must be obvious that the plaintiff, or the potential plaintiff, is going to know whether the story is true or not.

If anyone is going to know for certain that the story is accurate, it must be the person about whom it was written. John Munro certainly knew whether he had in fact engaged in the kind of corrupt behaviour that the *Sun* accused him of. If the potential plaintiff knows that what was published about her is true, it is unlikely she will sue. Why would anyone go to all the expense and bother if she knows that it will come out in court that the statements made about her were indeed accurate? Truth is a pre-emptive defence; the truth of a story ensures that there will not be a libel action.

Fair Comment

The next defence to consider is fair comment. It is important to understand the distinction between the use of justification, the defence of "truth," and the defence of "fair comment". If you are sued in respect of assertions of fact, you defend those assertions by attempting to prove that they are true. If you are sued in respect of an expression of an opinion, then you defend your opinion by seeking to establish that it was fair comment made in good faith and without malice on a matter of public interest. The law makes a distinction, then, between assertions of fact and expressions of opinion. As we shall see, this distinction can cause difficulties.

"Fair comment" can be an extraordinarily useful and broad defence, as was demonstrated in a case called *Pearlman v. Canadian Broadcasting Corp.*[464] This case arose out of an investigative piece that CBC Radio in Winnipeg did about a local person, Pearlman, who was both a lawyer and a slum landlord. It was a rigorous piece of reporting. Abuse after abuse and deficiency after

---

[464] (1981), 13 Man. R. (2d) 1 (Q.B.).

deficiency were meticulously catalogued in the report. At the end, the CBC said of Pearlman that he was a person who had "no morals, principles, or conscience." It is difficult to imagine anything worse that could be said about another person. The CBC successfully defended this statement as "fair comment". If fair comment allows you to say that someone has no morals, principles, or conscience and successfully defend that statement, it is an exceedingly useful defence.

We will catalogue the elements that make up the defence and note some of the difficulties that can arise. In the first place, a court must be persuaded that the allegedly libellous statements being defended as fair comment are indeed expressions of an opinion rather than assertions of fact. The difficulty is that, if a defendant tries to raise "fair comment" and the court decides that the libellous statement is not an expression of an opinion but an assertion of a fact, that defence will not be available. The only way to defend factual assertions is to prove that they are true. This was the problem in a well-known libel case from British Columbia, *Vander Zalm v. Times Publishers*.[465]

The Victoria *Times* ran an editorial cartoon about Bill Vander Zalm, later premier of British Columbia, who was at the time the province's minister of human resources. It was a simple, straightforward drawing of Vander Zalm seated at a table, a smile flickering across his lips, pulling the wings off flies. Vander Zalm sued. The paper's defence was "fair comment". But the trial court said the paper could not raise that defence because the cartoon was not an expression of an opinion but an assertion of a fact. What fact? The court said the newspaper was asserting as a fact that Vander Zalm was a cruel person. One would have thought that to say someone is cruel is to express an opinion. How can it be established as a matter of fact that someone is or is not cruel? Nonetheless, that was what the court said. The *Times* could not

---

[465] (1980), 109 D.L.R. (3d) 531 (B.C.C.A.).

prove that Vander Zalm was a cruel person and it lost at trial. The newspaper had the good sense, and also, of course, the resources, to appeal to the British Columbia Court of Appeal. The Court of Appeal reversed the trial court's decision and held that, almost by its nature, an editorial cartoon was an expression of opinion. Having decided that this cartoon was an expression of an opinion, the court had no difficulty in concluding further that it was "fair comment".

It is crucial to ensure that assertions of fact are clearly set out as such, that expressions of opinion are likewise set out as such, and that the two are demarcated from each other.

The next requirement in establishing the "fair comment" defence, and the next area where there can be some difficulty, is that the matter commented upon must be one of public interest. This makes sense. The law of libel is an ongoing attempt to "strike a fair balance between the protection of reputation and the protection of free speech."[466] There is an inherent tension between the two that manifests itself in libel law. Both are recognized as important—the reputations of individuals should be protected, but expression should also be free.

Libel law requires the courts to attempt to find the right balance. Thus, when it comes to matters of public interest, individuals and the mass media will be allowed to comment broadly and, obviously, adversely about other people. The protection of reputation will give way somewhat to the promotion of free expression.

The corollary is that fair comment may not be relied upon to defend public attacks on relatives or friends or former friends, or lovers, or associates, because none of these would be matters of public interest. How is the distinction made? We have another British Columbia case called *Pound v. Scott*.[467] Pound was a

---

[466] *Cherneskey* v. *Armadale Publishers Ltd.*, [1979] 1 S.C.R. 1067 at 1095.
[467] (1973), 37 D.L.R. (3d) 439 (B.C.S.C.).

physician who had left the United Kingdom allegedly out of disgust with its National Health Service. He came to Canada because of his opposition to a system of health care run by the state. He was of the opinion that Canada should not repeat the mistake made by the United Kingdom. Dr. Pound believed this so strongly that he contacted a reporter for the Victoria *Times* to express his point of view. He suggested that the reporter do a story about him and about his views on health care. The reporter agreed and a piece was duly published in the *Times*.

Scott, the defendant, was a columnist with the same newspaper and did not like Dr. Pound's views on health care. Scott wrote a column attacking Pound and his opinions. He wrote the following:

> *What I am saying is that Dr. Pound, to my own knowledge, was not at all fair in his presentation of these facts. As for his opinion, I find it equally suspect. Any man who describes health as "a commodity" and the doctor's role "as free trade with his customers," is hardly qualified to judge a national medical scheme based on the philosophy that good health is every citizen's right.*

He also said a number of other quite critical things about Dr. Pound. Pound sued. The defence raised was fair comment. Dr. Pound's response was that neither the paper nor Scott should be permitted to raise fair comment because this was not a matter of public interest. Pound was, in effect, saying:

> *I'm not a rock star, I'm not a professional athlete, I'm not a politician, I'm not a public figure; I'm just an ordinary, everyday, private citizen and you can't attack me and my opinions and defend your attack on the basis of fair comment because what I happen to think about*

> *health care is simply the personal view of one private*
> *citizen and not a matter of public interest."*

The court disagreed. It accepted that Dr. Pound was an ordinary private citizen, but it also noted that he had himself, and on his own initiative, voluntarily entered the arena of public controversy and public debate. Health care was clearly a matter of public interest. Dr. Pound involved himself as an ostensible expert in a public debate about health care and, therefore, his opinions on that subject were a matter of public interest. Criticism of those opinions could be defended as "fair comment". Fair comment would not have succeeded if, for example, Scott had gone to a purely social gathering, met Dr. Pound and chatted with him concerning his views on a state-operated health-care system, and then written a column attacking Pound and his ideas. Under those circumstances, Pound's opinions would not have been matters of public interest. But clearly when we talk about rock stars, professional athletes, politicians, and so on, what these people think and do are matters of public interest. The point—that when it comes to matters of public interest, individuals must be prepared to sacrifice some part of their reputations—was well expressed by the trial judge who commented of Dr. Pound:

> *Like a boxer, having entered the ring, he must accept*
> *the blows given him, provided always that none is*
> *'below the belt.'*[468]

The third point about fair comment is that the defendant is required to establish a factual basis for the opinion that is to be expressed. Built into the defence is the notion that opinions do not simply fall from the sky. In order to succeed with fair comment, the defendant must have set out the facts on which the

---

[468] *Ibid.*, at p. 442.

opinion is based or from which it is derived. As was noted in *Pearlman*, the Winnipeg slum landlord case, CBC Radio detailed all the salient facts. The factual foundation must be laid in the same piece as the one that contains the opinion. This is always required, except where the facts on which the opinion is based are so well known as to be notorious.

Libel law is simply a formalization of basic rules of good journalism. If you are going to express critical opinions about somebody in public, you should lay out a factual foundation before you do so. The facts must be set out and, of course, they must be set out accurately. It surely makes sense to require that a person may rely on "fair comment" to defend the expression of her opinion only if the facts on which she claims to base her opinion are accurate and accurately stated.

What is the crucial element in the fair comment defence? Having ensured that you are indeed expressing an opinion, having made sure that it has to do with a matter of public interest, having accurately set out all the facts on which the opinion is based, it becomes simply a matter of honestly expressing your real opinion. A defendant is not required to persuade the court to agree with her opinion. A defendant is not even required to persuade the court that her opinion is reasonable. All a defendant must do is persuade the court that it was her honestly held opinion. The court may think that the opinion is absurd or implausible. The court may be incapable of imagining why anyone would hold such an opinion. All this is beside the point. If it is an honest expression of the defendant's real opinion, it is fair comment. Passages from two old English cases, both of which have been quoted over and over again in Canadian courts, will illustrate this point. The first is from an 1887 decision called *Merivale v. Carson*:[469]

Every latitude must be given to opinion and to

---

[469] (1887), 20 Q.B.D. 275 at 281–282 (C.A.).

> *prejudice, and then an ordinary set of men with ordinary judgment must say whether any fair man would have made such a comment.... Mere exaggeration, or even gross exaggeration, would not make the comment unfair. However wrong the opinion expressed may be in point of truth, or however prejudiced the writer, it may still be within the prescribed limit. The question which the jury must consider is this—would any fair man, however prejudiced he may be, however exaggerated or obstinate his views, have said that which this criticism has said?*

And, in Silkin v. Beaverbrook Newspapers Ltd.,[470] cited in Cherneskey v. Armadale Publishers,[471] the judge said:

> *They must believe what they say, but the question whether they honestly believe it is a question for you to say. If they do believe it, and they are within anything like reasonable bounds they come within the meaning of fair comment. If comments were made which would appear to you to have been exaggerated, it does not follow that they are not perfectly honest comments.*
>
> *...could a fair-minded man, holding a strong view, holding perhaps an obstinate view, holding perhaps a prejudiced view—could a fair-minded man have been capable of writing this? ...that is a totally different question from the question: Do you agree with what he said?*

The law is that when you are honestly trying to say what you

---

[470] [1958] 2 All E.R. 516 at 518–520 (Q.B.), Diplock L.J., quoting from *R. v. Russell* (2 December 1905), (Q.B.) [unreported].
[471] Above note 38.

really think about a matter of public interest, your exercise of your freedom of expression will take precedence over my reputation. The Supreme Court of Canada removed the "honest belief" requirement in *WIC Radio* v. *Simpson*[472] which is discussed at greater length, and from a slightly different perspective, below. But if you are saying nasty things about me simply because you are motivated by a whim or by a desire to spread scandal about me, then protection of my reputation should take precedence over your freedom of expression.

Recent legislation in a number of the common law provinces has altered this fundamental aspect of fair comment. In 1978 the Supreme Court of Canada decided *Cherneskey v. Armadale Publishers Ltd.*[473] This litigation was between a local politician and the Saskatoon *Star-Phoenix* over a letter to the editor that had been highly critical of the politician, claiming he was a "racist". The paper raised fair comment as a defence, but did not join the two law students who had written the letter as co-defendants or call them as witnesses. The Court trapped itself in a conceptual dead end. Since the evidence given at trial indicated that none of the actual defendants in the action—officials of Armadale, which owned the *Star-Phoenix*, and of the paper itself—believed the plaintiff to be a racist, the Court concluded that the defence of fair comment could not be raised. The statement was not an honest expression of the real opinion of any defendant and, as a result, the newspaper lost. This conclusion required the Court to disregard the obvious point that the statements in the letter clearly represented the real opinions of the people who wrote it. Several of the common law provinces amended their legislation to avoid the result in *Cherneskey*. Section 24 of Ontario's *Libel and Slander Act* now reads:

---

[472] [2008] 2 S.C.R. 420.
[473] Above note 464.

Where the defendant published defamatory matter that is an opinion expressed by another person, a defence of fair comment by the defendant shall not fail for the reason only that the defendant or the person who expressed the opinion, or both, did not hold the opinion, if a person could honestly hold the opinion.[474]

A media defendant can now successfully raise fair comment with respect to an opinion that neither it, nor the author of the opinion, actually holds. This defence seems strange. The question of whether the defendant will succeed with the defence of fair comment seems to have been distilled down to one final question: "Could any fair-minded person honestly express that opinion on a proven fact?"[475]

There is one instance where fair comment does not allow such broad latitude for free expression. This is where, to use the legal jargon, the defendant imputes corrupt or dishonourable motives to the plaintiff. We find an example in another case from British Columbia, *Masters v. Fox*.[476] This case had to do with a letter to the editor published in a local newspaper, the Comox District *Free Press*. The letter was written during a local election campaign about two people who were candidates in that election. The letter read as follows:

Election time is here again with some of the same old types trying to get in on the action. During the past year the Communist Party Action Committee [the plaintiffs actually belonged to something called the Community Planning Action Committee] has managed

[474] Above, note 424. For comment, see Robert Martin, *Libel and Letters to the Editor*, (1983) 9 Queen's L.J. 188.
[475] *Grant v. Torstar Corporation* (2009) 92 O.R. (3d) 561 (C.A.).
[476] (1978), 85 D.L.R. (3d) 64 (B.C.S.C.).

to belch a lot of bile and in the process make every effort to con the people into believing they are concerned with local issues and the orderly progress of the community—when in point of fact they are much more interested in spreading their particular brand of political venom—all of it under the guise of community interests....

I would not think that the voter has much of a problem in selecting a suitable and worthwhile candidate. With a full time career lay about and an old maid would appear (at a glance) to be an excellent recipe for a loser—but in spite of all some of these loud mouth windbags are going to tell and show everyone how to be winners and whatever the problem—you name it and they will cure it. Not one of them could run a peanut stand without a grant or subsidy and I would even suggest that one of them should be careful that the natural vegetation doesn't slowly take over and immobilize all activity.

It would be unfortunate if the voter was misled by some of their published rubbish which might permit (by accident) a few to get their grubby hands onto the tail end of a few more tax dollars.

This letter raises important issues about the proper scope of libel law. It is clearly extreme. On the other hand, it was written to a newspaper during the course of an election campaign. Should individuals be permitted, without any legal sanctions, to write letters like that during an election campaign about candidates in the election? I do not, for example, believe I should be able to write letters to the editor like that about my neighbour. But this was an election and the plaintiffs were candidates.

There were a number of problems with this letter, but the most important, and the reason the plaintiffs won, had to do with this question of imputing corrupt or dishonourable motives. The letter suggested that these people were running as candidates in the election in order to get their hands into the public till and start embezzling the public's money. The statement "might permit (by accident) a few to get their grubby hands onto the tail end of a few more tax dollars" was taken to suggest that the plaintiffs ran for election for the purpose of putting themselves in a position where they could more successfully indulge their inclinations towards corruption.

The law about imputing corrupt or dishonourable motives is clear. If the defendant imputes such motives in the course of expressing an opinion, then the defendant will have to *prove* that the plaintiffs were indeed motivated in exactly the fashion suggested. In *Masters v. Fox* the court said that in order to succeed the defendant would have to prove that the "full time lay about" and the "old maid" were running for public office precisely because they wanted to get their "grubby hands onto the tail end of a few more tax dollars." It must be obvious how difficult it would be to prove that unless, of course, these two defendants had publicly admitted that was why they were running for office. Once again, libel law accords with the requirements of good journalism. As a matter of principle, journalists should not speculate about people's motives. Idle speculation has no place in good journalism. Thus, not only is it bad journalism, but it is dangerous, to speculate about motives. The practical answer is to avoid it.

The final point to note about fair comment is the question of malice. When fair comment is raised, the plaintiff can attempt to show that in expressing her opinion the defendant was motivated by malice. If the plaintiff can successfully persuade the court that this was the case, the defence is lost. The same principle arises in relation to the defence of qualified privilege, so a full discussion of malice will be left until that point.

Privilege

We now move to consider the third defence in libel actions—
privilege. The defence of privilege is conceptually different from
the other two defences of justification and fair comment. When
the defence of justification is raised, the defendant is saying to the
court that the statements complained of may look as if they are
libellous, but they are not. They are not libellous because they are
true. Similarly, when the defence of fair comment is raised, the
defendant is saying these statements may appear to be libellous,
but they are not because they are fair comment made in good faith
and without malice on a matter of public interest. Both defences
focus on the substance of the allegedly libellous statements.
Privilege is different. When the defence of privilege is raised the
defendant is, in effect, conceding that the statements complained
of are libellous and is basing her defence, not on the substance of
those statements, but on the circumstances under which they
were made. As the Supreme Court put it:

> [P]rivilege attaches to the occasion upon which the
> communication is made, and not to the communication
> itself.[477]

The obvious implication is that a statement may be defensible if
made on an occasion of privilege, but the identical statement
might not be defensible if repeated on another occasion, under
different circumstances, which were not privileged. The breadth
of the defence is indicated by the fact that documents prepared by
lawyers in contemplation of litigation will attract the privilege.[478]

---

[477] *Botiuk* v. *Toronto Free Press Publications Ltd.*, [1995] 3 S.C.R. 3 at 29
[hereinafter Botiuk].
[478] 1522491 *Ontario Inc.* v. *Stewart, Esten Professional Corp.* (2010) 100
O.R. (3d) 596 at 608.

The point about privilege is that, in trying to find the proper balance between protection of reputation and the promotion of free expression, the law recognizes that there are certain situations in which it is so important that people be able to express themselves freely that they require preferring free expression over the protection of reputation. An important illustration is the case of senators or members of Parliament speaking inside the chamber of the Senate or the House of Commons. There is a clear social interest in ensuring that senators and MPs feel free to say whatever they like on any subject. A member of Parliament, speaking inside the chamber of the House of Commons, is absolutely privileged in respect of anything she says. She can stand up in the House of Commons and tell a series of malicious lies about me for no reason other than to damage my reputation. There is nothing I can do because the law takes the view that on this occasion the freedom of the MP to say whatever she wishes to say is more important than my reputation.

The purpose of having the defence of privilege is said traditionally to be the "common convenience and welfare of society."[479] The common convenience and welfare of society require that MPs speaking in Parliament feel free to express themselves as they choose. As a result, the common convenience and welfare of society also require that, in that circumstance, my reputation take a back seat.

The defence of privilege makes a great deal of reporting possible. A journalist reporting what transpired on an occasion of privilege will have a defence to a libel action if the report is fair and accurate. For example, not everything that a Member of Parliament says in a speech in the House of Commons may be accurate. The speech may well contain lies or distortions or be the result of shoddy research. Nonetheless, regardless of the number

---

[479] *Shultz* v. *Porter and Block Brothers Ltd.* (1979), 9 Alta. L.R. (2d) 381 at 391 (S.C.) [Shultz].

of inaccuracies in the MP's speech, as long as the report of it is fair and accurate, there will be a defence.

The practical point about privilege as a defence in a libel action is that, under appropriate circumstances, it permits the mass media to report statements made by other people without having to worry whether what is being asserted in those statements is true.

Turning specifically to privilege as a defence to be raised by the media, there are two broad subcategories: absolute privilege and qualified privilege. The structure of privilege is set out in Figure 3.

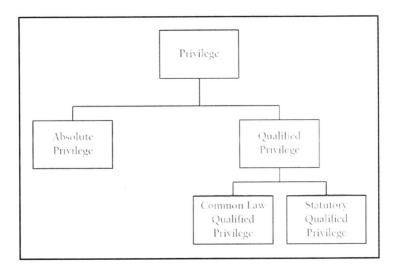

Figure 3: The Defence of Privilege

Absolute Privilege

Absolute privilege arises on one occasion and one occasion only: it will apply to a fair and accurate report of the public proceedings of a court. A reporter covering a trial does not have to trouble her mind whether what the witnesses or the judge or the lawyers are saying is true. Her only concern is that her report of what they are saying be fair and accurate.

Why does absolute privilege exist? Once again, the answer is that the common convenience and welfare of society require that the public be informed as fully as possible about what is happening in the courts. But this would not be possible if reporters and editors were required to establish the correctness of every assertion made in court before a report could be published. From a slightly different perspective, what we have here is another manifestation of the principle of the openness of the courts.

Absolute privilege results in the common law provinces from either the *Libel and Slander Act* or the *Defamation Act*. Certain difficulties may arise with the defence. First, all the statutes use the adverb "contemporaneously".[480] For the fair and accurate report of the public proceedings of a court to be privileged, it must be published *contemporaneously* with the proceeding in question. None of the statutes defines exactly what is meant by contemporaneously. The usual rule of thumb is that contemporaneously spans three to five days after the actual hearing or, if the publication in question is a weekly or a monthly, extends to the next issue after the proceeding. The general view is that after a week has passed, a report of the particular proceeding will no longer be contemporaneous and will, thus, not qualify for the privilege.

A second and important qualification is that in order to attract the privilege, the report of what went on in the courtroom must be "fair and accurate". The obvious point is that a reporter must get what witnesses and lawyers and judges are saying right. If something is wrongly reported and a story has a witness saying exactly the opposite of what the witness really said, it will not be a fair and accurate report and the defence of privilege will not be

---

[480] See, for example, the Ontario *LSA*, above, note 442, s. 4(1).

available. Once again, good reporting and good editing are key. However, it is clear that a fair and accurate report does not have to be verbatim. Nor does a fair and accurate report have to be a *precis* of what went on in the court. It is perfectly proper to select portions of what happened for reporting, or to focus on one witness or even one statement made by one witness. The report can still be fair and accurate. The standard that has been applied to determine whether a particular report is fair and accurate is to ask whether the impression created in the mind of a reader or a viewer of the report would be consistent with the impression that would have been created in the mind of somebody who was actually in the courtroom at the time. If the answer to the question is "yes," the report is fair and accurate. If the answer is "no," the report is not.[481]

An interesting issue arises with respect to language in *Libel and Slander Acts* or *Defamation Acts* to which few, if any, people have paid attention and whose meaning is, as a result, unclear. For example, section 4(1) of the Ontario *Libel and Slander Act* requires that, as a condition of raising the defence, the defendant must have been prepared to insert in its newspaper or broadcast a reasonable statement of explanation or contradiction by or on behalf of the plaintiff. This could mean, for example, as bizarre as it might appear, that if a reporter had covered the Paul Bernardo trial and, presumably, written some unpleasant things about Bernardo, that reporter might conceivably be under an obligation to afford some sort of right of reply to Bernardo. This provision has not, as far as I am aware, actually become an issue in litigation.

Why is absolute privilege called *absolute* privilege? Herein lies the basic distinction between absolute privilege and qualified privilege.

If the defendant has raised qualified privilege, the plaintiff can attempt to show that the defendant was motivated by malice in

---

[481] *Cook* v. *Alexander* [1974] Q.B. 279 (C.A.).

publishing the story. If the defendant was motivated by malice, the defence will be lost. By way of contrast, evidence of malice is irrelevant when the defendant relies on absolute privilege. This distinction is not entirely logical. If the defence raised is absolute privilege, it is difficult to see how a report that was motivated by malice could be regarded as fair and accurate. Nonetheless, that is the distinction.[482]

Qualified Privilege

There are two subcategories of qualified privilege—qualified privilege that arises under statute and qualified privilege that arises under common law. We will deal first with qualified privilege under statute and then turn to qualified privilege under common law.

Statutory Qualified Privilege

The various *Libel and Slander Acts* or *Defamation Acts* create extraordinarily broad bases for qualified privilege. They set out lengthy lists of occasions and circumstances about which the mass media may report and claim a defence of privilege, so long as the report in question is fair and accurate. The most significant of these are as follows. A fair and accurate report of the proceedings of any legislative body in the Commonwealth, or part or committee thereof that exercises either sovereign law-making power or delegated law-making power, is privileged. The most common example of a body that exercises delegated law-making power is a municipal council. Such a body has had the authority to

---

[482] Absolute Privilege was relied on to defend a document prepared by a lawyer in contemplation of litigation, even when the court concluded that the lawyer had been guilty of "malice and misconduct" in preparing the document. Note 476, above, at p. 603.

make laws which has been given or delegated to it by the provincial legislature. Thus, a fair and accurate report of proceedings in Parliament, or of the provincial legislature, or of a city council, or of any committee of Parliament, and so on, is privileged.

There is an interesting paradox here. Members of sovereign legislatures, when they are speaking inside the chamber of the legislature, are speaking on an occasion of privilege. Not only is the MP privileged in respect of what she says, but the media's fair and accurate report of what she said is also privileged. But because municipal councils are not sovereign law-making bodies, members of councils probably do not enjoy the same degree of privilege in respect of what they say during council meetings. So, if Councillor X were to stand up and call the Mayor a lying scoundrel, the Mayor might successfully sue Councillor X, but not the newspaper or broadcaster that published a fair and accurate report about the incident.

A fair and accurate report of the proceedings of any public administrative body in Canada is also privileged. That includes the proceedings, for example, of such bodies as the CRTC, or a provincial Workers' Compensation Board or Labour Relations Board. A fair and accurate report of the proceedings of any public commission of inquiry is privileged.

The Dubin Commission[483] which enquired into the use of drugs in sport would be a good illustration of the utility for the media of the defence of privilege. It sometimes seemed that every statement made by witnesses before the Commission was a libel of somebody or other. Many witnesses said such things as "he was supplying drugs", "she was using drugs", "someone else was prescribing drugs". If it had not been for the defence of qualified

---

[483] Canada, Commission of Inquiry into the Use of Drugs and Banned Practices Intended to Increase Athletic Performance, *Report*, Ottawa, Minister of Supply and Services, 1990.

privilege, it would have been impossible to publish reports about the proceedings of the Dubin Commission.

Indeed, a fair and accurate report of the proceedings of any lawful public meeting, whether admission to the meeting is general or restricted, is privileged. This category would include a shareholders' meeting from which members of the public were excluded. So, once again, if a reporter were to cover the annual general meeting of the Middlesex County Cat Fanciers' Association and all kinds of outrageous accusations were hurled round the room, that reporter's fair and accurate report about the meeting would be privileged. This means, to repeat a point made in relation to absolute privilege, that the accuracy of what is being reported must be ensured in the sense that this is indeed what the outgoing president of the Cat Fanciers' Association said, but the reporter is under no obligation to check that the substantive content of the outgoing president's statement was accurate.

A fair and accurate synopsis of any public statement or press release put out by any public or governmental body in Canada is also privileged. Thus, when the ministry of whatever sends out a press release, the media can report about it and not have to worry whether what is asserted in that press release is correct.

The defence is even broader. A fair and accurate report of any of the decisions, proceedings, or public statements of any association or body in Canada which is dedicated to any art, science, religion, or learning, or any trade, business, industry, or profession, or any game, sport, or pastime is privileged. It is useful again to think back to the Dubin Inquiry. The Canadian Track and Field Association, for example, regularly issued statements disagreeing with what certain witnesses before the Commission had said. Many of its press releases arguably libelled various people. But as long as the media produced fair and accurate reports of what was in one of those press releases, their reports were privileged.

If qualified privilege did not exist, a great deal of reporting would not be possible. How on earth, for example, could a reporter check the accuracy of every statement made by every member of a municipal council at every council meeting?

It is essential that the occasion in question actually be an occasion of privilege. For example, as has been noted, a fair and accurate report of a lawful public meeting is privileged. But it must have been a *bona fide* public meeting. In an old Saskatchewan case an individual rented a hall and invited the public in for no reason other than to give himself a platform from which to rail against various people he did not like. This occasion was held not to be a *bona fide* public meeting and, as a result, reports of it, even though they were fair and accurate, were not privileged.[484]

Qualified Privilege at Common Law

The question of qualified privilege under common law is especially interesting because it relates to the broader question of the direction Canadian libel law should be taking and, most important, whether it should become Americanized. At common law, privilege is attached to communications made under the following general circumstances. If the person making the communication was under a moral, social, political, legal, or professional duty to make it and the person to whom it was made was under a corresponding obligation to receive it, then the relation between them was regarded as one that gave rise to privilege.[485]

Privilege would attach to communications made during the course of that relation. For example, let us say a firm that was contemplating hiring someone engaged a psychiatrist to give an opinion about that person's emotional stability. The psychiatrist

---

[484] *Hefferman v. Regina Daily Star* (1930) 25 Sask. L.R. 148 (K.B.).
[485] *Adam v. Ward* [1917] A.C. 309 (H.L.).

would be under a professional duty to provide that information. Likewise, the firm would be under a corresponding obligation to receive it. Thus, a relation is created between the firm and the psychiatrist which gives rise to a qualified privilege surrounding communications made during the course of the relation. If the firm, having received a letter from the psychiatrist, showed that letter to an outsider, however, no privilege would attach to that communication.

How far can this principle be extended? Can it be argued that the mass media in a democracy are under an obligation to inform the public on matters of public interest and that the public is under a corresponding obligation to be informed? The result of accepting this argument would be that whenever the mass media speak to the public on matters of public interest, a relationship is created that gives rise to privilege. Thus, any plaintiff wishing to sue the mass media over a story that dealt with a matter of public interest would be met by the defence of qualified privilege; the plaintiff could only succeed if she were able to establish that the defendant was motivated by malice.

That, in fact, has been the basis of American libel law since a decision of the US Supreme Court in 1964 in a case called *N.Y. Times Co. v. Sullivan*.[486] Practically speaking, the result has been that the mass media in the United States are under no legal obligation to check their facts whenever they are dealing with a matter of public interest.

Such an approach was expressly rejected by the Supreme Court of Canada in 1961 in a case called *Banks v. Globe & Mail Ltd.*,[487] another piece of litigation arising out of the struggle between the Canadian Seamen's Union and the Seafarers' International Union. But the argument has been revived with the

---

[486] 376 U.S. 254 (1964).
[487] [1961] S.C.R. 474.

adoption of the *Charter* and, in particular, the guarantees of freedom of expression and freedom of the press in section 2(b).

Basing themselves on *N.Y. Times Co. v. Sullivan*, many in this country have argued that the defence of qualified privilege should be expanded to the point where any statement made by the mass media on any matter of public interest would attract a *Charter*-based privilege. This argument was expressly and unequivocally rejected by the Supreme Court in 1995 in *Hill v. Church of Scientology of Toronto*.[488] This decision, while it did not directly involve the mass media, set out important conclusions about the general direction the law of defamation should take in Canada.

The Court noted that the *Sullivan* approach had been widely criticized in the United States and, more important, had not been adopted by either the courts or the legislature of any other country. It further held that there was no compelling evidence to lead it to conclude that existing Canadian defamation law unduly limited freedom of expression. In addition, the Court saw nothing objectionable in the idea that the media should be legally responsible for the accuracy of what they publish. Finally, the court concluded that Canadian law struck an appropriate balance between the competing claims of expression and reputation.

At a more general level, the Supreme Court's decision in *Hill v. Church of Scientology of Toronto* can be seen as a definitive affirmation that the law of defamation is consistent with the standards of the *Charter*. Since the *Charter* was adopted in 1982, many people have suggested that Canadian defamation law limited freedom of expression and would have to be altered to bring it into conformity with the *Charter*. *Hill* would seem to have removed most of the basis for such arguments.

This is not to say that there is no common law qualified privilege in Canada. It is simply to say that it is substantially more limited than in the United States. One reason is that Canadian

---

[488] Above note 454.

courts have generally been unwilling to accord any special legal status to journalists. As justification for this restriction, the judges have often quoted a 1914 UK decision, *Arnold v. R.*:

> *The freedom of the journalist is an ordinary part of the freedom of the subject, and to whatever lengths the subject in general may go, so also may the journalist, but, apart from statute law, his privilege is no other and no higher.*[489]

An illustrative, if somewhat unusual, decision is *Camporese v. Parton.*[490] Ms. Parton was a reporter for the Vancouver *Province*. Under the headline "Importer Pushes Canning Lids That Could Spell Death," she wrote a story for the *Province* ostensibly to warn the public about the danger of food poisoning through the use of a certain brand of canning lid. There was, in fact, no such danger and the assertions about the canning lids which she made in her article were inaccurate. Nonetheless, a trial court upheld her claim to privilege. The court said the question of food poisoning was clearly one of general public interest and, moreover, the defendant was under a duty to communicate the imagined risk to the public. Most important, the defendant had an "honest belief" in the truth of what she had written about the particular brand of canning lid.

    Hill v. Church of Scientology of Toronto did extend the common law of qualified privilege[491] in one respect. The Supreme Court held that documents prepared for the purposes of litigation do

---

[489] (1914), 83 L.J.P.C. 299 at 300.

[490] (1983), 150 D.L.R. (3d) 208 (B.C.S.C.).

[491] There have been some interesting recent Canadian decisions on qualified privilege. See *Myers v. C.B.C.* (1999) 47 C.C.L.T. (2d) 272, *Leenen v. C.B.C.* (2000) 50 C.C.L.T. (2d) 213 and *Jones and Derrick v. Campbell*, [2002] N.S.C.A. 128.

attract the privilege even before they are filed with a court or read out in open court.

Malice

We turn now to the question of malice. Where the defendant raises either fair comment or qualified privilege, both defences can be defeated if the plaintiff can show that the defendant was motivated by malice. By way of contrast, malice is irrelevant when the defendant raises the defence of justification. Truth is a complete defence.

It may be useful, since we are addressing questions of motive, to digress slightly and ask whether truth should always be a complete defence in libel actions. Let us take an extreme case and say that there is someone who is a pillar of the community, universally loved, admired, and respected has enjoyed a wonderful working life and family life, and so on. A reporter discovers that thirty years ago this individual did one despicable thing. This reporter decides, for no other reason than to ruin our mythical character's reputation, career, and family life, to make the information public. The reporter and whoever publishes this story will have a complete defence. Should malice, or motive, which is what is at issue here, also be relevant to the defence of truth? Does it make sense to say that you may not express your opinions maliciously, but as long as you are telling the truth you can be as malicious as you like?

What is malice? The case law is clear. Malice will be found when the desire to injure is determined to be the dominant motive in publishing the defamatory material.[492] It is important to note that knowledge that publication may have the effect of injuring the plaintiff is not the same thing as the desire to injure. Go back to the *Pearlman* case. One would have to be naive not to

---

[492] *Shultz*, above note 477.

know that, when you say that someone has no morals, principles, or conscience, the statement is going to cause some injury. But that is not the issue. The issue is whether the defendant was motivated by the desire to cause injury. If the court is satisfied that the defendant was motivated by such a desire or was reckless whether injury resulted, that is malice, and the defences of fair comment and qualified privilege will be lost.

The case law makes a distinction between *recklessness* and *carelessness*. With qualified privilege it is essential that the defendant have an honest belief in the truth of what has been published. If it turns out that the assertions made are inaccurate or untrue, the defence will not necessarily be lost. It will be lost if the material was published recklessly, if the defendant neither cared nor considered whether it was true. It will not be lost if the defendant was merely careless—impulsive or irrational—about whether it was true. Recklessness amounts to malice; carelessness does not.[493]

Sloppy reporting may be held to be evidence of malice. The sloppiness, however, may have to be so extreme as to amount to recklessness. In *Camporese v. Parton*,[494] despite its conclusion that the defendant had prepared her article "without adequate research and with untimely haste," the trial court was still not prepared to find evidence of express malice on her part. On the other hand, deliberately keeping information favourable to the plaintiff out of a story may be regarded as malicious.

The point about good reporting and good editing is worth repeating. If there is good reporting and good editing, there should never be even the slightest question about malice. But where there is something other than good reporting and good editing, problems can arise. One of the things that helped to finish

---

[493] See *Botiuk*, above note 475.
[494] Above note 488.

the Toronto *Sun* in the *Munro*[495] case was evidence that the younger investigative reporter had, on occasion, walked around the newsroom announcing to anyone who cared to listen, "I've got that fucking Munro."[496] Statements like this did not help the *Sun* in its attempts to defend its story. The simple answer is that even if you happen to think things like this, keep them to yourself.

Courts have also held that where it is clear that the dominant motive in producing a particular story was the reporter's own personal ambition, that may amount to malice. Some of the case law seems to suggest that reporters must appear to be noble creatures concerned only with truth and the public interest.[497]

Both *Leenen v. CBC* and *Myers v. CBC* were responses to an investigative report, "The Heart of the Matter", which aired on the CBC TV programme, *The Fifth Estate*, on 27 February 1996. "The Heart of the Matter" purported to deal with what it regarded as the questionable behaviour of two physicians—Leenen and Myers—in relation to a heart medication called nifedipine. The *Fifth Estate's* contention was that nifedipine was an exceedingly dangerous medication and that the two physicians had demonstrated a callous and culpable disregard for the safety of patients who might use nifedipine. When each of the physicians sued, the CBC attempted to raise the defence of qualified privilege.

The element of the broadcast which led Dr. Leenen to sue was the airing of an interview with him, in which he had agreed to participate. The interview made Dr. Leenen look very bad.

When the CBC raised the defence of qualified privilege, the burden of proving that the CBC had acted with malice was shifted to Dr. Leenen. The court expounded at some length on the meaning of malice, noting that:

---

[495] Above note 458.

[496] 39 O.R. (2d) at p. 104.

[497] *Vogel*, above note 457.

> *Malice is commonly understood as spite or ill will towards someone. However, it also includes any indirect motive or ulterior purpose other than the sense of duty or the mutual interest which the privileged occasion created.* [498]

The Court noted certain aspects of the broadcast which it found to be evidence of malice. First, the CBC did not give Dr. Leenen a fair opportunity to defend himself against defamatory allegations which were made about him. Second, the fact that the piece which aired was completely one-sided and sought merely to validate preconceptions held by the CBC was seen to be evidence of malice. The person who produced the story originally wished to call it "Canada's Worst Drug Disaster." This fact, together with what the court saw as a general "good guy/bad guy" approach was taken to be evidence of malice. As the court observed further, "there was no quest for the truth here. The quest was for sound bites sufficient to fit the story line."[499]

Third, the court found that the CBC omitted evidence that was contrary to its thesis: "...an inference of malice may be drawn from the fact that the defendants wilfully misrepresented the facts by omitting significant evidence contrary to their thesis."[500] On this same point, the court observed about the CBC that, "Scandal was what they hoped would attract viewer interest and that attitude, in my view, was malicious."[501] The Court described the behaviour of the producer of the programme as "self-righteous arrogance".[502] It would be difficult, in my view, to imagine a more apt characterisation of "The Fifth Estate".

---

[498] *Leenen v. CBC*, above note 489 at 259.

[499] *Ibid.*, at p. 262.

[500] *Ibid.*

[501] 50 C.C.L.T. (2d) at p. 263.

[502] 50 C.C.L.T. (2d) at p. 266.

The *Myers* case was very similar to, and arose out of the same broadcast as, *Leenen*. Neither casts "The Fifth Estate" in a creditable light. The Court determined that the programme conveyed certain defamatory innuendoes about Dr. Myers. The CBC attempted to raise the defence of qualified privilege, a defence which the Court rejected, holding that the broadcast was not an occasion of privilege. The Court elaborated on the defence, stating:

> To succeed in making out the defence, the defendants must establish:
> 1. that they had an interest or duty to communicate the information; and
> 2. that the recipient had a corresponding duty or interest to receive the information.[503]

The Court noted an important difficulty that can arise when the mass media seek to raise the defence of privilege.

> Because of the notions of reciprocal interest and duty at the heart of the defence, confusion has surrounded the question of whether the privilege can arise in situations involving publication to the world at large.[504]

The Court noted further that:

> There is no general media privilege for the publication of matters of interest to the public, whether they be originated by the media or by members of the public. The media defendant is no different from anyone else

---

[503] *Myers v. CBC*, above note 378 at 295.
[504] *Ibid.* at 296.

and must show the relevant reciprocity of duty and
interest. [505]

The Court explored this point further, noting that

> ...qualified privilege can attach to a communication by
> the media published to the world at large if it is
> published in the context of a social or moral duty to
> raise the underlying issue; [506]

and, in particular, that:

> ...there is no general privilege available to the media
> at common law and that "special circumstances" will be
> required before the public interest in any given matter
> will be strong enough to impose a duty upon a
> newspaper to publish a defamatory matter.... It would
> appear that special circumstances may well exist when
> there is an urgent need to ventilate the subject matter,
> or perhaps when there is a health scare. [507]

It was not long before the *Fifth Estate* was involved in another libel
action. As a general principle of civil litigation, the defendant in
any torts proceeding is entitled to, and should, demand that the
plaintiff prove each and every element of her case. The *Fifth Estate*
became outraged by the ways in which some insurance companies
and their advisors, for example, Assessmed Inc., sought to
exercise this right in certain personal injury cases and prepared a
piece which was highly critical of Assessmed Inc.

The piece, called "Prove it if you can", aired on 10 November

---

[505] *Ibid.*

[506] *Ibid.*

[507] *Ibid.*

1998. Assessmed sued the C.B.C. for libel.[508] After a very lengthy trial, the Ontario Superior Court of Justice, in March of 2004, dismissed Assessmed's libel suit, holding that "Prove it if you can" was capable of conveying a defamatory meaning, but could be defended as fair comment. In June of 2006, the Ontario Court of Appeal denied Assessmed's appeal against this judgment[509] and, in September of 2006, the Supreme Court of Canada dismissed Assessmed's application for leave to appeal. In the Ontario Court of Appeal, Goudge, J.A. stated expressly that *Assessmed* should not be seen as comparable to either *Leenen*[510] or *Barltrop*[511].

The Court saw *Camporese v. Parton*[512] as a case in which these "special circumstances" existed, but concluded that the CBC could not rely on the defence of privilege in this case.

The chain of unfortunate events which led to the libel action in *Campbell v. Jones and Derrick*[513] was set in motion on 6 March 1995. On that date, Carol Campbell, a Constable in the Halifax Police, was called to a school in Halifax in connection with an alleged theft. The school was described as "... an inner-city school in a neighbourhood where many of the students are black and many are poor." Three teenagers suspected of the theft were in the school's guidance office. The respondent then searched these girls, each of whom was black. There was some controversy as to whether the girls were required to undress partially or completely during the course of the search. Stories about the searches appeared in the local media. The parents of two of the girls and the guardians of the third were upset and retained lawyers to assist

---

[508] (2004) 22 C.C.L.T. (3d) 89.

[509] *Assessmed Inc. v.C.B.C.* (2006) 211 O.A.C. 240.

[510] Above, note 489.

[511] Below, note 364.

[512] Above note 488.

[513] (2001) 197 N.S.R. (2d) 212. The appeal, *sub. nom. Jones and Derrick v. Campbell*, is reported at (2002) 209 N.S.R. (2d) 81.

them.

Two different lawyers were retained—Burnley A. "Rocky" Jones and Anne S. Derrick. Jones was a social activist, as well as a lawyer, and had played an important role in a Canadian Black Power movement which flourished briefly in the late 1960s. Anne Derrick had spent much of her legal career as a feminist activist. On 5 April 1995, Jones and Derrick held a press conference. Both Jones and Derrick described what had happened to the girls as "strip searches" and made reference to "systemic racism" in the Halifax Police Department.[514] Constable Campbell began a defamation action against Jones and Derrick. After a lengthy trial, a jury found in favour of Campbell and awarded her damages in the amount of $240,000.

Jones and Derrick raised the defence of privilege, but this was rejected by the trial court. They also attempted to introduce the evidence of a number of experts. This, too, was rejected. Jones and Derrick appealed. The Nova Scotia Court of Appeal delivered its decision on 24 October 2002. The central issue in the appeal was whether the press conference organized by the appellants on 9 April 1995 was an occasion of privilege. The Court of Appeal allowed the appeal. Roscoe J.A. discussed privilege at some length, noting that:

> There are certain occasions on which a person is entitled to publish untrue statements about another where he or she will not be liable even though the publication is defamatory. One such occasion is called a conditional or qualified privilege.... An occasion is privileged if a statement is fairly made by a person in the discharge of some public or private duty, or for the purpose of pursuing or protecting some private interest, provided it

---

[514] For a judicial discussion of racism in the Halifax police, see *R. v. R.D.S.*, [1997] 3 S.C.R. 484.

> is made to a person who has some corresponding interest
> in receiving it.... At the heart of the defence of
> qualified privilege is the notion of reciprocity or
> mutuality.[515]

The Court of Appeal was not willing to develop a new category of qualified privilege called "political information", whereby the publication of all such information would attract qualified privilege.

The Court was prepared to accept that the appellants were seeking to "...promote equality rights and to draw attention to violations of *Charter* rights." The appellants had argued that the searches of the girls were conducted in a manner which violated their *Charter* rights and that the girls had been searched only, or primarily, because they were young, black, and attending school in a poorer section of Halifax. The judge observed:

> I would conclude that in all the circumstances of the
> case, observed with today's eyes, in today's social
> conditions, that it is in the public interest that the press
> conference be found to be an occasion of qualified
> privilege.[516]

In this regard the Court emphasised the two appellants' professional interest in representing their clients. The decision in *Campbell* v. *Jones and Derrick* may be regarded as the first instance of the utilisation of the "contextual approach" in the resolution of

---

[515] *Sub. nom. Jones and Derrick v. Campbell*, above note 511 at 96.

[516] The dissenting judge in the Court of Appeal felt that the conduct of Jones and Derrick exceeded the limits of privilege. He said, "I regret to say that, in my opinion, their statements were high-handed and careless, void of any semblance of professional restraint or objectivity, were grossly unfair and far exceeded any legitimate purpose the press conference may have served." [*Ibid.* at 128.]

a libel action, which is to say, the first example of the politicisation of a libel action. One might say that, when a person acts in a fashion which could, from the perspective of the secular state religion of equality, be regarded as heretical or blasphemous, she is consigned to a state of quasi-outlawry, thereby losing her rights to her reputation. *WIC Radio* v. *Simpson*[517], discussed above in relation to fair comment, was a similar proceeding.

Kari Simpson was a "social activist" in British Columbia. She was unenthusiastic about the advocates of "gay rights" and, in particular, about their efforts to expose their propaganda to children in the public schools. Rafe Mair was a guardian of the public morals and the host of a talk radio show. He delivered himself of an "editorial" on 25 October 1999. The "editorial" was an attack on Simpson and on her views about homosexuals. He compared her to Hitler, to the KKK and to former Alabama Governor George Wallace. The editorial was stronger on venom than on historical accuracy. Mair had Wallace standing in a schoolhouse door declaiming that no Blacks would ever enter Alabama schools, when, in fact, the door was to the University of Alabama. Simpson sued for libel and the matter ended up before the Supreme Court of Canada. Mair sought to defend his remarks as fair comment. Before this decision, a defendant in a libel action, in order to make out the defence of fair comment, was obliged to satisfy the court as to her "honest belief" in the opinion expressed. The Supreme Court removed the "honest belief" requirement from the fair comment defence, offering this reasoning:

> *The traditional elements of the tort of defamation may require modification to provide broader accommodation to the value of freedom of expression.*[518]

---

[517] [2008] 2 S.C.R. 420.
[518] *Ibid.*, at p. 423.

I believe it is reasonable to interpret that last statement to mean, "Every possible latitude must be given to citizens who wish to denounce heretics and blasphemers".

As a necessary corollary to its having become a theocracy, Canada's public discourse has degenerated into a dismal and ritualistic morality play. Adherents of the secular state religion, by definition, think good thoughts and are, thus, good people. Anyone who deviates, or is seen to deviate, even slightly, from the one true faith, thinks bad thoughts and is, thereby, a thoroughly and hopelessly bad person.[519] It can readily be seen that this institutionalised manichaeanism[520] has functioned so as to create a political atmosphere in which democratic discourse has become impossible. If a certain point of view is defined, *a priori,* as good and any deviation from, or criticism of, that point of view, is, similarly, bad,[521] there is not, and cannot be, anything to talk about.[522] Stefan Braun grasped the existence and the significance of this Manichaean impasse and asserted:

> Today a kind of intellectual stalemate has developed beyond which thinking on these questions seems unable to move....Thinking becomes paralysed—in familiar

---

[519] James Bowman, *The Death of Politics* (2009) 27 The New Criterion, no. 7, 55.

[520] This phenomenon becomes most apparent on those rare occasions when someone ventures any public criticism of feminism or feminists. Any man sufficiently foolhardy to do so can expect to be anathemised and dismissed as a "misogynist", while any woman who does so will certainly be reviled as a "traitor". See, David Warren, *Extremist Thinking,* Ottawa Citizen 14 March 2010.

[521] See, below, note 568.

[522] James Bowman, *Unhappy is the Land,* (2010) 28 The New Criterion, no.6.

forms.[523]

As an example of institutionalised Manichaeanism, the Student Federation at the University of Ottawa, in March of 2010, refused to allow Ann Coulter, a conservative American columnist, to speak at the university, suggesting that her heterodox opinions amounted to "hate speech".[524] The university administration wrote an official letter to Ms Coulter which, as I interpret the letter, warned and threatened her concerning what she might, and might not, be permitted to say at a Canadian "university".[525] This letter cries out for further discussion and analysis. It was signed "Francois Houle, Vice-President Academic and Provost, University of Ottawa". I do realise that English is not Francois Houle's first language, but it is worth pointing out some of the many grade-school errors which the letter contained. These included using "different than" rather than "different from", "hopefully" rather than "I hope" and "restrictions to" rather than "restrictions on". The letter concluded with this memorable sentence:

> *Hopefully, you will understand and agree that what may, at first glance, seem like unnecessary restrictions to freedom of expression do, in fact, lead not only to a more civilized discussion, but to a more meaningful, reasoned and intelligent one as well".*[526]

As if to underscore the point about the Manichaean nature of

---

[523] *Democracy Off Balance, op. cit.,* p.7.

[524] Tony Lofaro, *Group attempts to silence U.S. right-winger's talk*, Ottawa Citizen, 20 March 2010.

[525] The *National Post* printed the text of the letter in its edition of 22 March 2010. See, *University's letter to Ann Coulter*, National Post, 22 March 2010.

[526] *Ibid.*

public discourse in Canada, Ann Coulter herself, during a speech which she gave at the University of Western Ontario, suggested that Francois Houle's letter to her amounted to a "hate crime".[527] As it turned out, Ms. Coulter's presentation at the University of Ottawa was cancelled.[528]

There has not appeared to have been, as the years 2010-2012 have unfolded, a substantial diminution in the Manichaean approach to public discourse in Canada. Expression which deviates, or appears to deviate, from established norms has continued to be anathemised as "hate". Sun Media applied for a licence to operate a television station in Canada. A group which claimed to be opposed to "American-style hate media" sought to forestall the issuing of the necessary licence and asked interested persons to sign a petition to that effect to "Canada's Radio and Telecommunications Commission" which, or so it appeared, is what the group believed CRTC to be short for.[529]

Christie Blatchford, who writes for the *Globe and Mail*, is, in my view, Canada's leading journalist. In 2006, Aboriginals from the Six Nations Reserve in southern Ontario, carrying the flag of the Mohawk Warrior Society, began a rampage through the neighbouring township of Caledonia. Blatchford wrote a book about the whole business.[530] In the course of her book, she said critical things about the Aboriginals involved. She was invited to

[527] Kenyon Wallace, *I'm the victim of a hate crime, Ann Coulter tells Canadian audience*, National Post, 22 March 2010.
[528] Robert Sibley, *Ann Coulter's event at the University of Ottawa cancelled over 'public safety' fears*, National Post, 24 March 2010. See also, Matthew Pearson, *Organisers, not university, cancelled Ann Coulter: U. of O.*, Ottawa Citizen, 24 March 2010.
[529] Kelly McParland, *Margaret Atwood's selective support for press freedom*, National Post, 2 September 2010.
[530] *Helpless: Caledonia's Nightmare of Fear and Anarchy and How the Law Failed All of Us*, Toronto, Doubleday Canada, 2010.

speak about her book at the University of Waterloo on 12 November 2010. Students disrupted the event and, shouting "racist" at her, made it impossible for Blatchford to speak. One student, who might well have read the Supreme Court of Canada's decision in *WIC Radio* v. *Simpson,* likened her to Julius Streicher. One articulate student summed up the purpose of the disruption, "...our goal was to not let her speak."[531]

If the reader will have accepted my having borrowed the judicial characterisation of the CBC's *Fifth Estate* as displaying "self-righteous arrogance"[532], she might be prepared to accept a characterisation of the University of Ottawa's behaviour as "sanctimonious pomposity".[533]

To return to the discussion of the defence of fair comment, removing the "honest belief" element from the defence seems strange. If my freedom to express my opinion on matters of public interest is to be preferred over your reputation, it does seem reasonable to require that I demonstrate my honest belief in what I am saying. As we have noted, evidence that the defendant was motivated by malice will vitiate the defence of fair comment. Returning, once again, to the litigation between Ms Simpson and Mr Mair, one might have thought that comparing someone to Hitler would be, in and of itself, sufficient evidence of malice.

Finally, neither a refusal by the defendant to apologize to the plaintiff, nor a determination to maintain the defence of justification—that is, continuing to assert that the story is true— will be taken as evidence of malice. Such would not, of course, be the case if it turned out that the defendant, in fact, knew the story to be false.

---

[531] Rex Murphy, *University of Waterloo ignoramuses accomplish their doltish goal*, National Post, 20 November 2010.

[532] See, above, p. 311.

[533] See, Robert Fisk, *Spare me the academics who only want a 'safe, positive' space*, The Independent, 3 April 2010.

Consent

The fourth defence, one that seldom arises, is consent. In many different contexts the presence or absence of consent will determine the legal character of an act. To touch another person without that person's consent is unlawful. It is both an assault that is actionable civilly and a criminal battery. To take a more concrete example, the practice of medicine is made legally possible because of consent on the part of patients. Just as an individual can consent to having someone else take a knife and cut her open, so too it is possible, in theory, to consent to being libelled. The problem is that it is difficult to imagine who, and under what circumstances, would be prepared to consent to this treatment. Do you mind if we call you a person of no morals, principles, or conscience?

One case that raised the issue was *Syms v. Warren.*[534] The plaintiff, who was the chair of the Manitoba Liquor Commission, went on an open-line radio show where a caller accused him of being an alcoholic. He sued the radio station and its defence was consent. The station said that since Syms had consented to appear on the program, he must be taken to have consented to these remarks, or, presumably, any others, being aired about him. The court agreed that a defence of consent existed, but said it did not arise in this case. The mere fact that this individual consented to appear on the open-line radio show could not be taken to mean that he consented to the publication of anything that anyone might conceivably say about him. It should be added that it is foolhardy for a radio station to air an open-line show without employing a delay mechanism.

As far as individual journalists are concerned, this question of consent can occasionally arise in relation to newspapers. Readers often write letters to the editor complaining about reporters or

---

[534] (1976), 71 D.L.R. (3d) 558 (Man. Q.B.).

columnists. Some newspapers have a practice that, before they print such a letter, they will show it to the staffer complained about. My view is that when an editor shows a reporter such a letter, by implication she is asking the reporter's consent to print it. And if the reporter is not enthusiastic about seeing the letter in print, she should say so, clearly and firmly.

Innocent Dissemination

An unusual defence is that of "innocent dissemination." This defence can be used in an attempt to negative the third element in the plaintiff's case—publication. In order to raise this defence, the defendant must establish that:

i)   the allegedly libellous material was disseminated in the ordinary course of business, and

ii)   that she had no knowledge of the libel, and

iii)   there was nothing in the material or the circumstances surrounding its dissemination which ought to have led her to suppose that it contained a libel.[535]

Professional Negligence and the Public Interest/Responsible Journalism Defence

It might be suggested that a libel action is the equivalent of a professional negligence action against a journalist. The analogy is not entirely apposite. It will be useful to look generally at the elements of an action for professional negligence.

---

[535] *Menear v. Miguna* (1996) 32 C.C.L.T. (2d) 37 (Ont. Ct. of Justice) at 39. It has been suggested that, when an I.S.P. is sued in respect of defamatory material published on the Internet, it might be able to raise the defence of innocent dissemination. See, Randy A. Pepper, *op. cit*, note 450, at p. 193.

In order to succeed the plaintiff must establish the basic requirements of a negligence action. First, the plaintiff must prove that the defendant failed to meet the requisite standard of care. Second, the plaintiff must prove that the defendant owed the plaintiff a duty of care. Third, the plaintiff must prove, on the balance of probabilities, that the defendant's negligent conduct was a cause of his or her injuries. Typically, in a negligence action, the defendant may raise such defences as contributory negligence, which decreases damages, or *novus actus*, which is a complete defence to a negligence action. The only defence of relevance in a professional negligence action is that of voluntary assumption of risk.

Historically, the word "profession" was confined to the three learned professions, the church, medicine, and law.[536] Courts, however, have given the word a broader meaning to include such occupations as architecture, engineering, and accounting *inter alia*. In order to be classified as a profession some special skill or ability was required to be exhibited, or some special qualifications derived from training or experience.[537] One must ask the question: "Would...the ordinary reasonable [person]...say...in the time in which we live, of any particular occupation, that it is properly described as a profession?"[538]

Journalism is not, strictly speaking, a profession in Canada, since it does not possess the legal attributes of a profession. This determination relies on whether or not a particular person is a member of an organized professional body with a recognized standard of ability enforced before she can enter it and a recognized standard of conduct enforced while she is practicing

---

[536] Commissioners of Inland Revenue v. Maxse, [1919] 1 K.B. 647 (U.K.C.A.)

[537] Carr v. Inland Revenue Commissioners, [1944] 2 All E.R. 163 at 166 (C.A.).

[538] *Ibid.*

it.[539] Professionals are expected to apply the degree of care that a normally skilled member of the profession might reasonably be expected to exercise.[540] Even though journalism is not, strictly speaking, a profession,[541] there do exist standards of behaviour to which journalists are expected to conform. When individual journalists fail to do so, a libel action is likely to occur. Standard of care is the most important element in a professional negligence action. This analysis will address professional negligence with respect to both the medical and legal professions.

Medical Profession

In *ter Neuzen v. Korn*,[542] the Supreme Court of Canada outlined the standard of care to be expected of medical professionals. In that case, the plaintiff was infected with HIV as a result of an artificial insemination procedure conducted by the defendant. Expert evidence indicated that the defendant complied with approved medical practice in screening sperm donors at the time of the procedure. Sopinka, J. for the majority, stated that physicians have a duty to conduct their practice in accordance with the conduct of a prudent and diligent doctor in the same circumstances, while specialists must act in accordance with the conduct of other ordinary specialists who possess the reasonable knowledge, competence, and skill expected of Canadian

---

[539] Currie v. Commissioners of Inland Revenue, [1921] 2 K.B. 332 (U.K.C.A.).

[540] *Larche v. Ontario* (1990), 75 D.L.R. (4th) 377 (leave to appeal to SCC refused).

[541] The International Labour Organisation has made a distinction between "regulated" and "non-regulated" professions. Journalism is clearly a non-regulated profession.

[542] [1995] 3 S.C.R. 674 [*ter Neuzen*].

professionals in that field.[543] Sopinka, J. acknowledged that courts do not typically have the expertise to tell professionals that they are not behaving properly in their field. Therefore, it is generally accepted that when a doctor acts in accordance with a recognized and respectable practice of the profession, he will not be found to be negligent.[544] While adherence to the practice of one's peers may be strong evidence of reasonable and diligent conduct, it is not determinative.[545] The standard practice itself may be found to be negligent where it is "fraught with obvious risks" such that anyone is capable of finding it negligent, without possessing any specific expertise.[546] As a general rule, where a procedure involves difficult or uncertain questions of medical treatment or complex scientific or highly technical matters that are beyond the ordinary experience and understanding of a judge or jury, a standard medical practice cannot be found negligent. On the other hand, as an exception to the general rule, if a standard practice fails to adopt obvious and reasonable precautions which are readily apparent to the ordinary finder of fact, then it is no excuse for a practitioner to claim that she was merely conforming to a negligent common practice.[547]

Legal Profession

A solicitor is expected to meet the standard of the ordinary competent solicitor and will be liable in negligence if she makes an error which the ordinary competent solicitor would not have made.[548] Expressing an opinion which turns out to be wrong will

---

[543] *Ibid.* at 693.

[544] *Ibid.* at 695.

[545] *Roberge v. Bolduc*, [1991] 1 S.C.R. 374 at 437.

[546] Above note 540 at 696–97.

[547] *Ibid.* at 699.

[548] *Glivar v. Noble* (1985), 8 O.A.C. 60 (C.A.) at 67.

not be sufficient to establish professional negligence. Counsel will only be guilty of gross negligence if she makes an elementary error.[549] While a solicitor must meet a reasonably high standard of care, she is not required by law to act as if she were infallible.[550] As is the case with medical professionals, compliance with the customary practice of her peers in the community is not conclusive that the solicitor has exercised reasonable care in carrying out the legal work in question.[551]

Once a particular occupation is classified as a profession, its members will be expected to apply the degree of care which a normally-skilled member of that profession might reasonably be expected to exercise. This is because professionals are expected to possess specialized knowledge upon which others are entitled to rely. As exemplified in *Ter Neuzen*, the courts are reluctant to second-guess the established practices of professionals unless the practice is fraught with risks.

A libel action is likely to result when the acts of a journalist fall below the standards normally expected of a professional journalist.[552]

The Ontario Court of Appeal recently adopted a somewhat similar analysis in constructing a new defence to be used in libel actions. The litigation in question was *Cusson v. Quan*.[553] The Court took the opportunity to conduct a thorough review of the existing common law of defamation, concluding that it was deficient in that it "...clearly favours the protection of reputation

---

[549] *Rondel v. Worsley*, [1969] 1 A.C. 191 at 287 (H.L.).

[550] *Karpenko v. Paroian, Courey, Cohen & Houston* (1981), 30 O.R. (2d) 776 (H.C.).

[551] Above note 540.

[552] See *Myers v. C.B.C.* (1999) 47 C.C.L.T. (2d) 272 and *Leenen v. C.B.C.* (2000) 50 C.C.L.T. (2d) 213.

[553] (2007) 87 O.R. (3d) 241 (C.A.).

over freedom of expression."[554] The plaintiff, Cusson, was a Constable in the Ontario Provincial Police who, after the attacks on New York City of 11 September 2001, went there to assist. For some reason, the Ottawa *Citizen* decided to publish a series of attacks on Cusson. The first of these was published on 25 September 2001 under the head, "Renegade O.P.P. officer under fire". This was followed on 26 September by "O.P.P. apologizes for Cusson 'Fiasco'" and, on 11 October 2001, by "O.P.P.'s Cusson faces internal investigation." Cusson sued for libel. The *Citizen* attempted initially to raise the defence of qualified privilege, saying that qualified privilege, in its traditional sense, placed undue restrictions on free expression and should be broadened. The Court appeared to accept the argument that the defence of qualified privilege restricted free expression unduly but expressly refused to extend the defence to "...all media reports on matters of public interest."[555] The Court was, nonetheless, prepared to recognise a new defence. This was the *"public Interest / responsible journalism"* defence, based on two decisions of the U.K. House of Lords.[556] The Court elaborated the elements of the defence:

> ...*where a media defendant can show that it acted in accordance with the standards of responsible journalism in publishing a story that the public was entitled to hear, it has a defence even if it got some of its facts wrong...to avail itself of the public interest responsible journalism test a media defendant must show that it took reasonable steps in the circumstances to ensure that*

---

[554] *Ibid.*, at p. 252.

[555] *Ibid.*, at p. 276.

[556] *Jameel* v. *Wall Street Journal* [2007] 1 A.C. 359 and *Reynolds* v. *Times Newspapers* [2001] 2 A.C. 127.

> the story was fair and its contents were true and
> accurate.[557]

The Court concluded that, since the new defence had not been litigated at the trial, it could not be available on appeal. In a decision released on 22 December 2009[558], the Supreme Court of Canada formally recognized the Responsible Journalism/ Public Interest defence. It appeared to have been impelled to this result by a belief that the existing law of libel restricted freedom of expression to a greater degree than was necessary.

Remedies

We turn now to remedies in civil libel actions. Concretely, we will investigate the question of what a successful plaintiff can expect to receive.

We can begin to address this matter through an analogy with criminal prosecutions. In every criminal prosecution, there are two separate and distinct stages. In the first, the court is concerned with the question of the guilt or innocence of the accused. If the accused is found not guilty, that is the end of the matter. If the accused is found guilty, however, the court moves to the second stage, which involves a determination of the appropriate punishment. Civil proceedings are not as clearly demarcated into two stages as are criminal proceedings, but there is at least a conceptual distinction. The first stage in all civil proceedings addresses the issue of liability. Who wins? Is the defendant liable to the plaintiff? If the defendant wins, if the court determines she is not liable to the plaintiff, that is the end of the matter. But, if the plaintiff wins, the question that must be answered is: What does the plaintiff get?

---

[557] (2007) 87 O.R. (3d) 241 at p. 279.
[558] *Grant* v. *Torstar Corp.* [2009] 3 S.C.R. 640.

People do not normally institute civil proceedings for the sole purpose of winning moral victories. They have some concrete goal in mind. In tort law the most common remedy is an award of money damages. It is also possible, under certain circumstances, that a plaintiff may seek an injunction to prevent the publication, or republication, of a libel. We will investigate issues relating to damages first and then turn to the matter of injunctions.

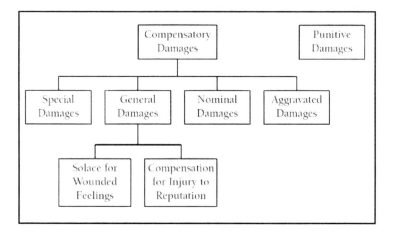

Figure 4: Damages in Libel Actions

Damages

What standard is used to determine how much money should be awarded as damages? A 1980 English decision restated the traditional principle:

> *The general object underlying the rules for the assessment of damages is, so far as possible by means of a monetary award, to place the plaintiff in the position*

> *which he would have occupied if he had not suffered the wrong complained of.*[559]

So what a court is trying to do is give the plaintiff a sum of money which will, as far as possible, restore the status quo that existed prior to the defendant's unlawful act. The goal is to put the plaintiff back where the plaintiff would have been had it not been for the defendant's unlawful act.

Unfortunately, the matter gets more complicated in practice. In tort law there are two broad heads or categories of damages. The first is called "special damages." Special damages are easy and straightforward. Their purpose is to compensate plaintiffs for directly quantifiable pecuniary loss—out-of-pocket monetary loss. We can use the example of a tort claim arising out of a car accident, at least as it would have been dealt with prior to the creation of "no-fault" systems. The sorts of things a plaintiff could claim under the head of special damages as a result of a car accident would include loss of income, car repairs, medical bills, wheelchairs, drugs and physiotherapy. These are all items for which a price can easily be ascertained. The calculation of special damages is largely a matter of arithmetic. You write down all the things the plaintiff had to pay for and add them up. Did the plaintiff have to pay for this or did she not? Did she have to rent a wheelchair? If she did, for how long and what did it cost?

It should also be clear that there can be no *a priori* limit or ceiling on "special damages". No one can say in advance that a particular sum is the maximum amount any plaintiff might claim by way of special damages. The only question is to determine the extent of the actual losses, which must, of course, be proved by the plaintiff. These are added up and the total is special damages.

---

[559] *Dodd Properties (Kent) Ltd.* v. *Canterbury City Council*, [1980] 1 All E.R. 928 at 938 (C.A.).

Having said all this, special damages are not common in libel actions. The more obvious examples would be instances where the plaintiff loses a job or business as the result of the publication of a libel. Claims for special damages in libel actions will largely be confined to claims for lost income. Again, there are no particular problems with special damages in libel actions. The one obstacle confronting a plaintiff is that this is the only area of libel law where she must prove actual loss. The plaintiff has to prove that she suffered this out-of-pocket, monetary loss as a direct result of the publication of the libel. If she can, the loss is compensable by way of special damages. If she cannot, it isn't.

The real difficulties in libel actions arise in relation to general damages. General damages are awarded in respect of non-pecuniary, non-quantifiable losses. Once more, it is useful to look at analogies with personal injury claims. Someone who is injured in a car accident might, under the rubric of general damages, be able to claim for such things as pain and suffering, loss of the enjoyment of life, and reduced life expectancy. The difficulty with all these losses lies in assigning a monetary value to them. This has been a deeply vexed problem in personal injury litigation. How much is the loss of one leg worth? What about the pain and suffering and loss of enjoyment of life that result from such a loss? How many dollars are they worth? If the plaintiff lost both legs, should that be worth twice as many dollars as losing one leg?

In 1978 the Supreme Court of Canada decided three personal injury cases that have come to be called "The Trilogy".[560] These were very difficult cases. In one a little girl was playing around her house in the summer and heard an ice cream vendor. The ringing bells had the intended effect. The little girl went running after the ice cream vendor—and was hit by a car. As a result, she was

---

[560] *Andrews* v. *Grand & Toy Alberta Ltd.*, [1978] 2 S.C.R. 229; *Thornton* v. *School District No. 57 (Prince George)*, [1978] 2 S.C.R. 267; *Arnold* v. *Teno*, [1978] 2 S.C.R. 287.

turned physically and mentally into a total vegetable. She would never do anything, never move, never think, never in any sense enjoy a human life, but would probably live another fifty years. The award of special damages was enormous, but the Court had to address the question of how much should be given as general damages. The Court said that the maximum that could be awarded as general damages in respect of these non-quantifiable, non-monetary losses was $100,000. That remains the ceiling today in personal injury cases, except, of course, that it must continually be adjusted for inflation.

The point is that, if it is difficult in personal injury litigation to assign a dollar value to things like pain and suffering and loss of the enjoyment of life, it is even more difficult with respect to the losses that general damages seek to compensate in libel actions. General damages in libel are said to be awarded to address two issues. First, there is to be compensation for injury to reputation and, second, solace for wounded feelings. How should a court go about determining a dollar amount to compensate for injury to reputation and to provide solace for wounded feelings? The difficulties are compounded by the principle that, apart from special damages, the plaintiff is not required to prove any actual loss.

These difficulties are further compounded because general damages in libel actions are said to be "at large". This means that, where a libel case is tried before a jury, the jury is entitled to select any figure it wishes. Toronto lawyer Julian Porter put the matter this way:

> *The magic of libel is that damages are at large and a jury can give whatever it sees fit....*
>
> *Consequently counsel must adopt a baroque attitude with tears if possible. One must abandon and gush with vibrato. My view is that unlike other cases a plaintiff's counsel can ill afford to be cheery or chirp*

witty asides to a jury. A jury must be slowly and
continually persuaded that the worst ailment on this
earth is to be buried with a sullied name. All speeches
should dwell on the illusory balm of money and the
eternal pain of losing the quality of life that has been
wrenched away by the monstrous libel. The great area
to exploit is that damages are at large and that actual
damages needn't be proved.[561]

To underline this point, we should refer again to *Hill v. Church of Scientology of Toronto.*[562] In this decision the Supreme Court affirmed the largest award of damages—$1,600,000—ever reached in a Canadian defamation suit. After deliberating for four hours, the jury had asked the trial judge for some direction concerning the appropriate award. In particular, the jury asked about "realistic maximums" in recent cases. The judge's reply, which was endorsed by the Supreme Court, was:

I have discussed the question with counsel and we are
all in agreement that the only answer that we can
provide to you is that by law neither the parties nor the
judge are entitled to advise the jury of maximums or
minimums in these kinds of cases. So, I'm afraid you're
on your own.[563]

If there is a case for a ceiling on the amount that can be awarded as compensation for non-pecuniary loss in personal injury litigation, it would seem there would be an even stronger one for such a ceiling in libel litigation. In both *Snyder v. Montreal Gazette Ltd.*[564] in

---

[561] J. Porter, *Tangents* (1981) 5 Canadian Lawyer 24.

[562] Above, note 454.

[563] [1995] 2 S.C.R. at p. 1195.

[564] [1988] 1 S.C.R. 494.

1988, and *Hill v. Church of Scientology of Toronto*, the Supreme Court has rejected the idea, basing its rejection on the general ground that there is too much variation in the facts and circumstances of individual defamation cases to justify the establishment of an *a priori* ceiling.

It is worth stressing that awards of general damages in Canadian libel cases are modest in comparison with awards in similar cases in the United States and the United Kingdom. In *Hill v. Church of Scientology of Toronto*, the Court noted that between 1987 and 1991 there were only twenty-seven reported—that is, reported in law reports—decisions in libel cases and that the average award of damages was $30,000. From 1992 to 1995 there were twenty-four judgments reported, with an average award of $20,000. And while *Hill* itself, as we have noted, saw the largest total award ever upheld by appellate courts, the award of general damages of $300,000 was consistent with existing Canadian standards. The Supreme Court made it clear that this was a figure either at or very near the upper end of the scale. In fact, it would not be unreasonable to view $300,000 as a *de facto* ceiling on general damages in libel actions.

The special role of the jury in determining the amount of a damage award must be emphasized. Where a libel action is tried with a jury, it is the jury's responsibility to determine exactly how much shall be awarded to the plaintiff. An appellate court will alter the figure awarded by a jury only if it is satisfied either that no reasonable jury could have awarded that amount or that the amount is so out of proportion to the libel as to shock the court's conscience and sense of justice.

General damages, and special damages are two of the headings under which compensatory damages may be awarded. Since there is little more that can be said about special damages, we will continue our analysis of compensatory damages by looking in more detail at nominal, general, and aggravated damages.

Compensatory Damages

Nominal Damages

A court may conclude that, while the defendant has indeed libelled the plaintiff, the extent of the injury to the plaintiff's reputation has been so slight as to merit only a minimal or nominal award of damages. The main factor that would lead a court to such an award is the actual state of the plaintiff's reputation at the time of the publication of the libel.

If it can be shown that the plaintiff had no reputation to speak of, a nominal award may follow. The defendant is permitted to introduce general evidence of the plaintiff's poor or non-existent reputation. "General", as used here, means evidence relating to matters other than what had been asserted in the original libellous statement about the plaintiff. This occurred in *Leonhard v. Sun Publishing Co.*[565] The Vancouver *Sun* had published an article in which it described the plaintiff as a "drug king". Although the *Sun* conceded that this assertion was libellous, it also introduced evidence showing that Jacob Leonhard was widely known as a gangster and had no reputation in the community. He was awarded $1 in damages. The risk in this tactic is that if the defendant's evidence as to the plaintiff's generally bad reputation fails to persuade the court, the defendant, as a result, may pay even more in damages.

General Damages

Here we will address the factors a court will look at in arriving at a final amount. We will look first at factors that relate to the plaintiff and then at factors that relate to the defendant.

It is unfortunate, but true, that in libel litigation some people

---

[565] (1956), 4 D.L.R. (2d) 514 (B.C.S.C.).

are more equal than others. The more socially prominent a plaintiff is, the greater the amount she is likely to be awarded as general damages. The reasoning underlying this inequality is roughly as follows. It is assumed that the more significant someone is, the better her reputation must be. The better someone's reputation, it must follow, the more serious the injury to it will be. And the more serious the injury to reputation, the more substantial the award of damages needed to compensate for that injury. Thus, the Nova Scotia Court of Appeal could conclude in *Barltrop v. Canadian Broadcasting Corp.*:

> *Here, a man of international reputation is vilified in the eyes of his professional confreres. He thus suffers greatly, though he may not lose a single dollar.* [566]

As we have seen, an incorporated organization can sue as a plaintiff in a libel action. But a successful corporate plaintiff can claim only special damages; it cannot seek general damages for injury to reputation.

Turning to the defendant newspaper or broadcaster, its exact nature and character are important. To begin with, other factors being equal, the extent of publication is important. The theory is that the more people who saw or read the libel, the more serious has been the injury to the plaintiff's reputation. This approach is not to be applied mechanically, however. In *Walker v. CFTO Ltd.*,[567] the jury awarded $1 in damages for each of the roughly 900,000 persons who had viewed the libellous broadcast. This amount was cut back drastically on appeal, the case being one of the few instances where an appellate court has interfered with a jury's award of damages.

The reputation of the defendant is also important. The better

---

[566] (1978), 25 N.S.R. (2d) 637 at 665 (C.A.).
[567] (1987), 59 O.R. (2d) 104 (C.A.).

the reputation the defendant newspaper or broadcaster has, the more likely it is people will believe what it publishes and, therefore, the more serious the injury it can cause to the plaintiff's reputation. This issue was addressed in *Vogel v. Canadian Broadcasting Corp.*,[568] where the court said:

> In terms of prestige, power and influence…[the CBC] is at the opposite end of the spectrum from the sleazy scandal sheet. Created and maintained by Parliament to inform the Canadian public, its news services are accorded great respect throughout Canada. They have a well-merited reputation for reliability. For that very reason, CBC has an enormous capacity to cause damage. The general run of right-thinking people tend to think that "it was on the CBC news, so it must be so."

Awards of general damages made by Canadian courts, taking inflation into account, continue to be modest. Courts have generally recognized that they "must be careful not to award damages which may tend more to stifle the free expression of opinion than to rehabilitate the reputation of the defamed."[569] And it is worth noting that, with some exceptions, the awards at the higher end of the scale have not generally been against media defendants.

Aggravated Damages

The terminology used by the courts in discussing damages in libel actions is often confusing. Aggravated damages are awarded in addition to general damages, but are still regarded as compensatory. Aggravated damages represent an additional

---

[568] Above note 457 at 178.
[569] *Derrickson v. Tomat* (1992), 88 D.L.R. (4th) 401 at 411 (B.C.C.A.).

amount of money awarded to the plaintiff to compensate her for a particularly serious injury to her reputation and, of course, to provide a more generous solace. The determining factor in leading a court to award aggravated damages is the conduct of the defendant.

In *Hill v. Church of Scientology of Toronto* the Supreme Court of Canada upheld an award of $500,000 as aggravated damages. The Court said such damages "take into account the additional harm caused to the plaintiff's feelings by the defendant's outrageous and malicious conduct." Other decisions have used words like "insulting", "high-handed", "spiteful", "malicious", or "oppressive" to describe the sorts of conduct that may result in aggravated damages.

A court will look at the entire course of conduct of the defendant from the time of the publication of the libel up until the conclusion of the trial. Among the factors to be considered, according to the Supreme Court, are whether the defendant sought widespread publicity for the libel; the presence or absence of a retraction or an apology by the defendant; repetition of the libel; and the conduct of the defendant and the defendant's counsel throughout the trial. This approach means, of course, that there can be a risk involved in mounting a vigorous, aggressive, and determined defence. If such a defence fails to persuade the court, the award may be higher than might otherwise have been the case.

Punitive Damages

Punitive damages, or exemplary damages, are awarded in addition to compensatory damages. Their primary purpose is to punish the defendant, not compensate the plaintiff, since that, of course, has already been done. They are also awarded to deter others from engaging in conduct similar to that of the defendant.

The whole idea of punitive damages in tort actions is anomalous. First, they cause the distinctions between criminal law and tort law to become blurred. Second, they represent a windfall for a plaintiff who has already been fully compensated for any loss she might have suffered. Nonetheless, punitive damages are recognized in libel actions. In *Hill v. Church of Scientology of Toronto* the Supreme Court upheld an award of $800,000 as punitive damages. A court will only award punitive damages where it finds the defendant's behaviour to have been "truly outrageous", "so malicious, oppressive and high-handed that it offends the court's sense of decency."

It is inexcusable for aggravated damages or punitive damages to be awarded against a media defendant. Observing the rules of good reporting and good editing should ordinarily guarantee that this does not happen. Where these rules are not followed, aggravated damages or punitive damages may result. The cases in which this has happened exemplify egregious failures to observe basic standards of journalism. We have already looked at some of these cases, so for present purposes we will address only what the judges had to say in awarding larger than usual damages.

In *Vogel v. Canadian Broadcasting Corp.*,[570] the court spoke of the "reckless and deliberately damaging actions of the defendants" in reaching its conclusion to award aggravated damages. In *Thomas v. Canadian Broadcasting Corp.*,[571] aggravated damages were awarded because of the CBC's failure to include in its broadcast information which it had in its possession and which tended both to be favourable to the plaintiff and to cast doubt on the CBC's interpretation of what had happened. In *Munro v. Toronto Sun Publishing Co.*,[572] punitive damages, although only in the amount of $25,000, were awarded, largely on the basis of the court's

---

[570] Above note 457 at 184.
[571] Above note 389.
[572] Above note 458.

conclusion that the two investigative reporters "did deliberately intend harm to Mr. Munro." Among the evidence that led the court to this conclusion was the comment by the younger investigative reporter at the *Sun*, "I've got that fucking Munro", and, more generally, "the lack of care as to accuracy of the story and the falsity of the contents."

Apology

The law gives a number of advantages to media defendants in libel actions. The most important of these have to do with an apology. A timely apology may permit a defendant effectively to avoid the consequences of libelling someone, and the procedural rules governing apologies give an advantage to a media defendant.

The law places certain obligations on a potential plaintiff, obligations that are strictly enforced. Although there is some variation from province to province, a plaintiff must, as a precondition to being able to sue, serve a libel notice on a media defendant within a specified period of time.[573] A libel notice must be in writing and must indicate the material that the plaintiff claims is defamatory. Apart from these requirements, no particular form is specified for a libel notice. In Ontario a libel notice must be delivered to the newspaper or broadcaster within six weeks of the libellous material coming to the plaintiff's attention. This time limit is the shortest statutory period. In all cases, these limits are strictly interpreted.[574] Furthermore, it will likely be assumed that the alleged libel came to the plaintiff's attention on the same day it was published, unless there is some evidence to show why this could not have been the case. Even if a newspaper or broadcaster does libel someone, if that individual does not have a libel notice delivered within the statutory period

---

[573] See Ontario, *LSA*, above note 442, s. 5(1).
[574] *Grossman v. CFTO-Television Ltd.* (1982), 39 O.R. (2d) 498 (C.A.).

specified by the law of the particular province, the newspaper or broadcaster is off the hook.

If a libel notice is received, the period immediately after its arrival is the most crucial of all. This period is when the decision to apologize, or not to apologize, must be made. The various *Libel and Slander Acts* or *Defamation Acts* give media defendants three days within which to decide to apologize. If the defendant apologizes—that is, publishes a "full and fair retraction"—within this period, the maximum amount that can be awarded against it is reduced to "actual damages". Actual damages means special damages and, since special damages are seldom awarded in libel actions, the practical result of an apology is that the matter is at an end. In the case of a defendant who operates a print publication other than a daily newspaper, an apology in the next regular issue after the receipt of the libel notice will suffice.

As soon as a libel notice is received, a lawyer should be called to review the material complained of carefully with the reporter and the editor who worked on it. Every aspect of this material should be checked. If, by the end of this review, it has become apparent that an error was made, an apology should be issued. If, however, it is clear that the facts complained of are accurate or that the opinions expressed are fair comment or that the assertions are a fair and accurate report of communications made on an occasion of privilege, there is no need to apologize. If a story is the result of good reporting and good editing, there is no reason to be intimidated by a libel notice. Far more libel notices are served than libel actions are instituted.

Even if a defendant fails, for whatever reason, to publish an apology within the three days provided by the statute, an apology made at any time prior to judgment actually being given by a court will have the effect of reducing the amount of money that can be awarded as damages. The longer the defendant delays in issuing an apology, however, the less benefit there is to be gained from it.

To be effective, an apology must be real and it must be sincere. To quote from an old British Columbia case:

> *That is surely not sufficient. It is not the offer nor even the publication of an apology at all, but an offer to offer an apology. And even in terms, it seems to reserve to the defendant a right of judging whether the plaintiff is reasonable in demanding any particular form e.g., it offers to make such an apology as the defendant thinks fit. Such an apology as merely "beg your pardon" or "sorry for it," is not sufficient in a case of libel. The defendant should admit that the charge was unfounded, that it was made without proper information, under an entire misapprehension of the real facts, etc., and that he regrets that it was published in his paper.... You should not offer to make, but actually make and publish at once, and unconditionally, such an apology, expressing sorrow, withdrawing the imputation, rehabilitating the plaintiff's character as well as you can; not stipulating that the plaintiff is to accept it; not making any terms but publishing it in the interests of truth, and because you are anxious to undo whatever harm which may have accrued from a wrong which you find you have been the unconscious instrument of inflicting.*[575]

In other words, for an apology to be legally effective, it must contain an amount of grovelling.

Furthermore, if a purported apology is not a real apology, not only may the defendant not derive any benefit from it, it may actually have the effect of increasing the amount of money

---

[575] *Hoste v. Victoria Times Publishing Co.* (1889), 1 B.C.R. (Pt. 2) 365 at 366 (S.C.).

awarded as damages. In *Brannigan v. S.I.U.*,[576] the publication *Canadian Sailor* claimed to have apologized to Brannigan for calling him a communist. In a subsequent issue, under the heading "We Have Blundered," the magazine expressed its sorrow to Brannigan for having printed a photograph that did not, as the magazine had originally claimed, prove that he was a communist. But on the same page another story asserted "Picture That Should Have Appeared," and showed a fresh photograph, the photograph that, the magazine said, really established that Brannigan was a communist. As the trial judge noted, this sort of "apology" would aggravate, rather than mitigate, the damages.

A number of technical points about apologies should be borne in mind. First, it is common practice that the plaintiff's lawyer will send a suggested apology along with the libel notice. It is not necessary to publish this apology in order to gain the benefit of the statute. As long as the apology published is a real apology, it will have the intended effect. Second, a general rule of thumb is that the apology should be given the same prominence as the material complained of in the libel notice. If the offending story was on page 1 of a newspaper, the apology should go on page 1; if it was the lead item in a network newscast, the apology should, likewise, be the lead item. Third, it is essential in drafting an apology not to repeat the defamatory statements. If this is done, not only will the benefit of apologizing have been lost, but a fresh libel will have been published.

A curious problem arose in the Ontario courts in the late 1980s. It was, for a time, feared that the practical value to media defendants of apologies might have been substantially eroded, but this appears not to have been the case.

The facts of *Teskey v. Canadian Newspapers Co.*[577] were decidedly unusual. A certain individual had been active in local

---

[576] Above, note 386.
[577] (1989), 68 O.R. (2d) 737 (C.A.).

politics in the Midland, Ontario, area. He was regarded as controversial and given to making sweeping and unsubstantiated statements about local issues and personalities. In order to get his views on a specific issue published in the weekly Midland *Free Press*, this individual sent them to the newspaper in the form of an advertisement. The difficulty with this course of action was that, while material to be published in the news or editorial pages of the newspaper was regularly vetted to determine whether it was libellous, advertising copy was not.

The advertisement was published and Teskey, a local lawyer who was the object of the unfavourable comment in the advertisement, sued. The editorial staff at the paper received Teskey's libel notice, took one look at the advertisement, and issued an apology at once. The newspaper presumably thought that was the end of the matter, but it was not.

Teskey continued with his action, basing his argument on section 5(2) of the Ontario *Libel and Slander Act*. This section stipulates that in order for a media defendant to gain the benefit of an apology, the original libel must have been published in "good faith". Teskey argued that because no one at the newspaper had checked the advertisement to determine whether it might be libellous, there had been a "complete disregard for whether it…[was] libel," which amounted to negligence. The court accepted this argument and held that the libel had not been published in good faith and that, as a result, the newspaper could not benefit from its apology.

Although facts like these are not likely to arise often, the *Teskey* decision should serve to reinforce the two principles set out at the beginning of our discussion of libel: that *anything* that appears in a newspaper or a broadcast can be the subject of a libel action; and that a newspaper or a broadcaster is responsible for everything it publishes.

The final point to note about apologies is that an apology will offer no assistance to a defendant if the libel complained of was an assertion that the plaintiff had committed a crime.

Injunctions

A plaintiff may seek an injunction to prevent the publication, or republication, of a libel. The force of an injunction derives from the fact that to breach it is to disobey an order of a court—that is, to commit the offence of contempt of court.

As we have already noted in relation to non-statutory publication bans, an injunction is an order issued by a superior court which seeks to prevent the commission of an unlawful act. In the case of publication bans, an injunction may be issued to prevent the commission of a crime—namely, contempt of court. But injunctions may also be issued in the course of civil proceedings. The general principle is that an injunction should be made only in the clearest of cases, where the likelihood is that the plaintiff would succeed were the matter actually to go to trial and, further, where the plaintiff would suffer irreparable loss, loss that could not be compensated through an award of damages, if the defendant were allowed to proceed with her proposed unlawful conduct.

There are, however, problems with injunctions issued in the course of civil proceedings, particularly in the course of libel actions.

The first is that a plaintiff can apply for an interim, or temporary, injunction without having to give notice of such application to the other party. Concretely this means that an injunction could be made against a newspaper or a broadcaster without that newspaper or broadcaster having been given an opportunity to argue against it. The second problem is that an injunction issued during a libel action is as clear an example as one could ask of a prior restraint on publication—censorship in its most basic form.

The encouraging aspect is that few such injunctions are

applied for and fewer are made. The reason few injunctions are applied for in libel actions is the obvious one that few plaintiffs know in advance that a libel is going to be published about them. This foreknowledge usually will happen only where there has been advance publicity concerning an upcoming television broadcast or an about-to-be-released novel or film. Most encouraging, however, are the established legal rules about the conditions that must be met before an injunction will be issued to restrain the publication of an alleged libel. These are:

a. the jurisdiction of the courts to make an interlocutory injunction is of a delicate nature and should only be exercised in the clearest of cases;

b. there must be no doubt that the material in issue is libellous of the plaintiff. Indeed the material before the court must be so evidently libellous that any jury would find it to be so, and that were a jury to find otherwise its verdict would be set aside as unreasonable;

c. an injunction will not be granted when the defendant indicates an intention to raise one of the recognized defences, unless such defence is, in the circumstances of the case, manifestly without foundation.[578]

Although the Supreme Court of Canada refused in *Hill v. Church of Scientology* to "constitutionalize" defamation law, its decision in *Dagenais v. Canadian Broadcasting Corp.*[579] is probably more relevant in this context. The clear direction of the *Dagenais* decision was that, as a matter of principle, courts should be very careful about issuing injunctions to prevent publication. There is no reason to imagine that this principle would not be followed in dealing with

---

[578] Robert Martin, *Interlocutory Injunctions in Libel Actions* (1982) 20 U.W.O. L. *Rev.* 129 at 131–32.

[579] [1994] 3 S.C.R. 835.

applications to prevent the publication of defamatory material. The result should be that the three rules set out above would be followed stringently. *Dagenais* also suggests that, because they involve limitations on freedom of expression, applications for publication bans should not be entertained by judges unless notice has been given to the party or parties against whom the ban is sought. I assume a similar approach would in future be followed in relation to applications for injunctions in libel actions.

The three rules set out above represent the position prior to the adoption of the *Charter*. Reading them together with the *Dagenais* decision, it is hard to imagine many circumstances under which a court would be prepared today to enjoin the publication of a libel. Indeed, the only conceivable circumstances would likely be as bizarre as those that arose in *Hill v. Church of Scientology of Toronto*. After a verdict was given against it at trial, Scientology repeated its original libel against the plaintiff. An injunction was issued to prevent further repetition.

Conclusion

There has been a great deal of talk over the last two decades about something called "libel chill".[580] The theory of libel chill is that the fear of being sued for libel intimidates the mass media, that many good stories are not published because of this fear.

This seems unlikely. I personally have never heard a reporter or an editor point to an actual story that was not published because of the fear of a possible libel action. As a matter of law, the Supreme Court of Canada appears to have decided in *Hill v. Church of Scientology of Toronto* that there is no such thing as libel chill. And such data as exist suggest that the extent of libel chill has been considerably exaggerated. In 1986, 1987, and 1988 the

---

[580] See, Robert Martin, *Does Libel Have A 'Chilling Effect' in Canada?* (1990) 4 Studies in Communications 143.

Canadian Daily Newspaper Publishers' Association (now the Canadian Newspaper Association) carried out *Libel Defence Costs Surveys*. Sixty-one daily newspapers responded in 1986, seventy in 1987, and eighty-five in 1988. In 1987 and 1988, 59 percent of these newspapers reported that they had spent absolutely nothing defending libel actions, and in 1988, 73 percent of all daily newspapers spent less than $5,000 defending libel actions. Forty-six percent of newspapers received no libel notices in 1988, and 71 percent did not have a libel action started against them. Most newspapers and broadcasters carry libel insurance. In 1988, 62 percent of the daily newspapers surveyed paid annual premiums under $5,000.

It is useful also to remember the many advantages the law gives media defendants in libel actions. Libel is highly technical, and a plaintiff might conceivably engage a lawyer who is not particularly knowledgeable in the area. A libel notice must be issued quickly. An apology effectively concludes the matter. If the plaintiff decides to go ahead and sue, the formal action must be commenced quickly, within a far shorter period than that allowed for most other civil claims. Libel actions are very expensive, and legal aid is ordinarily not available. In many instances the defendant in a libel action can frustrate the plaintiff's litigation by asking for "security for costs", a procedure that can result in the plaintiff being required to post a bond with the court before being allowed to continue. Even if a media defendant should lose a libel action, awards of damages in Canada, as has been noted, are modest.

The really important thing about libel actions, as far as the mass media are concerned, is to avoid them. I have argued that the most effective means for achieving this goal are good reporting and good editing. But there is an additional practical point worth noting. What follows is based on the 1985 Iowa Libel Research

Project,[581] but I suspect similar patterns and similar responses would be found in Canada. The first finding of this project was that people who believed they had been libelled in a newspaper tended to take the matter up with that newspaper before they went to a lawyer. The second, and crucial, point was that if such persons were treated by the newspaper with civility and respect, they would probably not contact a lawyer; if they weren't, they would. Once again, both the law and good journalism suggest the same result. The people who read newspapers and the people written about should both be treated in a professional and responsible manner.

A final point to note about libel actions relates to the individual journalist who did the story that led to the suit. It is overwhelmingly likely that the media corporation for whom that reporter works will be a defendant in the action and will, as a result, hire a lawyer to conduct the defence. This lawyer's professional duty is to represent her client, the employer, and not the reporter. Thus, this lawyer may well act in ways that are in her client's interests, but not necessarily in the interests of the reporter. There may well be situations, then, where it would be desirable for the reporter to retain her own lawyer to represent her own interests before the court.

Privacy

There is no general right to privacy in Canada. By that it is meant that there is no general principle of Canadian law which prohibits the publication by the mass media of personal or private information about individuals. Put another way, assuming it can be proven to be true; there is nothing that the mass media may not say about someone.

---

[581] See R.P. Bezanson, G. Cranberg, & J. Soloski, *Libel Law and the Press: Setting the Record Straight* (1985) 71 Iowa L. Rev. 215.

The *Canadian Charter of Rights and Freedoms*[582] appears to enshrine a certain notion of privacy. Section 8 creates protection against unreasonable searches, which would include both unreasonable searches of residences and other premises and the unreasonable interception of postal and electronic communications.[583] Section 7 has also been interpreted as addressing certain privacy issues in that it has been seen as guaranteeing individuals against state interference with either their bodily integrity or the making of personal and intimate decisions.[584] But this *Charter* right to privacy has so far been interpreted only as creating guarantees against the state, as protecting a certain personal sphere of action from interference by the state.[585] If this is the complete scope of any *Charter*-based right to privacy, it clearly says nothing about the ability of the mass media to publish private or personal information concerning individuals.

There is a federal *Privacy Act*,[586] and a number of provinces have similar legislation. With certain exceptions to be noted below, however, these statutes address the use by the state of personal information about individuals which is in the possession of the state. As a broad principle, the federal statute provides that "Personal information under the control of a government institution shall not, without the consent of the individual to whom it relates, be disclosed by the institution." But the Act says nothing about the use of "personal information" by non-state organizations such as the mass media. A similar approach is found

[582] Part I of the *Constitution Act, 1982*, being Schedule B to the *Canada Act 1982* (U.K.), 1982, c. 11 [*Charter*].
[583] *R.* v. *Nicolucci*, [1985] C.S. 1243 (Que.).
[584] *R.* v. *Morgentaler*, [1988] 1 S.C.R. 30.
[585] *R.* v. *Dyment*, [1988] 2 S.C.R. 417 and *Royal Bank of Canada* v. *Wetton* (2009) 93 O.R. (3d) 403 (C.A.).
[586] R.S.C. 1985, c. P-21.

in provincial privacy legislation.

The common law has not so far recognized a tort of invasion of privacy. A recent decision from Ontario contained a supremely equivocal discussion of this issue.[587] Although it might be relied upon in a variety of circumstances, such a tort, for present purposes, would give individuals some ability to protect themselves against the publication of certain kinds or categories of personal information. The recognition of such a tort would permit individuals to recover damages from persons or organizations who published protected information.

No Canadian superior court has expressly confirmed the existence of this precise tort, although a number of related claims have been upheld. In *Robbins v. Canadian Broadcasting Corp. (Que.)*,[588] the only one of the cases to be noted which involved the mass media, the plaintiff was awarded damages for what the court variously described as "humiliation", "invasion of privacy", "malicious mischief", and "nuisance". He had written a critical letter to the CBC television program *Tabloid*. After reading the letter on air, the host of the program invited viewers to write letters to Dr. Robbins to "cheer" him up. Robbins's mailing address appeared on screen. The result was that Robbins received an avalanche of harassing letters, telephone calls, and visits to his residence.

In a similar vein, it was held in *Motherwell v. Motherwell*[589] that to subject someone to an uninterrupted flow of harassing telephone calls and letters over a period of two years was to commit a tort that the court described as "nuisance by invasion of

---

[587] *Somwar* v. *McDonald's* (2006) 79 O.R. (3d) 172. The Court held both that "...there is no tort of invasion of privacy" (p. 180) and "...the time has come to recognize invasion of privacy as a tort in its own right" (at p. 182).

[588] (1957), 12 D.L.R. (2d) 35 (Que. S.C.).

[589] (1976), 1 A.R. 47 (C.A.).

privacy". There is also a related tort generally described as "appropriation of personality". This tort involves the unauthorized use of another person's name or likeness for a commercial purpose, as in, for example, an advertisement that falsely suggested that a well-known public figure had endorsed a particular product.[590]

One recent decision in Ontario, *Gould Estate v. Stoddart Publishing Co.*,[591] elaborated on the meaning and scope of appropriation of personality. The Court noted:

> *The few Canadian cases dealing with this tort have generally involved situations in which the name, or image of an individual enjoying some celebrity status has been used in the advertising or promotion of the defendants' business or products.*[592]

In this case the estate of a famous Canadian pianist sued a publisher in appropriation of personality for its use of an interview with the pianist, as well as photographs which had been taken at the same time as the interview. The interview had taken place with someone whose book about the pianist was then published forty years after the interview.

The Court dismissed the action of the pianist's estate, holding that it had "...no basis in law"[593] and that such a result was consistent with upholding freedom of expression.[594]

The closest a Canadian court has come to recognizing a tort of invasion of privacy committed through the publication of private information was in a 1982 Ontario County Court decision, *Saccone*

---

[590] *Krouse v. Chrysler Canada Ltd.* (1974), 1 O.R. (2d) 225 (C.A.).

[591] (1996) 30 O.R. (3d) 520 (Gen. Div.).

[592] *Ibid.* at 524.

[593] *Ibid.* at 531.

[594] *Ibid.* at 527.

v. Orr.[595] A plaintiff was awarded damages against a defendant who tape-recorded a telephone conversation between the two without the plaintiff's permission or knowledge and subsequently played the tape at a public meeting.

The privacy legislation in British Columbia, Manitoba, Newfoundland, and Saskatchewan creates liability in tort for certain infringements of privacy interests.[596] Among the forms of conduct these statutes address are eavesdropping, surveillance, wire-tapping, and the use of personal documents. The legislation also creates broad defences against claims of invasion of privacy. These defences include publishing any of the following: a matter of public interest; a fair comment on a matter of public interest; and anything that would be privileged under the law of defamation.

There has been little litigation under these statutes. An instructive case is *Silber v. British Columbia Broadcasting System Ltd.*,[597] a 1986 decision of the British Columbia Supreme Court. A strike was under way at a business owned by the plaintiff. On the day in question, the plaintiff discovered a camera crew from the defendant filming the strike from the parking lot of his business premises. He told the crew to leave the parking lot and, during the course of this exchange, he became involved in a physical struggle with some of its members. This struggle was videotaped, and tape that included the strike, the discussion, and the struggle was aired.

The plaintiff sued for invasion of privacy. His claim was dismissed, the court holding, first, that while the parking lot was

---

[595] (1981), 34 O.R. (2d) 317 (Co. Ct.).

[596] For B.C., see *Privacy Act*, R.S.B.C. 1979, c. 336; for Manitoba, *Privacy Act*, R.S.M. 1987, c. P125; for Newfoundland, *Privacy Act*, R.S.N. 1990, c. P-22; and for Saskatchewan, *The Privacy Act*, R.S.S. 1978, c. P-24.

[597] (1986), 25 D.L.R. (4th) 345 (B.C.S.C.).

private property, everything happening there was clearly observable and, as a result, the plaintiff had no "reasonable expectation of privacy" with respect to it; and, second, that the altercation between the plaintiff and the camera crew was a matter of public interest. As a final point on these statutory torts of invasion of privacy, if they were to be interpreted in such a way as to constrain the ability of the mass media to gather or publish information, the relevant portions of the statutes which created them could then be open to a constitutional challenge on the basis of the *Charter's* guarantee of freedom of expression.

In one British Columbia case a court did award damages arising out of an alleged breach of the province's *Privacy Act*.[598] The plaintiff had undergone surgery to alleviate his baldness. The organization which performed the surgery, L. Inc., videotaped the procedure and, largely because of the questionable behaviour of T.S., an employee of L. Inc., the videotape came into the possession of BCTV, which aired it. The plaintiff sued L. Inc., T.S., and BCTV for defamation, breach of confidentiality and invasion of privacy. The network raised the defence of justification to the libel action and succeeded. Because the reporter who obtained the videotape for BCTV had made careful inquiries about the propriety and legality of giving the tape to her, the court held that it had effectively discharged any duty of confidentiality it might have owed to the plaintiff. The court dismissed the actions against BCTV and awarded damages against L. Inc. and T.S. This decision suggests that, in this area, as in all areas of media law, newspapers and broadcasters are not likely to be held liable when reporters and editors behave in a careful and professional manner.

The *Quebec Charter of Human Rights and Freedoms* has been interpreted so as to include a right to privacy. In *Aubry v. Editions Vice-Versa Inc.*[599] a photographer took a photo of the plaintiff sitting

---

[598] *Hollinsworth v. B.C.T.V.* (1996) 34 C.C.L.T. (2d) 95 (B.C.S.C.).
[599] (1998) 157 D.L.R. (4th) 577 (S.C.C.).

on a step in front of a building on Ste-Catherine Street in Montreal. The photo was taken and, subsequently, published without her permission.

She sued for damages based on an alleged infringement of rights guaranteed under the Quebec *Charter*. The judges in the Supreme Court agreed that Canadian *Charter* protected individuals against invasions of privacy by the state, but not necessarily against the sort of thing that had happened here. Lamer C.J.C. noted that:

> ...there is a fundamental difference between a person's reasonable expectation of privacy in his or her dealings with the state and the same person's reasonable expectation of privacy in his or her dealings with ordinary citizens. [600]

There was no evidence that the plaintiff suffered any actual loss, but, because the publication of her photograph caused "humiliation", [601] she was awarded $2,000 in damages.

In 2000 Parliament enacted a statute called the *Personal Information Protection and Electronic Documents Act*. [602] The Act purports to create "...rules to govern the collection, use and disclosure of personal information in a manner that recognizes the right to privacy of individuals with respect to their personal information." [603]

The Act is probably unconstitutional, on two grounds. First, it is likely *ultra vires* Parliament, since it deals with the behaviour of private, non-state actors in their relations with other individuals and appears to create a civil cause of action. Thus, it would seem

---

[600] *Ibid.* at 582.
[601] *Ibid.* at 589.
[602] S.C. 2000, c. 5.
[603] *Ibid.*, s. 3.

that the true subject-matter of the Act is "property and civil rights in the province", a matter reserved exclusively to the provincial legislatures by section 92 of the *Constitution Act 1867*. Since the Act purports to place limits on the use of information, it could be seen as an infringement of the *Charter* guarantee of freedom of expression.

Legislation in Quebec places restrictions on the ability of corporations and businesses to deal with personal information about individuals. As a general principle, personal information about an individual may not be communicated to third parties without the consent of that individual.[604]

We will conclude the analysis of privacy issues with a discussion of the two situations that are of most practical concern to the mass media: the taking of photographs and the tape-recording of telephone conversations.

As a general matter, it is not necessary, outside of Quebec, to seek or receive a person's permission before taking or publishing her photograph. Certain issues can, however, arise. First, the person photographed might be able to bring an action in trespass if the photographer physically invaded her land or premises in the course of taking the photograph. Despite this possibility, courts have held that there was no trespass in flying over a plaintiff's residence to take a photograph, or in taking photographs in front of the plaintiff's house while visiting the house to ask for an interview.[605]

Second, it may amount to nuisance or harassment to subject a residence to constant surveillance in order to get a photograph. Third, the taking of a photograph may amount to the torts of

---

[604] *An Act Respecting the Protection of Personal Information in the Private Sector*, S.Q. 1993, c. 17.

[605] *Bernstein of Leigh (Baron)* v. *Skyviews and General Ltd.*, [1978] 1 Q.B. 479; *Belzberg* v. *British Columbia Television Broadcasting System Ltd.*, [1981] 3 W.W.R. 85 (B.C.S.C.).

assault or battery if it involves any physical restraint of or physical interference with the person being photographed. Fourth, the mass media may be restrained from publishing a photograph that has been obtained in breach of a confidence.[606] Finally, while this is not a privacy concern, any tampering with or alteration of a photograph may render it defamatory.

Once more, as a general matter, there is no need to seek someone's permission to tape-record a telephone conversation. However, two qualifications should be noted. First, regulations made under the *Broadcasting Act*[607] specify that if a tape-recording of a telephone conversation is to be aired, the other person must, as a pre-condition, be informed and her permission granted. Second, the *Criminal Code*[608] makes it an offence to intercept telephone communications without lawful authority.

Closely related to privacy questions are issues of confidentiality. If I receive confidential information from my employer, or from my spouse or from a client or patient, I may be under a legally enforceable obligation not to disclose that information to anyone else. If I were to disclose such information to a third party—obviously, in the present context, a reporter— the individual or organization to whom I owe the obligation of confidentiality might be able to take legal action against me and I might be subject to either criminal or professional disciplinary proceedings. But none of this is directly relevant to the reporter to whom the information was given. What legal liability, if any, might the reporter face?

There is no recognized principle of Canadian law under which the reporter can be made liable for breach of confidence in such a circumstance. There is no legal relation, no legal nexus, between the reporter and the individual or organization from whom the

---

[606] *Duchess of Argyll* v. *Duke of Argyll*, [1967] Ch. 302.

[607] Radio Regulations, 1986, SOR/86-982, s. 3(e).

[608] R.S.C. 1985, c. C-46, s. 184.

reporter's source—the person disclosing the information—received the information.

Problems might arise if the reporter actively encouraged the source to give her information that both she and the source knew to be confidential. The reporter might be open, depending on the precise circumstances, to a tort action of inducing breach of contract or a charge of criminal conspiracy.

But, to repeat, if the reporter, without offering inducement or persuasion, simply accepts the information that the source is proffering, no legal difficulties should result.[609]

FURTHER READING

As far as libel is concerned, good general introductions are A. Skarsgard, *Freedom of the Press: Availability of Defences to a Defamation Action* (1981) 45 Sask. L. Rev. 287, and G.A. Flaherty, *Defamation Law in Canada*, Ottawa, Canadian Bar Foundation, 1984. For a full and detailed statement of the law, R. E. Brown's *The Law of Defamation in Canada*, 2 vols., 2d ed. Toronto, Carswell, 1994 should be consulted. This work has now grown to a four-volume, loose-leaf service. Because of its size and its cost ($399), it is not possible to recommend Brown for students. For my analysis of the book, see Robert Martin, *Book Review*, (1989) 14 Canadian Journal of Communication, no. 1, 83. Roger D. McConchie and David A. Potts, *Canadian Libel and Slander Actions*, Toronto, Irwin Law, 2004 should now be regarded as the leading Canadian work in the field. Robert J. Sharpe, *The Last Day, the Last Hour: The Currie Libel Trial*, Toronto, Carswell, 1988 is a superb, richly-detailed account of Canada's best-known libel action. This volume is a

---

[609] There is an exhaustive discussion in G.H.L. Fridman, *The Law of Torts in Canada*, vol. 2, Toronto, Carswell, 1990 at 189–206. See also G.F. Proudfoot, *Privacy Law and the Media in Canada,* Ottawa, Canadian Bar Foundation, 1984, at 44–46.

shining beacon of scholarship in a dismal landscape of pseudo-history.

D. Gibson, ed., *Aspects of Privacy Law: Essays in Honour of John M. Sharp,* Toronto, Butterworths, 1980 provides an overview of privacy issues, but is very dated.

CHAPTER 5

Free Expression in a Multicultural Society

Introduction

CANADA AND CANADIANS are involved in a noble experiment. We are attempting to build a harmonious, multicultural democracy. Democracy, of course, means rule by the people. Kenneth Minogue has noted certain difficulties in the path towards multicultural democracy.

> *You cannot...have democracy without having a people, and they must be a population that treats each other as individuals rather than as collective enemies and rivals.*[610]

Thus,

> *The idea of democracy and the idea of cultural diversity (as promoted by multicultural doctrine) are...contradictory.*[611]

This experiment necessitates certain limits on unfettered free expression. If Canadians were free to run around promoting

---

[610] *The Servile Mind, op. cit.*, p.31.
[611] *Ibid.*, at p.30.

hatred and hostility against each other, the whole experiment could be fatally jeopardised.[612] The ostensible defenders of our experiment have, or so it seems to me, moved in this direction with an excess of zeal to a point where their zeal has become a major threat to the experiment.[613] A large part of this chapter will be devoted to analysis and explication of this zealotry.

The word *Multicultural* describes a society that contains a multiplicity of ethnic, linguistic, religious or cultural groups. From this perspective, most nations in today's world are multicultural, there being few completely homogenous societies. At this point it will be useful to make the distinction between a society which is, objectively, multicultural because it contains a multiplicity of ethnic, linguistic, religious or cultural groups, and one which has, as a matter of public policy, decided to adopt, in

---

[612] An interesting critical analysis of the Canadian experience can be found in, Neil Bissoondath, *Selling Illusions: The Cult of Multiculturalism in Canada*, Harmondsworth, Penguin, 1994. See also, William Kaplan, *Belonging: The Meaning and Future of Canadian Citizenship*, Montreal and Kingston, McGill-Queen's University Press, 1993. For a searching and thoughtful critical analysis of multiculturalism, see Munira Mirza, *Rethinking Race*, Prospect, Issue 175, 22 September 2010. Salim Mansur, *Delectable Lie: A Liberal Repudiation of Multiculturalism,* Brantford, Ontario, Mantua Books, 2011 is an original and powerful critical analysis.

[613] Mark Steyn identified the contradiction at the centre of the whole exercise, when he observed: "...the more Canada congratulates itself on its tolerance, the less it's prepared to tolerate." See, *True North strong not free*, Macleans, 8 April 2010. Contemporary Canada seems to affirm Karl Popper's observation that, "Unlimited tolerance must lead to the disappearance of tolerance." See his, *The Open Society and its Enemies, Volume 1, The Spell of Plato*, Princeton, N.J., Princeton University Press, 1971, p.265.

its constitution or in its laws, "multiculturalism".[614] The first attempt by the Canadian state to limit freedom of expression in the interests of multiculturalism occurred in 1970. Before moving to an analysis of this attempt, it will be useful to note that the simplest and most direct general observation which may be made about free expression in multi-culti Canada in 2011 is, there ain't none.

The Criminal Code

In 1970 Parliament amended the *Criminal Code*, creating two new offences. These offences were "advocating or promoting genocide" in section 318[615] and "wilfully promoting hatred" in section 319(2). Both offences proscribe statements *directed* at "an identifiable group", which means persons identified by "colour, race, religion or ethnic origin". Section 319(2), which created the offence of wilfully promoting hatred, was carefully drafted. The section created defences of truth, good faith and public benefit.

---

[614] Canada's formal commitment to "multiculturalism" is found in s. 27 of the Charter, which asserts that, "this Charter shall be interpreted in a manner consistent with the preservation and enhancement of the multicultural heritage of Canadians." A skeptical person might suggest that the most significant results of the adoption of an official policy of "multiculturalism" are, first, an institutionalization of relativistic ways of thinking (Allan Bloom, *The Closing of the American Mind*, New York, Simon and Shuster, 1987) and, second, the promotion of sanctimoniousness (Robert Martin, *A Lament for British North America* in Anthony A. Peacock, ed., *Rethinking the Constitution: Perspectives on Canadian Constitutional Reform, Interpretation and Theory*, Toronto, Oxford University Press, 1996, p. 3).

[615] The first charge under this offence was laid in July of 2010. See, Kathryn Blaze Carlson, *Canadian extremist Salman Hossain charged with promoting genocide*, National Post, 8 July 2010.

The first prosecution did not occur until 1977.[616] In its decision in this case, the Ontario Court of Appeal held that the adverb "wilfully" in section 319(2) meant that the Crown would have to establish the highest level of *mens rea* before there could be a conviction. Section 319 contains a further protection in that a prosecution may not be instituted without the consent of the Attorney General of the province. L.W. Sumner has argued that Parliament should have distinguished more precisely between the "promotion" of hatred, which does not, in his view, satisfy Mill's standard of "harm" and the "incitement" of hatred, which does.[617]

The second prosecution for wilfully promoting hatred involved a man named James Keegstra. The Keegstra matter is discussed in Chapter 1. By the time Keegstra was prosecuted, the *Charter* had become part of Canada's constitution and Keegstra decided to challenge the constitutionality of the *wilfully promoting hatred* offence on the basis of the *Charter* guarantee of freedom of expression. This challenge went, eventually, to the Supreme Court of Canada. In its decision,[618] the Court followed the approach set out in *Irwin Toy*,[619] its first decision on the *Charter* guarantee of freedom of expression.

In *Irwin Toy* the Court found that any material which had expressive content or which sought to convey a meaning qualified as constitutionally-protected expression. In *Keegstra* the Court held that section 319(2) of the *Criminal Code* infringed the freedom of expression guaranteed in section 2(b) of the *Charter*. All the

---

[616] *R. v. Buzzanga and Durocher* (1979) 101 D.L.R. (3d) 488 (Ont. C.A.).

[617] L.W.Sumner, *Incitement and the Regulation of Hate Speech in Canada: A Philosophical Analysis*, Extreme Speech, 204 at p. 217.

[618] [1990] 3 S.C.R. 697 *Keegstra*. See also, *R. v. Andrews et al* (1988), 65 O.R. (2d) 161 (C.A.), aff'd, [1990] 3 S.C.R. 870.

[619] [1989] 1 S.C.R. 927. This decision is analysed at length in Chapter One, above.

members of the Court agreed that, despite its message, hate speech did convey meaning and, therefore, qualified as expression under the *Charter*. However, the Court was divided as to whether or not section 319(2) constituted a reasonable limit on freedom of expression in a free and democratic society and could, therefore, be justified under s.1 of the *Charter*. By a decision of four to three, the court ruled against Keegstra. Stefan Braun believed that the Supreme Court went much further in this decision than it reasonably needed to. As he saw the matter, the preferable, and more efficacious, remedy would have been to dismiss Keegstra for having engaged in a gross misuse of his position as a teacher. Braun observed that the decision:

> ...*effectively reduces all Canadians to the status of a captive audience of impressionable schoolchildren and hate propaganda law to the role of in loco parentis over them.*[620]

The unusual aspect of the Court's decision in *Keegstra* lay in its embracing of what it called "free expression values". The Court seemed to say that suppressing freedom of expression in the name of "free expression values" was acceptable. Writing for the majority, Dickson, C.J. said "it is through rejecting hate propaganda that the state can best encourage the protection of values central to free expression...."[621] In my view, this comes close to doublethink, with the Court apparently holding that the way to protect freedom of expression is to suppress it.[622]

A recent, and disturbing, prosecution was *R. v. Harding*.[623]

---

[620] *Democracy off Balance*, *op. cit.*, p. 27.

[621] Above note 616 at 764.

[622] See, Terry Heinrichs, *Censorship as Free Speech: Free Expression Values and the Logic of Silencing*, (1998) 36 Alberta Law Review 835.

[623] (1998), 45 O.R. (3d) 207.

The accused, Mark Harding, had made statements in which he expressed his dislike for Muslims. Harding's statements were unpleasant and nasty, vicious even. But the offence in section 319 is stated to be "wilfully promoting hatred against" an identifiable group, not "making nasty and unpleasant statements about" an identifiable group. In the criminal law context, the distinction between "wilfully promoting hatred" and "making nasty and unpleasant statements" lies in the question of *mens rea*.

The Ontario Court of Appeal in *R. v. Buzzanga and Durocher* and the Supreme Court of Canada in *R. v. Keegstra* enunciated a very high standard for the *mens rea* which would have to be established before an accused could be convicted of wilfully promoting hatred. In *Keegstra*, Chief Justice Dickson asserted:

> *wilfully means an "...accused subjectively desires the promotion of hatred or foresees such a consequence as certain or substantially certain to result from an act done in order to achieve some other purpose.*[624]

One cause for concern with *Harding* lies in the fact that, as I interpret the judgment, the trial judge did not seem to have applied as stringent a standard for determining the presence of the necessary *mens rea*. The trial court seemed to be prepared to infer wilfulness from the circumstances surrounding Harding's making of the statements, particularly his unsatisfactory response to police when they asked him to explain his statements.

It is not encouraging to note that Canada has become a country in which the police can demand that people "explain" their public utterances. Harding argued that he had not intended to promote hatred. The statements about his intention which Harding gave as evidence during the trial contradicted what he

---

[624] *Keegstra*, above note 616 at 754.

had said to the police.[625] At the end of the day the court simply did not believe Harding's assertion that he had not intended to promote hatred.

The trial judge concluded that he was:

> ...convinced beyond a reasonable doubt that Mr. Harding either intended to promote hatred towards Muslims or was wilfully blind that such was a substantially certain consequence.[626]

The trial court went on to find that neither of the *Criminal Code* defences of "good faith" and "honest belief" was applicable. The court was of the view that, in a case where a court found that an accused intended to promote hatred, it would be "rare" to find that the accused had acted in good faith or upon an honest belief.[627]

There are aspects of the *Harding* decision which are, in my view, disturbing. Both the trial judge and the Court of Appeal seem to have interpreted s. 319 in such a way as to remove the crucial defences which are an important part of it. The decision came perilously close to turning "wilfully promoting hatred" into a strict liability offence.

Harding appealed his conviction to the Ontario Court of Appeal, which released its judgment on 17 December 2001.[628] The decision of the Court of Appeal is not ideal, but, in my opinion, the judges in that court did demonstrate a clearer understanding of the issues involved than did the trial judge. The Court of Appeal addressed the difficult question of *mens rea*. The court recognised that the existence of *mens rea* in this prosecution

---

[625] 45 O.R. (3d) at 215.

[626] *Ibid.* at 222.

[627] *Ibid.* at 223.

[628] *R. v. Harding* (2001), 57 O.R. (3d) 333 (C.A.).

was problematic. It noted that in *Keegstra*, Dickson, C.J. said that "wilfully" requires that the accused "…subjectively desires the promotion of hatred…."[629] The trial court had been unable to find this subjective desire to promote hatred, but was satisfied that Harding was "reckless" as to whether his remarks would lead to the promotion of hatred. This, in the view of the trial judge, was sufficient. The Court of Appeal was convinced that "mere recklessness" was not enough.[630] Harding, in the view of the court, had manifested "wilful blindness" as to whether his statements would promote hatred. This "wilful blindness" was more than "mere recklessness" and would satisfy the *mens rea* requirement.[631]

The Court of Appeal also dealt with the defences of "truth" and "good faith". The court rejected "truth", noting that, "this defence cannot be interpreted on a purely subjective basis" and that, "[t]here were no reasonable grounds to believe the statements were true."[632] On the matter of "good faith", the court inferred that because Harding's opinions were so extreme, he could not have been acting in good faith when he expressed them.[633] Apart from the *Harding* decision, the courts have dealt with prosecutions under section 319(2) in a careful manner which has shown a proper respect for freedom of expression.[634]

In one recent decision[635] the Ontario Court of Appeal dealt with a prosecution under s. 319 in a careful and meticulous

---

[629] *Keegstra*, above note 616 at 775.

[630] Above note 626 at 350.

[631] *Ibid.*

[632] *Ibid.*, at 344.

[633] *Ibid.*, at 344–46.

[634] For general background and an overview, see Robert Martin, *Group Defamation in Canada in Freedman and Freedman*, eds. Group Defamation and Freedom of Speech, Westport, Greenwood Press, 1995, 191–217.

[635] *R. v. Elms* (2007) 82 O.R. (3d) 415 (C.A.).

fashion. The accused, who "might have been" a "skinhead" was sitting at a table at which various CDs were offered for sale. Some of the words on the CDs were adjudged to amount to "promoting hatred". The question was whether the accused's acts in operating the table from which these CDs were being sold constituted the "wilful promotion of hatred". He was acquitted.

The way in which Canadians think and express themselves is constrained by the secular state religion of equality and, consequently, expression which appears to deviate from this orthodoxy has been suppressed.[636] Multi-culti Canada manifests many of the hallmarks of a tyranny. As often seems to be true of tyrannies, ours was constructed on a foundation of lies. Postmodern ideology, by undermining the very idea of truth, prepared much of the ground for this construction. For the devotee of postmodernism, there is no truth, only differing "narratives".

While everyone over the age of six understands that the very notion of truth is problematic, the fundamental distinction between truth-telling and lying must always be borne in mind. Canadians, as I understand them today, seem to prefer lying to truth-telling. A sweeping statement like that requires a degree of qualification or elaboration. I am convinced that the state's vast thought control apparatus has succeeded to the point where many Canadians feel afraid to give expression to their natural and instinctive thoughts. The process whereby one expresses one's natural, unconstrained and unrehearsed thoughts can be described as truth-telling. I am strongly inclined to the belief that describing spades as spades is the essence of truth-telling and that calling

---

[636] For an elaboration of this orthodoxy, see Robert Martin, *The Most Dangerous Branch: How the Supreme Court of Canada has undermined our Law and our Democracy*, Montreal and Kingston, McGill-Queen's University Press, 2003.

spades something less than spades is the first step in lying.[637]

In a similar vein, a process whereby one suppresses one's natural thoughts and expresses only thoughts and opinions which one has been coerced or manipulated into believing are acceptable can properly be described as lying. Melanie Phillips asserted that, "...the West has replaced truth with ideology."[638] The process of creating tyranny requires both cowards and bullies. Canada has both, in abundance. We have eschewed the hard tyranny of men in jackboots, prison cells and the gallows and embraced, rather, the soft tyranny[639] of sensitive and caring female lawyers and "human rights" commissions. In Phillips' words:

> *Hurtful thoughts and insensitive communications are brought relentlessly under surveillance, but such strong-arm tactics are masked as effusive caring or as resistance to prejudice.*[640]

It is profoundly unfortunate that the institutions—the universities,

---

[637] See, Dwight Garner, *In Pursuit of Prey, Carrying Philosophy*, New York Times, 2 May 2010. See below, p. 413.

[638] *The World Turned Upside Down, op. cit.*, at p. 406.

[639] See, Paul A. Rahe, *Soft Despotism, Democracy's Drift*, New Haven, CT, Yale University Press, 2009. One commentator spoke of "...a state backed by the coddling of the welfare state instead of brute force" and continued, "...it may be harder to resist a totalitarian state which relies on free milk and birth control clinics than one which relies on castor oil and concentration camps." Gerald J. Russello, *Christopher Dawson and the Coming Conflict*, (2010) 28 The New Criterion, no.7. Mark Steyn has suggested that, "...'diversity' and 'equity' and respect are merely the fashionable cloaks for muscle." See, *True North strong not free*, Macleans, 8 April 2010. In March of 2011, Anthony Daniels made the astute and accurate observation, "...everyone must conform in the name of diversity", National Review, 9 March 2011.

[640] *The World Turned Upside Down, op.cit.*, at p. 398.

the mass media, the legal profession and the judiciary—which one might expect to have offered some resistance, appear, to a substantial degree, to be the province of cowards.[641] In the quest to stamp out offensive speech, the two institutions in the vanguard of suppressing free expression have been human rights commissions[642] and universities. There have been two solid recent books on "human rights" commissions.[643] In Canada there is a human rights commission at the federal level, as well as one in each province. Strictly speaking, these might better be called anti-discrimination and equality commissions. Canadians are mesmerised by "equality" and nothing is allowed to stand in its way.[644]

---

[641] Mark Steyn observed: "For the corrosive effects of 'diversity', look no further than three critical societal institutions: the education system, law enforcement and the media.", note 27. Melanie Phillips has argued a similar point, suggesting that the, "...grand inquisitors are to be found within the intelligentsia—in the universities, the media, the law, the political and professional classes—...". loc. cit., note 35.

[642] Human rights commissions were established, initially, to provide redress to persons who experienced discrimination in housing and in employment. It is only recently that they have got into the thought police business.

[643] See, Kathy Shaidle and Pete Vere, The Tyranny of Nice: How Canada crushes freedom in the name of human rights (and why it matters to Americans), Toronto, the Interim Publishing Co., 2008 and Ezra Levant, Shakedown: How our Government is undermining democracy in the name of Human Rights, Toronto, McClelland and Stewart, 2009. See also, Rory Leishman, Against Judicial Activism: The Decline of Freedom and Democracy in Canada, Montreal and Kingston, McGill-Queen's University Press, 2006, pp. 105-135.

[644] Martin Loney, The Pursuit of Division: Race, Gender and Preferential Hiring in Canada, Montreal, McGill-Queen's University Press, 1998. See also, Ian Hunter, When Human Rights become Wrongs, (1985) 23 The University of Western Ontario Law Review, no. 2, 197.

Human Rights Commissions

As befits a theocracy, Canada has it very own *holy inquisition*, a standing organization with a broad mandate to identify and extirpate both heresy and blasphemy. Melanie Phillips has argued that, Western liberals [stamp out dissent] by social and professional ostracism and legal discrimination. It is a kind of secular inquisition.[645]

Since Canada is a federal theocracy, its holy inquisition is divided into bits along the lines of the general division of powers. These bits are called Human Rights Commissions.

Ontario was the first jurisdiction to adopt anti-discrimination legislation. It enacted a *Racial Discrimination Act* in 1944.[646] This statute prohibited the displaying of signs indicating an intention to discriminate on religious or racial grounds. Concretely, this provision was intended to prohibit signs, which were not unknown at the time, saying "No Jews Allowed". This provision has survived to become section 13 of the Ontario *Human Rights Code*,[647] which now states:

(1) A right under Part I (freedom from discrimination) is infringed by a person who publishes or displays before the public or causes the publication or display before the public of any notice, sign, symbol, emblem or other similar representation that indicates the intention of the person to infringe a right under Part I or that is intended by the person to incite the infringement of a right under Part 1.

(2) Subsection (1) shall not interfere with freedom of expression of opinion.

---

[645] Melanie Phillips, *The World Turned Upside Down, op. cit.,* at p.99.

[646] S.O. 1944, c. 51.

[647] R.S.O. 1990, c. H-19.

A provision similar to this is found in all provincial human rights legislation. The statutes in the three westernmost provinces—Alberta, British Columbia and Saskatchewan—go well beyond the position in the Ontario statute. Section 3(1)(b) of the *Alberta Human Rights, Citizenship and Multiculturalism Act*[648] prohibits any statement that is "likely" to expose a person or a class of persons to hatred or contempt on the basis of a prohibited ground of discrimination. Very similar provisions are found in section 7(1)(b) of the *British Columbia Human Rights Code*[649] and s. 14(1)(b) of the *Saskatchewan Human Rights Code.*[650]

Despite the inclusion of sub-section (2), these provisions have been the basis for interference with free expression by human rights commissions. In *Warren v. Chapman,* a Manitoba court ruled that the Manitoba Human Rights Commission did not have jurisdiction to hear and decide upon complaints against a Winnipeg newspaper columnist. In its decision, the court found that "the newspaper articles or editorials written by the applicant can[not] be said to come within the meaning of the words 'any notice, sign, symbol, emblem or other representation' used in section 2(1) of the Act."[651]

While the Canadian mass media have largely embraced the reigning secular state religion, one cheerfully and enthusiastically counter-orthodox publication was a monthly magazine called *Alberta Report.* The magazine ceased publication in July 2003. In a 2001 decision, a panel set up by the Alberta Human Rights and Citizenship Commission appeared to adopt the notion that expression becomes unacceptable at the point at which someone

---

[648] RSA, 2000, c. H-14.

[649] R.S.B.C., 1996, c. 210.

[650] R.S.S., 1979, c. S-24.1.

[651] (1985), 11 D.L.R. (4th) 474 (Man. Q.B.). See also *Iwasyk v. Saskatchewan (Human Rights Commission)* (1977), 80 D.L.R. (3d) 1 (Sask. Q.B.) rev'd (1978), 87 D.L.R. (3d) 289 (Sask. C.A.).

might find it to be offensive.[652] The panel concluded that:

> ...*discrimination is not about the intention of the publisher in this case; it is about the impact upon the vulnerable group, from their [sic] point of view.*

I interpret that to mean that if someone *feels* she has been discriminated against, that is sufficient to establish that "discrimination" has indeed occurred.

The panel then ordered the publisher of *Alberta Report* to seek expert advice to assist him in establishing an internal system of self-censorship designed to ensure that *Alberta Report* would never again publish anything unacceptable. The panel delivered this admonition:

> *Canada is a multicultural society. Respectful conduct is expected within [sic] our society and this includes prohibiting discrimination on the basis of race, colour, ancestry, religious beliefs, place of origin, etc.*

Amazingly enough, the panel allowed outsiders to intervene in the hearing. Amongst those intervenors was the Women's Legal Education and Action Fund (LEAF), the legal arm of Canadian feminism.[653] *Alberta Report* appealed the decision of the panel on the grounds that the panel had breached the rules of natural justice by relying on expert evidence given before another tribunal (in British Columbia) and quoted in cases provided by the intervenor, LEAF.

The court in this case agreed with *Alberta Report,* ruling that

---

[652] *Harvey Kane and Jewish Defence League of Canada v. Alberta Report, Link Byfield, Michael Byfield and Ted Byfield*, Calgary, 2001.
[653] For more on LEAF, see Robert Martin, *The Most Dangerous Branch, op. cit.*

administrative tribunals have a duty of fairness to those who appear before them. This includes the requirement of informing the parties about any evidence that they intend to consider, and allowing the parties to address the question of whether that evidence should be admitted, to challenge the weight to be accorded to the evidence and to submit other evidence in rebuttal. The panel did none of these things. As a result the judge allowed the appeal and sent the matter back for a new hearing.[654]

Human rights commissions first got into the thought police business because of the activities of a Toronto group called the Western Guard Party. This group was dominated by John Ross Taylor. Taylor was definitely the grand old man of Canadian Nazism, having been detained pursuant to the *War Measures Act* for continuing his pro-Nazi activities during the Second World War.

In the mid-1970s, Taylor and the Western Guard Party unveiled an innovation. This was a Dial-a-Hate Message service. Leaflets bearing a telephone number were distributed. Persons who called the number could listen to a recorded hate message. A flurry of correspondence between the government of Canada and the government of Ontario ensued, with both governments eager to "do something" about Taylor and the Western Guard Party. Consequently, s. 13(1) was added to the *Canadian Human Rights Act*. Section 13(1) ordained that it was a "discriminatory practice" to:

> ...communicate telephonically or to cause to be so communicated, repeatedly, in whole or in part by means of the facilities of a telecommunications undertaking within the legislative authority of Parliament, any matter that is likely to expose a person or persons to hatred or contempt by reason of the fact that that

---

[654] *Alberta Report v. Alberta (Human Rights and Citizenship Commission)*, [2002] A.J. No. 1539 (Q.B.).

> *person or those persons are identifiable on the basis of a*
> *prohibited ground of discrimination.*

Taylor and the Western Guard Party were brought before the Canadian Human Rights Commission (CHRC) because of a complaint that they had violated s. 13(1). The Commission found a violation of s. 13 and ordered that the recorded hate messages stop. The CHRC is given teeth by a provision in the *Act* which states that its orders may be entered in the judgment book of the Federal Court of Canada. Thus, breaches of an order made by the CHRC would amount to the offence of contempt of court.

Taylor and the Western Guard Party continued the hate messages in violation of the order made by the CHRC. They were brought before the Federal Court, which sentenced Taylor to be imprisoned for one year for contempt of court. The sentence was to be suspended if the hate messages stopped. The hate messages continued and Taylor was imprisoned.[655] When he was released, the hate messages resumed.

The process described above was recommenced. The entire hideous matter ended up before the Supreme Court of Canada.[656] The *Charter* had, by this time, become part of Canada's constitution and Taylor pleaded it before the Supreme Court, arguing that s. 13(1) infringed the freedom of expression guaranteed in s. 2(b) of the *Charter*. Following the *Irwin Toy* analysis, the Court was bound to conclude that s. 13(1) did, indeed, infringe upon freedom of expression. The bulk of the decision, as is generally true of cases involving freedom of expression, was taken up with the analysis of whether the infringement could be justified under s. 1 of the *Charter*.

The main judgment was delivered by Chief Justice Dickson,

---

[655] J. P. Boyer, *Political Rights: The Legal Framework of Elections in Canada*, Toronto, Butterworth, 1981, pp. 308-309.

[656] *Canada* v. *Taylor* [1990] 3 S.C.R. 892.

who, as I read the judgment, tied himself in logical and semantical knots in his attempt to find a justification for s. 13(1). What was the state's objective in creating s. 13(1)? It was the "furtherance of equality", undeniably pressing and substantial. The section 1 analysis was quickly disposed of by noting, "...the guiding principles in undertaking the s. 1 inquiry include respect and concern for the dignity and equality of the individual and a recognition that one's concept of self may in large part be a function of membership in a particular cultural group."[657] In subsequent years, the thought control sector has come to look upon the decision in *Taylor* as its charter and its licence.[658]

Given the vast number of outrages perpetrated by human rights commissions in recent years, it is not easy to decide where to start. It may be more enjoyable to begin with those that are merely laughable.

In May of 2007, Guy Earle was the host for a comedy evening at a restaurant in Vancouver. Two female patrons, who appeared to be drunk, began heckling him, even going to the point, it was alleged, of throwing drinks at him. Earle tried to shut them up and, surmising that they were lesbians, made some very unpleasant remarks to them. On 10 September 2007, one of the women, Lorna Pardy, complained to the British Columbia Human Rights Tribunal, which agreed to proceed with the matter. [659]

The nub of Pardy's complaint was that, by directing a stream of abuse at her, Earle had "discriminated" against her, both as a woman and as a lesbian.[660] As of February of 2010, this matter had

---

[657] *Ibid*, at p. 920.

[658] Karen Selick, *A golden opportunity to kill human rights commissions*, National Post, 3 November 2010.

[659] *Pardy* v. *Earle* [2008] BCHRT 241.

[660] Arendt asserted that, "Totalitarian domination...aims at abolishing freedom, even at eliminating human spontaneity in general". Origins, p.405.

still not been resolved and the hearing scheduled to take place before the British Columbia Human Rights Tribunal was not to begin until 29 March 2010. A hearing before the British Columbia Human Rights Tribunal did, indeed, begin in Vancouver on 29 March. The lawyer representing Guy Earle raised a series of legal questions going to the Tribunal's jurisdiction to proceed with the matter. The official chairing the hearing panel ruled that the questions concerning the Tribunal's jurisdiction to proceed with the hearing would be dealt with only at the conclusion of the hearing. At this point, the lawyer representing Mr Earle withdrew from the hearing.[661]

I have suggested (see p. 394), that human rights commissions operate in an "Alice-in-Wonderland" world. The ruling, mentioned above, made by the chair of the panel hearing the complaint against Guy Earle, appears to confirm this suggestion. That ruling, as I perceive it, could be interpreted as a determination that:

> *Mr Earle's counsel has raised certain objections concerning the jurisdiction of this Tribunal to conduct this hearing. We will proceed with the hearing and, after the hearing has been completed, we will address the questions going to its legality.*

Media reports about the hearing seemed to underline its Alice-in-Wonderland nature.[662] On 23 April 2010, the Tribunal issued a sort-of decision.[663] The decision is, with respect, baffling. Ms Pardy's complaint was brought under s.8 of the *British Columbia*

---

[661] Brian Hutchinson, *Lawyer walks out on comedian's rights hearing*, National Post, 29 March 2010.

[662] Brian Hutchinson, *Funny business at B.C. human rights hearing*, National Post, 2 April 2010.

[663] *Pardy* v. *Earle and others (No. 3)* [2010] BCHRT 128.

Human Rights Code[664] which purports to prohibit "discrimination" with respect to the provision of any "accommodation, service or facility customarily available to the public" because of, *inter alia,* "sex" or "sexual orientation". It is not easy to grasp how the master of ceremonies at an open mike comedy evening is engaged in the provision of a service or facility customarily available to the public. The Tribunal determined, quite plausibly, that the restaurant did, in fact, provide a service or facility customarily available to the public and that Mr Earle was its employee or agent in the provision of such a service or facility. It was also determined that, by his behaviour, Mr Earle had "discriminated" against Ms Pardy.

This determination seems to me to stretch the meaning of "discrimination" beyond any plausible limit. One might have thought that "discrimination", in this context, would have involved saying to Ms Pardy: "We surmise that you are a lesbian and, for that reason, we will not permit you to sit in our restaurant, nor will we serve you." The Tribunal also skated over the fundamental issue of jurisdiction. Jurisdiction is *the* threshold question in matters of this nature, since it addresses the issue of whether a public body possesses the lawful authority even to address a particular matter.

Earle argued that the Tribunal lacked the lawful authority to deal with the complaint. The Tribunal's decision, to the extent that I am capable of understanding it, seems to have been: we will proceed to hear the complaint and then, after we have completed the hearing, we will address the question whether we possess the lawful authority to do so. Earle argued, further, that s. 8 of the *Code* was an unjustifiable limit on the guarantee in s. 2(b) of the *Charter.* The member of the Tribunal who made the decision, and who has been identified as a lawyer, appeared to believe that s. 2(b) guaranteed "freedom of speech" rather than, as it does,

---

[664] R.S.B.C. 1996, c. 210.

"freedom of expression". The decision of 23 April 2010 did not set out a final resolution of the complaint raised by Ms Pardy, so, one must assume that such a resolution will be reached in the fullness of time.

Ted Kindos operates Gator Ted's Tap and Grill, a bar and restaurant in Burlington, Ontario. In May of 2005, a patron named Steve Gibson, who was authorised to smoke cannabis for medical reasons, was doing so just inside the entrance to the restaurant. Other patrons complained and Kindos asked Gibson to stop. Gibson complained to the Ontario Human Rights Commission, which sided with him. The Commission drew up a settlement under which Gibson would have been permitted to smoke cannabis in Kindos' establishment. Barbara Hall, who chairs Ontario's Human Rights Commission, offered her analysis:

> This is about the need to balance between the legal and medical rights of one person to smoke marijuana legally because of health issues and the rights of others impacted by that.[665]

Kindos then received word from Ontario's liquor licensing authorities that they did not make exceptions for the medical use of cannabis. If Kindos accepted the Human Rights Commission's settlement, or so he was informed, he would lose his licence to sell alcohol.[666] I have difficulty avoiding the sense that this incident was based on a Monty Python sketch.

The remaining stories aren't funny. We now turn to the most outrageous of all.

Stephen Boissoin was a Pastor in Red Deer, Alberta. He became concerned about the proselytising activities of

---

[665] Jordana Huber, *Clarification demanded on where medical marijuana smokers can light up*, Vancouver Province, 7 February 2009.
[666] Shaidle and Vere, *op. cit.*, p. 58.

homosexuals, which activities were directed at younger persons, particularly those in the public schools. In 2003 he wrote a letter to the Editor of the Red Deer *Advocate*. The letter was critical of the political activities of homosexuals, in particular of the advocacy of same-sex marriage. The newspaper decided to publish the letter. Ezra Levant described the letter as "…a rough piece of work, rude even, and it was certainly provocative."[667]

Darren Lund, then a teacher and now a Professor at the University of Calgary, made a complaint to the Alberta Human Rights and Citizenship Commission. It is relevant to note that Mr Lund was not then and is not now, homosexual. A hearing was held before the Human Rights Panels of Alberta. A lawyer for the government of Alberta appeared at the hearing and argued:

> …*if people were allowed to simply hide behind the rubric of political and religious opinion, they would defeat the entire purpose of the human rights legislation.*[668]

A decision was reached that the letter to the editor was in breach of the relevant provisions of Alberta's *Human Rights, Citizenship and Multiculturalism Act*. The "remedy" awarded against Boissoin and the *Advocate* is the horrifying part. The decision included this assertion:

> *The Panel does find that Dr. Lund…although not a direct victim, did expend considerable time and energy and suffered ridicule and harassment as a result of his*

---

[667] Levant, *op. cit.*, p. 83.
[668] Shaidle and Vere, *op. cit.*, p. 54.

complaint."[669]

There might be those who would take issue with my having characterized Canada as "totalitarian". It is undeniable that this country already manifests a definitive characteristic of a totalitarian system in that people are encouraged to spy on their fellow citizens and to report deviationists to the state.[670] Boissoin was ordered to "...cease publishing in newspapers, by email, on the radio, in public speeches, or on the internet, in future, disparaging remarks about gays and homosexuals...and is prohibited from making disparaging remarks in the future about Dr. Lund or Dr. Lund's witnesses relating to their involvement in this complaint."[671] Boissoin was also ordered to make a written apology to Lund and to ask the *Advocate* to print the apology. In addition to the apology, Boissoin was to pay Lund $5,000.00 and to pay the expenses of Lund's leading witness.[672]

When I read that order, the question that arises in mind is, why did the Panel stop short of ordering that Boissoin be burned at the stake? Stephen Boissoin sought judicial review of the decision that went against him. On 3 December 2009, he received justice according to law.[673] The judgment of Mr Justice E.C. Wilson was both scathing and witty. Wilson adumbrated the many errors, both substantive and procedural, which had been made by the Panel. These errors were sufficient to vitiate the Panel's decision and Wilson, J. quashed it.

Interestingly enough, the judge concluded that the *Act* itself

---

[669] *Lund* v. *Boissoin*, decision of Human Rights Panels of Alberta, 30 May 2008.

[670] Arendt saw "denunciation" as a core function of the subjects of a totalitarian system. Origins, p. 323.

[671] Note 667.

[672] *Ibid.*

[673] *Boissoin* v. *Lund*, (2009) 314 D.L.R.(4th) 70.

was both *intra vires* the Alberta legislature and consistent with the *Charter* and, thus, completely lawful. It was the lawless behaviour of the Panel which necessitated overruling its decision. Boissoin was, as a result, freed from the lifetime prohibition against making public or private "disparaging" remarks about homosexuals. There may well be people who have not been persuaded by my characterization of contemporary Canada as a "totalitarian theocracy". The case of Damian Goddard is both apposite and instructive. Goddard was a sports journalist in Toronto. In a private tweet to a hockey agent who had been critical of same-sex marriage, Goddard expressed his support for what he described as the "traditional and TRUE meaning of marriage". Goddard lost his job because he made this assertion.[674]

Much criticism of human rights commissions has focussed on their failure adequately to distinguish between expression which is merely offensive and expressions of "hate".[675] The ongoing conflation of hate and offensive expression must be the most serious failing of human rights commissions. Cram suggested a subcategory of offensive expression, which he described as "gratuitously offensive". He argued:

> *Little or no contribution to public debate or understanding is made or is intended to be made by groundless utterances and where gratuitously offensive speech is regulated, it could be argued that legal controls play a role in fostering a civilized and*

---

[674] Cathal Kelly, *Fired sports journalist Damian Goddard 'stands by' tweet*, Toronto Star, 11 May 2011.

[675] Ian Cram, *The Danish Cartoons, Offensive Expression, and Democratic Legitimacy*, Extreme Speech, p. 311.

> *respectful discourse among individuals who wish to
> participate in public discourse.*[676]

Whatever one might think of Cram's distinction, it must be clear that Boissoin's statements were sincere and heartfelt and anything but gratuitous.

Despite this victory, nothing was done to mitigate the financial burden which the entire proceeding had imposed on Boissoin. It is important to stress the extent to which the decisions in *Boissoin, Owens* and both *Whatcott* matters manifest the crucial role which real courts, staffed by real judges, can play as guardians of free expression.

On 29 March 2010, Darren Lund filed a notice of his intention to appeal this decision to the Alberta Court of Appeal.[677] In 2006 the Canadian writer Mark Steyn published a book called *America Alone*.[678] The purpose of the book, it seems, was to warn Canada and the United States and other countries of the threat which he believed to be posed by Islam. On 23 October 2006 *Maclean's* magazine published an article *The Future belongs to Islam* also by Steyn. The article repeated many of the themes raised in the book. Individual Muslims, as well as Islamic organisations, made complaints to the Canadian Human Rights Commission and

---

[676] *Ibid.,* at p. 325.

[677] See, Joseph Brean, *Judges grapple with Canada's legal test for hatred*, National Post, 9 April 2010. See also, Sarah McGinnis, *Eight-year legal battle continues over hate law*, Calgary Herald, 7 April 2010. It has already been noted that Lund is not, himself, homosexual (see p. 381). EGALE (Equality for Gays and Lesbians Everywhere) is the leading national advocacy and political organisation for homosexuals. It is worth noting that EGALE does not support Lund's actions. See, Gilles Marchildon, *Freedom for all means freedom for each*, InQueeries 3 November 2005. This piece, written by the President of EGALE, was a solid, well-founded and well-thought out argument in favour of free expression.

[678] Washington, DC, Regnery Publishing.

to three provincial commissions—in Alberta, British Columbia and Ontario.

It is important to note significant recent changes in the way Human Rights Commissions (HRCs) operate. There was a time when HRCs performed a filtering function. Aggrieved individuals would make complaints to HRCs. Those complaints would be investigated by HRC staff who would determine whether a particular complaint should go to a formal hearing before a Human Rights Tribunal. In an effort to make procedures more "user friendly", the filtering process has been removed and complaints now go directly to a hearing before the tribunal.

On 10 October 2008, the BC Human Rights Tribunal dismissed the complaint against *Maclean's*.[679] It is a discouraging experience to read the Tribunal's decision. The decision is, as I read it, pompous and overblown. The Tribunal dismissed freedom of expression in one or two turgid sentences. "Freedom of expression is not an absolute right…competing values of freedom of expression and the right of marginalised groups in our society to live free from discrimination." The Tribunal quickly skated over "a meeting" between *Maclean's* editors and three Muslim law students which degenerated into a blatant attempt at extortion. The Tribunal demonstrated deference to the "experts" trotted out by the complainants. Had I ever received work of such poor quality from a student, I would have given it a failing grade.

Maclean's was represented before the BC Tribunal by Toronto lawyer Julian Porter, Q.C., probably Canada's leading media law practitioner. He argued, in part:

> *Against the argument that you cannot cry fire in a crowded theatre: "Oh yes you can—you must, if in your*

---

[679] *Elmasry and Habib* v. *Rogers Publishing and MacQueen* [2008] B.C.H.R.T. 378.

> *considered view there is a fire. In that case there is a*
> *duty to cry fire.* [680]

If I may be forgiven for extending the metaphor, we in Canada, as I see it, now live in a crowded theatre surrounded by fire, which is already racing up and down the aisles, and the state has decreed that we may not cry fire.

Both the BC and Alberta tribunals dismissed the complaints and the Canadian and Ontario Commission each determined that it did not have jurisdiction to deal with the content of a publication like *Maclean's*.

Barbara Hall, who chairs the Ontario Commission, issued a statement in which she ruled her Commission had no jurisdiction to deal with the matter, but, nonetheless, concluded that the article in question was an "...example of racism and Islamophobia."[681]

The confluence of official multiculturalism and of identity politics has resulted in a Canada which is deeply tribalised. Social cohesion and harmony have been eroded to such an extent that, or so it appears, if one is a person of Aboriginal, African or Asian ancestry and one has an experience which one perceives to be less than ideal, one will, almost reflexively, be inclined to view the unfortunate occurrence as the result of "racism".[682]

---

[680] Shaidle and Vere, *op. cit.*, p. 42.

[681] Shaidle and Vere, *op. cit.*, p. 37 and Joseph Brean, *Ontario rights commission dismisses complaint*, sort of, National Post, 10 April 2008.

[682] Joseph Brean, *Law Dean Candidate alleges Racism*, National Post, 10 September 2010. In a 2010 decision, *Knoll North American Corp. v. Adams* (2010) 104 O.R. (3d) 297, the Ontario Divisional Court appeared to adopt precisely this perspective. The litigation arose out of a workplace dispute between a black worker and his Caucasian(sic) supervisor. The Court concluded, on the basis of no direct evidence, that the supervisor had been motivated by anti-black racism, with which "...society is permeated". (at p.309) and further, again without any evidence, that

In 2009, the Faculty of Law at the University of Windsor began its search for a new Dean. A law professor who was a woman of South Asian ancestry applied for the position in November of 2009. In February of 2010, the search committee published a short list of two candidates, one of whom was the aforementioned law professor. The search committee eventually decided not to recommend that either candidate on the short list be appointed Dean. The female law professor made a complaint under the Ontario *Human Rights Code* to the effect that, in deciding not to offer her the post of Dean, the Law Faculty had "discriminated" against her both on the ground of race and of sex. In April of 2010 the Law Faculty appointed an Acting Dean and established a fresh search committee. The complaint went to the Human Rights Tribunal of Ontario which released an Interim Decision on 27 September 2010.[683]

Even though it did not hold a full hearing, the tribunal was, nonetheless, able to conclude that the university had "discriminated" against the complainant. The Tribunal neither expressed nor entertained any doubt as to its authority to interfere in the internal administration of a university to the extent of ordering that a particular candidate be appointed the Dean of a faculty. The tribunal, further, had no doubt concerning its authority to grant an "interim remedy" against a respondent in a case where there had not been a hearing.[684] In the event, the tribunal declined to grant an "interim remedy". As time passed, this matter gave every indication of escalating into one of those blood feuds which make teaching in a Canadian university such a

---

this racism is "…subtle, pervasive and unconscious." (104 O.R.(3d) at 310.) Althia Raj, *Senator urges blacks to 'rise up and claim our rightful place'*, Montreal Gazette, 27 June 2011 presents a full exposition of the "racism is everywhere" worldview.

[683] *Carasco* v. *University of Windsor* 2010 HRTO 1968.

[684] *Ibid.*, para 22.

delightful experience.[685]

Canadians can take pride in the fact that we have succeeded in establishing a society which is completely beyond parody. An embryonic Canadian John Cleese or Spike Milligan would throw up his hands in abject surrender, recognising the utter impossibility of creating anything funnier than the CBC, or the *Globe and Mail,* or our human rights commissions, or our judiciary or our universities. A graduate student of social work at Ryerson University in Toronto recently complained to the Human Rights Tribunal of Ontario that she was being discriminated against because of her commitment to "ethical veganism".[686] The student's supervisor had declined to recommend her for a Ph.D. programme on the ground that "animal rights" were not "clearly related" to social work. The complainant argued that she had been "...attacked and treated unfairly because of my belief in ethical veganism and because I am a member of a marginalized community, vegan animal rights activists."

As a further consequence of the confluence of multiculturalism and identity politics, zero-sum thinking has become widespread. Zero-sum thinking, which I would describe as a pernicious intellectual indulgence, has afflicted many social institutions and relations, including free expression.

One commentator suggested that zero-sum thinking inheres in the discourse of equality.[687] When all the complaints against *Maclean's* failed, certain Muslims contrived to see the result as

---

[685] Joseph Brean, *University of Windsor fires back at failed law dean candidate,* National Post, 10 November 2010.

[686] Joseph Brean, *Ryerson student takes veganism discrimination dispute to Human Rights Tribunal of Ontario,* National Post, 8 November 2011.

[687] Peter Foster, *The Equality Obsession,* National Post, 17 September 2010.

"Europeans win, Muslims lose."[688] Khurrum Awan, now a lawyer, played a central role in bringing the complaints against *Maclean's*. He subsequently asserted that the "strategic objective" behind the complaints was to "...increase the cost of publishing anti-Islamic material".[689] Khurrum Awan's observation raises an important question about the purpose of human rights legislation. Is this legislation, to put the question in lawyers' language, intended to function as a "sword" or as a "shield"?

Looking at the matter historically, it seems that shield is probably the better answer. Ontario was the first jurisdiction in Canada to enact human rights legislation. Its early legislation was designed to protect persons against discrimination in accommodation, in employment and in respect of the provision of public goods and services and to provide a forum in which persons who claimed to have suffered such discrimination might seek redress. That formulation, emphasising the word protect, suggests that the legislation was, indeed, intended to function as a shield. When individuals or groups seek to use the legislation as a means, either of attacking their enemies, or of achieving broader political goals, they are, thereby, seeking to use it as a sword.

Not content with having reached a conclusion in the *Maclean's* matter without holding a hearing, Barbara Hall called for the creation of a national press council to act as a "filter" for the media.[690] Angered by media reports about ministerial corruption and about the extravagant sexual behaviour of the country's President, the South African government created a Media

---

[688] Joseph Brean, *Muslims told to insist on equal voice*, National Post, 9 June 2008.

[689] Robert Sibley, *Ezra Levant sued in 'Jihad Chill' Case*, Ottawa Citizen, 26 January 2010.

[690] Levant, *op. cit.*, p. 183.

Tribunal to exercise supervision of the media.[691]

It would not be accurate to seek to analyse the role of human rights commissions without adverting to Richard Warman. The behaviour of certain persons connected with the Canadian Human Rights Commission has been disturbing. The unusual, if not to say bizarre, activities of certain persons have recently attracted attention. Richard Warman is an Ottawa lawyer who was employed by the CHRC from 2002 to 2004. It seems that Warman spends a substantial amount of time prowling the Internet, looking for questionable websites. When he found a website that gave the impression of promoting unacceptable ideas, he would, or so it seems, log on to the website using a pseudonym and himself post hateful material on the website.[692] The next step in this practice would be to make a complaint to the CHRC about the statements which he himself, in fact, had published.

Between 2003 and 2009 the vast majority of s.13 complaints to the CHRC were made by Warman.[693] Since the CHRC almost always finds in favour of the complainant in complaints made under s.13, Warman has been very successful and has received substantial sums of money in awards of compensation.[694] In one ruling[695] the Canadian Human Rights Tribunal did advert to some of Warman's activities, describing him as "...an experienced lawyer who has spent a good deal of time and effort researching

---

[691] R.W.Johnson, *Johannesburg: Hard Pressed*, Standpoint, 30 September 2010.

[692] "...Mr Warman admitted (after initially denying) that he had participated in communicating messages on Internet Websites similar to the Northern Alliance Website utilizing pseudonyms...". *Warman* v. *Ouwendyk* (2009) CHRT 10, Para 59. Reference should also be made to Paras 60 and 61 of the same decision.

[693] *Ibid.*, para. 99.

[694] *Ibid.*

[695] *Warman* v. *Ouwendyk* (2009) C.H.R.T. 10. The Tribunal was also critical of several aspects of Warman's behaviour. See Note 690, above.

and pursuing persons or groups of persons whom he believes are responsible for hate messaging."[696]

Warman has, on occasion, allowed himself to be associated publically with a street gang called Anti-Racist Action and has demonstrated that he is not reluctant to institute libel actions against people who oppose him.[697] On 6 July 2005, Warman gave a speech to the Annual General Meeting of Anti-Racist Action. The title of the speech was "Maximum Disruption",[698] a phrase which can be taken as encapsulating Warman's approach to those persons whom he regards as his opponents.

In May of 2009, the Parliamentary Subcommittee on International Human Rights invited me to testify before it as a witness to address the matter of human rights commissions and freedom of expression. On 18 June 2009, I appeared before the Subcommittee in Ottawa and, as invited, addressed, *inter alia,* the work of the Canadian Human Rights Commission. In the course of my remarks, I made certain critical observations about Mr Warman. As a result, Mr Warman wrote a letter of complaint,

---

[696] *Ibid.*

[697] *Warman* v. *Grosvenor* (2009) 92 O.R. (3d) 663, and *Warman v. Fromm* [2007] O.J. No. 4754. In one of his defamation actions, in this case against the proprietors of a website, Mr Warman attempted to persuade the judges to require that the operators of websites reveal the identities of people who posted allegedly defamatory material. See, Don Butler, *Court to decide web posters' ability to remain anonymous,* National Post, 12 April 2010. In this libel action, the Ontario Superior Court of Justice rejected Mr Warman's attempt to persuade it to order that the operators of a website reveal the identities of persons making postings on the website. *Warman* v. *Wilkins-Fournier et al.* (2010) 100 O.R. (3d.) 648. In 2009, the Ontario Superior Court of Justice had been prepared to order that an ISP disclose the identities of persons who used its services. *York University* v. *Bell Canada Enterprises et al.* (2009) 99 O.R. (3d) 695.

[698] *Warman* v. *Winnicki* (2006) CHRT 20, para. 151.

dated 4 July 2009, about me to the Law Society of Upper Canada, the professional governing body for lawyers in the Province of Ontario.

In his letter[699] as I interpret it, Mr Warman implied that I was a neo-Nazi, a liar and lacking in integrity. It will be helpful at this point to mention Dean Steacy, a sometime "investigator" with the CHRC. Testifying during a hearing, he asserted that, "Freedom of speech is an American concept"…to which he did not give "any value".[700] There is an obvious question which a lawyer must ask: How did the CHRC acquire jurisdiction over the internet? It will be recalled that s.13 of the *Canadian Human Rights Act* makes it a "discriminatory practice" to "communicate telephonically…by means of the facilities of a telecommunication undertaking within the legislative authority of Parliament, (prohibited matter)." The Canadian Human Rights Tribunal appears to have convinced itself that the internet comes within this definition.[701]

On 2 September 2009, the Canadian Human Rights Tribunal released a decision[702] of vast significance. The tribunal held that s.13(1) of the *Canadian Human Rights Act* created a limit on the freedom of expression guaranteed in s. 2(b) of the *Charter* and, further, that reading s. 13(1) together with s. 54 of the *Act,* this was a limit which could not be justified in a free and democratic society. Section 54, which was added to the *Act* after the Supreme Court of Canada's decision in *Taylor,* authorised the imposition of fines as punishment for breaches of s. 13(1). The very existence of s. 54, as I read it, seriously undercuts the reasoning of Chief Justice Dickson in *Taylor.* Because it was bound by an earlier

---

[699] Letter in the possession of the author.

[700] Shaidle and Vere, *op. cit.*, p.7. See, also, John Ivison, *Laws should protect against hate, not against being offended*, National Post, 2 April 2010.

[701] *Warman* v. *Ouwendyk* (2009) C.H.R.T. 10. See also, Joseph Brean, *Internet rendered hate law 'outdated'*, National Post, 22 February 2010.

[702] *Warman* v. *Lemire* (2009) CHRT 26.

Supreme Court of Canada decision concerning the powers of administrative tribunals[703], the CHRT stopped short of issuing a declaration that s. 13(1) was invalid.[704] *Warman* v. *Lemire* could well mean the end of human rights commissions acting as thought police.

It will be useful at this juncture to observe that the thought police role of human rights commissions, sometimes described as "protecting 'vulnerable' groups", and so-called "equity"[705] may be viewed as the two sides of a coin of pity and condescension.[706]

One might have thought that the ruling in *Warman* v. *Lemire* was all that needed to be said, but apparently not. Pearl Eliadis of Montreal, who describes herself as a "human rights" lawyer, took

---

[703] *Cuddy Chicks Ltd* v. *Ontario Labour Relations Board* [1991] 2 SCR 5.

[704] For commentary, see Joseph Brean, *Hate Speech Law unconstitutional: Rights Tribunal,* National Post, 2 September 2009.

[705] For my views on "equity", see *Opposing Racism by Racist Means,* (1994) 3 *Inroads 88; Challenging Orthodoxy: A Critical Analysis of Racially-Based Job Quotas* (1993) 1 Canadian Labour Law Journal 409; and *Employment Equity Simply Wasn't Necessary,* Toronto Star, 26 July 1995. "Equity" is the obfuscating term for Canadian efforts to go beyond affirmative action and create quota systems in education, employment and many other economic and social spheres. For analysis and explication of "equity", see Robert Martin, *Challenging Orthodoxy: A Critical Analysis of Racially-Based Job Quotas,* (1993) 1 Canadian Labour Law Journal 409.

[706] This perspective was suggested by Dambisa Moyo's wonderful book, *Dead Aid: Why aid is not working and how there is another way for Africa,* London and New York, Allen Lane, 2008. Pascal Bruckner argued that the "culture of apology" which has gripped much of the West, is "…above all, a culture of condescension". *The Tyranny of Guilt,* at p.42. He has also asserted that looking on whole groups of people as "victims of perpetual oppression" necessarily involves seeing them "as inferiors".(at p. 145) Philip Gourevitch has elaborated and explicated the many ways in which pity and condescension may, and have, led to disaster. See his, *Alms Dealers,* The New Yorker, 11 October 2010.

to the pages of the *National Post*[707] in order to provide an authoritative interpretation, but succeeded only in muddying the waters. There was, as she saw it, "confusion" because A. Hadjis, the member of the Canadian Human Rights Tribunal who wrote the decision, "erred" and this was compounded because "the media" interpreted his reasons "badly". The media culprit was reporter Joseph Brean of the *National Post* who had written a story[708], in Eliadis' opinion, full of errors and misunderstanding. Why did Brean get it all so wrong? Because, in Eliadis' words, he "misconstrue[d] what I said to him". It was not encouraging, in reading Eliadis' writing, to discover that the "human rights lawyer" did not grasp the distinction between a fine imposed as punishment and "punitive damages". There was one superb piece of media analysis of the whole business.[709] In January of 2010 the Canadian Human Rights Commission applied to the Federal Court of Canada[710] for judicial review of this decision. I have great difficulty grasping whence an administrative tribunal derives the standing to seek judicial review of its own decision, but, in what can only be described as the Alice-in-Wonderland world of human rights commissions, just about anything is possible. The hearing before the Federal Court began in October of 2010. A number of parties intervened in the proceeding, thereby causing it to become politicized.[711]

We can now turn to the good news, an unusual HRC matter

---

[707] Pearl Eliadis, *What the tribunal ruling really means*, National Post 4 September 2009.
[708] Joseph Brean, *Tribunal backs off Hate provision*, National Post 3 September 2009.
[709] David Warren, *Kafka Comes to Canada*, Ottawa Citizen 4 September 2009.
[710] T. −1640—09.
[711] Joseph Brean, *Ottawa withdraws from clash of interests over hate speech law*, National Post 23 October 2010.

that reached a resolution in accordance with the law. Hugh Owens lived in Saskatoon. He was not impressed with "gay activists" nor with "gay pride" week. In order to express his lack of enthusiasm, he ran an ad in the Saskatoon *Star-Phoenix*. The ad featured two stickmen holding hands, over which was printed the standard "not permitted" symbol, a circle with a line running diagonally across it. A number of biblical passages condemning homosexuality were reproduced below this figure. The ad appeared on 30 June 1997.

Predictably enough, there was a complaint to the Saskatchewan Human Rights Commission. The complainants, who identified themselves as "gay men", averred that the ad caused them "anger, hurt and frustration". A Board of Inquiry concluded that the ad "discriminated" and ordered Owens to cease any further display of bumper stickers connected to the ad and to pay $1,500.00 to each of the three complainants.

Owens appealed the Board's decision to the Saskatchewan Court of Queen's Bench which agreed with the Board. He appealed further to the Court of Appeal.[712] The Court of Appeal adverted specifically to context, noting that the ad was published "...in the middle of an ongoing national debate about how Canadian legal and constitutional regimes should or should not accommodate sexual identities."[713] The Court characterised the advertisement as "...a position advanced in a continuing public policy debate rather than...a message of hatred or ill will."[714] Owens' appeal was allowed.

The question of the ability of persons who disapprove of homosexual proselytising in the public schools to express their disapproval publically has continued to be a difficult one. In 2001 and 2002 William Whatcott distributed flyers in Saskatoon in an

---

[712] *Owens* v. *Saskatchewan* (2006) 267 D.L.R. (4th) 733.

[713] *Ibid.*, at p. 756.

[714] *Ibid.*, at p. 757.

attempt to express his opposition to these practices. Complaints that Whatcott was acting in violation of s. 14(1) of the province's *Human Rights Code* were made to the Saskatchewan Human Rights Commission.

A Human Rights Tribunal concluded that Whatcott had, indeed, violated the provisions of the *Code*. The province's Court of Queen's Bench dismissed his appeal against this decision and he appealed further to the Court of Appeal. That court's decision[715] upholding Whatcott's appeal was released on 25 February 2010. The decision of Hunter, J.A. is important. She asserted, "Anything that limits debate on the morality of behaviour is an intrusion on the right to freedom of expression". Stressing the importance of looking at Whatcott's acts in context, she concluded that he had not infringed s. 14 of the *Code*.

I feel confident in predicting that, eventually, a "climate-change denier"[716] (I have heard the phrase) will be dragged before a human rights commission, as will someone who wishes a neighbour or a co-worker Merry Christmas.

In its 2009 policy statement, discussed above, the CRTC argued strongly against the state continuing to perform a thought police role. Commissioner Timothy Denton presented a learned and cogent argument in favour of free expression:

> *The history of the regulation of speech in this country does not engender confidence that such power will be used wisely...regulatory authorities charged with combating racism, hatred and other evils have consistently expanded their mandates, have abused their powers and eroded fundamental liberties. Wherever there is official orthodoxy, disagreement is heresy, and*

---

[715] *Whatcott* v. *Saskatchewan Human Rights Tribunal*, (2010) 317 D.L.R.(4th) 69.
[716] Melanie Phillips, *The World Turned Upside Down*, *op. cit.*, at p.113.

> *where there is heresy, there is usually an inquisition to*
> *root it out. After centuries ridding ourselves of thought*
> *control agencies, 20th century Canada re-invented*
> *them.*[717]

Shortly after Denton wrote these words, the CRTC announced that they were "additional" and disappeared them.

If we recall Pierre Trudeau's best-known aphorism, "the state has no business in the bedrooms of the nation", then, *a fortiori*, the state has no business in the computers of the nation.[718]

Various events in 2007 in what I believe can accurately be described as the persecution of Mark Steyn and Ezra Levant led to a sort of public outcry against the excesses of HRCs. What follows contains criticism of the Canadian Human Rights Commission and of its Chair, Jennifer Lynch.

There is no intention to engage in a personal attack against Ms Lynch. I believe strongly that both the behaviour and the capabilities of highly placed and highly paid public servants are, in a democracy, important and legitimate subjects for critical analysis. The Canadian Human Rights Commission decided to attempt to reply to its critics. In June of 2009, it released a document called *Special Report to Parliament: Freedom of Expression and Freedom from Hate in the Internet Age*[719]. The document can, as I see it, be characterised briefly as a compendium of postmodern "ideas" written in opaque postmodern jargon.

It spoke of a "Matrix of Rights", as if the imagined right not to be offended were to be accorded the same respect as freedom of

---

[717] Broadcasting Regulatory Policy, CRTC 2009-329.

[718] See, George Jonas, *Censors of the World Unite—and ruin the Internet*, National Post, 27 January 2010. This article provides a convincing demonstration of the similarities in official attitudes towards the Internet in Canada and in the People's Republic of China.

[719] Ottawa, 2009

expression. It staked out a serious claim to being recognised as a monument to banality with assertions such as "Words and ideas have power". In the end the *Report* had little to offer but arrogance, arguing, as I interpret it, that, because they might abuse it, which abuse could lead to people having their feelings hurt, Canadians should really not be trusted with free expression. Jennifer Lynch, Q.C., who chairs the CHRC, took to the pages of *The Globe and Mail* to argue in favour of the *Report*.[720] She treated the judgment of Dickson, C.J. in *Taylor* as if it were holy writ which provided a blanket justification for everything that HRCs do. She suggested that those who criticise HRCs are merely attempting to further a "new agenda" and raised the bogeymen of "absolute freedom of expression". For someone who regularly uses the letters "Q.C." after her name, she demonstrated a shaky knowledge of the law, asserting that s.13 of the *Canadian Human Rights Act* gave the CHRC jurisdiction over the internet and arguing that:

> *HRCs and Tribunals provide access to the justice system and remedies for those who believe they are victims of discrimination. As is the case with all administrative law bodies, they ensure that all parties are protected by the rules of natural justice and that frivolous complaints are effectively disposed(sic).* [721]

The only plausible conclusion I can reach, on reading those words, is that Ms Lynch knows little either of administrative law or of the practice of HRCs, including her own. She concluded that debate over free expression and human rights is a "passionate topic", whatever that might be. It emerged, towards the end of June

---

[720] Jennifer Lynch, *The Debate is out of Balance*, Globe and Mail, 12 June 2009.
[721] *Ibid.*

2009, that Jennifer Lynch keeps an "enemies list".[722] The CHRC spent $167,000.00 on public relations consultants. These consultants wrote speeches for Ms Lynch and helped prepare her before public appearances.[723]

On 30 May 2010, Ms Lynch delivered an address to the Council of Canadian Administrative Tribunals, 5th International Conference held in Montreal. As I interpret the speech[724], Ms Lynch was seeking to reply to critics of Canada's HRCs. The speech manifested many deficiencies, to some of which I now feel obliged to turn. She was not pleased with critics, observing of them:

> ...some individuals, are seeking to erode trust in public institutions by spreading campaigns of misinformation that dishonestly attack the practices and the people in these institutions.

She appeared to accept the existence of an inherent contradiction between freedom of expression and equality, listing, as "competing" rights, "the right to freedom of expression vs. the right to equality". She was not pleased with the tactics of critics, asserting, "They deliberately misrepresent or fabricate information to discredit or vilify people and organizations." I would surmise that English is probably Ms Lynch's first language, so it might be useful to note several widespread errors which crept into her address. These included using "concerning", rather

---

[722] Joseph Brean, *Canadians 'misinformed' on hate speech*, National Post, 22 June 2009. See also, Mark Steyn, *Name the date, Jennifer. I'll be there*, Maclean's 25 June 2009.

[723] Brian Lilley, *Top bureaucrat paid big bucks for spin doctors: Docs*, Toronto Sun, 13 November 2010.

[724] Text downloaded from the Canadian Human Rights Commission website. www.chrc-ccdp.ca.

than "cause for concern", using "most importantly" rather than "most important", using "within" rather than "in", using "as such" rather than "therefore" and stating "Social media *has*".

The Universities

Beginning in the 1990s, Canadian universities became active in suppressing the expression of both their faculty and their students. This was done primarily through the adoption and enforcement of what were called "speech codes."[725] In November of 2008 Queen's University took thought control to unprecedented depths. It announced plans to create a cadre of students to spy on other students. These "dialogue facilitators" would eavesdrop on the conversations of other students and, were anything blasphemous or heretical to be said, attempt to steer the conversation in an acceptable direction.[726]

It is my personal opinion that it would be exceedingly difficult to name a government ever and anywhere in Canada that was as hostile towards free expression as the N.D.P. one, led by the Honourable Robert K. Rae, P.C., O.C., Q.C., to give him his complete, formal title, which ruled Ontario from 1990 to 1995.

In October of 1993 that government issued two secret *ukases* called, first, *Framework Regarding the Prevention of Harassment and*

---

[725] For general discussion of speech codes, see: John Fekete, *Moral Panic: Biopolitics Rising*, (2d ed.). Robert Davies, Montreal, 1994, and Peter C. Emberley, *Zero Tolerance: Hot Button Politics in Canada's Universities*, Penguin Books, Toronto, 1996. Each university now has its own horror story about speech codes. See J. L. Granatstein, *The Decline and Fall of Free Speech*, (1994) 3 Literary Review of Canada, no. 6, 9 and Robert Martin, *Speech Codes in Action*, (1995) 44 University of New Brunswick Law Journal 65.

[726] Joseph Brean, *Queen's New Dialogue Monitors*, National Post, 19 November 2008.

Discrimination in Ontario Universities and, second, *Framework Regarding the Prevention of Harassment and Discrimination in Ontario Colleges*. These "frameworks" were to apply to faculty, staff, and students at universities and colleges, as well as to persons who had contracts with colleges or universities, and even to casual visitors. These documents declared "a policy of zero tolerance of harassment and discrimination" at Ontario's universities and colleges and included a "minimum expectation" regarding the kind of policies that the universities should adopt. These would embrace conduct both on and off university and college campuses, including at social functions and in telephone conversations. According to the documents, the definition of harassment included:

> *"one or a series of vexatious comments…that is known or might reasonably be known to be unwelcome/unwanted, offensive, intimidating, hostile, or inappropriate."*

As I interpret them, the two *Frameworks* would effectively have prohibited the discussion of most things involving human beings in universities and colleges in Ontario. The Canadian Civil Liberties Association agreed with this interpretation. In its brief to the Minister responsible for the *Frameworks*, the Association wrote:

> *Unfortunately, this definition suffers from both vagueness and overbreadth. Subjective concepts such as "unwelcome," "unwanted," and "offensive" could operate so as to make one person's thin skin the condition of another person's free speech. Thus, this definition is capable of catching within its net varieties of expression that it would simply be unconscionable for an academic*

community to suppress or even imperil.[727]

With rules like this in force, it's hard to imagine forthright discussions on many controversial issues such as ethnicity and crime, allegations of anti-Semitism in Quebec, or the possibility of a genetic component in sexual preferences. At the same time, it is not difficult to imagine how any of these topics could trigger formal complaints.

Since neither document was made public, there was little opportunity for discussion of them.[728] The universities *Framework* was eventually withdrawn, but the one for colleges remained in effect.[729]

Into 2010 the universities continued to be places which did not welcome original thought. A professor at the University of Alberta denounced a speaker for having "assimilationist and Eurocentric opinions" and suggested that she should not have been permitted to speak.[730]

The *Criminal Code* Again

At this point it will be useful to say something about the law and public statements which are critical of individuals because of their sexual orientation. Discussing this matter under the rubric

---

[727] *Framework Regarding Prevention of Harassment and Discrimination in Ontario Colleges and Universities*, Toronto Ministry of Education and Training, 1993.

[728] I am proud to say that I was the first person to be publically critical of the "frameworks." See, Robert Martin, *Ontario universities should refuse to adopt Minister's vile 'anti-racism' policies*, The Lawyers Weekly 17 December 1993.

[729] The universities Framework was dropped shortly after Robert Fulford wrote a critical article about it in the *Globe and Mail* (see *Defending the Right to be Offensive*, Globe and Mail, 2 February 1994).

[730] Andrew Hanon, *A lesson in racism*, Edmonton Sun, 9 March 2010.

"multicultural society" only makes sense if one imagines that, in contemporary Canada, homosexuals and heterosexuals belong to different cultures.[731] Eric Heinze has argued in favour of the near-limitless expansion of the number of groups "protected" by prohibitions against "hate speech" directed at them.[732] He was positively rhapsodic in his support for "massive censorship"[733], arguing that derogatory remarks directed at persons on the basis of mental or physical disability, age or obesity, even though he could find no evidence of actual social harm arising from such remarks[734], should be proscribed as "hate".

In 2001, Bill C-250, legislation to expand the wilfully promoting hatred offence, was introduced in Parliament. Bill C-250 was a private member's bill introduced by Svend Robinson, an openly homosexual M.P. from British Columbia. In 1995 he published an article in the *University of New Brunswick Law Journal*[735] in which he noted that, in one university class which he attended, an instructor said things which caused his (Robinson's) feelings to be hurt. His conclusion was that universities should, therefore, have speech codes which limit what might be said in the classroom.

Bill C-250 proposed to amend section 318 of the *Criminal Code*, the section which makes "advocating genocide" against an "identifiable group" a crime. Clause 1 of Bill C-250 amends

---

[731] This appears to be the premise underlying the Supreme Court's decision in *Little Sisters Book and Art Emporium v. Canada (Minister of Justice)*, [2000] 2 S.C.R. 1120. The same question is discussed by Gertrude Himmelfarb in her *One Nation, Two Cultures*, New York, Vintage Books, 2001.

[732] *Cumulative Jurisprudence and Hate Speech: Sexual Orientation and Analogies to Disability, Age and Obesity*, Extreme Speech, pp. 265- 285.

[733] At p. 285.

[734] *Ibid.*, at pp. 278, 283.

[735] *The Collision of Rights*, (1995) 44 University of New Brunswick Law Journal 61.

section 318(4) of the *Code* so that "identifiable group" now means "…any section of the public distinguished by colour, race, religion, ethnic origin or sexual orientation." Bill C-250 does not, in its terms, amend the companion section 319(2), which creates the offence of "wilfully promoting hatred against an identifiable group." But Bill C-250 inevitably has this effect. Section 319(7) states that "'identifiable group' has the same meaning as in section 318." Thus, the amendment to the definition of "identifiable group" in section 318(4) necessarily amends the meaning of "identifiable group" for the purposes of section 319. Based on the Supreme Court's decision in *Keegstra*, I assume that a court would decide that the new, expanded section 319 created a limit on freedom of expression. Is this still a limit which can be justified in a free and democratic society? Reading the Supreme Court's judgments in *Vriend*,[736] *Little Sisters*,[737] and *T.W.U. v. B.C.C.T.*,[738] I think it is possible to predict what the answer would be.

Before a court may find that a particular limit on a *Charter* right is justified in a free and democratic society, the court must be satisfied that the state's objective in creating the limit was "pressing and substantial, of sufficient importance to warrant overriding a constitutional right." It is not immediately apparent that making sure no one ever says anything that might hurt Svend Robinson's feelings, which I take to have been the objective underlying Bill C-250, is pressing and substantial.[739]

---

[736] *Vriend v. Alberta*, [1998] 1 S.C.R. 493.

[737] [2000] 2 S.C.R. 1120

[738] [2001] 1 S.C.R. 772.

[739] The Bill was given first reading on 22 November 2001 and passed by the House of Commons on 17 September 2003.

Equality

It will now be useful to comment on the current meaning of "equality".

There was a time when Canada was governed in accordance with the Rule of Law. "Equality before the law" was regarded as a central element of the Rule of Law. Many, particularly feminists, became enraged at the way "equality before the law" was applied, especially by the Supreme Court of Canada.[740] The demand began to be made for "substantive equality"[741] as opposed to "equality before the law". "Substantive equality", to the extent that it had any meaning, was a demand for concrete equality of outcomes, rather than formal, legal equality.[742] This notion shaded over into a demand for equality of self-esteem which turned, eventually, into institutionalised solipsism:

---

[740] See, Lynn McDonald, *The Supreme Court of Canada and the Equality Guarantee in the Charter*, in Robert Martin, ed., Critical Perspectives on the Constitution, (1984) 2 Socialist Studies 45.

[741] See, Margaret Denike, Fay Faraday and M. Kate Stephenson, *Making Equality Rights Real: Securing Substantive Equality under the Charter*, Toronto, Irwin Law, 2006. Theodore Dalrymple observed that, "It is not enough that formal legal barriers should have been removed, only absolute statistical equality will satisfy", *The New Vichy Syndrome*, below, note 798, at p. 55.

[742] On the relentless expansion of the meaning of "equality" and its aggressive enforcement by human rights commissions, see Ian Hunter, *The Dangerous Evolution of Human Rights Legislation*, National Post, 18 February 2010. Signing herself Chief Commissioner, Ontario Human Rights Commission, Barbara Hall wrote a letter to the editor in reply to this article. See, Barbara Hall, *Why we still need HRCs*, National Post, 19 February 2010. As seems generally to be true of the official efforts which HRCs have made to reply to critics, the letter, as I interpret it, was unconvincing.

> *If human dignity is at bottom a matter of how I feel*
> *about myself, then I myself become both the measure*
> *and the measurer of human dignity.*[743]

This amorphous notion of human dignity has expanded to the point where it now seems to be imagined that everyone has a right to be thought well of and to be assured that she is thought well of.[744]

Equality was transformed into a religion after the adoption of the *Charter*, s.15 of which can be regarded as the scriptural foundation for the secular state religion of equality.

Section 15(1) of the *Charter* states:

> *Every individual is equal before and under the law and*
> *has the right to the equal protection and equal benefit*
> *of the law without discrimination and, in particular,*
> *without discrimination based on race, national or*
> *ethnic origin, colour, religion, sex, age or mental or*
> *physical disability.*

The judges of the Supreme Court of Canada determined that the enumeration, in the text of s. 15, of prohibited grounds of discrimination was not exhaustive and that they, consequently, possessed the authority to recognize what they described as "analogous grounds".[745] The notion of "analogous grounds" is

---

[743] Douglas Farrow, *Rights and Recognition* in Daniel Cere and Douglas Farrow, eds, *Divorcing Marriage: Unveiling the Dangers in Canada's New Social Experiment*, Montreal and Kingston, McGill-Queen's University Press, 2004, p. 102.

[744] *Ibid.*, at p. 104.

[745] See, *Andrews* v. *Law Society of British Columbia*, [1989] 1 S.C. R. 143 and *Corbiere* v. *Canada (Minister of Indian and Northern Affairs)*, [1999] 2 S.C.R. 203.

similar to what Heinze described as "cumulative jurisprudence".[746] The careful reader will have noticed that neither "sexual orientation", nor "sexual preference" appears in the listing of prohibited grounds of discrimination found in the text of s. 15(1). The judges of the Supreme Court of Canada decided to rewrite s. 15 so as to add these two to the list of prohibited grounds of discrimination.[747]

> It should be a simple matter to see that hostility
> towards free expression inheres in the solipsistic religion
> of equality.[748]

This view of equality, as expressed above, underlies the "dictatorship of relativism" which defines the limits of permissible thought and expression today.[749]

The dominance of relativism does follow logically, since, if any person were ever to say that one thing was better than another, why, then, someone's self-esteem might be injured.

Theodore Dalrymple has offered this explanation for the triumph of relativism:

> ...unprecedentedly large numbers of people, who would
> once have had little exposure to philosophical
> arguments, have now been exposed to epistemological
> relativism. It is probably true to say that, in proportion
> as their numbers increase, so their critical faculty
> decreases. They are, therefore, likely to accept on
> authority that there is no such thing as truth, that

---

[746] See, note 730, above.

[747] See, *Vriend* v. *Alberta*, [1998] 1 S.C.R. 493.

[748] See, notes 740 and 741.

[749] Roger Kimball, *Introduction, The Dictatorship of Relativism*, (2009) 27 The New Criterion 4.

*everything depends upon one's initial point of view,
and that one opinion is as " valid" as another (the
weasel word "valid" has almost replaced the word
"true".) They accept on authority that there is no
authority: except, of course, what they themselves think,
which is as good as what anyone else thinks.
Intellectual weight is replaced by egotism.[750]*

None of the developments discussed above bodes well for free
expression. Free expression, like everything else, must give way
to the secular state religion of equality.[751]

Self Censorship

Censorship is not only imposed externally by the state. It can
come from within and be imposed on one's self. Canadians, as I
understand them, are gripped by terror at the prospect of thinking
or expressing or even appearing to express, anything that might
possibly be construed as a negative observation about any group of
people. Consequently, a regime of self-censorship[752] which
constrains the way Canadians, think, express themselves and,
even, understand their own history has been created.

The use of the circumlocution "community", is easily, as I
view it, the most pathetic and risible manifestation of Canadians'
horror at the possibility of being seen to be saying anything

---

[750] Theodore Dalrymple, *The New Vichy Syndrome: Why European
Intellectuals Surrender to Barbarism*, New York and London, Encounter
Books, 2010, p. 53.
[751] Dickie v. Dickie [2007] 1 S.C.R. 346.
[752] Arendt asserted that, "…totalitarianism has discovered a means of
dominating and terrorizing human beings from within.", Origins, p.325.
"The human rights commission inside my head" would be a good brief
definition of self-censorship.

improper about any group of people. Consequently, we no longer have Jews, but, rather, "members of the Jewish community". The use of the word "homosexuals" is now impermissible, so that we have, "members of the lesbian, gay, bisexual and transgender (sic) community". The use of the word "Indians" is also effectively prohibited. Individuals who hold the legal status "Indian" under the *Indian Act*[753] are now "first nations people" and persons from the Republic of India are "members of the South Asian community". This usage can often be taken to absurd lengths. I recall once seeing the writer Naomi Klein on television discussing computer hackers. She could not quite bring herself to say "hackers" and, instead, ventured "members of the hacking community". I have no doubt that I shall one day hear both "members of the axe-murdering community" and "members of the serial-raping community". It does seem that words or phrases which might, even conceivably, cause anyone to be upset or offended have all been rendered impermissible. Consequently, prostitutes are no longer prostitutes, but "sex trade workers"[754]; impotence is no longer impotence, but either "erectile difficulty" or "erectile dysfunction"(sic) and drug addiction and alcoholism are no longer drug addiction and alcoholism, but "substance abuse". I feel confident in predicting that pimps will one day be known as "sex trade facilitators".

The sense of horror and outrage at anyone ever expressing negative feelings about any group underlies a book, [755] which can, in my view, only be described as "foolish". The author managed to be outraged at the fact that, during the course of the Great War, there actually were Canadians who experienced, and manifested,

---

[753] R.S.C. 1985, c. I-5.

[754] Her Majesty's judges have adopted the phrase "sex trade workers". See, *R. v. Powell* (2010) 99 O.R.(3d) 671 at 673, 675 and 676.

[755] Robert Rutherdale, *Hometown Horizons, Local Responses to Canada's Great War*, Vancouver, University of British Columbia Press, 2004.

feelings of hostility towards Germans.[756] *Hometown Horizons*, which is written in a fashion so encrusted with postmodern jargon as to be near-incomprehensible, displays a tone of relentless condescension.[757] The volume demonstrates a central characteristic of pseudo-history, which is to say, a disregard for context. The author appeared not to grasp the fact that, between 1915 and 1918, German soldiers caused the deaths of 51,700 Canadians.[758] Rutherdale understood so little about Canadian participation in the Great War that he referred to highland regiments as "kilties".[759]

What, exactly, is it that we are so afraid of? Why have we sacrificed free expression? As is so often the case when we look at our current predicament, the search for an answer must take us back to Pierre Trudeau. Prior to Trudeau, "Canadian" was a generally recognised synonym for "staid, dull and boring". Trudeau made us hip. We actually had a Prime Minister who was romantically involved with Barbra Streisand. The secular state religion of equality is a way of proclaiming to the world that, "Despite the passing of Trudeau, Canadians are still hip."

Twas not ever thus.

I was born at the end of July 1939. On 1 September, Germany invaded Poland and the Second World War began, so, consequently, I spent a substantial part of my childhood in a country at war. Many little boys my age had a father, or a brother or an uncle who was off fighting the war. We were not wracked by fears that we might harbour unpleasant thoughts about Germans. Every little boy knew these words, sung to the tune of a

---

[756] *Ibid.*, at pp 121, 193.

[757] *Ibid.*, at p. 200.

[758] G.W.L. Nicholson, *Canadian Expeditionary Force, 1914-1919*, Ottawa, Queen's Printer, 1962, p. 546.

[759] *Hometown Horizons* at p. 193.

British march called "Colonel Bogey."[760]

> *Hitler has only got one ball.*
> *Goering has two, but they are small.*
> *Himmler has something similar,*
> *But Dr. Goebbels has no balls at all.*[761]

Summary and Conclusions

The activities of HRCs, particularly at the provincial level, raise a host of constitutional questions. There is, from the outset, the little matter that the Constitution of Canada, in section 2 (b) of the *Charter*, contains an explicit guarantee of freedom of expression. In those instances where tribunals and courts have perceived that there might be a problem, they have tended to define it out of existence. I like to think that I have a lot of imagination, but I cannot begin even to conceive how grown-ups might conclude that ensuring no-one's "self-esteem" is ever bruised is a pressing and substantial objective in a free and democratic society.

It is worth recalling the discussion in Chapter 1 of the Supreme Court of Canada's decision in the *Alberta Press Bill* matter. That decision appeared to have established the principle that a provincial legislature lacked the authority to enact laws which placed limits on freedom of expression. Human Rights Tribunals would seem to offend against the limited separation of powers found in the Constitution of Canada.[762] They are also a

---

[760] "Colonel Bogey" is what the British prisoners of war are whistling when they march into the camp at the beginning of the movie *The Bridge on the River Kwai*.

[761] This is clearly incorrect. Josef Goebbels and his wife Magda had six children, all of whom they poisoned in Berlin in April of 1945.

[762] Reference re Residential Tenancies Act, 1979 [1981] 1 S.C.R. 714.

blatant denial of the guarantee in section 11 of the *Charter*. The Ontario Human Rights Tribunal concluded in July of 2009, that "unconscious discrimination" could amount to a breach of the Ontario *Human Rights Code* and, further, that a person accused of breaching the *Code* is obliged to establish her own innocence.[763]

We urgently need a full dress judicial evaluation of the constitutionality of HRCs. As might be expected in a country governed according to a secular state religion of equality, some people are definitely more equal than others.[764] It is instructive, by way of illustrating the notion that some people are more equal than others, to look at the activities of one Salman Hossain, a university student in Toronto. He has written that Jews are the "scum of the earth" and argued that "a genocide should be perpetrated against the Jewish populations of North America and Europe."[765]

While the thought police of Canada's "human rights" commissions were prosecuting Guy Earle, Ted Kindos and Stephen Boissoin, they seem to have failed to notice Salman

---

[763] Margaret Wente, *Guilty of unconscious Racism*, Globe and Mail, 28 July 2009.

[764] R. v. Turpin [1989] 1 S.C.R. 1296 at p. 1333. See also, Martin Loney, *The Pursuit of Division: Race, Gender and Preferential Hiring in Canada,* Montreal and Kingston, McGill-Queen's University Press, 1998. The primary constitutional guarantee of equality in Canada is found in s. 15(1) of the Charter. That section begins with the telling words "Every individual is equal…". In Turpin the Supreme Court of Canada declined to give these words their clear and obvious meaning and decided that only persons who were members of a "historically disadvantaged group" might claim equality rights.

[765] Editorial, *A case study in hate*, National Post, 6 March 2010. Salman Hossain has also urged the killing of Canadians. See, Stewart Bell, *Killing Canadians 'best way'*: student, National Post, 30 January 2008.

Hossain.[766] Salim Mansur is, like Salman Hossain, a Canadian of Bangladeshi origin. Mansur has argued in favour of protecting "...this despicable young man's right to speak freely, even offensively."[767] It appeared, by July of 2010, that Salman Hossain would be charged with wilfully promoting hatred. He did, in fact, become the first person to be charged with "advocating genocide".[768]

> At a public gathering held in a large Canadian city in January of 2009, a man, presumably a Canadian citizen, asserted that, "Hitler did not do his job". At the same gathering an adult woman, also presumably a Canadian citizen, shrieked at a nine year old girl, "Die fucking Jewish child.[769]

Both these people were able to do what they did with impunity. I have little doubt that, had I had the temerity to criticise this behaviour, I would have been dragged before a human rights commission. Ujjal Dosanjh is a Sikh. In 2000 he took office as the Premier of British Columbia, thereby gaining the distinction of being the first Canadian of South Asian ancestry to become

---

[766] As of May of 2010 police were investigating a website to which Salman Hossain was believed to be connected. See, Stewart Bell, *Police working 'flat out' investigating anti-semitic website*, National Post, 3 May 2010.

[767] Salim Mansur, *Protect free speech, even if offensive*, London Free Press, 6 March 2010.

[768] Stewart Bell, *Ontario police set to charge Muslim extremist*, National Post, 8 July 2010. See also, Joseph Brean, *Genocide charge will test hate crime laws*, National Post, 9 July 2010.

[769] For background to these events, see Kevin Libin, *United under the Swastika*, National Post, 12 January 2009 and Reuven Poupko and Chaim Steinmetz, *Bashing Israel right here at home*, National Post, 6 January 2009.

Premier of a province. He has serious doubts about the desirability of our thought control apparatus, believing that it often functions so as to frustrate and inhibit our ability to engage in public debate about significant social issues. As a general principle, Dosanjh believes that, "We must never be too sensitive to call a spade a spade."[770] It is apparent that our thought control apparatus, in both its explicit (human rights commissions) and implicit (self-censorship), forms has limited our ability to address important social concerns, like so-called honour killing.[771] In March of 2011 Justin Trudeau, M.P. opined that an official document which described honour killing and female genital mutilation as "barbaric" was "offensive".[772]

The current state of free expression in multi-culti Canada may, as I view the matter, be summarised in a series of rules. What follows should not be regarded as an authoritative statement, but is, simply, my attempt to summarise and synthesise the results of the decisions.

1. No Christian may publically disagree with or criticise or say anything that might in any way offend or annoy any person who is an atheist or an adherent of another religion.

2. No person of European ancestry may publically disagree with or criticise or say anything that might in any way offend or annoy a person of Aboriginal, African or Asian ancestry.

The veracity and accuracy of this assertion are

---

[770] Ujjal Dosanjh, *We are complicit in our silence*, National Post, 17 June 2010.

[771] Barbara Kay, *Honour killings must be confronted here at home*, National Post, 7 July 2010.

[772] Stephen Taylor, *Trudeau fears barbaric might offend barbarians*, National Post, 15 March 2011.

confirmed regularly in a dismal and predictable ritual that unfolds whenever it is alleged that someone has expressed a "racial slur". In a National Hockey League game played on 31 December 2011 an altercation between an African player on one team and a European player on the opposing team broke out. Words were exchanged. The African player had fallen to the ice and the European player suggested that he, the African player, might have slipped on a banana peel. These words were interpreted as a "racial slur". The NHL responded by suspending the European player for one game. There was a minor outbreak of sanctimoniousness, with the words used by the European player being characterised as "inappropriate", "offensive" and "unacceptable". An opinion piece in the *Globe and Mail* applauded the action of the League, particularly since it "...serve[d] notice to all NHL players to be careful of (sic) their language...".[773]

3. No heterosexual person may publically disagree with or criticise or say anything that might in any way offend or annoy a homosexual person.

4. No male person may publically disagree with or criticise or say anything that might in any way offend or annoy a female person.

There are no limits concerning what may be said publically about Christians[774], persons of European ancestry, heterosexuals and

---

[773] David Shoalts, *Is the NHL tough enough on racism?*, Globe and Mail, 6 January 2012.

[774] See Brian Lilley, Gilles Duceppe, Pat Martin: *Still bigots, still creepy*, Canada Politics Examiner 5 June 2010. See also, Marci McDonald, *The*

males.

> *A belief in the goodness and desirability of abortion is,*
> *as I see it, a significant tenet of the secular state*
> *religion of equality.*[775] *Feminists have succeeded in*
> *persuading themselves, and many others, that the*
> *equality of women is connected to the unfettered ability*
> *of each woman to kill*[776] *or injure*[777] *a foetus which she*
> *might be carrying.*[778]

Given the centrality of abortion to the secular state religion of equality, it probably does follow that the freedom of expression of persons who are unenthusiastic about abortion has been curtailed. University students who oppose abortion have systematically been prevented from expressing their opposition on university

---

Armageddon Factor: The Rise of Christian Nationalism in Canada, Toronto, Random House Canada, 2010.

[775] M. J. Sobran, *Abortion: the Class Religion*, National Review 23 January 1976. See also, Charles I. Lugosi, *The Law of the Sacred Cow: Sacrificing The First Amendment to Defend Abortion on Demand*, (2001) 79 Denver University Law Review 1.

[776] *R. v. Morgentaler* [1988] 1 S.C.R. 30. The position, by the mid-1970s, was that, "Canadian feminists...fiercely embraced the abortion issue as their own and Morgentaler as their martyr-hero." F.L. Morton, *Morgentaler v. Borowski: Abortion, the Charter and the Courts,* Toronto, McClelland and Stewart, 1992, p.71. The Supreme Court's 1988 *Morgentaler* decision ushered in the era of unfettered "choice" in Canada. The pro-"choice" position was set out most strongly in the judgment of Madam Justice Bertha Wilson. Her judgment was couched very much in the language of women's rights. See, Ibid., pp. 237-239.

[777] *Dobson v. Dobson* [1999] 2 S.C.R. 753 and *Winnipeg Child and Family Services v. G. (D.F.)* [1997] 3 S.C.R. 935.

[778] See, Tobi Cohen, *Shut the fxxx up on abortion file, counsels Tory senator*, National Post, 4 May 2010.

campuses.[779] Picketing at abortion "clinics" or at the residences of abortionists, oops, members of the abortion provider community, has been restricted.[780]

A grotesque form of "abortion" was practised at Foothills Hospital in Calgary in the late 1990s. A full-term foetus would be delivered alive and simply left to die. There were nurses who objected to the fact that they were not permitted to come to the aid of these tiny creatures who had been left alone to scream out their lives. The hospital sought, and received, an injunction to preclude the release of information about what was going on.[781] A nurse in Saskatchewan who took part in an anti-abortion demonstration was disciplined for professional misconduct.[782]

Anyone who doubts the accuracy of my suggestion that contemporary Canada may best be understood as a totalitarian theocracy, would do well to look into the case of Linda Gibbons. Gibbons is a 63 year-old grandmother who feels a deep moral abhorrence towards abortion, which she regards as murder. In 1994, the New Democratic Party government of Ontario obtained an injunction to create a "bubble zone" around abortion

[779] Charles Lewis, *Arrest of Carleton students over anti-abortion posters framed as free speech issue*, National Post, 4 October 2010.

[780] *Ontario* v. *Dieleman*, (1994) 2 O.R. (3d) 229. The legislature in B.C. enacted a statute in 1996 called the *Access to Abortion Services Act*. This created a "bubble zone" around "clinics". See, Ian Mulgrew, *Bubble zone around abortion clinics upheld by court*, Vancouver Sun, 27 April 2009.

[781] Marni Ko, *What really goes on at Foothills Hospital?*, Calgary Herald, 11 August 1999 and Richard Cairney, *Leak of Abortion Information creates Turmoil at Foothills*, (1999) 161 Canadian Medical Association Journal 424.

[782] The nurse sought judicial review of this order. The Saskatchewan Court of Appeal overturned the disciplinary decision and returned Whatcott to his duties. *Whatcott* v. *Saskatchewan Association of Licensed Practical Nurses* (2008) 289 D.L.R. (4th) 506.

mills.[783] The "bubble zone" prohibited picketing or protests within 25 metres of an abortion "clinic". This injunction was issued by a civil court in the course of a civil proceeding, so any breach of it should, technically, have been treated as a civil, rather than as a criminal, contempt. Gibbons had the temerity to stand outside abortion mills praying silently. She even went so far as to hold up a sign saying, "Why, Mom, when I have so much love to give?" She has been arrested many, many times and has spent more than nine years behind bars, often under conditions that have been tantamount to torture. One supporter of abortion offered this thoughtful justification for the treatment meted out to Gibbons, "What people like her do is creepy". Gibbons' courage and determination seem to be without limit and she has refused to bow to the attempts by the Canadian state to break her.[784]

In 2008 the Ontario Human Rights Commission announced that it would regard a refusal by a physician to perform an abortion as a breach of the *Ontario Human Rights Code*.[785]

---

[783] See note 778.

[784] Ian Hunter, *Adding cold insult to injustice*, National Post, 13 February 2011; Charles Lewis, "Anti-abortion activist Linda Gibbons gets her day in Canada's top court", *National Post*, 13 December 2011.

[785] See, Canadian Physicians for Life, "Policy Statement", 11 September 2008. What is commonly described as our "health-care" system appears to have acquired a status which verges on the sacramental. Consequently, physicians in Alberta had been subject to state-imposed limits on their ability to engage in public questioning or criticism of that system. See, Tom Blackwell, *Alberta doctors win right to free speech*, National Post, 26 June 2010.

CONCLUSION

THIS BOOK WAS designed to achieve two goals. First, it aimed to provide practical information, especially to working journalists. This information is necessary for a clear understanding of stories that raise legal issues. It is also essential if journalists are to avoid problems for themselves and for their employers. Second, the book sought to raise a number of important theoretical and social issues. Each of these issues has some connection with the way we understand free expression and the devices employed in our legal system both to protect it and to limit it.

The most crucial of all these issues and the starting point in any discussion of freedom of expression must be: Why does it matter? Our courts have not provided a coherent and consistent answer to this question. Recent decisions, especially those of the Supreme Court of Canada, are not only difficult to understand, but manifest a variety of points of view. They often contradict each other. Indeed, it is not at all clear that the judges themselves are persuaded of the importance of free expression.

In the *Keegstra*[786] decision, for example, then Chief Justice Brian Dickson appeared to suggest that free expression "values" should be accorded precedence over freedom of expression itself. In contrast, the judgment of Chief Justice Lyman Duff, in the *Alberta Press Bill* decision, set out a justification for freedom of

---

[786] *R. v. Keegstra*, [1990] 3 S.C.R. 697.

expression that was both clearly stated and well-rooted socially. He said:

> *[The] right to free public discussion of public affairs is the breath of life for parliamentary institutions.*[787]

Indeed, this assertion provides, at the same time, a definition of free expression and an argument in its favour. The essence of free expression is seen to be political expression. Its justification is a corollary to this definition. Freedom of expression is important because, without it, democratic institutions and, therefore, democratic politics would not be possible. Freedom of expression is an essential precondition to democracy.

The most unfortunate result of recent decisions by the Supreme Court of Canada has been a diminution in the clarity of thinking and in the significance imputed to free expression. This is a direct consequence of the Court's decision in *Irwin Toy*[788] to accord constitutional protection to virtually all forms of expression.

Despite this tendency, one Canadian tradition has continued: the notion that free expression is not absolute, that it may be limited in favour of other socially significant goals. In practice, litigation about free expression in Canada has been about balancing the imperative of free expression against competing social claims. The bulk of the book has been devoted to explication and analysis of how that balancing has been carried out. Chapter 2 addressed the balance between certain claims of the state and free expression. Chapter 3 investigated the balance between the integrity of the judicial process and free expression. Chapter 4 looked, in part, at the balance between the protection of reputation and free expression.

---

[787] *Reference Re Alberta Legislation*, [1938] S.C.R. 100.

[788] *Irwin Toy* v. *Quebec (A.G.)*, [1989] 1 S.C.R. 927.

It may be that the precise balance reached in each instance by our legal system is not ideal. There is always, in a democracy, room for disagreement on issues of this nature. And what is seen as an appropriate balance in one era may not be acceptable in another. But if debate on these matters is to flourish and if the mass media themselves are to play a role in that debate, it is essential that individual journalists maintain an active personal commitment to free expression. To achieve this commitment they need a theoretical understanding of free expression and a practical determination to make it a living reality in their day-to-day working lives.

It is not always easy to maintain this knowledge and this determination. Many influences and pressures work against it. Two seem especially important. The first is the most obvious and the most direct: the pressure, by no means always subtle, that employers can and do exert. An obituary in the *Economist* made the point with great force:

> *He was the sort of character Humbert Wolfe had in mind when he wrote:*
>
> > *You cannot hope to bribe or twist,*
> > *thank God! The British journalist.*
> > *But seeing what the man will do*
> > *unbribed, there's no occasion to.*
>
> *George Malcolm Thomson was his master's pen, the obedient leader-writer who did the bidding of Lord Beaverbrook, press baron and politician manqué.* [789]

The law does not address this matter. Owners and managers have substantial proprietary authority and the limits on this authority

---

[789] *The Economist*, 1 June 1996, 86.

come down in practice to the integrity and courage of individual journalists.

The second pressure is orthodoxy and, in particular, pressure to make one's thoughts and one's writing conform to the demands of orthodox thought. The power of orthodoxy is obvious in Canada's mass media. Again, the extent of this power often comes down to a matter of the honesty and integrity of the journalist. Orwell expressed this point with his usual clarity:

> ...the controversy over freedom of speech and of the press is at the bottom a controversy over the desirability, or otherwise, of telling lies. What is really at issue is the right to report contemporary events truthfully, or as truthfully as is consistent with the ignorance, bias and self-deception from which every observer necessarily suffers. [790]

Canada's Constitution and laws create substantial protection for free expression. But no one, least of all working journalists, should imagine that this protection is the end of the matter. It is not enough to sit back confidently and assume that lawyers and judges can look after free expression, that it is not an issue of ongoing concern. At the end of the day, free expression demands from each journalist both nurturing and jealous protection. It is important, in this regard, to welcome the formation of a group called, Canadian Journalists for Free Expression. The CJFE has begun, sensibly enough, to publish an annual report on the state of free expression in Canada. The report for 2009 contained an

---

[790] *"The Prevention of Literature", The Collected Essays, Journalism and Letters of George Orwell, Vol.4: In Front of Your Nose, 1945–1950* (Harmondsworth: Penguin 1970), 83.

article on the current state of free expression and the law.[791] It is unfortunate, but necessary, to point out some significant errors made by the authors of the article. They spoke of a journalist being "guilty of defamation"[792], as if a defamation suit were a criminal, rather than a civil, proceeding. It was in their discussion of "hate speech"[793] that the authors demonstrated a serious failure to understand their subject matter. They appeared to believe in the existence of something called the *Human Rights Act,* which managed to operate, simultaneously, at both the federal and provincial levels.

The authors were clear on the distinctions between the restrictions on free expression imposed on the one hand by the *Criminal Code* and, on the other, by human rights legislation. There was an error in the apparent conflation of the offences of "willfully promoting hatred" and "seditious libel". The authors seemed to believe that, before a person may be convicted of the offence of willfully promoting hatred, the Crown must establish that she intended to "incite violence".[794] They were unhappy with the kinds of restrictions on expression that have been imposed by human rights tribunals and, consequently, applauded the decision of the Canadian Human Rights Tribunal in *Warman* v. *Lemire.* Their conclusion in this regard was solid and admirable.

> *We believe that when the statements of racists do not promote violence, the best way to deal with those statements is to forcefully and publicly denounce them...the answer to hateful or offensive speech that is*

---

[791] Terry Gould and Bob Carty, *Freedom of Expression on Trial*, 2009, *Canadian Journalists for Free Expression*, The 2009 Free Expression Review, Toronto, 2009, p.6.

[792] *Ibid.,* at p.9.

[793] *Ibid.,* at pp.9-11.

[794] *Ibid.,* at p.9.

> *not intended to incite violence is more speech, not censorship*[795]

It is encouraging to discover that there remain Canadian journalists capable of both grown-up and independent thought. Writing, amazingly enough, in the *Globe and Mail,* Lysiane Gagnon[796] addressed many of the matters that are at the heart of this book. She began her analysis by asserting that "hate" was an unacceptably amorphous and subjective standard for defining the point at which the state might legitimately seek to limit expression. She did believe that the state might properly proscribe expression which involved "Direct calls for violence against a person or a group…". She was displeased with the current situation, noting that:

> *Canada…has become a 'mommy state' in the grip of a vast clique of moralizers who encourage people to be extraordinarily sensitive to the slightest insult…*

Her conclusion definitely bears repeating:

> *A civilized, progressive society should opt for freedom of speech, period.*

The Gagnon article, as good as it is, should not be seen as signifying the outbreak of clear thinking at the *Globe.* Anyone inclined to imagine that should look at an article by Erna Paris[797] which appeared in the same paper a week-and-a-half later. The Paris article was something of a tour de force, since it managed, in the space of a few hundred words, to set out the most common and widely accepted arguments against free expression.

---

[795] Ibid., at p.11.
[796] *Why we must tolerate hate*, Globe and Mail, 17 October 2011.
[797] *There *are* limits to free expression*, Globe and Mail, 28 October 2011.

BIBLIOGRAPHY

Legislation—Federal Statutes

Access to Information Act, R.S.C. 1985, c. A-1.

An Act to amend the Criminal Code (Sexual Assault), S.C. 1992, c. 38, amending R.S.C. 1985, c. 46.

An Act to Amend the Young Offenders Act, the Criminal Code, the Penitentiary Act and the Prisons and Reformatories Act, R.S.C. 1985 (2d Supp.), c. 24, amending R.S.C. 1985, c. Y-1.

Anti-Terrorism Act, S.C. 2001, c.41.

Broadcasting Act, S.C. 1958, c. 22.

Broadcasting Act, 1968, S.C. 1967-68, c. 25.

Broadcasting Act, S.C. 1991, c. 11.

Canadian Bill of Rights, S.C. 1960, c. 44, reprinted in R.S.C. 1985, App. III.

Canadian Broadcasting Act, S.C. 1936, c. 24.

Canadian Charter of Rights and Freedoms, Part I of the Constitution Act, 1982, being Schedule B to the Canada Act 1982 (U.K.), 1982, c. 11.

Canadian Human Rights Act, R.S.C. 1985, c. H-6.

Canadian Radio Broadcasting Act, S.C. 1932, c. 51.

Canadian Radio-television and Telecommunications Commission Act, S.C. 1974-75-76, c. 49.

Criminal Code of Canada, R.S.C. 1985, c. C–46.

Criminal Law Amendment Act, 2001, S.C. 2002, c. 13.

Emergencies Act, S.C. 1988, c. 29 (now R.S.C. 1985, c. 22 (4th Supp.).

Indian Act, R.S.C. 1985, c. I-5.

Juvenile Delinquents Act, R.S.C. 1970, c. J-3, as rep by Young Offenders Act, S.C. 1980–81–82–83, c. 110.

Official Secrets Act, R.S.C. 1985, c. O-5. Renamed Security

of Information Act by S.C. 2001, c. 41, s. 25(1).

Personal Information Protection and Electronic Documents Act, S.C. 2000, c. 5.

Privacy Act, R.S.C. 1985, c. P-21.

Security of Information Act, R.S.C. 1985, c. O-5. Originally enacted under title: Official Secrets Act; renamed Security of Information Act by S.C. 2001, c. 41, s. 25(1).

Young Offenders Act, R.S.C. 1985, c. Y-1, as rep. by S.C. 2002, c. 1, s. 199.

Youth Criminal Justice Act, S.C. 2002, c. 1.

War Measures Act, S.C. 1915, c. 2, as rep. by the Emergencies Act, R.S.C. 1985, c. 22 (4th Supp.).

Federal Regulations

Cable Television Regulations, SOR/86–831, as rep. by the *Broadcasting Distribution Regulations*, SOR/97-555, s. 57.

Consolidated Orders Respecting Censorship, P.C. 1918–1241, C. Gaz. 1918.4376.

Defence of Canada Regulations, P.C. 1939–2891, C. Gaz. 1939.1126.

Privacy Act Extension Order, No. 2, SOR/89–206.

Public Order Regulations, SOR/70-444.

Radio Regulations, SOR/86–982.

Television Broadcasting Regulations, SOR/87–49.

Alberta

Alberta Human Rights Act, RSA 2000, c A-25.5.

British Columbia

Human Rights Code, R.S.B.C., 1996, c. 210.

Privacy Act, R.S.B.C. 1979, c. 336.

Manitoba
Privacy Act, R.S.M. 1987, c. P125.

Newfoundland
Privacy Act, R.S.N. 1990, c. P-22.

Ontario
Courts of Justice Act, R.S.O. 1990, c. 43.
Child Protection Act, R.S.O. 1990, c. C.11 (now *Child and Family Services Act*).
Human Rights Code, R.S.O. 1990, c. H.19
Juries Act, R.S.O. 1990, c. J.3.
Libel and Slander Act, R.S.O. 1990, c. L.12
Racial Discrimination Act, S.O. 1944, c. 51.

Quebec
An Act Respecting the Protection of Personal Information in the Private Sector, S.Q. 1993, c. 17. (now R.S.Q. c. P-39.1)

Saskatchewan
The Jury Act, 1981, S.S. 1980–81, c. J-4.1, as rep. by S.S. 1998, c. J-4.2.
Privacy Act, R.S.S. 1978, c. P-24.
Saskatchewan Human Rights, R.S.S., 1979, c. S-24.1.

United States (Federal)
Communications Decency Act of 1996, Pub. L. No. 104-104, 110 Stat. 133 (1996).

United Kingdom
British North America Act, (U.K.), 30 & 31 Vict., c. 3

Monographs and Reports

Anderson, Brian C. and Adam D. Thierer. *A Manifesto for Media Freedom* (New York: Encounter Books, 2008).

Anisman, P. and A. M. Linden, eds. *The Media, the Courts, and the Charter* (Toronto: Carswell, 1986).

Appleby, Joyce, Lynn Hunt & Margaret Jacob. *Telling the Truth about History* (New York: Norton, 1994).

Arendt, Hannah. *The Origins of Totalitarianism* (Orlando, Florida: Houghton-Mifflin, Harcourt Publishing Company, 1985).

Article 19 and Alexander de Waal. *Starving in Silence: a report on censorship and famine* (London: Article 19, 1990).

Australia, Law Reform Commission. *Reform of Contempt Law (Issues Paper No. 4)* (Sydney: The Commission, 1984).

Bala, Nicholas and Sanjeev Anand. *Youth Criminal Justice Law*, 2nd ed. (Toronto: Irwin Law, 2009).

Bercuson, David A. and S.F. Wise, eds. *The Valour and the Horror Revisited* (Montreal: McGill-Queen's University Press, 1994).

Bissoondath, Neil. *Selling Illusions: The Cult of Multiculturalism in Canada* (Harmondsworth: Penguin, 1994).

Blatchford, Christine. *Helpless: Caledonia's Nightmare of Fear and Anarchy and How the Law Failed All of Us* (Toronto: Doubleday Canada, 2010).

Bloom, Allan. *The Closing of the American Mind* (New York: Simon and Shuster, 1987).

Boyer, J.P. *Political Rights: The Legal Framework of Elections in Canada* (Toronto: Butterworth, 1981).

Braun, Stefan. *Democracy off Balance: Freedom of Expression and Hate Propaganda Laws in Canada* (Toronto: University of Toronto Press, 2004).

Brown, D.H. *The Genesis of the Criminal Code of 1892* (Toronto: University of Toronto Press, 1989).

Brown, R.E. *The Law of Defamation in Canada*, 2 vols., 2d ed. (Toronto: Carswell, 1994).

Bruckner, Pascal. *The Tyranny of Guilt: An Essay on Western Masochism* (Princeton, New Jersey: Princeton University Press, 2010).

Bruser, R.S. and B.M. Rogers. *Journalists and the Law: How to Get the Story without Getting Sued or Put in Jail* (Ottawa: Canadian Bar Foundation, 1985).

Canada, Advisory Committee on Broadcasting. *Report* (Ottawa: Queen's Printer, 1965) (Chair: Robert Fowler).

Canada, Commission of Inquiry into the Use of Drugs and Banned Practices Intended to Increase Athletic Performance. *Report* (Ottawa: Minister of Supply and Services, 1990) (Chair: Charles Dubin).

Canada, House of Commons, Special Committee to Inquire into the Administration of the Canadian Radio Broadcasting Act, 1932. *Report, Official Report of Debates of the House of Commons*, vol. 3 (Ottawa, 1936) 3077.

Canadian Human Rights Commission. *Special Report to Parliament: Freedom of Expression and Freedom from Hate in the Internet Age* (Ottawa, 2009), online: Canadian Human Rights Commission http://www.chrc-ccdp.ca/pdf/srp_rsp_eng.pdf

Canadian Radio-Television and Telecommunications Commission. *Annual Report, 1986–87.* (Ottawa: Supply and Services Canada, 1987).

Cere, Daniel and Douglas Farrow, eds. *Divorcing Marriage: Unveiling the Dangers* in Canada's New Social Experiment (Montreal: McGill-Queen's University Press, 2004).

Coloroso, Barbara. *The Bully, the Bullied and the Bystander: from preschool to high school—how parents and teachers can help break the cycle of violence* (New York: Harper Collins, 2003).

—*Extraordinary Evil: A Brief History of Genocide* (Toronto, Viking Canada, 2007).

Conrad, Margaret and Alvin Finkel, with Veronica Strong-Boag. *History of the Canadian Peoples,* vols. 1-2 (Mississauga: Copp Clark Pitman, 1993).

Denike, Margaret, Fay Faraday and M. Kate Stephenson, eds. *Making Equality Rights Real: Securing Substantive Equality under the Charter* (Toronto: Irwin Law, 2006).

Dalrymple, Theodore. *The New Vichy Syndrome: Why European Intellectuals Surrender to Barbarism* (New York and London: Encounter Books, 2010).

Emberley, Peter C. *Zero Tolerance: Hot Button Politics in Canada's Universities* (Toronto: Penguin Books, 1996).

Emerson, T.I. *The System of Freedom of Expression* (New York: Random House, 1970).

Federal Cultural Policy Review Committee. Report (Ottawa: Supply and Services Canada, 1982) (Co-chairs, Louis Applebaum and Jacques Hébert).

Fekete, John. *Moral Panic: Biopolitics Rising*, 2d ed. (Montreal: Robert Davies, 1994).

Flaherty, David H. and Frank E. Manning, eds. *The Beaver Bites Back? American Popular Culture in Canada* (Montreal: McGill-Queen's University Press, 1993).

Flaherty, G.A. *Defamation Law in Canada* (Ottawa: Canadian Bar Foundation, 1984).

Fontana, J.A. *The Law of Search and Seizure in Canada*, 3d ed. (Toronto: Butterworths, 1992).

Freedman, Monroe H. and Eric M.Freedman, eds. *Group Defamation and Freedom of Speech* (Westport: Greenwood Press, 1995).

Fridman, G.H.L., *The Law of Torts in Canada*, 2 vols. (Toronto: Carswell, 1990).

Gibson, D., ed. *Aspects of Privacy Law: Essays in Honour of John M. Sharp* (Toronto: Butterworths, 1980).

Gillmor, Don, Achille Michaud and Pierre Turgeon. *Canada: A People's History* (Toronto: McClelland and Stewart, 2001).

Gottfried, Paul Edward. *Multiculturalism and the Politics of Guilt: Toward a Secular Theocracy* (Columbia, Missouri: University of Missouri Press, 2002).

Granatstein, J.L. *Canada's Army: Waging War and Keeping the Peace* (Toronto: University of Toronto Press, 2002).

—*The Last Good War* (Vancouver: Douglas and McIntyre, 2005).

—*Who killed Canadian History?* (Toronto: Harper Collins, 1998).

Greene, Ian. *The Charter of Rights* (Toronto: Lorimer, 1989).

Haggart, R. and A.E. Golden. *Rumours of War*, 2d ed. (Toronto: New Press, 1979).

Hare, Ivan and James Weinstein, eds. *Extreme Speech and Democracy* (Oxford: Oxford University Press, 2009).

Hartley, L.P. *The Go-Between* (New York: New York Review Books, 2002).

Himmelfarb, Gertrude. *On Looking into the Abyss: Untimely Thoughts on Culture and Society* (New York: Knopf, 1995).

—*One Nation, Two Cultures* (New York: Vintage Books, 2001).

Hogg, P.W. *Constitutional Law of Canada*, 3d ed. (Toronto: Carswell, 1992).

Hogg, P.W. *Constitutional Law of Canada*, 5th ed., 2 vols., looseleaf (Toronto: Carswell, 2007).

Kaplan, William. *Belonging: The Meaning and Future of Canadian Citizenship* (Montreal: McGill-Queen's University Press, 1993).

Kramer, Hilton and Roger Kimball, eds. *The Betrayal of Liberalism* (Chicago: Ivan R. Dee, 1999).

Lasch, Christopher. *The Revolt of the Elites and the Betrayal of Democracy* (New York: W.W. Norton, 1995).

LaMarsh, Judy. *Memoirs of a Bird in a Gilded Cage* (Toronto: McClelland and Stewart, 1969).

Law Reform Commission of Canada. *Contempt of Court* (Report 17) (Ottawa: Minister of Supply & Services, 1982).

—*Crimes against the State* (Working Paper 49) (Ottawa: Law

Reform Commission of Canada, 1986).

—*Defamatory Libel* (Working Paper 35) (Ottawa: Minister of Supply and Services, 1984).

—*Public and Media Access to the Criminal Process* (Working Paper 56) (Ottawa: The Commission, 1987).

Leishman, Rory. *Against Judicial Activism: The Decline of Freedom and Democracy in Canada* (Montreal: McGill-Queen's University Press, 2006).

Levant, Ezra. Shakedown: *How our Government Is Undermining Democracy in the Name of Human Rights* (Toronto: McClelland and Stewart, 2009).

Loney, Martin. *The Pursuit of Division: Race, Gender and Preferential Hiring in Canada* (Montreal: McGill-Queen's University Press, 1998).

MacKinnon, Catharine. *Only Words* (Cambridge, Massachusetts: Harvard University Press, 1993).

MacMillan, Margaret. *The Uses and Abuses of History* (Toronto: Viking Canada, 2008).

Macpherson, C.B. *Democracy in Alberta: Social Credit and the Party System*, 2nd ed. (Toronto: University of Toronto Press, 1962).

Mansur, Salim. *Delectable Lie: A Liberal Repudiation of Multiculturalism* (Brantford: Mantua Books, 2011).

Martin, Robert. *Critical Perspectives on the Constitution* (1984) 2 Socialist Studies. (Winnipeg, Manitoba: Society for Socialist Studies, 1984).

—*The Most Dangerous Branch: How the Supreme Court of Canada Has Undermined Our Law and Our Democracy* (Montreal: McGill-Queen's University Press, 2003).

—*Speaking Freely: Expression and the Law in the Commonwealth* (Toronto: Irwin Law, 1999).

Martin, Robert and G.S. Adam. *A Sourcebook of Canadian Media Law*, 2d ed. (Ottawa: Carleton University Press, 1994).

Martin, Robert and Estelle Feldman. *Access to Information in*

Developing Countries (Berlin: Transparency International, 1998).

McConchie, Roger D. and David A. Potts. *Canadian Libel and Slander Actions* (Toronto: Irwin Law, 2004).

McDonald, Marci. *The Armageddon Factor: The Rise of Christian Nationalism in Canada* (Toronto: Random House Canada, 2010).

McNairn, C.H. and C.D. Woodbury. *Government Information: Access and Privacy* (Toronto: Carswell, 1992).

Mill, John Stuart. *On Liberty* (Chicago: Henry Regnery Company, 1947).

Minogue, Kenneth. *The Servile Mind: How democracy erodes the moral life* (New York: Encounter Books, 2010).

Moon, Richard. *Constitutional Protection of Freedom of Expression* (Toronto: University of Toronto Press, 2000).

Morton F.L. *Morgentaler v. Borowski: Abortion, the Charter, and the Courts* (Toronto: McClelland & Stewart, 1992).

Moyo, Dambisa. *Dead Aid: Why aid is not working and how there is another way for Africa* (London: Allen Lane, 2008).

Nicholson, G.W.L. *Canadian Expeditionary Force, 1914-1919* (Ottawa: Queen's Printer, 1962).

Canadian Civil Liberties Association. *Framework Regarding the Prevention of Harassment and Discrimination in Ontario Colleges* (Toronto: Ministry of Education and Training, 1993).

Ontario Press Council. *Annual Reports* (Ottawa: Ontario Press Council, 1972/73-).

Orwell, George. *The Collected Essays, Journalism and Letters of George Orwell, volume 4: In Front of your Nose, 1945-1950* (Harmondsworth: Penguin, 1970).

Peacock, Anthony A. *Rethinking the Constitution: Perspectives on Canadian Constitutional Reform, Interpretation and Theory* (Don Mills, Ontario, Oxford University Press, 1996).

Phillips, Melanie. *The World Turned Upside Down: The Global Battle over God, Truth and Power* (New York and London: Encounter Books, 2010).

Popper, Karl. *The Open Society and its Enemies, Volume 1: The*

Spell of Plato, (Princeton, N.J.: Princeton University Press, 1971).

Proudfoot, G.F. *Privacy Law and the Media in Canada* (Ottawa: Canadian Bar Foundation, 1984).

Raboy, Marc. *Missed Opportunities: the Story of Canada's Broadcasting Policy* (Montreal: McGill-Queen's University Press, 1990).

Rahe, Paul A. *Soft Despotism, Democracy's Drift* (New Haven, CT.: Yale University Press, 2009).

Roberts, J.V. and R.M. Mohr, eds. *Confronting Sexual Assault: A Decade of Legal and Social Change* (Toronto: University of Toronto Press, 1994).

Robertson, S.M. *Courts and the Media* (Toronto: Butterworths, 1981).

Rodal, Alti. *Press Councils in Canada* (Ottawa: n.p., 1983).

Royal Commission on Broadcasting. *Report* (Ottawa: Queen's Printer, 1957) (Chair: Robert M. Fowler).

Royal Commission on National Development in the Arts, Letters and Science. *Report* (Ottawa: King's Printer, 1951). (Chair: Vincent Massey).

Royal Commission on Newspapers. *Newspapers and the Law* (Ottawa: Minister of Supply & Services, 1981).

—*Report* (Ottawa: Minister of Supply and Services, 1981). (Chair: T. Kent).

Royal Commission on Radio Broadcasting. *Report* (Ottawa: King's Printer, 1929). (Chair: Sir John Aird).

Russell, N., ed. *Trials and Tribulations: an Examination of News Coverage Given Three Prominent Canadian Trials* (Regina: School of Journalism and Communications, University of Regina, 1986).

Rutherdale, Robert. *Hometown Horizons, Local Responses to Canada's Great War* (Vancouver: University of British Columbia Press, 2004).

Shaidle, Kathy and Pete Vere. *The Tyranny of Nice: How Canada Crushes Freedom in the Name of Human Rights (and Why It Matters to Americans)* (Toronto: The Interim Publishing Company, 2008).

Sharpe, Robert J. *The Last Day, the Last Hour: The Currie Libel Trial* (Toronto: Carswell, 1988).

Singer, Benjamin D., ed. *Communications in Canadian Society*, 3d ed. (Scarborough, Ontario: Nelson, 1991).

Steyn, Mark. *America Alone; the End of the World as We Know It* (Washington, D.C.: Regnery Publishing, 2006).

Sumner, L.W. *The Hateful and the Obscene: Studies in the Limits of Free Expression* (Toronto: University of Toronto Press, 2004).

Task Force on Broadcasting Policy. *Report* (Ottawa: Supply and Services Canada, 1986).

U.K., Committee on Contempt of Court. *Report, Cmnd. 5794* (London: Her Majesty's Stationery Office, 1974).

Vaver, David. *Intellectual Property Law: Copyright, Patents, Trade-Marks* (Toronto: Irwin Law, 1997).

Wigmore, J.H. *Evidence in Trials at Common Law*, vol. 8, 3d ed. rev. by J.T. McNaughton (Boston: Little, Brown, 1961).

Windschuttle, Keith, *The Fabrication of Aboriginal History, Volume Three, The Stolen Generations 1881-2008* (Paddington, NSW: Macleay Press, 2009).

Articles and Essays

Anand, S. *Expressions of Racial Hatred and Racism in Canada: An Historical Perspective* (1998) 77 Canadian Bar Review 181.

Arkes, Hadley. *Liberalism and the Law* in Hilton Kramer and Roger Kimball, eds., *The Betrayal of Liberalism* (Chicago: Ivan R. Dee, 1999) 93.

Bernstein, Andrew and Rima Ramchandani. *Don't Shoot the Messenger: A Discussion of I.S.P. Liability* (2002) 1:2 Canadian Journal of Law and Technology 77.

Bezanson, R.P., G. Cranberg & J. Soloski. *Libel Law and the Press: Setting the Record Straight* (1985) 71 Iowa Law Review 215.

Boivin, Denis W. *Accomodating Freedom of Expression and Reputation in the Common Law of Defamation* (1996) 22 Queen's Law Journal 229.

Bowman, James. *The Death of Politics* (2009) 27:7 The New Criterion 55.

——*Unhappy is the Land* (2010) 28:6 The New Criterion 57.

Cairney, Richard. *Leak of Abortion Information Creates Turmoil at Foothills* (1999) 161 Canadian Medical Association Journal 424.

Calamai, P. *Discrepancies in News Quotes from the Colin Thatcher Trial* in N. Russell, ed., Trials and Tribulations: an Examination of News Coverage Given Three Prominent Canadian Trials (Regina: School of Journalism and Communications, University of Regina, 1986), 1.

Cram, Ian. *The Danish Cartoons, Offensive Expression, and Democratic Legitimacy* in Ivan Hare and James Weinstein, eds. Extreme Speech and Democracy (Oxford: Oxford University Press, 2009), 311.

Farrow, Douglas. *Rights and Recognition* in Daniel Cere and Douglas Farrow, eds., Divorcing Marriage: Unveiling the Dangers in Canada's New Social Experiment (Montreal: McGill-Queen's University Press, 2004) 97.

Dalrymple, Theodore. *It's All Your Fault* New English Review, September 2010, online: New English Review.org http://www.newenglishreview.org.

Dworkin, Ronald. *Foreword* in Ivan Hare and James Weinstein, eds. Extreme Speech and Democracy (Oxford: Oxford University Press, 2009).

Feldthusen, Bruce. *Awakening From the National Broadcasting Dream: Rethinking Television Regulation for National Cultural Goals* in David H. Flaherty and Frank E. Manning, eds., The Beaver Bites Back? American Popular Culture in Canada (Montreal: McGill-Queen's University Press, 1993) 42.

Fox-Genovese, Elizabeth. *From Separate Spheres to Dangerous Streets: Postmodernist Feminism and the Problem of Order* (1993) 60

Social Research 235.

Goldman, Irvin and James Winter. *Mass Media and Canadian Identity in Benjamin D. Singer*, ed., Communications in Canadian Society, 3d ed. (Scarborough, Ontario: Nelson, 1991) 146.

Gourevitch, Philip. *Alms Dealers* The New Yorker 86:31 (11 October 2010), 102, online: The New Yorker.com http://www.newyorker.com

Gould, Terry and Bob Carty. *Freedom of Expression on Trial, 2009* in The 2009 Free Expression Review 6.

Granatstein, J.L. *The Decline and Fall of Free Speech* (1994) 3:6 Literary Review of Canada 9.

Heinrichs, Terry. *Censorship as Free Speech: Free Expression Values and the Logic of Silencing* (1998) 36 Alberta Law Review 835.

Heinze, Eric *Cumulative Jurisprudence and Hate Speech: Sexual Orientation and Analogies to Disability, Age and Obesity* in Ivan Hare and James Weinstein, eds. Extreme Speech and Democracy (Oxford: Oxford University Press, 2009) 265.

Himmelfarb, Gertrude. *Where Have all the Footnotes Gone?* in On Looking into the Abyss: Untimely Thoughts on Culture and Society (New York: Knopf, 1995) 122.

Hunter, Ian. *When Human Rights become Wrongs* (1985) 23:2 *The University of Western Ontario Law Review* 197.

Jeffrey, Brooke and Philip Rosen. *The Protection of Human Rights in Canada* (1979) 2:3 *Canadian Parliamentary Review* 37.

Johnson, R.W. *Johannesburg: Hard Pressed* Standpoint (September 2010), online: Standpoint http://standpointmag.co.uk

Kent, Tom. *The Significance of Corporate Structure in the Media* (1985) 23 The University of Western Ontario Law Review 151.

Kimball, Roger. *Introduction: The Dictatorship of Relativism* (2009) 27:5 *The New Criterion* 4.

Lederman, S.N., P. O'Kelly & M. Grottenthaler. *Confidentiality of News Sources* in P. Anisman & A.M. Linden, eds., The Media, The Courts, and The Charter (Toronto: Carswell,

1986) 227.

Loring, John. *Force for CHANGE: Toronto Police Chief Bill Blair breaks from* [sic] *the past* (Spring 2010) 37:3 U of T Magazine 36, online: U of T Magazine.ca http://www.magazine.utoronto.ca.

Lugosi, Charles I. *The Law of the Sacred Cow: Sacrificing The First Amendment to Defend Abortion on Demand* (2001) 79 Denver University Law Review 1.

MacDougall, Bruce. *Outing: The Law Reacts to Speech about Homosexuality* (1996) 21 Queen's Law Journal 79.

Marchildon, Gilles. *Freedom for all means freedom for each* InQueeries (3 November 2005).

Martin, Robert. *Bill C-49: A Victory for Interest Group Politics* (1993) 42 University of New Brunswick Law Journal 357.

——Book Review of *Charter of Rights* by Ian Greene, (1992) 23:3 Interchange 327.

——Book Review of *The Law of Defamation in Canada*, 2 vols., 2nd ed. by Raymond E. Brown, (1989) 14 Canadian Journal of Communications 83.

——*Case Comment: R. v. Sharpe* (2001) 39 Alberta Law Review 585.

——*Challenging Orthodoxy: A Critical Analysis of Racially-Based Job Quotas* (1993) 1 Canadian Labour Law Journal 409.

——*Does Libel Have A 'Chilling Effect' in Canada?* (1990) 4 *Studies in Communications* 143.

——*The Great War and Canadian Memory, Part 2* Canadian Military History (Summer 2005), Book Review Supplement, Issue 18, 1.

——*Group Defamation in Canada* in Monroe H. Freedman and Eric M. Freedman, eds. Group Defamation and Freedom of Speech (Westport: Greenwood Press, 1995) 191.

——*Interlocutory Injunctions in Libel Actions* (1982) 20 *The University of Western Ontario Law Review* 129.

——Judicial Proceedings: Media Bans, Case Comment on Dagenais v.Canadian Broadcasting Corporation (1995), 74

Canadian Bar Review 500.

——*A Lament for British North America* in Anthony A. Peacock, ed., Rethinking the Constitution: Perspectives on Canadian Constitutional Reform, Interpretation and Theory (Toronto: Oxford University Press, 1996) 3.

——*Libel and Letters to the Editor* (1983) 9 Queen's Law Journal 188.

——*The Meteoric Rise and Precipitous Fall of Clara Brett Martin: Thoughts on the Misuse of History* (1995) 4 Inroads 182.

——*Notes on Emergency Powers in Canada* (2005) 54 University of New Brunswick Law Journal 161.

——*Opposing Racism by Racist Means* (1994) 3 Inroads 88.

——*Promoting Freedom of Expression in the Commonwealth* (2002) 366 The Roundtable 521.

——*Speech Codes in Action* (1995) 44 University of New Brunswick Law Journal 65.

McDonald, Lynn. *The Supreme Court of Canada and the Equality Guarantee in the Charter* in Robert Martin, Critical Perspectives on the Constitution (1984) 2 Socialist Studies (Winnipeg, Man.: Society for Socialist Studies, 1984) 45.

Meisel, John. *Stroking the Airwaves: The Regulation of Broadcasting by the CRTC* in Benjamin D. Singer, ed., Communications in Canadian Society, 3rd ed. (Scarborough, Ontario: Nelson Canada, 1991) 217.

Mirza, Munira. *Rethinking Race* Prospect, Issue 175, (22 September 2010), 30, online: Prospect http://www.prospectmagazine.co.uk

Orwell, George. *The Prevention of Literature* in The Collected Essays, Journalism and Letters of George Orwell, Volume 4: In Front of Your Nose, 1945-1950 (Harmondsworth: Penguin, 1970) 83.

Pepper, Randy A. *Internet Defamation: Canadian vs. American Perspectives* (2002) 25 Advocates Quarterly 190.

Porter, Julian. *Tangents* (1981) 5 Canadian Lawyer 24.

Prang, Margaret. *The Origins of Public Broadcasting in Canada* (1965) 46 Canadian Historical Review 1.

Robinson, Svend. *The Collision of Rights* (1995) 44 University of New Brunswick Law Journal 61.

Russello, Gerald J. *Christopher Dawson and the Coming Conflict* (2010) 28:7 The New Criterion 14.

Sandall, Roger. *Aboriginal Sin?* (2010) 28:10 The New Criterion 75.

Savage, Ryan. *Between a Rock and a Hard Place: Defamation and I.S.P.s* (2002) 2 Asper Review of International Business and Trade Law 107.

Schauer, F. *Social Foundations of the Law of Defamation: A Comparative Analysis* (1980) 1:3 Journal of Media Law and Practice 19.

Schneiderman, David. Book Review of *Rethinking the Constitution: Perspectives on Canadian Constitutional Reform, Interpretation and Theory* by Anthony A. Peacock, (1997) 22 Queen's Law Journal 531.

Skarsgard, A. *Freedom of the Press: Availability of Defences to a Defamation Action* (1981) 45 Saskatchewan Law Review 287.

Steyn, Mark. *The Future belongs to Islam* Maclean's (23 October 2006).

——*Name the date, Jennifer. I'll be there* Maclean's (25 June 2009).

——*True North strong not free* Macleans (8 April 2010).

Sumner, L. W. *Incitement and the Regulation of Hate Speech in Canada: A Philosophical Analysis* in Ivan Hare and James Weinstein, eds. Extreme Speech and Democracy (Oxford: Oxford University Press, 2009) 204.

Tarnopolsky, W.S. *Freedom of the Press* in Newspapers and the Law (Ottawa, Minister of Supply & Services, 1981), 1.

Newspaper Articles

Adenekan, Shola. *Chakufwa Chihana* The Guardian (13 July 2006).

Bell, Stewart. *Killing Canadians 'best way': student* National Post (30 January 2008).

——*Ontario police set to charge Muslim extremist* National Post (8 July 2010).

——*Police working 'flat out' investigating anti-semitic website* National Post (3 May 2010).

Blackwell, Tom. *Alberta doctors win right to free speech* National Post (26 June 2010).

Blatchford, Christie. *A thin line between abuse and discipline* National Post (11 July 2002).

——*Judge who demands silence speaks out* National Post (2 July 2002).

——*Parents urge media ban be lifted* National Post (12 June 2002).

Bourrie, Mark. *Judge flip-flops on publication ban* Law Times (27 November 2000).

Braun, Stefan. *Free Speech: Beware of the 'system works' test* Winnipeg Free Press (8 May 2010).

Brean, Joseph. *Canada's 'addiction to rule-making'* National Post (7 August 2010).

——*Canadians 'misinformed' on hate speech* National Post (22 June 2009).

——*Genocide charge will test hate crime laws* National Post (9 July 2010).

——*Hate Speech Law unconstitutional: Rights Tribunal* National Post (2 September 2009).

——*Human rights commission calls for media council* National Post (12 February 2009).

——*Internet rendered hate law 'outdated'* National Post (22 February 2010).

——*Judges grapple with Canada's legal test for hatred* National Post (9 April 2010).

——*Law Dean Candidate alleges Racism* National Post (10 September 2010).

——*Muslims told to insist on equal voice* National Post (9 June 2008).

——*Ontario rights commission dismisses complaint, sort of* National Post (10 April 2008).

——*Ottawa withdraws from clash of interests over hate speech law* National Post (23 October 2010).

——*Queen's new dialogue monitors* National Post (19 November 2008).

——*Ryerson student takes veganism discrimination dispute to Human Rights Tribunal of Ontario* National Post (8 November 2011).

——*Sumo suits instruments of 'oppression': Queen's student govt* National Post (29 March 2010).

——*Tales from the Hate Crime Underworld* National Post (5 February 2010).

——*Tribunal backs off Hate provision* National Post (3 September 2009).

——*University of Windsor fires back at failed law dean candidate* National Post (10 November 2010).

Butler, Don. *Court to decide web posters' ability to remain anonymous* National Post (12 April 2010).

Carlson, Kathryn Blaze. *What happens when the heroes of the past meet the standards of today?* National Post (14 May 2011).

——*Canadian extremist Salman Hossain charged with promoting genocide* National Post (8 July 2010).

Castelo, Vasco. *Why not accommodate feelings?* London Free Press (30 October 2010).

Codeivilla, Angelo M. *America's Ruling Class—And the Perils of Revolution* The American Spectator (17 July 2010).

Cohen, Tobi. *Shut the fxxx up on abortion file, counsels Tory senator* National Post (4 May 2010).

Conway, John F. *Regina 16 say common folk won freedoms* Calgary Herald (6 April 2010).

Daniels, Anthony. *The Dismaying Johns Fostering Case* National Review (9 March 2011).

Dosanjh, Ujjal. *We are complicit in our silence* National Post (17 June 2010).

Dubinski, Kate. *Charges fly over venue's snub of author* London Free Press (22 October 2010).

Editorials

——*Remarks over Muslims cost top US radio host his job* National Post (22 October 2010).

——*A bittersweet day for Press Freedom* National Post (8 May 2010).

——*A case study in hate* National Post (6 March 2010).

——*Much ado about racism* National Post (19 March 2010).

Eliadis, Pearl. *What the tribunal ruling really means* National Post (4 September 2009).

Fisk, Robert. *Spare me the academics who only want a 'safe, positive' space* The Independent (3 April 2010).

Foster, Peter. *The Equality Obsession* National Post (17 September 2010).

Fulford, Robert. *Defending the right to be offensive* Globe and Mail (2 February 1994).

——*The latest from the anti-racism industry* National Post (3 April 2010).

——*Lessons of 9/11* National Post (11 September 2010).

——*The threatening honesty of Ayaan Hirsi Ali* National Post (12 June 2010).

Gahtan, Alan. *I.S.P.s protected from liability* Law Times (15 July 2002).

Gagnon, Lysiane. *Why we must tolerate hate* Globe and Mail (17 October 2011).

Garner, Dwight. *In Pursuit of Prey, Carrying Philosophy* New York Times (2 May 2010).

Gunter, Lorne. *Liberals defend sanctity of free speech for liberals only* National Post (22 October 2010).

Hall, Barbara. *Why we still need HRCs* National Post (19 February 2010).

Hanon, Andrew. *A lesson in racism* Edmonton Sun (9 March 2010).

Huber, Jordana. *Clarification demanded on where medical marijuana smokers can light up* Vancouver Province (7 February 2009).

Hunter, Ian. *Adding cold insult to injustice* National Post (13 February 2011).

——*The Dangerous Evolution of Human Rights Legislation* National Post (18 February 2010).

Hutchinson, Brian. *Funny business at B.C. human rights hearing* National Post (2 April 2010).

——*Lawyer walks out on comedian's rights hearing* National Post (29 March 2010).

Ivison, John. *Laws should protect against hate, not against being offended* National Post (2 April 2010).

Jonas, George. *Censors of the World Unite—and ruin the Internet* National Post (27 January 2010).

Kay, Barbara. *One punch, one MOWP = more campus outrage* National Post (2 April 2010).

——*Honour killings must be confronted here at home* National Post (7 July 2010).

Kay, Jonathan. *White and guilty* National Post (3 April 2010).

Kelly, Cathal. *Fired sports journalist Damian Goddard 'stands by' tweet* Toronto Star (11 May 2011).

Klavan, Andrew. *Name-Calling* City Journal (27 August 2010).

——*Juan Williams told the truth* City Journal (22 October 2010).

Ko, Marni. *What really goes on at Foothills Hospital?* Calgary Herald (11 August 1999).

Krauthammer, Charles. *When in doubt, blame bigotry* National Post (28 August 2010).

Lewis, Charles. *Anti-abortion activist Linda Gibbons gets her day in Canada's top court* National Post (13 December 2011).

—*Arrest of Carleton students over anti-abortion posters framed as free speech issue* National Post (4 October 2010).

Libin, Kevin. *United under the Swastika* National Post (12 January 2009).

Lofaro, Tony. *Group attempts to silence U.S. right-winger's talk* Ottawa Citizen (20 March 2010).

Lefore, Ernie. *Speech and Harm* New York Times (7 November 2010).

Lilley, Brian. *Lack of historical knowledge threatens Canada's future: Minister* Toronto Sun (18 November 2010).

—*Gilles Duceppe and Pat Martin: Still bigots, still creepy* Canada Politics Examiner (5 June 2010).

—*Top bureaucrat paid big bucks for spin doctors: Docs* Toronto Sun (13 November 2010).

Lynch, Jennifer. *The Debate is out of Balance* Globe and Mail (12 June 2009).

Mansur, Salim. *Protect free speech, even if offensive* London Free Press (6 March 2010).

Martin, Robert. *Employment Equity Simply wasn't Necessary* Toronto Star (26 July 1995)

—*How I lost my father—twice* Globe and Mail (11 November 1991).

—*Ontario universities should refuse to adopt Minister's vile 'anti-racism' policies* Lawyers Weekly (17 December 1993).

Mansur, Salim. *Stifling Free Speech is not really free* Toronto Sun (10 February 2010).

McGinnis, Sarah. *Eight-year legal battle continues over hate law* Calgary Herald (7 April 2010).

McParland, Kelly. *Margaret Atwood's selective support for press freedom* National Post (2 September 2010).

Moore, Oliver. *Ontario Judge Lifts Veil on Spanking Trial* Globe and Mail (29 June 2002).

Mulgrew, Ian. *Bubble zone around abortion clinics upheld by court*

Vancouver Sun (27 April 2009).

Murphy, Rex. *University of Waterloo ignoramuses accomplish their doltish goal* National Post (20 November 2010).

Obituary for George Malcolm Thomson. *The Economist* (1 June 1996) 86.

Paris, Erna. *There *are* limits to free expression* Globe and Mail (28 October 2011).

Pearson, Matthew. *Organisers, not university, cancelled Ann Coulter: U. of O.* Ottawa Citizen (24 March 2010).

Plotinsky, Benjamin A. *The Varieties of Liberal Enthusiasm* (2010) 20 City Journal, no.2, online: City Journal.org http://www.city-journal.org

Poupko, Reuven and Chaim Steinmetz. *Bashing Israel right here at home* National Post (6 January 2009).

Raj, Althia. *Senator urges blacks to 'rise up and claim our rightful place'* Montreal Gazette (27 June 2011).

Robertson, Grant and Matt Hartley. *CRTC new media hearings* Globe and Mail (17 February 2009).

Selick, Karen. *A golden opportunity to kill human rights commissions* National Post (3 November 2010).

Sher, Jonathan. *'Weak, opportunistic' Islam will fell West, Steyn says* London Free Press (2 November 2010).

Shoalts, David. *Is the NHL tough enough on racism?* Globe and Mail (6 January 2012).

Sibley, Robert. *Ann Coulter's event at the University of Ottawa cancelled over 'public safety' fears* National Post (24 March 2010).

——*Ezra Levant sued in 'Jihad Chill' Case* Ottawa Citizen (26 January 2010).

Sobran, M.J. *Abortion: the class religion* National Review (23 January 1976).

Taylor, Stephen. *Trudeau fears barbaric might offend barbarians* National Post (15 March 2011).

Tibbetts, Janice. *Court wades into Internet speech debate with hyperlinks case* National Post (1 April 2010).

University of Ottawa. *University's letter to Ann Coulter* National Post (22 March 2010).

Wallace, Kenyon. *I'm the victim of a hate crime, Ann Coulter tells Canadian audience* National Post (22 March 2010).

Warren, David. *Extremist Thinking* Ottawa Citizen (14 March 2010).

——*Kafka Comes to Canada* Ottawa Citizen (4 September 2009).

Wente, Margaret. *Guilty of unconscious Racism* Globe and Mail (28 July 2009).

——*The Menace of Free Speech* Globe and Mail (26 March 2010).

——*Motherhood, the new oppression* Globe and Mail (25 June 2010).

Other Sources

Bill C-250, *An Act to Amend the Criminal Code (hate propaganda),* 2nd Sess., 37th Parl., 2003 (as passed by the House of Commons 17 September 2003).

Bill C-19, *Criminal Law Reform Act, 1984*, 2nd Sess., 32d Parl., 1984 (1st Reading, 7 February 1984).

Broadcasting Regulatory Policy, CRTC 2009-329.

Canadian Newspaper Association. *The Press and the Courts* (Legal Resources), online: Canadian Newspaper Association http://www.newspaperscanada.ca/public-affairs/the-press-and-the-courts

Canadian Physicians for Life. *Policy Statement*, 11 September 2008 [unpublished].

Canadian Radio-television and Telecommunications Commission. *Broadcasting Regulatory Policy*, CRTC 2009-329 (4 June 2009), online: Canadian Radio-television and Telecommunications Commission http://www.crtc.gc.ca/eng/archive/2009/2009-329.htm

——Licence renewals for the television stations controlled by Global (2 August 2001), Broadcasting Decision CRTC 2001-458.

—Radio Frequencies are Public Property: Public Announcement and Decision of the Commission on the Applications for Renewal of the Canadian Broadcasting Corporation's Television and Radio Licences (31 March 1974), Decision CRTC 74–70.

—Re CHOI-FM (13 July 2004) Broadcasting Decision CRTC 2004-271.

House of Commons Debates, 19th Parl. 1st Sess., (20 May 1940), 17 at 51 (M.J. Coldwell).

Transcript of pre-trial hearing (*R.* v. *Keegstra*), 10 October 1994, (Alta. Q.B.) [unreported].

INDEX

386, 387, 390, 399, 401,
402, 405, 408, 411, 415

Warman, Richard, 95, 389,
390, 391, 392, 422

ABOUT THE AUTHOR

Robert Ivan Martin is Professor of Law, Emeritus at the University of Western Ontario. In addition to Western, he has taught law at universities in France, Ireland, Kenya, Lesotho, Mauritius and Tanzania.

He is a graduate of the Royal Military College of Canada (BA, 1961); the University of Toronto (LL.B., 1967) and the School of Oriental and African Studies, London (LL.M. with Distinction, 1971) From 1985-2000 he was Secretary-Treasurer of the Commonwealth Association for Education in Journalism and Communication, and, from 1997-2007, a Bencher of the Law Society of Upper Canada.

In 2007 he was elected an Honorary Fellow of Trinity College, Dublin, a distinction he is the only Canadian to hold. *Free Expression in Canada* is his 11th book. He speaks English, French and Swahili and may be reached at babaivan1@live.ca.

CPSIA information can be obtained at www.ICGtesting.com
Printed in the USA
LVOW06s1923011213

363412LV00004B/596/P